Human–Animal Relations and the Hunt in Korea and Northeast Asia

Encounters in the Middle East and Asia
Published in association with Archiv Orientální

Series Editors: Nicola Di Cosmo, Táňa Dluhošová and Stefano Taglia

Titles published in the series

Human–Animal Relations and the Hunt in Korea and Northeast Asia
George Kallander

edinburghuniversitypress.com/series/emea

Human–Animal Relations and the Hunt in Korea and Northeast Asia

George Kallander

EDINBURGH
University Press

Edinburgh University Press is one of the leading university presses in the UK. We publish academic books and journals in our selected subject areas across the humanities and social sciences, combining cutting-edge scholarship with high editorial and production values to produce academic works of lasting importance. For more information visit our website: edinburghuniversitypress.com

© George Kallander, 2023, 2024

Edinburgh University Press Ltd
13 Infirmary Street
Edinburgh EH1 1LT

First published in hardback by Edinburgh University Press 2023

Typeset in 10.5/13 Goudy Old Style by
IDSUK (DataConnection) Ltd

A CIP record for this book is available from the British Library

ISBN 978 1 3995 1209 1 (hardback)
ISBN 978 1 3995 1210 7 (paperback)
ISBN 978 1 3995 1211 4 (webready PDF)
ISBN 978 1 3995 1212 1 (epub)

The right of George Kallander to be identified as author of this work has been asserted in accordance with the Copyright, Designs and Patents Act 1988 and the Copyright and Related Rights Regulations 2003 (SI No. 2498).

Contents

List of Illustrations	vi
Acknowledgements	vii
List of Kings	ix
Introduction: Why Animals and the Hunt?	1
1 Wild Beasts on a Premodern Peninsula	26
2 Koryŏ and the Empire of the Hunt	59
3 Growth, Transformation and Challenge in the Late Fourteenth and Early Fifteenth Centuries	88
4 Confucian Beasts: Human–Animal Relations in Early Chosŏn	110
5 Stalking the Forests: The Military on the Chase in the Mid-Fifteenth Century	138
6 Challenges to the Royal Military Kangmu Hunt	164
7 Public Animals, Private Hunts and Royal Authority in the Fifteenth Century	185
8 Release the Falcons: A King in a Confucian Court	209
9 Taming Wild Animals and Beastly Monarchs	236
Conclusion: Legacies of the Hunt in Politics, Society and Empire	271
Bibliography	282
Index	300

Illustrations

Map I.1	Topographic map of the Korean peninsula, fifteenth century	4
Map 3.1	Northern regions of the Korean peninsula and its topography, fifteenth century	105
Map 4.1	Locations of known royal hunts from the late Koryŏ and early Chosŏn dynasties	115
Figure 2.1	Presumably Yi Chehyŏn, *Crossing a River on Horseback*	78
Figure 8.1	Attributed to Yi Am, *Goshawk Standing on a Perch*	213
Figure 8.2	Prince Anp'yŏng, *Painting of a Falcon*	221
Figure 9.1	Yi Am, *Mother and her Pups*	241
Figure 9.2	Artist unknown, *Painting of a Dog*	242
Figure C.1	Kim Hongdo, *Noble Falcon Hunt*	279

Acknowledgements

This book would not have been possible without the assistance of a number of people and institutions around the world, near and far. Foremost, I would like to thank Professor Nicola Di Cosmo at the Institute for Advanced Study (Princeton, NJ) and Táňa Dluhošová and Stefano Taglia at the Oriental Institute, Czech Academy of Sciences for their positive support and generosity for including my book in their series Encounters in the Middle East and Asia. I am humbled to initiate the series. I extend my sincere gratitude to the editorial board and the team at Edinburgh University Press (Louise Hutton, Rachel Bridgewater, Isobel Birks and Eddie Clark) for helping me through this rigorous process. I wish to thank Sue Dalgleish and Tracy Stober for copyediting the manuscript and Alex Martin at the University of Pennsylvania for producing the maps.

As I worked on this project over the years, a number of colleagues have helped me along the way. I am indebted to David Robinson at Colgate University for reading the book thoroughly and providing me with discerning comments that improved the final product. His expertise and careful eye greatly strengthened the focus and arguments. Thanks also to Jay Lewis at the University of Oxford for his sharp eye, helpful insight and encouragement. I would like to extend my gratitude to Donald Baker (University of British Columbia), Michael Pettid (Binghamton University), Jisoo Kim (George Washington University) and Edward 'Ned' Shultz (University of Hawai'i). Their suggestions and advice improved the book and their friendship made the process more bearable. While presenting a chapter at a workshop at the University of Helsinki, I received supportive feedback from Andrew Logie (University of Helsinki) and John Lee (Durham University). I am grateful to John for inviting me to join his panel at the Association for Korean Studies in Europe (La Rochelle University, France), where I presented on the book. Thank you too to Juhn Ahn for inviting me to present my research at the University of Michigan when I first began this project. Special thanks to

Charlotte Horlyck (SOAS, University of London) for her research, writing, publishing advice and friendship. I want to extend my deep gratitude to Morris Rossabi (Columbia University) for his constant guidance and sincere support throughout my graduate studies and academic career. My appreciation also goes out to colleagues and the staff at Syracuse University, especially Susan Branson, the chair of the History Department, and Norman Kutcher, my fellow East Asian historian down the hall from me.

My year at the Institute for Advanced Study (IAS) afforded me the time to expand the scope of my study and served as a springboard for the book. The support and inspiration of my colleagues and the staff at IAS helped me extend it into animal and environmental studies. This includes Professor Di Cosmo and my fellow colleagues in the East Asia dinner group: Wendy Swartz, David Bello, Richard Simmons, Asaf Goldschmidt, Poshek Fu, Teemu Ruskola, Danian Hu and Xin Luo. Other institutions I would like to thank include the InterLibrary Loan staff at Bird Library, Syracuse University as well as the staff of the Cornell University Library Annex, the Columbia University libraries, the National Assembly Library of Korea and the Academy of Korean Studies Library. Funding for research trips to Korea and for writing the book were generously provided by the W. Terry Pigottt Faculty Research and Development Fund, the Department of History, and the East Asia Program, the Moynihan Institute of Global Affairs, the Maxwell School, Syracuse University. I want to extend my gratitude to the institutions that granted me permission to reproduce images: the National Museum of Korea, Kansong Art Museum and the Museum of Fine Arts Boston.

Thank you to my wife Amy Aisen Kallander (Syracuse University) and my daughters Mona and Sabrina for their constant support and patience. Amy also read and commented on the introduction – thanks so much for everything you do. My sister Nancy has supported me throughout my life, warm traits she acquired from our late parents. I extend deep appreciation to her and them. I am fortunate to live around and visit the mountains, rivers and streams of upstate New York and Korea, places that constantly inspire me. In many ways, the wild animals that inhabit these lands or in my backyard have fuelled my interest in this study. Final thanks go out to my former advisor, the late Professor Gari Ledyard, as well as the late Professor JaHyun Kim Haboush, both formally of Columbia University. They have and will always be major influences on my life and scholarship. I am forever indebted to them.

Author's Note

For the romanisation of Korean names and terms, this book follows the McCune-Reischauer system used in libraries and by scholars outside of Korea. Dates adhere to the original lunar year, unless otherwise stated.

Kings

Late Koryŏ Kings

Ch'ungnyŏl	1274–1308
Ch'ungsŏn	1308–13
Ch'ungsuk	1313–30; 1332–9
Ch'unghye	1330–2; 1339–44
Ch'ungmok	1344–8
Ch'ungjŏng	1348–51
Kongmin	1351–74
Sin U	1374–88
Ch'ang	1388–9
Kongyang	1389–92

Early Chosŏn Kings

T'aejo	1392–8
Chŏngjong	1398–1400
T'aejong	1400–18
Sejong	1418–50
Munjong	1450–2
Tanjong	1452–5
Sejo	1455–68
Yejong	1468–9
Sŏngjong	1469–94
Yŏnsan'gun	1494–1506

Introduction: Why Animals and the Hunt?

In the late fifteenth century, King Sŏngjong's (r. 1469–94; 成宗) interest for hunting worried officials at the Korean court over questions of morality, conservation and safety. On one occasion in the second lunar month of 1472, he donned a military uniform and travelled to T'owŏn, roughly fifteen kilometres (10 mi.) northeast of the palace to meet the Three Great Queens – the grandmother of King Sŏngjong, Queen Chŏnghŭi wanghu (1418–83; 貞熹王后); the mother of King Sŏngjong, Queen Dowager Insu Sohye wanghu (1437–1504; 昭惠王后); and the wife of the former king, Queen Ansu wanghu (1445–99; 安順王后). While travelling, the king encountered an old man by the side of the road who had a quail hanging from his clothes. The king was so impressed by this sign of the man's skills that he bestowed on him a new set of clothes. The king and the queens subsequently proceeded to Somangol mountain pass, where King Sŏngjong and Queen Dowager Insu participated in a ring hunt, a type of group chase where soldiers and other 'beaters' encircled an area, beat gongs, and generated other noises as they walked inward to flush out game for the hunting party to catch on the other side. It was a particularly bountiful day as the group killed eight deer as well as fox and hare. The king and Queen Dowager Insu also observed falconry. The commander of the inner palace guards, Ch'oe Han'mang (?–?; 崔漢望), shot one deer with an arrow and presented it to the king, who rewarded him with a bow. The king told him, 'The ring hunt today was for the Queen Dowager [Insu]. I will offer her this freshly killed game. I am very happy that you were able to kill some deer.'[1]

I begin with this expedition, one of many recorded in the various sources, to demonstrate some of the political and social meanings of the hunt. By the late fifteenth century, hunting was an activity that cut across social status and

---

[1] *Chosŏn wangjo sillok* [Veritable records of the Chosŏn Dynasty] (Seoul: Kuksa p'yŏnch'an wiwŏnhoe, 1955–8), 8: 638. Hereafter CWS.

reinforced social hierarchies, as kings and commoners, such as the elderly quail hunter, travelled to the mountains in search of game. On these trips, diverse groups might encounter each other, communicate, exchange pleasantries, and interact in ways that were ordinarily forbidden or frowned upon. The hunter, through the display of his talents via the quail hanging from his chest and his age being senior to the king, garnered royal respect. This encounter shows how hunting could bring together old and young, high and low, through bonding over time spent in the field. As indicated by the presence of the three most senior women of the court, women took part by occasionally observing the hunt and accompanying the king to an area well beyond the comforts of the palace grounds. However, their participation was gendered as the hunt rearticulated their roles as participants in the violence while acting as matronly guides for the young king. While the group hunted safely in the mountain pass, and not in the forested hills above, an element of danger still existed due to the presence of nearby predators, such as tigers and leopards. The senior palace guard, ostensibly present to protect the king and royal family, not only participated but benefited from killing the deer by offering it to the king's mother as tribute, reaffirming and fortifying relationships among the palace elite. Hunting excursions like this were more than simple pleasure outings. Rather, they expressed an intricate web of relations among states, people and animals, however unequal, that operated beyond the control of court officials.

Between the end of the thirteenth and the beginning of the sixteenth centuries, massive change swept through Northeast Asia as the arrival of the Mongol Yuan Dynasty (1271–1368) and the rise of the Chinese Ming Dynasty (1368–1644) unleashed new political, military and social forces across the region. The Korean peninsula, swept up in these dramatic events, was tied to the Mongols through blood – first, through war and then through intermarriage between the Korean and Mongol ruling families. The Korean kingdoms of Koryŏ (918–1392) and Chosŏn (1392–1910) entwined with the Mongol and Chinese worlds in a delicate cultural, political and military tapestry of power and influence.

This study focuses on the transitional period of Northeast Asia from the reign of Koryŏ Dynasty's King Ch'ungnyŏl (r. 1274–1308; 忠烈) to the Chosŏn Dynasty's King Yŏnsan'gun (r. 1494–1506; 燕山君). During roughly these two centuries, as these peninsular leaders expanded their governing influence over people and the environment through taxation, conscription and resource extraction, human–animal relations became increasingly significant to politics, national security and elite identities unlike any time before. The central bureaucracy in the capital consolidated authority by extending control over wild animals, converting hunting grounds into agricultural lands, and restricting private and military access to them for fur, feathers, hides, medicine and food. The Confucian transformation of Korea – the adaption of Neo-Confucian laws and institutions during early Chosŏn – shaped how individuals and animals interacted thanks to its belief in the civilising nature of scholarship over military matters and the ritual requirements of animal sacrifice. Due to a strong prejudice that hunting was a distraction from governance, scholarly elites sought to regulate the actions of the royal family by controlling access to animals. Kings should not hunt, some insisted, as it displayed overindulgence, and was a distraction from governance that bode poorly for the future of the state. Ideally, kings should be isolated from the wild to demonstrate their distinction from non-human animals. At the very least, wild animals should be sacrificed only for state ritual, rather than hunted and consumed in feasts at the court.

Hunting was an important tradition on the Korean peninsula and in Northeast Asia. The earliest written records about hunting date to the tenth century when people from all social groups, from villages and towns adjacent to forests, hunted. They included professional hunters in the military, lowborn mountain men, peasants, scholarly elites, royal family members and kings. They hunted for a variety of purposes, from hare and pheasants for sustenance to the clearing of animals considered to be agricultural pests, such as birds and wild boar, to sport as in the sometimes-unexpected chase of tigers and leopards. The quarry became food, medicine, gifts, gestures of diplomacy, and Confucian ritual sacrifices at both home and state altars.[2] Encounters between male hunters and wild beasts were more than simple momentary acts of violence. These encounters between people and animals represented a complicated network of agency among those who hunted, those who depended on the game, and the animals. Hunting straddled the boundaries of acceptable and unacceptable forms of violence.

Through kingship paintings and texts imported from China, peninsular elite families governing from the capital (*sadaebu*; 士大夫) were well aware of the images of Chinese imperial hunting parks, though it is unlikely that all Korean elites had access to forested lands. Unlike other provincial elites, the *sadaebu* were based in areas located around the capital where land was scarce. As the population began rising in the capital region, lands were transformed into agricultural fields. Tensions over land ownership were exacerbated as

---

[2] An Myŏngsu, 'Hanjungil ŭi siksaenghwal munhwa pigyo yŏn'gu 14–19 segi, chirijŏk, yŏksajŏk hwan'gyŏng kwa siksaeng kwallyŏn sŏji rŭl chungsim ŭro' [Study on the comparison among Korean, Chinese, and Japanese food culture from the fourteenth to the nineteenth century, focusing on the environments of geography, history, and bibliographies], *Han'guk siksaenghwal munhwa hakhoeji* 12, no. 3 (1997): 356–7.

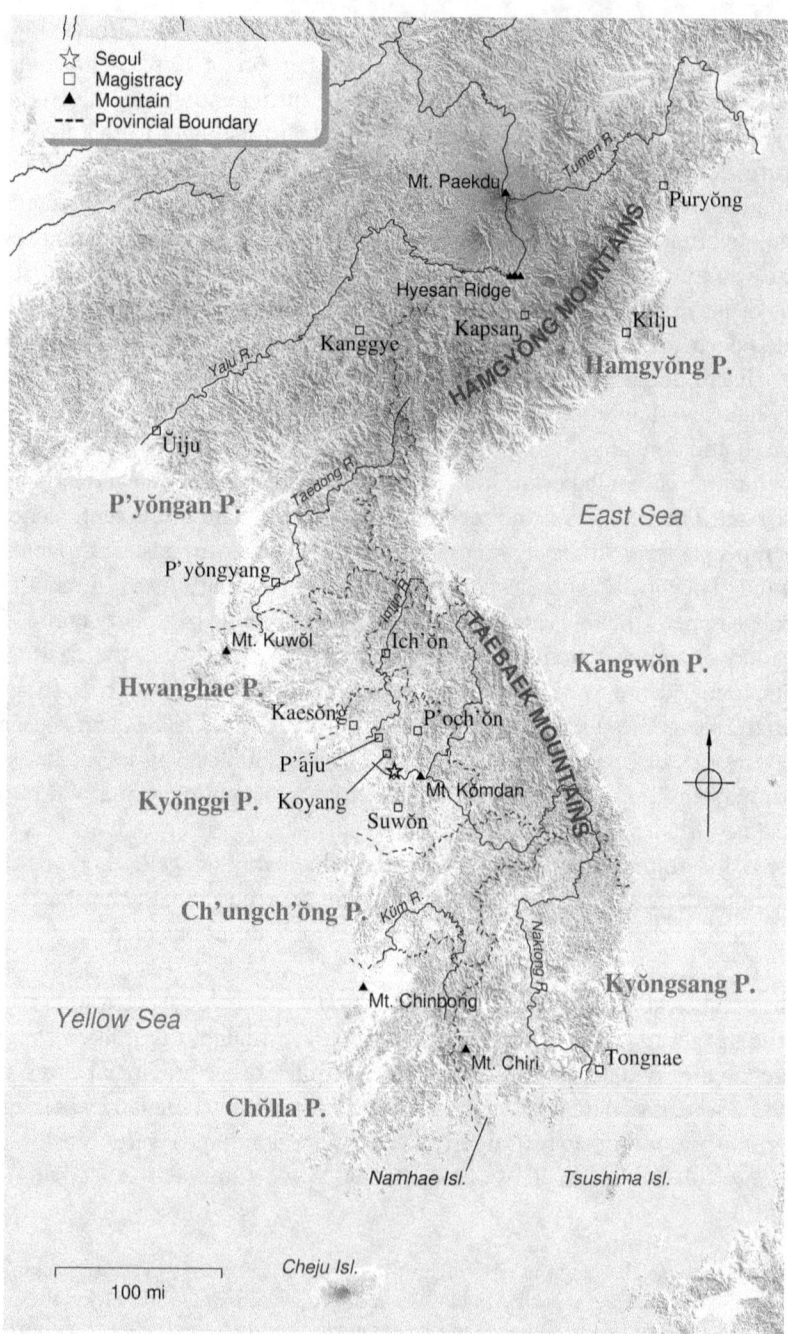

Map I.1 Topographic map of the Korean peninsula, fifteenth century.

individual farmers lost land to the royal family who, in turn, bequeathed it to merit subjects (*kongsin*; 功臣) who had been awarded high status for their support of the founder of the dynasty or their later descendants. Opposing the hunt, a small but vocal group of early Chosŏn bureaucratic leaders unified around a desire to regulate access to wild animals partly energised by taking sides in matters of land allocation for farmlands. By the beginning of the sixteenth century, these capital elites pushed to eliminate hunting entirely, first with commoners and lowborn then extending it to the king and his royal family members who, they argued, should serve as moral examples for others in society.

In the wake of Mongol collapse and the rise of the Ming Dynasty, hunting grew intertwined with definitions of civilisation and barbarity in Korea. As part of their competition for authority versus non-Korean tribes in the north, such as the Jurchen, scholarly elites in Chosŏn, by claiming to be more civilised, stigmatised hunting for food and pleasure and drew associations with peoples living along the northern frontier who they labelled as nomadic or barbarian. In fact, the mostly Jurchen tribes living on both sides of the Yalu and Tumen rivers in the northern part of the peninsula hunted frequently. As the Chosŏn court expanded the boundaries of the kingdom northward, Chosŏn encroached on Jurchen land conquering long-established Jurchen hunting grounds and prevented the tribes from accessing these forests by patrolling the region and moving settlers onto the land. In combination with harsh winters, this threatened the livelihood of these people, pressing the Jurchen south of the Yalu and Tumen rivers to hunt for food. These increasing, sometimes violent, encounters between the Jurchen and the Koreans worried the court. Korean civil elites associated hunting and its practices with the Jurchen crossing the frontier 'illegally'. Growing interactions with Jurchen hunting groups stigmatised the royal hunt with these 'uncivilised' violent practices. Wild animals encountered on hunts enticed kings, other elites who supported hunting, and soldiers to lands far away from the capital, including the expanded wilderness in the north and coastal zones along the peninsula. These hunts were potentially destabilising to central control and national security. Soldiers and others who hunted in contested territories sometimes collided with Jurchen tribes in the north and Japanese raiders along the coasts and islands in the south, all hunting for the protein of ungulates or the potential wealth of sable and fox fur.

As hunting was primarily a male activity, the concerns of Confucian bureaucrats about such animal encounters illustrate the courtly debates over the nature of elite masculinity and the terms through which elite men defined the ideal male. For one, the largely homosocial nature of hunting reflected Koryŏ and Chosŏn understandings of gender roles and gendered spaces. Men travelled together into dangerous terrain, bonding over the hardship and the struggle to pursue game and deploying weapons to display their skills in shooting and killing animals. Frequent feasting, drinking and sharing stories after a hunt provided opportunities for male bonding. Among the elite in particular, women worked, studied and tended the affairs of the family but remained largely within domestic spaces, while men engaged in scholarship, politics, warfare and the hunt in the public sphere. Women of lower social status may have hunted for food and sport and most certainly interacted with domesticated animals, such as pigs and chickens. They may have also encountered beasts in the wild, but their stories have been lost, as are those of commoners and lowborn who may have engaged in hunting. At issue here is elite understandings of masculinity, which were in opposition to the lives of commoners. For the elite, the experience of hunting interactions among men pushed the boundaries of the public and political space into wilderness areas on the margins of Koryŏ and Chosŏn control. These ideas about gender roles certainly informed human–animal encounters, politics, status, hunting and the construction of elite identities that I discuss in this book.

The hunt did not endure as a projection of royal authority or martial vigour. Over the fifteenth and sixteenth centuries, limited access to land, the migration of animals away from settled populations, and higher demands on the time of the monarch contributed to fewer occasions for grandiose royal hunting parties. Two hundred and fifty years after the founding of the Chosŏn Dynasty, reigning over an era of relative political stability in the aftermath of Manchu attacks and the founding of the Qing Dynasty (1644–1912), King Hyojong (r. 1649–59; 孝宗) pondered the disappearance of elite hunting practices, particularly the large-scale royal military chase: 'Our country used to have a system of royal military hunts. Now, they have been abandoned for quite some time. I don't really understand why. But after the Japanese invasion [1592–98], isn't it because we don't make time for these royal military Kangmu hunts?'[3] An official at court spoke up and explained to the king that he had never heard of the Kangmu hunt, attesting to the diminished status of this once important type of human–animal encounter that had elevated the reputation of the king as a militarised monarch. Suppressed by the bureaucracy and the needs of the state, the hunting of animals by the court was no longer a spectacle of kingly display of status or an activity necessary for military training. Put simply, my study investigates how and why the chase disappeared between 1270 and 1506, and what its disappearance meant for the political culture, royal authority, and the people and animals in Korea and the region.

[3] CWS, 35: 615.

Why Animals?

The outbreak of COVID-19 has once again drawn attention to the precarious nature of human–animal relations. A range of contemporary diseases are in fact zoonotic, transmitted from animals to people – from respiratory viruses such as SARS (bats) and MERS (camels) to MPV (monkeys), the plague (fleas), influenzas (birds), Lyme disease (ticks) and mosquito-borne viruses including Zika and the West Nile. Such diseases remind us of the intimate connections that exist between humans and animals, and the ways in which these relationships benefit, harm, or even upend the world as they pass from animals to humans. Beyond the immediacy of the sicknesses that arise from these ailments, as Luke Hunter argues, close interactions between animals and humans are some of the most important relationships that make us human.[4] The study of human–animal relations examines the complex and telling bonds between humans and animals and what these interactions expose about both. Recognising an integrated approach to studying animals – that is, the need for scholars to break out of isolation and work across fields – a number of important works have been published over the past twenty years that expand our understanding of the way human societies and animals impact each other. *Human–Animal Relations and the Hunt* seeks to contribute to this literature. To provide fresh insight into Korean and East Asian history, as well as offer an opportunity for comparative scholarship, this multidisciplinary study on the hunt in premodern Korea examines how the animals and the environment influenced and even shaped human politics and societies on the peninsula, impacting how people understood themselves and other people living beyond Korea.

To casual observers, the bond between humans and animals appears too obvious to demand critical scrutiny. Humans and animals have interacted with each other since the beginning, developing symbiotic relationships. As humans evolved with animals, animals evolved with humans, and both profited and suffered from each other. Some of these bonds have clear reasons, such as the domestication of animals for war (horses), consumption (pigs), farming (water buffalos), trade/transportation (mules or camels) and hunting (dogs and hawks). The list of animals that humans have and continue to dominate is staggering. Other relationships, such as those with pets (dogs, cats and other animals that have been adopted) seem less economically and politically significant to the human experience but are equally as important to us for companionship, both in the past and the present. Suggesting that animals are

---

[4] Luke Hunter, *Wild Cats of the World* (London: Bloomsbury Natural History, 2015), 196.

deserving of historical investigation, or that animals act as agents of historical change, touches on morality and ethics because it presumes that humans have and continue to mistreat animals. These inquiries raise deeper philosophical and religious debates about what defines humanity or what separates humanity from animals, especially when introducing issues such as the inhumane treatment of animals as test subjects or the slaying of animals for their meat or fur. These are issues I return to in my book in light of Korean historical experiences.

While the study of human–animal relations in the humanities first emerged with a focus on the West, the 'animal turn' in scholarship now includes consideration of humans and animals in a global perspective. Across the globe, our human ancestors would have lived alongside animals, hunting them for their meat, bones and fur. This relationship with the natural world has been lost in urban societies in particular. This loss is typical in most countries, including such places as Korea and China, where successive dynasties and the modern state have a long history of transforming the land and clearing animals away from population centres. Both China and Korea, as well as other countries across the globe, have reduced animals to pets, to carcasses prepared in supermarkets, to displays in zoos, and to pests to be eliminated. As Magnus Fiskesjo notes, the wide reduction in the diversity of animal species, combined with deforestation, air and water pollution, and a growing human population that consumes greater resources have negatively impacted human cognitive health.[5]

In the case of Japan, contemporary writers have criticised the poor treatment of the environment today. Others, however, argue that depictions of animals in Buddhist and Shinto art and literature contribute to the nation's unique cultural traits, which include a respect for animals. If the reality of the Japanese treatment of animals and the environment is more nuanced – as it was in premodern Japan when animals were considered animated beings with magical, divine and artistic qualities, while paradoxically living in a hierarchy where humans dominated them – such debates over human benevolence versus destruction inspire caution. When exploring the cultural, philosophical and religious concepts of animals in East Asia, unlike in pre-Darwinian Western Jewish and Christian teachings where a clear divide existed between the two, classical Chinese thought considered humans and non-human animals strands of the same continuum. Such issues will be considered throughout this text.

---

[5] Magnus Fiskesjo, 'China's Animal Neighbours', in *The Art of Neighbouring: Making Relations Across China's Borders*, eds Martin Saxer and Juan Zhang (Amsterdam: University of Amsterdam Press, 2017), 224.

The study of human–animal relations teases out the behaviour of people and the animals that live with and around us. At times these interactions were friendly and intimate for humans, as with livestock or pets, while at other times these exchanges were dangerous or uncertain, as with human encounters with animals in the wild – either through the deliberate tracking and hunting of animals or chance meetings. The overlapping of human and animal geographies – the territories where both live – can have deadly consequences for one or both. In addition to diseases passing from one species to another, violence can erupt on either side. Where the territories of hunters and game overlap, the brutal nature of human–animal interaction is most often to the detriment of the animals. Humans deliberately travel into wilderness areas to hunt. They slay game, and sometimes those same animals will stalk and kill hunters. Other times hunters are injured or die from hunting accidents. Hunting is a subjective and varied experience. No hunt is identical. 'Intangibles' like the terrain, weather, weapons, hunting partners and particular animal behaviours never remain the same. On top of all these complexities, even the landscape matters as it too transforms the way people and animals interact and respond to each other. Studying these relationships during the premodern era is especially fruitful because human and animal encounters developed in new and deeper ways. By examining these interactions through the Korean experience – when the state came into contact with novel and competing cultural ideas of rulership and hunting (the Mongols, Chinese and Jurchens), the slow centralisation of authority over new lands where the central bureaucracy competed with disparate groups (including kings) over finite resources (animals and hunting grounds), and the struggle over notions of rulership – we gain a better awareness of the fluctuating nature of these relationships and discover that animals have and continue to shape human histories.

Considered here too are ecological questions about land use and overhunting, the impact of human settlements on forests and animals, and the environmental consequences of state expansion. Animals are prime subjects of study to address these themes because the Korean peninsula continues to sustain a great diversity of indigenous animal life. These themes resonate with earlier scholarly attention on the distribution, development and management of agriculture, especially rice, and its impact on the economies, governments and lifestyles in the region by broadening the scope of environmental analysis. As a non-indigenous plant, rice requires a tremendous amount of time and energy in the Northeast Asian climate. Animal products, both wild and domestic, formed another facet of food production, similar to rice and other crops and grains, as they also fed the population (although to a much smaller extent) and were submitted as tax obligations that sustained the government and military.

The gradual transformation of the environment to build homes, agricultural fields, irrigation systems and spaces to raise domesticated animals reduced wilderness habitats, straining the relationship between people and wild animals. Korean states slowly transformed the land, especially from the fifteenth century, by shifting populations and reallocating lands, altering the way people and indigenous species interacted and how people identified themselves, a form of slow-motion ecological imperialism that had powerful consequences for wild birds and beasts and the people who hunted them. *Human–Animal Relations and the Hunt*, the first account to address hunting, animals and the environment in the context of Korea and Northeast Asia, speaks to these broader concerns that resonate across societies past and present.[6]

Shifting perceptions of wild animals demonstrate how regional interactions, political competitions and migrations informed the development of local cultural practices. Through detailing and navigating animals and the hunt, a theme Korean- and English-language scholarship has overlooked, I elucidate Korea's place in regional and Eurasian history. Attention to animals and the hunt allows us to recast the peninsula's relations to rejoin Eurasia as a whole.

Arguments and Structure

What began as a history of premodern Korea through a regional and global lens, focusing on elite hunting practices, came to include forays into the larger topic of human–animal affairs and environmental history in Northeast Asia. In my view, the royal and elite hunt, human–animal relations, and environmental history are all interrelated topics and cannot be discussed in isolation. Insight from these sources sharpen our understanding on how people, animals and the environment intersected. This builds on the scholarship of human–animal geography, an interdisciplinary field, which seeks to uncover new ways humans and animals react to one another and impact human spaces and cultures. Both co-exist together, create spaces and significance, and struggle together.

---

[6] For example, see Julie Hughes, *Animal Kingdoms: Hunting, the Environment, and Power in the Indian Princely States* (Cambridge, MA: Harvard University Press, 2012); Vijaya Mandala, *Shooting a Tiger: Big-Game Hunting and Conservation in Colonial India* (New Delhi: Oxford University Press, 2019); Edward Steinhart, *Black Poachers, White Hunters: A Social History of Hunting in Colonial Kenya* (Athens: Ohio University Press, 2006); Matt Cartmill, *A View to a Death in the Morning: Hunting and Nature through History* (Cambridge, MA: Harvard University Press, 1993); and Matthew Canepa, *The Iranian Expanse: Transforming Royal Identity through Architecture, Landscape, and the Built Environment, 500 BCE–642 CE* (Oakland: University of California Press, 2018).

Jacob Bull and Tora Holmberg write, 'animals are active place-making agents: Animals are active in the production of materialized meanings around certain places (wilderness, farm, home, laboratory, for example) ... Thus, as animals navigate in and between places, they stir our social imagination and disturb our social orders and create certain stories rather than others.'[7]

A number of arguments and themes weave their way simultaneously through the narrative of my book. Most apparently, I argue that court officials sought to temper the martial tendencies of the monarch by limiting his access to wild game and preventing him from attending hunts. These vociferous debates between scholars and kings about proper conduct stemmed from tensions surrounding Korea's contacts with regional and Eurasian empires, whether to adapt and assimilate or maintain distinct practices and customs. As a study of political transformation and cultural exchange, attention to hunting depicts how a multiplicity of cultural references – Sinic, Korean, Northeast Asian and steppe land – existed in tension with each other and served as a battleground for defining politics and elite masculinities. As Harriet Zurndorfer explains, 'Performing manliness has several dimensions: first, a man's adherence to the normative roles defined by the structures of marriage, fatherhood, and filial piety, and second, a man's pursuit of homosocial relations that take part outside the home.'[8] Among many features, the hunt and the military intersected offering a space for male homosocial camaraderie, one that challenged the hierarchical structures of the Confucian bureaucratic worldview and threatened scholarly influence at court.

Animals, especially undomesticated ones, like deer, wild boar and tigers, stirred imaginations and legends and helped define, in part, premodern elite concepts of governance and society. Through fables and written texts, elites relied on the animal world to help define social status, arguing for instance that there were no sharp divisions between the lowest members of society – slaves and people living north of the frontier – and animals. In texts that circulated among elite families and in written court documents that reflected contemporary understanding, writers in late Koryŏ and early Chosŏn described animal hierarchies that reflected those in human society. Tigers, for example, while

---

[7] Jacob Bull and Tora Holmberg, 'Introducing Animal Places', in *Animal Places: Lively Cartographies of Human–Animal Relations*, eds Jacob Bull, Tora Holmberg and Cecilia Asberg (New York: Routledge, 2018), 2. For another important study, see Samantha Hurn, *Humans and Other Animals: Cross-Cultural Perspectives on Human–Animal Interactions* (New York: Pluto Press, 2012).

[8] Harriet Zurndorfer, 'Polygamy and Masculinity in China: Past and Present', in *Changing Chinese Masculinities: From Imperial Pillars of State to Global Real Men*, ed. Kam Louie (Hong Kong: Hong Kong University Press), 14.

feared, were considered the elite of the animal world. At the same time, many royal family members, military men and civil elites interacted directly with animals. Some kept horses, others hunting dogs and falcons, while others spent time in the mountains and forests or in hunting parks and military training grounds pursuing deer or pheasants. By considering the royal hunt, human–animal relations, and environmental history in tandem, I hope to revise our understanding of late Koryŏ and early Chosŏn political and cultural history to place animals in a new light.

Another theme is the transnational nature of this moment. The period between the thirteenth and the early sixteenth centuries experienced greater movement of people in the region and their growing interest for and interactions with animals. The Mongol Empire propelled the movement of people in and around the peninsula more so than in previous eras. While armies came to conquer, others moved in response. Koreans, Chinese and Jurchens in particular traversed the region hunting, trapping and trading horses, hides and pelts. People from the Japanese islands sometimes reached the coast as raiders, other times as hunters. Koreans interacted with Ryukyu Islanders observing their hunts. While the majority of Koreans on the peninsula did not leave their home villages, they were exposed to these migrations via the greater number of soldiers traversing the country, many on large-scale military hunts. Among the elite, scholars and military officials travelled around and beyond the peninsula as well. Members of the royal family moved around too driven by the military, political, cultural and economic links threading through the peninsula and beyond. Hunting animals in the wild was a significant aspect of this transnational moment, along with the heightened interest in trained animals such as falcons and dogs that hunted alongside humans or served as gifts or diplomatic gestures in the regional gift economy.

In the fifteenth century, state interest in the environment also expanded, including greater attention to animals that resided on the land near the capital and in the mountainous northeastern part of the peninsula. The court began codifying Confucian ritual laws that placed greater economic and ritual demands over animals (namely wild deer or domesticated oxen and sheep) that were used as sacrifice for rituals and ancestral worship. Many of these ritual practices most likely existed earlier than the fifteenth century and may have arisen in tandem with indigenous shamanistic beliefs. Nevertheless, the Chosŏn government began codifying these rituals into law to limit and regulate access to these animals in order to maximise control over and protect the economic interests and religious authority of the state.

One important theme of this book is Neo-Confucianism. I provide a concrete sense of the Neo-Confucian transformation, especially in the fifteenth and early sixteenth centuries, through an examination of the royal hunt and human–animal relations. The central narrative of the Chosŏn Dynasty, and Korean history more broadly, has tried to explain how the country became overwhelmingly Confucian in its political culture, social practices and moral values. Confucianism in Chosŏn refers to a variant of Confucian thought and practice that initially formed in China during the eleventh and twelfth centuries and gradually won acceptance as state orthodoxy in Korea in the fifteenth century as Neo-Confucianism.[9] My book examines much the same period but adopts a different vantage point by tracing how hunting, which had been a core element of royal identity for most of the thirteenth and fourteenth centuries, came under progressively sharp criticism by a growing number of Korean elites in the fifteenth and sixteenth centuries. I offer a reinterpretation of the Confucian transformation debate through a discussion of the royal hunt. A small group of committed elite men, utterly convinced of their moral and cultural superiority, came to impose their worldview not only on men of similar socio-economic status but also on the royal house itself. Through agitation, sustained and loud protests, efforts at shaming, denunciations, and more, this small crowd gradually pushed its particular interpretation of Neo-Confucian thought and practice on the centre of Korean politics and, in the process, transformed the kingship and country. Rather than focusing on abstract Neo-Confucian thought and metaphysics, my book provides readers with a detailed and concrete reconstruction of specific restrictions, such as where the king was allowed to go, with whom and with what, and for what purposes. Successive kings struggled with new moral imperatives, while individual kings strained against the increasing limitations on their daily activities, on their circle of companions, and on their relations with their civil officials. *Human–Animal Relations and the Hunt* reveals a human, poignant, and more understandable history than studies on the metaphysics of Neo-Confucian thought.

Rather than simply viewed through the lens of Neo-Confucian ideology, a parallel argument explains the central government's desire to control the king's involvement in hunting and resources, including the land and wild beasts, in terms of state expansion in the fifteenth and sixteenth centuries. The initial abundance of animals, especially near the capital, fuelled an era of overhunting in a period when the government began consolidating control on the peninsula. In time, shifts in population into former hunting grounds and changing environmental conditions, especially in the south, compelled the central government to regulate hunting and enact stronger measures to convert hunting

---

[9] For instance, see Martina Deuchler, *The Confucian Transformation of Korea: A Study of Society and Ideology* (Boston, MA: Brill, 1995).

grounds into agricultural fields. At the same time, the state looked elsewhere on the peninsula for animals for rituals and medicine, namely in the distant northern provinces. Rather than simply interpreted as an ideological clash, Neo-Confucian laws, rites and regulations facilitated the administrative needs of an expanding state. In other words, to compete with a unifying Ming influence and challenges along the frontiers, the administrative and economic needs of an expansionist Korean state drove these changes. The Neo-Confucianisation narrative privileges ideology and rhetoric and is largely domestically oriented in the capital. The idea that governing values might shift because of territorial expansion allows us to tease out other factors – such as administrative growth, increased mobility of people on the peninsula, and interactions with animals and the Mongols and Jurchen hunting groups, who were viewed as animal-like Others – in the creation of an early Chosŏn identity. These arguments are not mutually exclusive. Rather, the singular focus on Neo-Confucian ideology obscures essential elements of change through other means.

To provide background for a deeper discussion on the royal and elite hunts, Chapter 1 journeys through the environmental conditions, animal populations and hunting practices on the Korean peninsula. Buddhist, Confucian and popular folk views of animals are explored here as well, illuminating the complexities and contradictions of the philosophical and moral belief systems humans held about animals in premodern Northeast Asia. Chapter 2 begins by contextualising the hunt in global and regional terms before turning to animal and human connections from the thirteenth through the fourteenth centuries under the Mongol Empire. When the Koryŏ Dynasty submitted to Mongol rule in the late thirteenth century, the Mongol Yuan emperor tipped the balance of politics in favour of the kings for almost a century, exacerbating tensions between the central bureaucracy and the royal family. Within the shifting political landscape of the capital, debates over the royal hunt, and the rise of a martial, neo-nomadic ethos, reveal a clash of political values between the Koryŏ civil bureaucracy and Mongol-backed royal family members and their supporters.

Human–animal relations in the Koryŏ–Chosŏn transition are the focus of Chapters 3 and 4. For the final few generations of Koryŏ sovereigns, the royal hunt was a source of empowerment enacting their mastery over men, women and beasts. In the wake of the Mongol collapse and the rise of the Ming Dynasty, new political and military forces in Northeast Asia – along with the challenges of a cooling climate and growing population – began reshaping Korean society. Bureaucratic elites and monarchs established laws and practices based on Neo-Confucian principles of governance and morality, rejecting nomadic and Mongol precedents. Not until the adaptation of

Neo-Confucianism in the late fourteenth century after the founding of the Chosŏn Dynasty did officials begin restricting hunting, first at the non-elite level, and later at the highest levels of the state: the kingship, his family, and military and civil elites. Animals were more plentiful in a vastly expanded domain and thus more readily provided to the state as a tribute tax. At the same time, they were increasingly sacrificed on the altars of both the state and private homes. Animals, wild and domestic, helped define Chosŏn identity, becoming the blood and bones of the dynasty's political legitimacy.

Because the demands of hunting collided with the needs of a growing state, the second half of this book spends more time examining the era of King Sŏngjong (r. 1469–94). Chapters 5 and 6 study hunting through the lens of the royal military Kangmu hunt to demonstrate the growing intersection of hunting, animals and politics. After the founding of Chosŏn, similar to many government institutions, the new dynasty reorganised the military to remove vestiges of the previous era. This was meant to signal to the new Ming Chinese state that the Chosŏn military would no longer be involved in the domestic politics of Korea or destabalise the new peace in Northeast Asia. However, officials contested removing the king from military affairs over the next century as threats from the north persisted in the form of Jurchen hunting groups along the frontier. Early kings of the Chosŏn Dynasty embraced a martial identity rooted in the violence of the previous century and the martial masculinity, a neo-nomadic ethos, that re-emerged during the Mongol Yuan–Koryŏ alliance.

Chapters 7 and 8 continue exploring the fifteenth century through the lens of the private hunts of the king, royal family members, and like-minded elites when tension between the Confucian bureaucracy and kingship over hunting practices intensified. A small group of vocal scholars criticised King Sŏngjong for what they called his indulgence in the hunt. Represented by his fondness for falcon hunting, King Sŏngjong attempted to re-establish the importance of the army and military practices in times of growing contact with Jurchen tribes in the north. Through small group hunting parties, he sought to project an image of himself as a martial king reminiscent of the likes of early Chosŏn leaders. Here too I explore the tradition of falconry in Korea and Northeast Asia. Conflict between the bureaucracy and the royal authority came to a head during King Yŏnsan'gun's reign (1494–1506), the subject of Chapter 9. Yŏnsan'gun returned to a hunting model not seen since the days of Koryŏ's King Ch'ungnyŏl. King Yŏngsan'gun's attempt to expand the royal hunting preserves around the capital conflicted with the powerful Confucian bureaucracy. A disagreement ensued over the bureaucratic constraints of royal authority, including access to hunting dogs in the royal palace and the king's desire to hunt outside the palace. In particular, Confucian bureaucrats targeted Yŏngsan'gun for his excessive hunting and love of entertaining during a time of growing political turmoil in the capital, shifting climate conditions, and the outbreak of pestilence throughout the peninsula. By tracing the connections between the loss of access to wild animals and the loss of royal power and mobility to the bureaucracy, *Human–Animal Relations and the Hunt* concludes by exposing the contradictory nature of human–animal relations as the demand for state animal sacrifices rise, wild animals grow scarce, and royal elite hunts fade at the turn of the sixteenth century.

Animals in the Archives

When I began work on this project, my former advisor Professor Gari Ledyard at Columbia University seemed confused. 'The hunt?' he mused. 'Why? You won't find anything on hunting!' Professor Ledyard's initial response to the subject of my book is understandable. In Korean and Northeast Asian historiography, almost nothing has been written on hunting.[10] Even outside of Korea, the hunt has been largely invisible to the historian.[11] This was excusable because animals were not considered to be agents of history until recently. The scholarship that did touch on animals and the hunt offered blanket statements based on religious and cultural reductionism.[12] Also, historiography on Korea has tended to follow institutional histories that studied the impact of Neo-Confucianism, which emphasised book learning over physical activities, including hunting and warfare, farming and manual labour. The tendency to perceive the Korean peninsula as a monolithic Confucian society has discouraged examining Korean history through other themes.[13]

---

[10] Two books provide useful descriptions of hunting in Korea. See Sim Sŭnggu, Im Changhyŏk, Chŏng Yŏnhak and Cho T'aesŏp, *Sanyang ŭro pon sam kwa munhwa* [Seeing life and culture through hunting] (Kyŏnggido kwach'ŏnsi: Kuksa p'yŏnch'an wiwŏnhoe, 2011); and Kim Kwangŏn, *Han Il Tong Siberia ŭi sanyang: Suryŏp munhwa pigyoji* [The hunt of Korea, Japan, and Eastern Siberia: Comparative notes of their hunting cultures] (Seoul: Minsogwŏn, 2007).

[11] Dorothee Brantz, *Beastly Natures: Animals, Humans, and the Study of History* (Charlottesville: University of Virginia Press, 2010), 2.

[12] For example, since ancient times Koreans adopted strong attitudes towards protecting life, including animals, and disdained hunting because of Buddhist and Confucian teachings, while wars by foreign invaders, such as the Japanese and the Manchu, devastated the environment, including the flora and fauna. 'Koreans considered sport hunting vulgar, except for hawking and falconry.' Yeong-Seok Jo, John Baccus, John Koprowski and Yo-han Ji, *Mammals of Korea* (Seoul: Life Science Publishing, Company, 2018), 19.

[13] See John Duncan, 'Maintaining Boundaries: The Military and Civil Branches in the Koryŏ and Early Chosŏn', *Taiwan Journal of East Asian Studies* 8, no. 1 (June 2011): 24–5.

To investigate animals, I undeniably have to rely on human accounts. The central sources for my book are multi-volume collections of dynastic records written in classical Chinese (*hanmun*) on the peninsula, namely the *Koryŏsa* (History of the Koryŏ Dynasty), *Koryŏsa chŏryo* (Essential history of the Koryŏ Dynasty), and the *Chosŏn wangjo sillok* (Veritable records of the Chosŏn Dynasty). Consisting of 139 volumes, the *Koryŏsa* was compiled by Confucian scholars in the decades following the end of the dynasty, but it was not completed until 1451. The more modest thirty-five-volume *Koryŏsa chŏryo* was finished around the same time and intended to augment the *Koryŏsa*. The 1,893-volume *Chosŏn wangjo sillok* records the Chosŏn Dynasty, while also offering insights on Koryŏ-era figures and events. Incorporating views on the hunt outside the court and the central bureaucracy, I also utilise literary collections (*munjip*), religious texts and falconry manuscripts – as well as visual sources – from late Koryŏ and early Chosŏn scholars and artists both inside and outside the court from the thirteenth through the sixteenth centuries. These sources describe human–animal encounters as well as human-to-human discussions, laws, and concerns about animals and the hunt.

Historical records such as these, many composed by Confucians and some by Buddhists, reflect their authors' disapproval of hunting, especially when it involved members of the royal family. Much as in China, Confucian officials disdained non-scholarly activities for interfering in governance, arguing that such pastimes placed the dynasty at risk by distracting the king from his moral responsibility to govern the people from inside the palace. However, the constant reiteration of this call for royal abstention illustrates the latter's continued participation in such activities. For these officials, not only did hunting pose a threat to governing practices by their absence from court and limit scholarly access to political power as the royal family fraternised with soldiers and other escorts, its inherent physical activity also contradicted the notion of the Confucian gentleman or superior man or *kunja* (C. *junzi*). Whereas hunting and feasting on game were ways for kings to demonstrate their royal authority and status, this martial masculinity conflicted with the scholar and moral sage-king ideals of Neo-Confucian scholars in the court and bureaucracy.[14] Though these sources almost exclusively convey an elite, male-centred worldview, such military and civil officials were the ones allowed to travel, deal with changes in the dynasty, and connect with other cultures, making them ideal sources for understanding Korea's place in regional political culture and intellectual currents.[15]

[14] JaHyun Kim Haboush, *Heritage of Kings: One Man's Monarchy in a Confucian World* (New York: Columbia University Press, 1988).
[15] Along with these primary sources, I rely upon a wide variety of secondary sources from across many disciplines, particularly anthropology and zoological studies.

Korean sources refer frequently to hunting and to interactions with animals, especially undomesticated creatures encountered in the mountains, valleys and plains. These accounts are so numerous that the real challenge is cataloging, interpreting and contextualising them. Primary sources from the late thirteenth to the beginning of the sixteenth centuries in particular are rich with references to animal–human encounters in wilderness areas. These references illustrate the peninsula's links to empires and peoples on the continent and how the regional and even global forces impacted the area. Kings, their royal family members, military personnel and other elites sometimes travelled to the imperial centre at Beijing carrying gifts of animals (sometimes live, sometimes as animal products) for the emperor and other Mongol leaders; other times they observed and participated in hunting or talked about animals while in China and Mongol lands or, once back on the Korean peninsula, they practised Eurasian hunting techniques, all of which demonstrates connections to the region. With its rituals and elaborate entourages, hunting expeditions, especially by members of the royal family, emerged as an important definer of identity and political legitimacy. These royal hunts differed from those of the average soldier, commoner or slave as they often involved groups of central officials and soldiers. The growing presence of wild animals in the sources suggests a state and elite concerned about animals as the human population, especially the royal family, soldiers and others, moved and travelled into the wild regions of the country. The shifting status of hunting as a royal activity is an example of the regional dynamics among the Ming, Yuan, Koryŏ and Chosŏn dynasties and the multiplicity of responses people had to the flourishing connections in the region.

While this book appears to mainly focus on the royal hunt, it also touches on the hunting practices of other elites, commoners and slaves. One way to describe the variety of hunts in premodern Korea is to imagine a spectrum. On one end of the spectrum were kings and royal family members. Their royal outings involved formalised hunts, such as seasonal hunts held two or three times a year, as well as the much grander, more formidable, royal military Kangmu hunts. Classical texts dictated the rules and regulations of these types of hunts. Kings led these hunts, but elites from the civil and military branches, non-elite soldiers and slaves participated. Next along the spectrum of hunting practices were the personal, private hunts of the king and the royal family. These hunts were smaller outings free from the rules of engagement dictated by the classical texts. Again, like the royal military Kangmu hunts, elites and non-elites, as well as civil and military officials, took part in them with the king. Following the spectrum, we find the private and personal hunting practices of the capital region and countryside elites.

Their outings resembled that of the personal, private hunts of the royal family. These leaders sometimes hunted alone or in small groups. Like kings, these men rode horseback into the wilderness, at times escorted by like-minded elites and non-elites who either hunted, carried weapons, or handled hunting dogs and falcons. Female servants (as represented in Figure C.1, *Noble Falcon Hunt* (*Hogwiŭngnyŏp to*; 豪貴鷹獵圖) by Kim Hongdo (1745–1806?; 金弘道), on page 279) sometimes accompanied them carrying and serving food and alcohol in the field. These lower-level elites appear in the sources when they are described as having hunted with kings and in reports when the central government began passing laws to limit hunting practices. At the far end of this spectrum are the hunting practices of the many commoners, soldiers and slaves who would have hunted for themselves and their families' sustenance or for tribute products for the central government. Put differently, the sources referenced in my study illuminate the royal experiences of the hunt, while also clarifying that all levels of society hunted during the Koryŏ and Chosŏn eras.

Setting the Stage: The Eve of the Fourteenth Century

For readers unfamiliar with the history of the peninsula, a brief overview sets the stage for the arguments of this book and can help to place Korea in a wider regional context. In global terms, Korea's Koryŏ (918–1392) and Chosŏn (1392–1910) dynasties were two of the longest enduring polities in world history. Koryŏ and Chosŏn leaders ruled the peninsula for one thousand years, lasting into the modern era. Few regions of the world have replicated such political stability and cultural continuity. This longevity can be attributed to patterns of governance and scholarship adopted from the Chinese Han, Tang, Song and Ming dynasties, which Koreans melded with indigenous patterns, practices and thought. Another reason for Korea's stability was its flexible relations with China and other Northeast Asian neighbours. These early peninsular states consolidated power by adopting cultural practices – writing, scholarship, and a centralised government around a kingship and bureaucracy – from China. While the kingship was hereditary, passing the civil service examination based on Confucian teachings was required of small groups of elite scholars before they could serve in the government. In addition to Confucianism, Buddhism and Daoism also permeated these two different societies, as in other parts of East Asia. Developments in China impacted the peninsula, and Korean scholars and Buddhist monks often admired Chinese civilisation. However, indigenous systems such as regional autonomy that resisted centralisation and a powerful social status system clashed with the teachings of Buddhism and Confucianism, and shamanistic beliefs that permeated society both high and low.[16]

In Koryŏ and Chosŏn, kings were neo-religious authority figures, the highest-ranking people in the state. To enhance their political authority, early Koryŏ kings claimed to be Bodhisattvas, individuals who, according to Buddhist traditions, had achieved nirvana (enlightenment) but had remained present in the world to help others. Later rulers from the Chosŏn Dynasty adopted the ideals of the 'sage king' or a moral governor of the people, based on Confucian principles. Regardless, kings believed in a strong centralised monarchy supported by a capable bureaucracy of loyal officials. Kings, in theory, held total power over everything, but they could not govern alone. In practice and reality, the bureaucracy from the Koryŏ era, limited to elite classically educated scholars, was formidable. Discussions at court, often intense and highly charged for political gain, was where politics played out among the king and his bureaucracy. For Koryŏ, access to elite status was hereditary, which was a matter of fate, not choice. In other words, one could not become a member of the elite class but had to be born into it. The status system was hierarchical and maintained through the Confucian and military examination systems; only those with the economic means and political connections had the time and resources to learn the Confucian Classics and sit for the exams.

Below the king and the royal family were the *yangban* elites. The yangban consisted of two branches – the military (*mu*; 武) and civil officials (*mun*; 文). Adopted from ancient Chinese practices, where both were core hereditary classes, the military and civil orders held prestige in Korea. The term 'yangban' existed in Koryŏ but took on new meaning during the Chosŏn Dynasty. As a safeguard to the dynasties, the military was an important element of the system, while the scholarly branch ascended at times of peace when the apparent need for a strong military faded. Sometimes, this focus on bureaucracy and the downgrading of the military were to the detriment of political stability and national security.

The super elite of the yangban were the '*sadaebu*', a term used when referring to the small ruling class in the capital that held government posts, served in a number of positions, struggled in their leadership, and faced both purges by the king and the loss of their statuses. Mostly members of the scholarly branch, *sadaebu* owned the land given to them from the government and

---

[16] For more, see Jae Woo Park, 'Early Koryŏ Political Institutions and the International Expansion of Tang and Song Institutions', *Korean Studies* 41 (2017): 9–29; and H. W. Kang, 'Institutional Borrowing: The Case of the Chinese Civil Service Examination System in Early Koryŏ', *Journal of Asian Studies* 34, no. 1 (November 1974): 10–25.

earned their salaries from land grants, the wealth produced on that land. As a land-owning aristocracy, *sadaebu* were taxed, but they pushed these fees to the peasants who farmed their lands.

While the instruments of government changed somewhat from the thirteenth to fourteenth centuries, and the percentage of Confucian officials working in the government grew, these leading families of the state staffed a government that was divided into three major divisions. First was the set of officials who helped decide policy and settled government issues before the royal throne. These constituted the highest political order, the State Council, the highest realm of civil government that met with the king daily. Next were six boards: personnel, rites, revenue, punishment, war and works. Each board had numerous subordinate organisations. For instance, the largest of these boards was the Board of Personnel and perhaps the most important board was the Board of Rites, which dealt with Confucian rituals of education, foreign relations, ritual relations and ceremonies with China, the Ryukyu Islands, Japan and tribes north of the frontier. The next major division included the Censorate Office, which consisted of overseer inspector generals who ensured that royal orders were carried out; the admonition council, whose members ensured the behaviour of senior officials, prevented corruption, and uncovered officials not following laws or rituals; the royal censors, who checked the king, as the king must be held accountable for ritual; and the classics mat, where Confucian experts instructed the king daily in the tenants of Confucianism, established in the late Koryŏ and strengthened in the early Chosŏn. The classics mat scholars were usually the most senior-ranking officers who doubled as tutors to the king and crown prince. Classics mat officials used their writing skills to admonish the king. The concept of remonstration – the Confucian critique of the king – and the officials who provided more checks than balances, promoted social stability.

The regional administrative system of the seven provinces around the capital expanded during the early Chosŏn from five provinces, two northern frontiers, and the capital region around Kaesŏng (present during Koryŏ times). The king appointed a governor to each province and magistrates to the fifty to sixty districts per province. There were subdistrict levels as well with no royal authority appointing personnel. There, men of local influence, with a large amount of autonomy in their affairs, held sway over villages. Elite yangban living outside the capital travelled to the capital to take the civil service exams every three years. In time, given the result of their exams, they could move to the capital and take part in governing. Countryside yangban had leadership responsibilities, following Confucian family codes. These men held great authority in their home villages but had no official posts in the government.

A large part of society consisted of farmers or peasants, the 'good people' (*yangin*; 良人).[17] As the agricultural foundation of the state, these commoners had no access to the government examination system. Commoners in Koryŏ and Chosŏn included peasants and merchants. While not a highly developed merchant state, Koryŏ carried out international trade with China, the Mongols, and others, all of which stimulated the economy, particularly during the fourteenth century.[18] Geographic and social mobility for commoners was limited by law, allowing the aristocracy to rule over society relatively efficiently. The lowest level of society included the lowborn or slaves (*nobi*; 奴婢), roughly 20–30 per cent of the population by early Chosŏn. Slaves had no self-determination and did not own their lives. Commoners could own land and slaves, while slaves had no personal choices.

Because the government survived on taxes, some of which were on items made from domesticated animals or hunted beasts, understanding the tax obligations of Korean society is essential. Each of these social groups held different tax obligations during both Koryŏ and Chosŏn. Ideally the elite were the ones required to pay land taxes. Formidable land-holding families towards the end of the Koryŏ Dynasty had to pay taxes but were powerful enough to be landlords and had numerous tenants whom they made pay in their stead. In reality, many of these elites did not pay taxes themselves. At the beginning of the Chosŏn Dynasty, some powerful families gained special status as merit subjects because they contributed to the founding of the state. The state gave these merit subjects hereditary land rights that they could then pass onto their descendants, and they had no tax obligations. Families that had special status could lose their rights and privileges if the government accused later generations of state crimes. While the king owned all the land in the dynasty in theory, less than thirty years after the founding of the Chosŏn Dynasty, families were buying and selling land. The tax burden fell on the commoners who paid not only various taxes that supported the central bureaucracy but also paid for and served in the military. These taxes included a cotton cloth tax and military and corvée labour service fees. Another tax paid by the community was contribution in kind. The state held a list of necessary items – military, bureaucratic and practical products. At times, the state demanded a certain product on a specified date from a particular region, such as bamboo in the south or fur pelts in the north, placing a considerable burden on the localities.

---

[17] Nan-ok Kim, 'Low-Class Commoners during the Koryŏ Dynasty', *International Journal of Korean History* 6 (December 2004): 87–111.

[18] Kang Hahn Lee, 'Koryŏ Trade with the Outer World', *Korean Studies* 41 (2017): 52–74.

The local magistrate was responsible for mobilising the community – the commoners and slaves – to collect this in-kind tax, which he sent to the capital.

Another aspect of Koryŏ and Chosŏn societies was the visible clashes between the governing status groups. The elites, the yangban – the military and scholarly – were often in conflict for proximity to royal authority and the resources and wealth of the state. In 1126, for instance, Yi Chagyŏm (?–1127), a leading civil official, insisted on marrying three of his daughters to the king to provide three generations of control over the royal family. His overreach for power led to civil war in the capital and the destruction of his clan. Crises like this convinced King Injong (r. 1122–46) to seek political advisors among Buddhist monks outside the Confucian bureaucracy. On one particular occasion, a monk named Myoch'ŏng (?–1135) exerted powerful control over the king. Using his proximity to the throne, Myoch'ŏng rose up against the central officials and encouraged the king to move the capital to P'yŏngyang and to proclaim a new kingdom in 1135. The aristocracy, enraged by his moves, acted swiftly, and killed him and his supporters.

After the Myoch'ŏng insurrection, military leaders grew alienated from the aristocratic scholarly elites as civil officials passed laws downgrading and denigrating the military class. From 1135 to 1170, tensions intensified, fuelled by discrimination the military men faced from the scholarly order. The military had slowly been deprived of property and humiliated until 1170, when tensions exploded as a well-planned coup that killed many scholarly elites, unleashing a turbulent time until 1196. Kings were held captive by military families, while generals and their house armies fought each other for domination. With a society out of control, civil war closed the doors on government, and politics slipped into disarray. This period saw a transfer of wealth and power to those in the military ranks. More than merely a coup, the military men took control of bureaucratic positions, from which they were normally excluded, and transferred land to themselves. From 1173, the kingship served as a puppet under the control of the military for nearly a century. Without royal authority, the aristocracy suffered. Some scholarly elites survived because of close friendships with military families, but many others were slain. Disorder came to an end in 1196 with the rise of General Ch'oe Ch'unghŏn (1149–1219) and his house army, a group of soldiers holding loyalty to a single clan. As the state repositioned itself and established governing institutions under a stable military regime, order began to reappear.[19] General Ch'oe, his sons

---

[19] For more, see Edward Shultz, *Generals and Scholars: Military Rule in Medieval Korea* (Honolulu: University of Hawai'i Press, 2000).

and his grandsons served as overlords of the Koryŏ Dynasty – but increasingly relied on civil officials to assist in governance – until the Mongol invasions of the thirteenth century when a foreign power facilitated the end of the military government.

The Mongols began appearing along the northern frontier from 1206 to 1219. The sizeable Mongol invasion of 1231 pressured Koryŏ with greater demands. Mongol leaders insisted that the powerful families of Koryŏ send thousands of sons and daughters to the Mongol capital as hostages. In response, the members of the Koryŏ bureaucracy and General Ch'oe's family relocated to Kanghwa Island in 1232. Furthermore, the court encouraged the population to retreat to the hundreds of large islands located in the Yellow Sea as a means to disperse the Korean population. Some travelled as refugees while the Mongols captured and brought others into Manchuria to farm, promoting the spread of ethnic Koreans beyond the peninsula. Even though the military still held power, the Koryŏ army had been fragmented by the Ch'oe military and was unable to defend the peninsula. Loyalty was to clan rather than to national defence. Over the course of three decades, from 1231 to 1259, the Mongols invaded Koryŏ scores of times unobstructed, seizing people and booty and returning north. In one attack, the Mongols burned the *Tripitaka* (K. *Taejangkyŏng*; C. *Daizangjing*; 大藏經), the complete wooden set of the Buddhist sutras, to punish the Koryŏ officials and demoralise the people. As a measure of strength, the bureaucracy encouraged the re-carving of the sutra in the middle of the invasion, which was completed years later in 1252.[20] The final major Mongol invasion in 1259 pressured King Kojong (r. 1213–59) who had sent his son, the crown prince and future King Wŏnjong (r. 1259–74), to the Mongols. The Ch'oe military house ended in 1259, and the court returned to the peninsula. However, strongmen continued to try to decide policy and challenged Wŏnjong once he returned from Mongol lands in 1260. In essence, Mongol intervention reinstated scholarly aristocracy and royal rule, returning Korea to its earlier political patterns.

While the political institutions, king and court officials returned to the capital, the Mongols controlled Korea through uxorilocal marriage rather than through a military government. Yuan Mongol princesses married Korean kings and princes. Mongol households raised young Korean crown princes in the Yuan Dynasty where they learned about Mongol customs and spoke Mongol, their children learned Mongolian too, and then the prince moved back to Korea after the Koryŏ king died. In the uxorilocal relationship, the husband lived in the wife's household raising their children with the wife's

---

[20] The *Tipitaka* is a massive and hugely important full collection of the Buddhist canon carved into more than 80,000 wood blocks.

parents. During the Koryŏ Dynasty, this meant that the crown prince brought his Mongol wife and their children back to Koryŏ. Some family members remained in Mongol Yuan lands, a pattern that repeated for seven kings from 1259 to 1356 until King Kongmin (1351–74) led a rebellion and weakened ties with the Mongol court.

Through relations like these, the Mongols governed Koryŏ passively, allowing a new aristocracy to rise to power. The court ruled through old and new talent. After the initial period of resistance in the thirteenth century, Mongol demands were not as onerous. Koreans still ruled Koryŏ, and Koryŏ institutions survived. Many ordinary Koryŏ elite men married Mongol women, which improved the situation of these men by giving them economic and social opportunities in the Yuan, with the intermingling of Mongol and Koryŏ blood. The civil bureaucracy functioned, and the kingdom was safe and secure. In 1274 and 1281 the Mongols demanded the assistance of Koryŏ in their attempted invasions of the Japanese islands. Koreans did not oppose these demands as the Mongols paid for what they needed, such as timber, horses and supplies, allowing some Koreans to grow wealthier. Many Koreans who travelled to the Yuan Dynasty learned Mongolian and returned to Koryŏ with a wider worldview. In the Yuan capital, Beijing, the Mongols held a worldly perspective. They tolerated all religions, the presence of Europeans as merchants and other craftsmen, and encouraged cultural exchanges. The capital of the Yuan had an air of cosmopolitanism that found its way to the Korean peninsula. This expansion of worldviews included a revival of hunting practices among the royal family and elite.

1
Wild Beasts on a Premodern Peninsula

This chapter explores the peninsular environment as the backdrop for the wild animals that live on it. To argue that not all wild animals were equally important to hunters or the state, I categorise the beasts most frequently encountered in the mountains, valleys, plains and pages of the historical records. Some held more significance in terms of protein, others for ritual needs, and yet more for medicinal, economic, or symbolic purposes. Some beasts were outright dangerous and a threat to people regardless of social class. The second half of this chapter studies the social role of animals in premodern Korea. How did people think about and 'use' animals in non-material ways? Part of the answer includes the adoption of animals as symbols of legitimacy and power by early political leaders, commoners and the lowborn. These beasts of the wild helped people from all social status groups make sense of their worlds.

About 70 per cent of the Korean peninsula is covered in mountains, including the Chiri, Hamgyŏng and T'aebaek ranges in addition to a number of minor mountain ranges.[1] The tallest mountains are located in the northeast, part of a spine of mountains along the eastern region stretching to the south. The T'aebaek range is the longest. The east coast and north to the Yalu and Tumen rivers are more heavily mountainous than the southwest. A number of these mountains reach 1,700 metres (5,500 ft) tall and continue to this day to be difficult to access. Mongol demands for wooden ships, during the two failed invasions of Japan in the 1270s and 1280s, may have

---

[1] Some geographers have attempted to redefine the number of mountain ranges in Korea because Japanese scientists initially classified the ranges in the early twentieth century. Chŏng Yongsŭng and Kim Haksŏng, 'Hanbando sanmaek ŭi chejosa wa pullyu mit taegi hwan'gyŏng e mich'inŭn yŏnghyang' [Classification of mountains on the Korean peninsula and the influence of the atmospheric environment], *Han'guk chiguhak hoeji* 37 (2016): 21–8.

resulted in the deforestation of some areas around the capital region near present-day Kaesŏng.² The founding of the new capital, Hanyang (Seoul), in the early fifteenth century further upset this equilibrium as the government demanded greater supplies of timber for buildings, temples and warships. Noting the impact of such a demand, officials put in place government policies and attempted to counterbalance this effect by nurturing pine forests.³ However, areas in the north were most likely heavily forested in the late Koryŏ and early Chosŏn eras. Throughout the sixteenth century, forests remained self-sustaining as demand did not outpace new growth.⁴ While potentially fragmented from human development and deforestation, the forests present during the late Koryŏ and early Chosŏn dynasties were vast and contiguous by today's standards; many connected by mountain chains that fanned across the peninsula like veins on a hand.

The steep topography of these mountain ranges restricted significant settlement in the interior. Villages and towns grew along the valleys or at the foot of mountains or plains. The forests that surrounded these settlements sustained the villagers by providing game and timber, much of it pine. The land northward was more mountainous and offered less space for population growth but more opportunities for habitat and animal diversity. Villagers settled in meadows, locations where the mountain ranges ended and waterways began from streams coming from nearby hills and highlands. In these locations, where the slopes were gentle, villagers relied upon the resources of

---

[2] See K. Tak, Y. Chun and P. M. Wood, 'The South Korean Forest Dilemma', *International Forestry Review* 9, no. 1 (June 2007): 549. For work on forest resources in late Chosŏn, see John S. Lee, 'Postwar Pines: The Military and the Expansion of State Forests in Post-Imjin Korea, 1598–1684', *Journal of Asian Studies* 77, no. 2 (May 2018): 319–32.

[3] Han Chŏngsu, 'Chosŏn T'aejo-Sejong tae sup kaebal kwa chungsong chŏngch'aek' [The development of forests and the formation of policies for cultivating pine trees from Chosŏn kings T'aejo to Sejong], *Sahak yŏn'gu* (September 2013): 44–6. Han Hŭngsun argues that the problem with government forest policies during the Chosŏn Dynasty was that the legal codes did not clearly identify ownership of land in the mountains. This contributed to the destruction of many forest regions by the eighteenth and nineteenth centuries as commoners and other groups, pressed by social and economic troubles, struggled with each other over control of these lands and their resources. See Han Hŭngsun, 'Sijang chuŭijŏk koch'al kwa kŭe tahan pigyo: Chosŏn hugi sallimjŏngch'aek mit sallim hwangp'ehwa' [Forest policies and forest devastation in the late Chosŏn: a review of the market principle critique], *Han'guk chiyŏk kaebal hakhoe* 20, no. 2 (June 2008): 172–3.

[4] Kim Tongjin, '15–19 segi hanbando sallim ŭi min'gan kaebang kwa sup ŭi pyŏnhwa' [Fifteenth- through nineteenth-century open door policy on the forests of the Korean peninsula and the transformation of forests], *Yŏksa wa hyŏnsil* 3 (2017): 77–118.

the nearby mountains, rivers and streams for their livelihoods.⁵ Rather than randomly selecting locations for settlements, these villagers took into consideration *P'ungsu* (wind and water), a means of reading the geography of the mountains and water or what is commonly referred to as feng shui, when placing their dwellings and towns.⁶ Surrounded by hills, these village watersheds, or areas where rainfall, streams and other running water collects, were self-sustaining ecosystems. Villagers worked the fields and cut timber from the mountains to build with and use as firewood. Building materials and firewood were also obtained from village forests, a type of public land, that separated settlements. Wildlife of all kinds thrived in the mountains and the development of new towns and villages at the foot of mountains promoted the frequency of wild encounters.⁷

One example of the type of terrain appropriate for hunts in the fifteenth century was Mt Pojang. Seventy-eight kilometres (48 mi.) northeast of the capital Hanyang, a full day's journey, Mt Pojang had imposing hills, rising over 500 metres (1,600 ft) high, fifteen *li* (60 km/37 mi.) west of the village of Yŏngp'yŏng, approximately eleven kilometres (7 mi.) from the modern-day city of P'och'ŏn.⁸ Offering intimate contact with prey, the dense terrain was typical of mountains where kings and other elites hunted. The great King Sejong and his hunting party frequented Mt Pojang. An expansive plain with a meandering river climbs upward nearly a kilometre before reaching a rapidly ascending mountain with a steep forested peak. The hills, forests and fields beyond Mt Pojang were much the same, with mountains and valley streams as far as the eye could see. The densely forested mountains that surround the river, where animals congregate, were roughly twenty-five square kilometres (15 sq. mi.) in circumference. As early as the Chosŏn times, the salubrious

---

⁵ Kim Pyŏngju and Yi Sanhae, '"*Taedong yŏjido*"rŭl t'onghae pon Chosŏn, sidae ssijok maul ŭi ipchi hwangyŏng' [Location and natural environment of lineage villages in the Chosŏn Dynasty based on the Taedong yŏji], *Taehan kŏnch'uk hakhoe nongmunjip kyehoekkye* 22, no. 1 (2006): 165–6.

⁶ Kim Pyŏngju, 'Yongmaek kwa sugu ro pon Chosŏn hugi toso ipchi hwan'gyŏng ŭi pyŏnhwa yŏn'gu' [A study on the location of village settlements in the late Chosŏn as reflected in the mountain ranges and watersheds], *Taehan kŏnch'uk hakhoe nongminchip* 31 (2015): 111–21.

⁷ Hong Hyŏngsun, 'Hwan'gyŏngsa kwanjŏm esŏ pon Chosŏn sidae kunggwŏl e pŏm kwa p'yobŏ ŭi ch'ulmul' [The emergence of tigers and leopards in the royal palace in the Chosŏn Dynasty from an environmental perspective], *Han'guk chŏnt'ong chogyŏng hakhoeji* 36, no. 3 (September 2018): 13–14.

⁸ *Chŭngbo munhyŏn pigo* [Documents for reference, revised and updated] (Seoul: Tongguk munhwasa, 1971), che-21-yŏjigo 9.

area produced a thriving deer population, which must have attracted hunters and predators.[9]

Another location, Mt Ch'ŏnggye, favoured by King Sŏngjong, offered similar wildlife habitat and hunting opportunities. Twenty *li* east of the town of Puryŏng, only fifteen kilometres (10 mi.) south of the capital, Mt Ch'ŏnggye was conveniently accessible and a less arduous journey for kings and his followers. Heavily forested, with copious rugged peaks reaching over 500 metres (1,600 ft), the terrain of Mt Ch'ŏnggye must have supported the vibrant and varied wildlife attractive to hunters. In both areas, the villages and paddy fields of the plains were distant, providing enough isolation from human communities for the natural world to thrive.

Beasts of the Wild

The vegetation, forests and foothills supported exceptional biodiversity throughout the region; a myriad of species inhabited the regions on the periphery of human settlements and beyond. Some of these species occurred sympatrically, living side by side with villagers and townspeople or surrounding the Buddhist monasteries deep in the mountains. Within this terrain, animals crisscrossed the environment more easily than the human population. Humans had limited social and geographical mobility, while animals moved freely without restriction. The mountains, many interconnected with streams and rivers from the summer rains, supported a vibrant ecosystem. Based on descriptions of animals in the sources, the fauna that kings, scholars, military men and others hunted – deer, hare, boar, tigers and pheasants, for example – appear to have changed little over the centuries. While some species are thought to be extinct, for example tigers and leopards, others thrive. Deer thrive now, much like they did during the Koryŏ and Chosŏn dynasties; while their habitats have been reduced, their natural predators, wolves, tigers and leopards, have been hunted to extinction.[10]

---

[9] Pak Sun (1523–89) and Kim Sanghŏn, *Saamjip* [Collected works of Saam], Chosŏn original manuscript, Ch'ŏlchong year 8, 1857. Held at Columbia University.

[10] The only controls of the deer population are human hunters and automobile collisions in South Korea. See Yi Kyŏngju, T'ak Chonghun and Pak Sŏnil, 'Urinara kosoktoro esŏ yangsaeng tongmul rodek'il e kwanhan sigongan ch'ui punsŏk' [Spatial and temporal patterns of wildlife road-kills on highways in Korea], *Han'guk imsangsuŭihak hoeji* 31, no. 4 (2014): 284. In North Korea, the government does not publish data on this issue. Most likely, numbers are low in North Korea because of a loss of habitat from deforestation and human hunting during times of famine.

Deer, elk, moose

Sources depict deer – *chang*, 獐; *ajang*, 牙獐; *sahyang*, 麝香; *nok*, 鹿; and *taerok*, 大鹿 – as one of the most significant game animals on the Korean peninsula. *Ayang* deer (*ayangnok*; 阿羊鹿), apparently hunted for their antlers, no longer appeared in the records after the middle of the fifteenth century. Unfamiliar with the beasts described to them, court scribes conflated subspecies, confused the types of deer hunted or offered for ritual sacrifice, or simply were unaware or unconcerned by the differences in species. Deer appear to have been categorised based on appearance – fanged or without fangs – and body size; rather than true fangs, these deer have tusks. Body size and fangs were two of the most immediately recognisable qualities used to identify a deer. Vernacular descriptions of deer were hard to depict in the classical Chinese expressions, and it was not until the late Chosŏn when Neo-Confucian scholars began to express a deeper awareness of deer species.

Chang included a number of deer species. The Korean water or river deer (*Hydropotes inermis argyropus*) was and continues to be one of the most widely dispersed deer on the peninsula. Found throughout forested lowlands, these fanged deer weigh between ten and fifteen kilogrammes (20–30 lb) and measure 75–100 centimetres (2 ft 6 in.–3 ft) long and only 45–55 centimetres (3 ft 6 in.–4 ft) tall when full grown.[11] While attracted to thick grasses and slopes with shrubs, they prefer heavy forests found in the lowland mountains. Their diet varies from shrubs and trees to forest undergrowth, reflecting their preference for mixed forest habitats. The home range of the female water deer averages two and a half square kilometres (1.5 mi.), whereas the males range on average three and a half kilometres (2 mi.), suggesting a high density of deer in heavily forested areas because of relatively limited ranges. Water deer are most active in the evenings from sunset to sunrise when they forage for food, the ideal time to hunt them. They tend to rest during the daytime; however, sometimes they can be found foraging during this time. Water deer also tend to increase their home range from June through August. They are attracted to agricultural areas as well as mountains and are found throughout the peninsula, especially areas close to water.[12]

---

[11] For reference, the North American white-tailed deer (*Odocoileus virginianus*; eastern USA) is more than twice the size of the water deer at 81–91 centimetres (2 ft 8 in.–3 ft) and range 95–220 centimetres (3 ft 1 in.–7 ft 2 in.) long and weigh up to fifty kilogrammes (110 lb).

[12] Baek Jun Kim and Sang-Don Lee, 'Home Range Study of the Korean Water Deer Using Radio and GPS Tracking in South Korea: Comparison of Daily and Seasonal Habit Use Pattern', *Journal of Ecology and Field Biology* 34, no. 4 (2011): 365–70; and

A small species of roe deer, the 'tooth deer' (*ajang*; 牙獐), was also fanged like the water deer. Their size and dark brown colour made them easily distinguishable from more common Siberian roe deer. Feeding on tree roots dug up with their hooves, they inhabited the alpine regions along the T'aebaek mountain range through to the coastal city of P'ohang. Generally, they moved along the southern side of mountains near foothills where forests were dense. Hunting them demanded that hunters stay along the narrow valleys of higher mountains and wait for them to emerge at closer ranges. If surprised, these roe would flee the area and tended not to return. Their blood was highly prized as medicine and their venison considered in late Chosŏn to be some of the highest quality meat of any animal.[13]

Also described as *chang*, but more commonly as *sahyangjang* (麝香獐), were the Korean musk deer (*Moshus moshiferus*). This species mostly inhabited and continues to inhabit coniferous or mixed forest habitats 1,000 metres (3,200 ft) above sea level. They especially favour rugged terrain. In the vernacular, they were called *hyang noro* or scented deer, because they were 'hunted for the perfume contained in a sac in the abdomen of the males'.[14] These animals consume plants, moss on tree bark and fruits of trees, and average 65–90 centimetres (25–35 in.) long and 75–105 centimetres (30–40 in.) tall, weighing a mere 7–15 kilogrammes (15–30 lb). One striking feature is their pair of long fangs protruding from their upper jaws that measure up to ten centimetres (4 in.). Korean musk deer are solitary most of the year, but groups of three or four will begin to gather during the breeding season. These groups consist of a doe and fawns. Beginning in October through December, bucks release

---

Kim Haek-Jun, Dae-Hyun Oh, Seung-Hoon Chun and Sang-Don Lee, 'Distribution, Density, and Habitat Use of the Korean Water Deer (*Hydropotes inermis agyropus*) in Korea', *Landscape and Ecological Engineering* 7 (2011): 291–7. See also Horace H. Underwood, 'Hunting and Hunters' Lore in Korea', *Transactions of the Korea Branch of the Royal Asiatic Society* 6, no. 2 (1915): 24.

[13] Yi Sango, *Suryŏp pihwa* [Secret stories of hunting] (Seoul: Pagusa, 1965), 269–71. Yi Sango (1905–69; 李相昈) was a professional hunter throughout his life, as well as an independence fighter against the Japanese. Yi is credited with helping transform hunting into a sport in Korea during the early and middle twentieth century. With a wealth of hunting experience throughout his life, Yi hunted extensively on the peninsula, including on 'Paekdu, Kŭmgang, Chiri, and all the famous mountains of Korea . . . There was not a place he did not go.' For these brief Yi obituaries see *Tonga ilbo*, 16 August 1969: 7; and *Kyŏngsang sinmun*, 16 August 1969. *Suryŏp pihwa* was first published as *Suryŏp pŏnwi Han'guk yasaeng tongmulgi* [Origins of hunting Korean wild animals] in 1965. Yi's insights, himself having learned hunting from late Chosŏn Dynasty-era hunters, offer a glimpse into an otherwise undocumented history of rural life, animals, and hunting strategies.

[14] Underwood, 'Hunting and Hunters' Lore in Korea', 24.

musk from glands on their bellies during the mating season to attract mates. While rutting, the males consume very little and wander outside their territories until after mating when they settle down again. Does give birth from May to July. Unlike other species of deer, the musk deer, originally found throughout the peninsula, are currently endangered because of over hunting and loss of habitat.[15] In the first half of the twentieth century, there were attempts to protect them.[16] While the venison is considered poor quality, the taste being overpowered by the odour of musk permeating the meat, the musk gland itself has been valued for its medicinal qualities. Because of the rocky alpine terrain they preferred, which was unlike the river deer, hunters and other predators had difficulty tracking them. One technique was to scare them by rolling rocks down from the tops of mountain slopes they were known to inhabit. Surprised, the musk deer would flee down the cliff where hunters waited.

Medium deer (nok; 鹿) most likely referred to several species based on body size and lack of 'fangs'. Siberian roe deer (*Capreolus pygargus*) are sizeable, averaging 150 centimetres (4.8 ft) in length and weighing in at sixty kilogrammes (130 lb). These deer can be distinguished by their slender tails. The males have small antlers in relationship to their body size.[17] The antlers of Siberian roe and other deer are used to fight other stags during the mating season. Beginning in spring, after shedding their antlers, new antlers begin growing over the old antler cast, reaching peak size at the end of the summer when the velvet is brushed off before they drop their antlers in the winter. Roe deer inhabit forested zones in mountains and hillsides. More than other species of deer on the Korean peninsula, they prefer shade, even in the winter, because of a species of fly that lay their eggs in the skin of the deer in the fall. The eggs hatch in the winter. Sunlight activates the larvae and irritates the deer; the larvae emerge from the deer in spring. Deer produce offspring around the fifth day of the fifth month of the lunar calendar during the early summer months. Roe does give birth to one or two offspring that are able to walk within one hour and flee predators on their own within two or three days, typical of all these deer species.

---

[15] The musk deer is endangered or extinct in many parts of Eurasia due to poaching. The musk gland is not only prized as perfume but musk deer antlers and other parts are also used in Chinese medicine in South and North Korea and other parts of Asia. Kim Chingt'aek, Kim Kŏnjung and Kim Hyŏnch'ŏl, 'Myŏljching wigijong Han'guk sahyang noru ŭi sŏsikji chosa' [Investigation of the natural habitat for Korean musk deer], *Han'guk kach'uk wisaeng hakhoeji* 30, no. 3 (2007): 460.

[16] The Japanese colonial government outlawed hunting roe deer. Yi Sango, *Suryŏp pihwa*, 271–2.

[17] Underwood, 'Hunting and Hunters' Lore in Korea', 25.

When escaping predators, roe deer have powerful strides – reaching 6–7 metres (20–22 ft) with each bound – and are known to migrate closer to human habitats around mid-June to avoid predators that grow more active deeper in the mountain forests. Mating season begins between late May and late June. These deer move about the area grunting, wildly chasing each other. If one of a pair is harvested, the mate will remain in the area crying for days. In addition to humans, roe deer are hunted by tigers, leopards, wolves and eagles. Roe would stop fleeing if they were unable to see their attacker and would hesitate for a moment roughly 200–300 metres (660–960 ft) from the hunter.[18] This is within the striking distance of arrows released from composite bows. In general, the meat of deer is flavourless in the spring and summer because animals have less fat. By the autumn and winter, they have stored fat by feeding on vegetation and the fat provides a richer flavour. However, roe deer have better flavour in the spring and summer than other times of the year, most likely because the sex organs become active in the fall and winter, overpowering the flavour. The fur was considered inferior, but the leather hide was considered high quality. Other parts of the animal, such as the bones and deer horn, were used as medicine but only for a limited number of ailments.[19]

The roe deer is one of the most adaptable deer species, exhibiting strong behavioural flexibility, and can survive in fragmented landscapes where habitats are disconnected because of human settlements. It responds well to changes in environmental conditions and structure of the landscape. This plasticity helps the species adapt to predation, changes in habitat and alterations to the environment. Roe deer are not timid about moving into areas with diminishing ranges or those spaces human encroachment disturb. As a consequence, they have remained abundant regardless of the pressure humans or predators place on them. Deer emerged from the mountains and fed on the grain in the fields at night, often in pairs. When hunters followed deer trails from the mountains into the fields, this was when deer were most vulnerable.[20] Pursued from behind, roe deer tended to descend mountain slopes, cross into open valleys, and ascend up the opposite ridge, habits that made them vulnerable to hunters waiting in the valley. Deer such as these tended to stay out of mountains fearing predation, but the animals were squeezed between two threats: the risk of tigers, leopards and wolves deep in the forest and the threat of humans hunting along the periphery of settlements.

---

[18] Yi Sango, *Suryŏp pihwa*, 261–4.
[19] Yi Sango, *Suryŏp pihwa*, 263.
[20] Yi Sango, *Suryŏp pihwa*, 264.

Also of this category were the red deer (*Cervus elaphus*). Given the adaptability of red deer to changing climate and environmental conditions, they appeared throughout the peninsula and were hunted throughout premodern times.[21] Measuring up to two metres (7 ft) long and weighing up to 180 kilogrammes (400 lb), they have been described like a small horse. Populating the many pine forests on the peninsula, red deer are seasonal in their habitat selection – adults preferring open coniferous stands in warmer weather and closed coniferous, usually around the edges, during the winter when they also avoid deeper forests.[22] Their antlers can reach eighty centimetres (30 in.) in size. In the spring and summer months, their fur turns red, and it darkens in the fall and winter months. From October until November, the stags fight over does in the mating season when their rutting calls can be heard throughout the forests. Their antlers were prized for their medicinal qualities.[23]

Another medium-sized deer was the sika deer often referred to as the Japanese deer or the spotted deer (*Cervus nippon mantchuricus*). Inhabiting such mountainous regions as Kangwŏn Province, these deer have red fur that turns spotted white in the summer. The body length of bucks reaches 155 centimetres (61 in.) long and 110 centimetres (43 in.) at the shoulder, and they can weight up to 110 kilogrammes (242 lb). Does are slightly smaller. Bucks grow antlers measuring up to eighty centimetres (32 in.). Like other deer species, they are most active from dusk until dawn. Hunting them can take days in the mountains. Even during Chosŏn times, this species' population thinned because of over hunting by villagers.[24]

Large deer (*taerok*; 大鹿) may have included several species. One was the Manchurian wapiti (*Cervus canadensis xanthopygus*).[25] This formidable ungulate is referred to as the Paekdu Mountain elk today. The Paekdu Mountain elk is one of the largest species of deer on the peninsula – the males average 2.5 metres (8 ft) long and weigh 320 kilogrammes (700 lb) – with a historical

---

[21] For more on red deer, see D. G. Drucker, *et al.*, 'Evolution of Habitat and Environment of Red Deer (*Cervus elaphus*) during the Late Glacial and Early Holocene in Eastern France (French Jura and the Western Alps) using Multi-Isotope Analysis (δ 13C, δ 15N, δ 18O, δ 34S) of Archaeological Remains', *Quaternary International* 245, no. 2 (2011): 268–78.

[22] A. M. Licoppe, 'The Diurnal Habitat Used by Red Deer (*Cervus elaphus* L.) in the Haute Ardenne', *European Journal of Wildlife Research* 52, no. 3 (2006): 164–70.

[23] Yi Sango, *Suryŏp pihwa*, 274–76; and Valerius Geist, *Deer of the World: Their Evolution, Behavior, and Ecology* (Mechanicsburg: Stackpole Books, 1999).

[24] Yi Sango, *Suryŏp pihwa*, 285–8.

[25] The Manchurian wapiti (*Cervus canadensis xanthopygus*) is a subspecies of the elk (*Cervus canadensis*).

range that covers the northern provinces and extends into northeast China. The Paekdu Mountain elk turn reddish brown in the spring and summer and dark brown in the autumn and winter to help camouflage them. The bulls grow antlers, which can reach over 1.2 metres (4 ft) long and weigh ten kilogrammes (20 lb) each, for the mating season in late January and February, before shedding them. Like other deer species, Paekdu Mountain elk begin growing antlers again in the summer and their length could determine the age of the bulls. After the age of three, they grow an additional branch each year. When they begin to rut in October and November, their antlers harden and the bulls grow violent, competing loudly with each other for females, their calls sounding like trumpets in the mountains. The reproductive period lasts for about two months when the bulls avoid food and lose about a third of their body weight. Despite growing enormous antlers by the age of ten, bulls have no trouble manoeuvering through dense forests. These antlers were and continue to be valued as medicine. The best season to hunt them was in the summer during the Koryŏ and Chosŏn dynasties when the vegetation was lush and hunters could shoot them from close range, 100–200 metres (330–660 ft).

Because of their size and speed and the range of these Paekdu Mountain elk reaching into uninhabited forested mountains, the use of chasers (men who flush out the animals) to hunt this sizeable deer species was difficult, unlike when hunting other species of deer. To successfully locate them, hunters had to prepare one to two months of supplies before entering the mountains. Hunters would build makeshift hunting lean-tos near deer tracks and wait months for the deer to return. Because other deer, like the sika, were easily frightened, hunters had to remain stationary for long periods of time. Salt, which the deer could smell from great distances, was sometimes deployed to attract them. Once killed, hunters had to work quickly to harvest the elk as the smell of the kill, deep in uninhabited mountains, attracted other predators, such as tigers and leopards. Even bears chased away hunters from their kills.[26]

Another large deer species included in the *surok* category was the Urasian moose (*Alces alces cameloides*), the largest deer species on earth. Bulls weigh in at 800 kilogrammes (1,500 lb) and measure 2.3 metres (7.5 ft) at the shoulder with a body length of 3.5 metres (11 ft) with antlers of a mature bull reaching up to 1.5 metres (5 ft) in length. The sizable animals inhabited the northern part of the T'aebaek Mountains, but their numbers declined rapidly during the late Chosŏn.[27]

---

[26] Yi Sango, *Suryŏp pihwa*, 282–4.
[27] Yi Sango, *Suryŏp pihwa*, 289.

Wild swine

Another important animal hunted for game was wild boar (*chŏ*; 猪). While two subspecies of boar have been identified (*Sus scrofa ussuricus* and *Sus scrofa coreanus*) on the peninsula, like several of the deer species, the sources do not differentiate between them. Koryŏ- and Chosŏn-era hunters tracked deer and wild swine at different times and in different areas and required different hunting skills. The species exchanged habitats, moving up and down the mountain seasonally. Deer rely not only on their sight and hearing but also scent, while wild boar have a limited sense of smell and rely on their sight and sense of hearing.[28] Deer can become aggressive and sometimes injure hunters, but adult wild boar are powerful and unpredictable animals often known for charging hunters as a means of defence.[29] As formidable animals, they range between eighty and 300 kilogrammes (175–660 lb).[30] Wild swine brought predators of all kinds together. Because the habitats of wild boar often overlap with humans and the animals sometimes damage crops and injure people, they have been frequently hunted. As noted by one observer in the early twentieth century, wild boar were nuisances to farmers and dangerous to individuals unaware of them:

> The animals are very plentiful in the mountain regions and are on the increase. They are a great pest to the farmers, as one large boar is said to be quite capable of ruining the crops in a day's plowing in one night. What they do not eat they root up, and I have seen fields which looked as though someone had been hard at work getting ready to plant trees ... They quite often travel in herds; the Koreans reporting having seen fourteen or fifteen in a herd ... The larger ones go by themselves, and it is these that are supposed to be dangerous ... and only last fall a Japanese [person] was ... almost killed by one not far from [Hanyang]. [The] biggest ones are found in inaccessible mountains.[31]

Descriptions like these resonate with earlier sources. Wild boar damaged crops, property and lives. The court dealt with these incidents. Like deer,

---

[28] Yi Sango, *Suryŏp pihwa*, 285.
[29] Even today, wild boar descend from the mountains into villages, towns and cities, destroy property and injure citizens.
[30] Youngjin Kim, Soyeon Cho and Yeonsook Choung, 'Habitat Preference of Wild Boar (*Sus scrofa*) for Feeding in Cool-Temperate Forests', *Journal of Ecology and Environment* 43, no. 30 (2019): 297–304.
[31] Underwood, 'Hunting and Hunters' Lore in Korea', 34.

wild boar were plentiful on Mt Namhan during the first half of the fifteenth century.[32] To provide some background, in 1431, for instance, the court prohibited the hunting of deer and wild boar near the royal Kangmu hunting grounds, but shortly after, it was rescinded because of the growing number of boar damaging the grain supplies.[33] One modern hunter details how before the twentieth century, wild boar inhabited the peninsula from deep in the mountains and hills to foothills near farming villages and towns.[34] They are omnivores and feed on a variety of smaller animals, roots and shrubs. Sows are social and (both infertile and fertile females) will congregate in groups called sounders. Males will leave their sounder when they come of age (15–18 months). During the mating season in December and January, solitary males congregate, usually in groups of seven or eight males, to rally for one female. In the spring, females give birth to between seven to thirteen squeakers. The high number of offspring is thought to be a counterbalance to the high mortality rate as young boar are prey for a variety of predators.

Once fully grown, their formidable size and strength protects them from wolves and leopards. Boar do not live in permanent dens but rather construct an overnight bed and move on the next day, thus increasing their range. Successfully hunting wild boar, a challenging task then and now, required a number of experienced 'beaters' or 'chasers', people along on the hunt who produced sounds and walked towards the animals to scare game towards the waiting hunters. It also required experienced trackers capable of traversing the many slopes and mountain forests. Boar are nocturnal and emerge at night to feed, resting during the day.[35] Like deer, the meat of the wild boar, flavourful from September to December, was considered an important source of nutrition. Starting in April, they begin losing their fat which diminishes the flavour. Like deer, the blood of wild boar was prized as an ingredient of Chinese medicine (*Hanyak*; 漢藥) that Koreans consumed.[36]

Sable

Sable (*ch'o*; 貂; *Martes zibellina*) were found in the northern part of the peninsula during the Koryŏ and Chosŏn dynasties. Males range between 180 and 1,800 grammes (1.9–3.9 lb) and measure 380–560 millimetres (15–22 in.),

---

[32] CWS, 2:375.
[33] CWS, 3:335.
[34] Yi Sango, *Suryŏp pihwa*, 229–31.
[35] Yi Sango, *Suryŏp pihwa*, 229–31.
[36] Yi Sango, *Suryŏp pihwa*, 217–22.

while the females are slightly smaller. Their tail length reaches 120 millimetres (4.7 in.). Living in dense forest areas of flatlands or mountains, they only avoid extreme alpine regions.[37] Their numbers have been known to reach up to 10,000 individuals in protected mountain ranges.[38] Sable were highly sought after, hunted for their glossy, black fur which was used as a luxury item in Korean clothes and traded with Jurchens across the Korean frontier.

Hare

Three species of hare (*t'o*; 兔), the Korean hare (*Lepus coreanus*), the Manchurian hare (*Lepus mandschuricus*) and mountain hare (*Lepus timidus*) inhabit the peninsula and were commonly hunted during premodern times. Hares do not reproduce as frequently as rabbits, producing only two or three offspring two or three times a year. Bark, weeds and leaves, which are abundant throughout the peninsula, provide ample food. Hares are prey to many animals. The meat was considered to have low fat content and the texture light with low nutritional value.[39] Regardless, hare was an important ingredient in Chinese medicine and the fur a source of warmth because it is light and soft. However, hunting them does not appear to have been prestigious. Usually, hunters killed them while in the field looking for other game. Once finding an area plentiful with hare, it was easy to return to hunt them, since hare will return to their burrows when chased away by hunters or other animals. While fast moving, hare were easy to catch and could be found near settlements, which was helpful to single, elderly or female hunters because they did not have to travel far into the forest or mountains to hunt.[40] Hares can be easily tracked in the winter snow and, unlike more sizable game, are not aggressive and do not charge hunters.

Fowl

Like hooved animals, birds enticed humans to explore the wild. Pheasants, quail, ducks (*ap*; 鴨) and wild geese (*am*; 雁), migrated up, down and through

---

[37] Sergei Ivanovish Onev, *Mammals of Eastern Europe and Northern Asia* (Jerusalem: Israel Program for Scientific Translations, 1962), 2: 415–35.

[38] As a comparison, when unprotected by laws, sable hunting resulted in 4,000–5,000 skins collected in three Mongolian mountain ranges between 1910 and 1920. See Jonathan Baillie, *et. al.*, *Mongolian Red List of Mammals* (London: Zoological Society of London, 2006), 106.

[39] Yi Sango, *Suryŏp pihwa*, 360.

[40] Yi Sango *Suryŏp pihwa*, 360–1.

the peninsula. Pheasants and quail (*ch'i*; 雉), the two most commonly hunted fowl, nested in mountains and forests nearby human settlements. A variety of pheasant and quail species lived on mountain tops around the capital. Pheasants consume fruits, acorns and insects in the wild as well as grain from fields intended for human consumption. Because homes and settlements were close to the fields, the birds often lived on the southern sides of mountains, areas thick with young pine trees. They also inhabited mountain tops that were close to human settlements but only when water was nearby. Young pheasants hatch in high weeds in late spring and roam, watchful of predators in the area and when the weather turns severe. Male pheasants can be aggressive to ward off predators and humans.[41] While hunted for sport and chased by falconers, wild birds, including pheasant, were not commonly consumed.[42] This is understandable considering how difficult it was to hunt birds such as pheasants before the introduction of hunting rifles. Pheasant was a game of royalty, or for the elite and commoners lucky enough to have hawks; in other words fowl were reserved for those with trained birds of prey.

Bears

The Asiatic bear (*ung*; 熊; *Ursus thibetanus*) lived throughout the peninsula in alpine and forest regions but were more often found in the north before the twentieth century in the less accessible mountains. With body lengths ranging from 120 to 220 centimetres (50–90 in.) and weighing between ninety and 180 kilogrammes (200–400 lb), these medium-sized black bears were known as moon bears because of a whitish patch of hair on the collar.[43] Solitary animals and harder to encounter, bears were not commonly offered to the court as gifts. In 1417, when one man from western Hwanghae Province captured a cub (*unga*; 熊兒) and presented it to the court alive as a tribute gift, the king angrily rejected it, saying, 'I do not appreciate these kinds of beasts!'[44] While bears captured like this were unappreciated at the court, people from all social backgrounds apparently hunted them for meat or medicine. In 1439, during another occasion in North Hamgyŏng Province, a hunter (*yŏpcha*; 獵者)

---

[41] Yi Sango, *Suryŏp pihwa*, 101–2.
[42] Kim Taehong, 'Uri nara kkwŏng kogi choribŏp ŭi yŏksajŏk koch'al' [Historical study of pheasant cooking in Korea], *Han'guksik saenghwal munhwa hakhŏiji* 11, no. 1 (1996): 83–96.
[43] Information on the taxonomy of the moon bear can be found at www.speciesplus.net/api/v1/documents/11091.
[44] *CWS*, 2:168.

pursued bears in the mountains near his village.[45] On one royal hunt in 1456, the soldiers in the hunting party killed a bear.[46] While encounters with bears were much less common than with deer and other types of wild animals, all levels of statuses, especially the royal family and elites in the capital, relied on herbal and animal medicines, some produced of animal parts – including bear gallbladder – to help prevent or cure sickness.

Predators

Found throughout the peninsula, natural predators to deer, boar, hare, fowl and, in some cases, humans were the tiger (*ho*; 虎) and the leopard (*p'yo*; 豹).[47] The Korean Amur tiger (*Panthera tigris altaica*) is one of the largest big cats and is mostly a solitary animal. Male tigers can weigh up to 320 kilogrammes (700 lb) and their bodies measure two metres (6 ft 6 in.). The female, or tigress, is significantly smaller weighing 130 kilogrammes (290 lb) with a length of eighty centimetres (6 ft). The range of male tigers are sizeable and overlap slightly with the ranges of females. Females generally remain in their territories for their lifetimes while male tigers roam until they return to mate. Tiger density in an area is usually determined by the availability of prey or the reduction in prey from human hunting. Population estimates range from one to three tiger per three square kilometres (1 sq. mi.) and depend greatly on the availability of large ungulates such as wild swine and deer.[48] Tigers are nocturnal hunters. During the day, they sleep or rest in steep rocky areas out of the wind and direct sunlight. They prey on all types of animals from oxen to hares and have been known to harm and kill people. However, tigers generally fear humans and only attack when surprised. They may also strike back when injured by a hunter. People entering forests were advised to make loud noises to scare them away.[49] Professional hunters pursuing tigers utilised two techniques: hunting with beaters and chase hunting. While popular in other regions of the continent, bait hunting – setting up snares and traps for tigers – was not a favoured technique on the peninsula to flush out tigers. When called upon to kill tigers sighted in particular areas, hunters

---

[45] CWS, 4:223.
[46] CWS, 4:223, 7:154.
[47] Underwood, 'Hunting and Hunters' Lore in Korea', 37.
[48] David Macdonald and Andrew Loveridge, *The Biology and Conservation of Wild Felids* (Oxford: Oxford University Press, 2014), 325–39; Ronald Tilson and Philip Nyhus, *Tigers of the World: The Science, Politics, and Conservation of* Panthera Tigris (Amsterdam: Elsevier/Academic Press, 2010). See also Luke Hunter, *Wild Cats of the World* (London: Bloomsbury Publishing, 2015).
[49] Yi Sango, *Suryŏp pihwa*, 175–80.

pursued them into the mountains to locate and kill them rather than rely solely on passive traps. When pursuing tigers, hunters worked either alone or in pairs traversing significant distances from fifty to 100 kilometres (30–60 mi.) or more for up to six days. Because of their thin skin and low body fat, tigers could be taken down with arrows and spears. However, after being wounded, the animals could sprint up to 100 metres (330 ft) and attack.

While their bodies are smaller than those of tigers, Amur leopards (*Panthera pardus orientalis*) were considered to have been more ferocious because they fought back more aggressively when confronted. The camouflage of their coats made them hard to see whether in the rocks or in the trees. Once injuring the animal, if it survived, skilled hunters could locate the wounded leopard by searching for its tail, which tended to swing about, making the cat easier to find. Like tigers, hunting leopards was challenging as these felines also had formidable territories and bait hunting was unpredictable. Hunting with hounds was effective. Traps were another way to capture these animals. At least from the late fifteenth century, villages were equipped with either pits or cages dug around villages to trap predators such as leopards and tigers. At times, leopards fell victim to hunters who were hunting other game, such as pheasant. Other times leopards were known to come into villages and prey on sheep and dogs. Hunted for their fur, which was reserved for royalty, the cats, like tigers, were vulnerable to arrows because of their thin bodies and limited body fat.[50] Into the twentieth century, leopards and tigers were most likely hunted into extinction.

Other carnivores that Koreans hunted and competed with for game included the red fox (*ho*; 狐; *Vulpes vulpes*) and the grey wolf (*si*; 豺; *Canis lupus*) which were found throughout the peninsula. Foxes measure up to seventy centimetres (2 ft 2 in.) and weigh less than six kilogrammes (13 lb). They, like the sable, were hunted for their fur, which was prized for its beauty and warmth. Wolves – measuring up to 160 centimetres (62 in.) and weighing up to forty kilogrammes (80 lb) – threatened wildlife and human settlements. Because wolves travel and hunt in packs in the same areas hunters frequented, sometimes wolves attacked hunters.[51] Stories of wolves descending from mountains to feed on livestock (pigs, sheep and horses) and even children survived into the late Chosŏn.[52]

In the woodlands, forests and mountains of the realm, kings and elites hunted these wild animals with help of domesticated and trained animals including

---

[50] Yi Sango, *Suryŏp pihwa*, 175–80.
[51] Yi Sango, *Suryŏp pihwa*, 303.
[52] Yi Sango, *Suryŏp pihwa*, 305.

horses, birds of prey and dogs.[53] War and work horses, including a number of different species, some native, others imported from Jurchen or Mongols, were the most available of these animals. Horseback riding was an important skill many kings and elites learned. Royal leaders and other hunters rode horses to the hunting grounds to hunt boar and other animals and would mount them to get a panoramic view of the hunt from a safe distance. Hawks, eagles and falcons were rare and refined animals that required huge investments of time and money; sometimes the creatures were offered as tribute gifts to the Chinese and the Mongols.[54] Professional falconers captured the young birds from their nests and painstakingly trained them. The sources suggest that kings observed the birds and their handlers and interacted with these trainers on a regular basis. Other elites practised falconry too, though most likely they did not handle the birds themselves, but rather owned slaves or employed commoners who raised, trained and tended to the birds even while on hunts for fowl and hare. Finally, hunters most likely took dogs along with them at times, such as the Sapsali and Chindo as well as a mixture of other breeds.[55] Raised by knowledgeable dog breeders and trainers, probably from all social status groups, hunting dogs played a vital role in heavily forested terrain hunts as they tracked and flushed out game such as deer and wild boar that humans were unable to locate or track. While the sources say little about hunting dogs in premodern times, unlike the detailed information found on falcons, they could have been bred in greater numbers and served not only as hunting companions but also as pets, as depicted in Chosŏn artwork in Chapter 9. On the Korean peninsula, dogs have held a complex relationship with humans in the past and present because some species were companions on the hunt while others were raised and consumed as food. Sometimes using dogs, sometimes using snares and traps, hunters trapped or tracked down and killed otters, lynx, racoon dogs, sable, bears and leopards, killing them for pelts and the ingredients for medicine.

---

[53] The South Korean government officially recognised falconry as an intangible cultural asset in 2010. See Hwang Kyŏngsun, 'Illum muhyŏng yusan taep'yo mongnong 'maesanyang' kongdong tŭngjae ŭi t'ŭksŏng kwa ŭiŭi' [The significance of the joint inscription of falconry to the intangible cultural heritage of humanity], *Munhwajae* 51, no. 4 (2018): 208–23.

[54] More will be said about birds of prey in Chapter 8.

[55] Today, South Korea has a number of dog breeds. In addition to the Chindo, the Sapsali is a well-known breed. However, the pre-twentieth century origins of dog breeds on the Korean peninsula are unclear. These pure-bred dogs differ from the mixed dogs raised and consumed for meat today. More will be said about dogs in Chapter 9.

Perceiving Animals

So far, this chapter has focused on the animals of the peninsula and some techniques premodern people employed for hunting them. This section overviews perceptions of animals by looking at textual sources and oral tales. It is in no way an exhaustive examination, but rather it introduces the various ways Koreans and others in the region perceived and represented animals. Hunting was not the only interaction people had with beasts. While animals saturated the mountains, fields, rivers, streams, oceans and air, people on the peninsula told stories and wrote about the wild beasts they observed and encountered. For some, like the farmers, wild animals must have been nuisances at times. Crows flew into the fields and ate the ripening crops. Field mice chewed their way into storehouses, consuming grain, while snakes in the grasses or biting flies, mosquitos or fleas pestered or sickened people. Oxen, horses, chickens and pigs made life easier for farmers, at least for those who could afford them – they lived near or within human homes and their faeces, along with human waste, was used as a fertilizer, increasing crop production. Life must have been more bearable for households with these domesticated animals, which would have helped with human effort and provided warmth in winter, fertilizer for the fields, and protein. Insects, like the mosquito, did not only favour the rural people, the yangban elite would also have suffered from insect bites, but their status allowed them the benefit of riding a horse over a mountain pass, somewhat protected from the wildlife around them by the height of their steed.

Social status often drove these types of wild animal encounters and impacted perceptions of animals. Animals did not distinguish class – a tiger could kill a yangban as easily as it could a slave – but commoners and slaves encountered them more frequently because of their occupations and residences. While forbidden by law to travel and explore, commoners and slaves spent more time in the fields, valleys and mountains near their home villages. One legal stipulation for Chosŏn slaves was that their huts, often made from mud with straw-thatched roofs, could not have surrounding walls (which elite homes had), leaving them more vulnerable to the environment and animal intrusions. What elites and non-elites thought about the animals that shared the world around them came from precedent and centuries of experience living among wildlife and wildlands. Much of this knowledge connected to regional, locally specific practices and occupations while other learning came from local belief systems and philosophies or wider regional teachings. Ways of thinking about animals and how to interact with or avoid them were transmitted over the centuries; this knowledge passed down from generation to generation, as oral stories for commoners and slaves and orally and textually for the elite.

While animals roamed the physical environment, they also inhabited the textual environment of stela, essays, art, poems, government policies, legends and tales of premodern religious leaders, scholars, officials, commoners and slaves. Shamanistic and indigenous customs passed down through oral stories helped people of all social statuses make sense of the world around them. This included their relationship to animals. Buddhist scripture, Confucian classics and Daoist thought – originally from China – acquired local meaning and blended together with shamanism as Koreans applied these teachings to their own lives. While these texts were often produced in China, they helped listeners and readers on the peninsula better understand beasts.

Confucianism, Buddhism and Daoism held contradictory views about animals. Largely concerned about relations between humans, Confucian teachings stressed the formation of a harmonious society for good governance, seeking to recreate the idealism of an era in ancient Chinese history that had been lost and now reimagined. Buddhist works, more attentive to helping the individual develop one's moral nature and achieve nirvana, were less interested in the workings of government and more interested in individual salvation in the next life. Daoism exerted an indirect influence and was never widely adopted as a religious or philosophical practice. Yet Daoism taught about the duality of the natural world through the concept of yin and yang and located meaning in uncovering the Way, the undefinable essence of the natural world. Yin and yang expressed balance and interdependence. Daoism also informed Buddhist, Confucian and shamanistic beliefs. In the twelfth and thirteenth centuries, Neo-Confucian teachings blended Confucianism, Buddhism and Daoism into new forms that stressed personal enlightenment through ideas such as 'quiet sitting', a meditation done while reciting the Confucian classics, to regulate the self, the home, the village and the country. All of these teachings helped guide individuals and families to find peace and solace in life and assisted states to better regulate social relationships.

Confucian teachings regulated human affairs and encouraged the practice of removing oneself from the world to study or meditate, but they also held distinctive views of animals. Early Confucian philosophical texts from China, known on the Korean peninsula at least since the Three Kingdom's period (the fourth to the seventh centuries), relied on animals to help them understand the patterns of life and the working of the world. For instance, some birds represented the ideal Confucian family relationship as certain species share in the feeding of their nestlings and mate for life, a practice Confucians aspired to emulate. Other times, the language of birds was used to denote the language of non-Chinese communities. Confucians saw no real division between humans and non-humans, as both were part of all things under heaven.[56] Despite the recognition of this close affinity between humans and animals, in Confucian practices, animals were offered as ritual sacrifice and butchered at the altar as a way to appease spirits and ancestors.[57]

While Confucian texts demanded the sacrifice of animals, Buddhist works, such as the *Tripitaka*, embraced the sanctity of all life and taught passive ways to demonstrate kindness to animals through vegetarianism and active means through the practice of liberating beasts (C. *fangsheng*; 放生) by setting captive animals free.[58] At least by Tang Dynasty times (618–907 CE), animals were significant to Chinese Buddhists thinkers. Monasteries were places animals and humans interacted for economic and moral needs.[59] While the concept of reincarnation joined humans with animals, early Buddhists considered animals inferior to humans.[60] Other monks began noting the complexities of wildlife, reinforcing the connection between humans and animals. The seventh-century Chinese monk Daoxuan classified all living things into five groups: humans who have two legs; animals with four legs; creatures that fly; those that live in the water; and creatures that move on the ground without legs.[61] While inferior, beasts helped monks define humans as superior to other forms of life.

Like texts from the early Chinese tradition, Korean Buddhist works took note of wild animals. Animals, like humans, were lower creatures according to the Buddhist hierarchy of existence. Granted, in traditional Buddhist societies of South and East Asia, animals, whether for consumption or work, were not considered sacred creatures, while treating animals with kindness

---

[56] For a comprehensive summary of recent scholarship on human-animal relations in Chinese cosmology, see Dagmar Schafer, Martina Siebert and Roel Sterckx, 'Knowing Animals in China's History: An Introduction', in *Knowing Animals in China's History: Earliest Times to 1911*, eds Roel Sterckx, Martina Siebert and Dagmar Schafer (New York: Cambridge University Press, 2020), 5–6.

[57] James Serpell, 'Animals to Edible: The Ritualization of Animals in Early China', in *Knowing Animals in China's History: Earliest Times to 1911*, eds Roel Sterckx, Martina Siebert and Dagmar Schafer (New York: Cambridge University Press, 2020), 46. See also James Serpell, *In the Company of Animals: A Study of Human–Animal Relationships* (New York: Cambridge University Press, 2014).

[58] Chengzhong Pu, *Ethical Treatment of Animals in Early Chinese Buddhism: Beliefs and Practices* (Newcastle upon Tyne: Cambridge Scholars Publishing, 2014), 4.

[59] Huaiyu Chen, 'A Buddhist Classification of Animals and Plants in Early Tang Times', *Journal of Asian History* 43, no. 1 (2009): 32.

[60] For a summary, see Chen, 'A Buddhist Classification of Animals and Plants in Early Tang Times', 34.

[61] Chen, 'A Buddhist Classification of Animals and Plants in Early Tang Times', 35.

generated rewards.⁶² Despite the Buddhist precepts against the killing of beasts, the outcome of which would result in recompense and retribution, there were no universal prohibitions against the consumption of meat in Korea. While recognised in the Buddhist teachings, animals were not universally elevated to a sacred status that prohibited them from being overworked in the fields, hunted, killed or consumed. Vegetarianism, a passive method of showing kindness to animals, was a well-established principle of Buddhist teaching and the Buddhist scriptures taught similar notions about the sanctity of animal life. One passage argued for treating caged animals with kindness by returning them to the wild: 'Now I urge all sentient beings to light lamps, make banners, set captive animals free, and cultivate good fortune to overcome hardship and distress, and not encounter numerous disasters.'⁶³ Doing so would improve the life of the practitioners but appeared more performative than substantive.

The Buddhist practice of non-killing inspired a few Korean kings to prohibit the slaughter or hunting of animals. King Pŏphŭng (r. 514–40; 法興王) of Silla (57 BCE–668 CE) and King Pŏp (r. 599–600; 法王) of Paekche, early Buddhist leaders of the Three Kingdoms era (roughly fourth–seventh centuries CE), promulgated laws that prevented the killing and consumption of animals.⁶⁴ King Munjong (r. 1046–83; 文宗), the eleventh king of the Koryŏ Dynasty, attempted to prohibit hunting to protect all life.⁶⁵ The prohibition of killing and consuming animals was established on the memorial day for the death of the royal concubine (wangbin; 王嬪), most likely as a way to commemorate her death and promote the karma of observers of the festivals. King Sŏnjong (r. 1083–94; 宣宗) followed King Munjong and insisted that animals not be killed and refused dishes with meat, as did King Kojong (r. 1213–59; 高宗) in 1254.⁶⁶ Despite the widespread acceptance of Buddhism, Buddhist monastic practices in Korea differed from the written doctrine.⁶⁷ Except for

---

⁶² Katherine Wills Perlo, *Kinship and Killing: The Animal in World Religions* (New York: Columbia University Press, 2009), 116.

⁶³ This is one of many similar quotes about the sanctity of life in the *Tripitaka*. For more, see the SAT Daizokyo Text Database, https://21dzk.l.u-tokyo.ac.jp/SAT/index_en.html.

⁶⁴ See Kim Pusik, *Wŏnmun Samguk sagi* [History of the Three Kingdoms] (Kyŏnggido P'aju-si: Han'guk haksul chŏngbo, 2012); and Iryŏn, *Samguk yusa* [Memorabilia of the Three Kingdoms] (Seoul: Han'guk chŏngsin munhwa yŏn'guwŏn, 2003).

⁶⁵ *Koryŏsa* [History of the Koryŏ Dynasty] (Seoul: Asea munhwasa, 1990), 1:188b. Hereafter KS.

⁶⁶ KS, 2:424a and 1:486c.

⁶⁷ See Sung-Eun Thomas Kim, 'Perception of Monastic Slaves by Scholar Officials and Monks in the Late Koryŏ and Early Chosŏn Periods', *Journal of Korean Religions* 7, no. 1 (2016): 6.

a small group of devotees, most people, including ordinary monks, did not adhere strictly to the guidelines expressed in the Buddhist teachings.[68] Koryŏ society did not adhere to the Buddhist precepts against killing and consuming animals.[69]

For Buddhist writers, as part of the cycle of birth, death and rebirth, animals are one of the six 'modes of existence'. Several examples illustrate this point. Death was the moment that humans and animals shared, where one could transcend or decline into the form of the other. Gods, demi-gods and humans were higher modes, while ghosts and animals were lower forms on the same Samsaracakra, or wheel of transmigration.[70] As part of the cycle of life, wild beasts became metaphors for the power of Buddhist teachings to win over even the most dangerous animals. Astounding the followers around him, a tiger approached the Buddhist monk Chin'gam (774–850; 眞鑑) on Mt Chiri and, without a sound, led him to the monastery.[71] When monk Pŏpkyŏng (?–965; 法經) died and achieved nirvana, the wild beasts and birds of the mountains and streams joined together with human beings to mourn his passing.[72] Monks such as eighth-century Taehyŏn (大賢), in his expositions on the Buddhist sutra, recognised the difference between the life of a human and an animal and reiterated that the two each have value and that killing either is a sin.[73] Discussing animal desires, and the potential human sexual desire for animals, he insisted that sex should be abstained from, especially with female animals, because sexual desire is a sin never satisfied. Taehyŏn also asserted the importance of releasing captive animals into the wild. He commented on the practice of releasing animals as a means to do away with the 'agent and object of slaughter, the suffering of the present', emphasising that everyone must contemplate 'all beings being our mothers and fathers'.[74] In other words,

---

[68] Yi Pyŏnghŭi argues that only a small Buddhist votary (kŏsa) of elite laymen in government posts excelled at Buddhist teachings and practices. See Yi Pyŏnghŭi, 'Koryŏ sidae kŏsa ŭi saenghwal pangbŏp kwa kŭ ŭimi' [Buddhist votary of the Koryŏ era and their significance], Sahak yŏn'gu 116 (December 2014): 200–1.

[69] For a fascinating study, see Man-Shik Kong, 'A Reconsideration of Koryŏ Meat-Eating Culture', Seoul Journal of Korean Studies 33, no. 1 (2020): 99–126.

[70] Stephen Teiser, 'The Wheel of Rebirth in Buddhist Temples', Arts Asiatiques 63 (2008): 139–53.

[71] John Jorgensen, ed., Anthology of Stele Inscriptions of Eminent Korean Buddhist Monks, trans. Patrick Uhlmann (Seoul: Jogye Order of Korean Buddhism, 2012), 81.

[72] Jorgensen, ed., Anthology of Stele Inscriptions of Eminent Korean Buddhist Monks, 201.

[73] A. Charles Muller, ed. and trans., Exposition of the Sutra of Bramna's Net (Seoul: Jogye Order of Korean Buddhism, 2012), 264.

[74] Muller, ed. and trans., Exposition of the Sutra of Bramna's Net, 355–6.

killing was unjustified because humans and animals shared the same desire to live, procreate and raise families. When monk Muŭija Hyesim (1178–1234; 無衣子 慧諶) observed the world, including the people and animals in it, he wondered why there were 'countless differences' among them all.[75] To monks like Muŭija Hyesim, animals and humans were equally worthy of observation and wonder. While seemingly random examples, an underlying theme threading through them is compassion. Animals serve as metaphors for human society. Rather than feared or mistreated, beasts of all kinds should be respected based on their perceived similarities with humans.

By the late Koryŏ and early Chosŏn dynasties, when the state performed more animal sacrifices and royal family members and elites took part in more hunting, the renown and influential monk Kihwa (1376–1433; 己和) was one of the most critical writers about the practice. At a time when kings and elites began hunting in earnest, and Neo-Confucian scholars began advocating greater adoption of ritual animal sacrifice, Kihwa, who was also well versed in Confucian learning as a former Confucian student, opposed such trends. In his work on the harming of life, Kihwa highlighted the fundamental inconsistencies between Confucian and Buddhist teachings on animal cruelty. While Confucians argue that 'people eat creatures and living creatures sustain people' and 'the method of hunting in spring, summer, fall, and winter are means by which the ancient kings helped the people avoid difficulty', Kihwa insisted that,

> the doing of violence to heaven's creatures is something in which the sage will have no part ... Killing life in order to nourish life is like one's own child killing a sibling in order to nourish itself. If children are killing each other in order to nourish themselves, how are the parents going to feel about this? To have their children killing each other is certainly not the wish of their parents. So how could the mutual inflicting of harm between human beings and the other creatures be the will of heaven and earth?[76]

Borrowing the language of Confucianism, Kihwa claims that the man who becomes a sage avoids killing animals, not out of concern for salvation in the Buddhist sense, but because the sage wishes to avoid destroying the family, the pillar of Confucian society. He also attacked the practice of hunting. According

---

[75] Roderick Whitfield and Young-Eui Park, eds and trans., *Seon Poems: Selected Works* (Seoul: Jogye Order of Korean Buddhism, 2012), 9, 72.

[76] A. Charles Muller, ed. *Doctrinal Treaties: Selected Works*, trans. A. Charles Muller and Richard McBride II (Paju: Jogye Order of Korean Buddhism, 2012), 448 and 467–8.

to Kihwa, humans and animals shared the same love, life and fear of death. He went on to argue,

> Even though the variations of hunting in spring, summer, fall, and winter are customs established by the kings of antiquity, there are presently places between the great mountains and within the islands and seas where the practice of hunting has not reached. Human beings and animals each pursue their own lives, each at home in their own places, living out their naturally ordained years with satisfaction. Observing this, why should it be necessary for these people to depend on hunting to be able to live their lives well?[77]

Zeroing in on the specific details of the Confucian practice of royal hunting during the four seasons, Kihwa criticised such practices arguing that not all lands in the realm have been Confucianised. Yet, the people and animals lived harmoniously in these areas, the goal of Confucian teaching. He went on to say that hunting should only be out of necessity and the killing of animals for ancestral sacrifice abandoned. For monks such as Kihwa, borrowing the language of Confucian texts was the most effective way to promote the Buddhist non-killing of animals.

While some wrote about animals to highlight their commonality with humans to justify not killing them, other writers elevated animals by transforming horses, hawks, dogs and cranes into artistic icons in poetry, prose and art.[78] In some of his work, the Confucian scholar Kim Chongjik (1431–92; 金宗直) used animals such as deer, birds and mythical creatures like the *luan* (鸞), a phoenix-like bird, to explain the transformation of life and the commonality of how all things unintentionally influence everything, quoting the *Book of Songs* (*Shijing*; 詩經) to highlight the role of the hunt in governance.[79] Such works suggest the usefulness of animals for artistic expression and as symbols of communicative ideas, to teach moral lessons to the human observer, while also reinforcing the command humans have over the animal world by insisting that they be hunted. Like humans and their social bonds to

---

[77] Muller, ed., *Doctrinal Treatises*, 475.
[78] Sin Yŏngju, 'Kihoek chuje: Chungse ŭi tongmul e taehan inskik kwa munhakjŏk hyŏngsang: Chosŏn sidae chisikindŭl ŭi tongmul aeho wa munhakchŏk hyŏngsang-ŭng, kyŏn, hak, ma rŭl chungsim ŭro' [Planning subject: The perception and literary form of animals in the Middle Ages: Focusing on falcons, dogs, cranes, and horses], *Tongbang hanmunhak* 1 (2014): 55–87.
[79] Kim Chongjik, 'Sugunyŏ kŭmsan', in *Kim Chongjik chakp'umjip*, Kim Chongjik [Collected works of Kim Chongjik] (P'yongyang: Munhak yesul ch'ulp'ansa, 2017).

each other, humans bonded with animals. The only morally responsible way for the state to hunt them was to follow ritual protocol.

A genre of Confucian poetry is dedicated to praising and describing the natural world as a way of reflecting on the imperfection of human society. However, Confucians, for the most part, accepted the inferior status of animals and their use as ritual and hunting objects. Cruelty, however, could be a symbol of excess, a sign of uncivil behaviour and depravity. At least one writer appraised the senseless killing of animals. A poem 'On Observing a Hunt', by Yi Chu (1468–1504; 李胄), critiqued the military-like nature of a hunt for wild boar, roe deer, fox and birds and the violent nature of human–animal encounters:

> The ancient, venerable wild boar advances forward
>   and meets death …
>   the poor roe deer and fox die,
>   an arrow draws blood,
>   spraying the grass red.
>   Suddenly,
>   all the birds and animals become a mass of bones.
>   The court captures ten young baby animals,
>   as senior-ranking generals turn in the saddle
>   to watch and laugh.[80]

For Yi, the large-scale hunts described here, which the government promoted, demonstrated the unruly and violent nature of human encounters with animals in the wild. The mass killing of these creatures and their young senselessly wasted the resources of the country and illuminated the military's cruel sway over the court, a subtle critique of the king for failing to educate his military personnel.

The metaphor of the wilderness, where wild animals resided, was popular among other Confucian works. In Confucianism, removing oneself from the public life of politics and pursuing a life of scholarship in the wilderness with deer and wild boar, largely idealistic, exemplified scholarly Confucian dedication in retirement. Alternatively, the wilderness and wild animals were a form of punishment. Forcing Buddhism into mountains during the early Chosŏn, or exiling scholars, officials and members of the royal family who have committed crimes in the eyes of the court to frontier lands and distant islands, suggested

---

[80] Yi Chu, 'Kwan'gun paeknyŏpsu', in Manghŏn sŏnsaeng munjip, Yi Chu [The collection of Manghŏn's work] (Hwasan: Pan'gyujŏng, Toju myŏnggye sŏwŏn, [kapchae 1804]), original manuscript.

that the punishment was not only to live on the margins of civilisation but also in areas where these people were forced to have more encounters with beasts. Confucian practices about animals relegated them to ritual resources. The butchering of animals was common. Animals, sacrificed at state altars and offered as meat at ancestral ceremonies, reflected the needs of the growing Confucian state.[81] Deer, roe deer and leopards entered monasteries, fortresses, the capital and the royal palace grounds.[82] The appearance or actions of animals in unexpected locations were signs of portents both good and bad. What is remarkable in these examples is that they represent a whole range of responses to animals. While there was a diversity of views among scholars, for the most part Confucian views differed considerably from those of Buddhists. Animals were useful in helping define the civilised from the uncivilised.

In the stratified society of premodern Korea, the line between animals and humans was vague. Humans at the lowest margins of the social order were seen as being kin of the animal world. Illustrating the economic reality of this point, one 1392 petition argued, based on Confucian morality, that slaves, who made up between 20 and 30 per cent of the population at the beginning of Chosŏn, were worth less than domesticated animals, determining that three slaves were less valuable that a single horse or ox.[83] Other animals illuminated the anti-social demeanour of people. Scholars accused of inappropriate behaviour, affronts to the king, or subverting Confucian ethics were accused by other elites of being pigs and worms to question their morality and crimes. Buddhists too compared those who were unable to fathom the Buddhist teachings as being 'the same as an animal'.[84] Below the elites, storytellers passed down folklore reinforcing the notion of commonality between humans and animals. Orally transmitted stories usually involved wild beasts such as tigers, roe deer, deer, pheasants, snakes, big cats and elk. Demonstrating kindness to animals resulted in the animal bringing unforetold grace to people while showing them harm brought punishment. I think the diversity of views that all these people held indicates the importance the animal world had for helping people make sense of their social, economic and political realities.

While numerous tales investigated the relationship between humans and animals, one of the most famous folk tales that demonstrates the way commoners and outcasts made sense of their world and the animals around them was the tale 'Heavenly Maiden and the Wood Cutter (Sŏnyo wa namukkun)'.

---

[81] More will be said about animal sacrifices in Chapters 2 and 4.
[82] See KS, 2:232a–234a.
[83] See Kim, 'Perception of Monastic Slaves by Scholar Officials and Monks', 14–15.
[84] Muller, ed. and trans., Exposition of the Sutra of Bramna's Net, 415.

One version is set in the heavily forested and mountainous Kangwŏn Province. A poor young man climbed into the mountains each day to cut down and collect firewood to sell to the people of his village:

> One day, when he was cutting firewood on the mountains as usual he heard something running towards him over the fallen leaves. This was most unusual, and he stopped work for a moment. He saw a terrified young deer running towards him. When it reached him, it implored him earnestly to help it, for it was in great danger. He was touched and immediately hid it under the pile of firewood he had cut . . . Almost at once, a hunter came panting toward him and said to him, 'My man! I have been chasing a deer, and it ran up here somewhere. Have you seen it?' The burly hunter stood in front of the woodcutter, with his bow and arrow in his hands. He was familiar enough with the mountain paths, but among the trees and on the steep slope, he moved only with difficulty. So, the woodcutter looked at him and said, 'Yes, I did see it. It came running past and went off down the valley over there' . . . The hunter rushed back down the mountain without delay. Then the young deer came out from under the pile of wood where it had been hiding, not daring to breathe, and thanked the woodcutter for his kindness. Weeping in its gratitude it said to him,
> 'You saved my life from deadly peril, and I am most deeply grateful to you.
>   To repay your kindness I will tell you something that will bring you great success and happiness. Go up the Diamond Mountain tomorrow afternoon . . . Then you will see eight heavenly maidens come down from the corner of heaven to bathe in the lakes. While they are bathing, they will hang their silken undergarments on the pine trees by the shore . . . go secretly and hide one of the garments. Then, when they finish bathing, one of them will not be able to return to heaven. Go to her and welcome her, and she will go with you. You will live happily with her, and children will be born to you.'

The mystical deer goes on to warn the hunter not to return the undergarments of this heavenly maiden until after they had had four children together. Otherwise, she would escape up to heaven with their sons and never return. The young man follows the deer's advice, and the story unfolds as the deer had promised. After bearing their third child, the maiden tricks the woodcutter into returning her undergarments, when immediately she ascends to heaven with their children. The woodcutter manages to find his way into heaven, and the heavenly king, the father of the maiden, grants him permission to remain with his family. Wishing to see his mother one last time, out of a sense of filial duty, the woodcutter returns to earth astride a dragon-horse. However, on the brief visit, frightened by a hot bowl of porridge accidentally dropped on it, his mystical dragon-horse flies off into heaven without him. The woodcutter

> never went back to heaven and used to stand every day in tears looking at the sky. At last, he died of grief, and was transformed into a cock. So, tradition says that the reason why cocks climb to the highest part of the roof and crow, with their necks stretched out to heaven, is that the woodcutter's spirit has entered into them, and he seeks the highest place it can find.[85]

The story recognises two types of occupations for common men of the mountains, the woodcutter harvesting firewood to sell to the commoners in the village below, and the hunter pursuing deer and other animals to kill, butcher, and sell or provide to the state as tax. Both were very familiar with the terrain, suggesting their long experience in the mountains. However, rather than comradery, where they both assist each other, the woodcutter sides with and conceals the deer and tricks the hunter into believing the deer has run off, saving its life. This compassion for animals – which appears to be uncommon among humans – warrants a heavenly gift be bestowed to him in the form of human companionship and family when the deer reveals the secrets of the forest and the bathing location of the heavenly maidens.

Stories of human–animal and animal–human reincarnation or communication were inspired by shamanistic beliefs and Buddhist thought, while shamanistic and folk practices inspired tales of human–animal transformation and animal interaction with humans. Oral histories like these, while documented in modern times, touch on the concerns of ordinary people and should not be discounted as important sources of human ideas about animals.[86]

In popular folk stories – as suggested by the heavenly king in the 'Heavenly Maiden and the Woodcutter', which depicts an encounter between a common woodcutter and the celestial leader in heaven and his inability to find a home at the court – and Confucian texts, animals were closely aligned with rulership. Emperors and kings held power over everything under heaven, including both people and animals. In China, for instance, the boundaries between animals and humans blurred. As Roel Sterckx explains 'early Chinese

---

[85] For this and many more folk tales about human animals, see In-Sob Zong, *Folk Tales from Korea* (London: Routledge and Kegan Paul, 1952), 21–5.

[86] See Hŏ Wŏn'gi, 'In'gan tongmul kwan'gyedam ŭi saengt'aejŏk yangsang kwa ŭimi' [The meaning of the ecological aspect of human-animal relations], *Tonghwa wa pŏnyŏk* 23 (2012): 255–82.

texts portray the animal realm as a constituent part of an organic whole in which the mutual relationship among the various species were characterized as contingent, continuous, and interdependent' where the sage-ruler 'exerted his moral command and control over the animal world'.[87]

Korea adopted some of these values through their absorption of Confucian texts. Confucian bureaucrats and kings identified with the sage-ruler, and Confucians may have identified with Kija (1,000 BCE; 箕氏), a legendary, though probably inaccurate, figure. Kija, a Chinese prince, purportedly fled China with his followers, migrated to the Korean peninsula, and usurped an ancient Korean state, bringing Chinese civilisation into the peninsula. While a historical figure, Kija symbolised the intellectual and cultural union of China and Korea.[88] Classical Confucian works spoke of sage rulers who controlled all living things under heaven. The Confucian elite embraced these texts, and the writings were further legitimised through acceptance from Korea's indigenous and independent peninsular traditions. One such legend was that of Tan'gun, the mythical ancestor of the Korean race and the most famous animal story in Korean history. According to the well-known tale, Hwanung (桓雄), the son of the deity Hwanin (桓因), in order to lead his many thousands of human followers, descended from heaven to reside in the highest mountain on the Korean peninsula. Two female animals – one bear and one tiger – desired to become human. They prayed to Hwanung who, in response, gave them each some mugwort and garlic to consume and instructed them to remain inside a nearby cave for one hundred days as a test and that after consuming the herbs for one hundred days, they would transform. The tiger was impatient and unable to follow Hwanung's diet and emerged from the cave. The she-bear had been diligent and was rewarded by becoming human. She then procreated with Hwanung and birthed their son Tan'gun, the founder of political and social order on the peninsula.[89]

---

[87] Roel Sterckx, 'Transforming the Beasts: Animals and Music in Early China', *T'oung Pao*, Second Series 86, Fasc. 1/3 (2000), 2–3.

[88] Weiguo Sun, 'Legend, Identity, and History: The Historiographic Creation and Evolution of Tangun Choson and Kija Choson', *Chinese Studies in History* 44, no. 4 (Summer 2011): 20–46.

[89] Tan'gun has produced an impressive amount of interest. For instance, see James Grayson, 'Tan'gun and Chumong: The Politics of Korean Foundation Myths', *Folklore* 126, no. 3 (December 2015): 253–65; James Grayson, 'The Myth of Tan'gun: A Dramatic Structural Analysis of a Korean Foundation Myth', *Korea Journal* 37, no. 1 (Spring 1997): 35–52; Michael Seth, 'Myth, Memory, and the Reinvention in Korea: The Case of Tan'gun', *Virginia Review of Asian Studies* 10 (Fall 2007): 55–67; Kim Myŏngok, 'Tan'gun sinhwa insik e taehan yŏksajŏk koch'al' [Historical examination of the awareness of the Tan'gun myth], *Yŏksa wa yunghap* 3 (2018): 45–86; and Yi Sŭngho, 'Tan'gun: Yŏksa wa sinhwa, kŭrigo minjok' [Tan'gun: History, myth, and nationalism], *Yŏksa pipyŏngsa* (November 2016): 224–51.

Most likely recorded in nonextant texts retold from oral histories, the Tan'gun legend first appears in the written records of the late thirteenth century. This corresponded with the end of Mongol attacks during the 1270s when Koryŏ's royal family began merging with, and hunting alongside, the Mongol leaders of the Yuan. While the legend was a compelling reminder of Korea's independence during the Mongol era and popularised at the end of the nineteenth century as a way to shore up Korean national identity in the face of foreign threats, the veracity of the tale is less important than the social and political context of its telling. The story of the Korean people emerging from a union of a male deity and female bear transformed into a woman demonstrates a powerful foundation legend that highlighted an identity separate from the new one being created from the union of the Koryŏ king and crown prince with Mongol princesses. The story also underscores the ruler's control over nature. As James Grayson points out, the name Tan'gun literally means 'Prince of the Sandalwood Tree' (Tan'gun; 檀君).[90] Such titles illuminate the way early leaders, or those who created such stories, sought legitimacy by associating rulership with the environment and natural world.

While Tan'gun is the most well-known today, other foundation myths of early Korean states display the significance of animal–human relations to people on the peninsula. Chumong (鄒蒙) was the mythical founder of the Puyŏ (夫餘) people (early Koguryŏ, 高句麗), one of the ancient confederacies arising in what is now North Korea and Jilin Province, China. In this legend, the earliest extant version in the *History of the Sui Dynasty* (*Suishu*; 隋書), a Chinese source dating to the seventh century, illuminates the connection between animals and early political legitimacy of tribal groups in Northeast Asia.

> Sunlight caressed her, and she gave birth to a large egg. A boy broke open the shell and came out. He was called Chumong. The people of Puyŏ said that Chumong was unnaturally born. They all requested [the king] to kill him, but the king did not listen to them. [Chumong] was courageous. When he hunted, he bagged everything. After Chumong fled south to escape soldiers trying to catch and kill him, he came to a great river which was too deep to cross over. Chumong said, 'I am the maternal grandson of Habaek, the Child of the Sun. I am fleeing; [enemy] soldiers are near; how can I cross over?' At this, the fish and terrapin clustered together and made a bridge. Chumong crossed over. The pursuing cavalry was not able

---

[90] James Grayson, *Myths and Legends from Korea: An Annotated Compendium of Ancient and Modern Materials* (New York: Routledge, 2001), 38.

to cross over and returned [home]. Chumong established a nation. He called it Koguryŏ.⁹¹

The union of humans and the natural world produced a boy, who emerged from a bird-like egg with powerful skills over animals, and lead him south, where the boy eluded the soldiers hunting him, himself resembling an animal fleeing through the forests, to establish a new state. Storytellers legitimised early tribal leaders by highlighting their supernatural births and animal-like origins.

Other oviparous foundation myths include Kaya, another confederacy of tribes in the southernmost tip of the peninsula, involving Kaya kings and egg births, and Pak Hyŏkkŏse (r. 57 BCE–4 CE; 朴赫巨世), the founder of Silla, an early Korean kingdom in the southeast. The people of the land, wanting a king,

> looked south to the Najŏng well, at the base of the mountain Yangsan. They saw a strange vapor and a flash shining by the ground. There was a white horse nearby that seemed to be bowing. They went to that spot and found a red egg … The horse, upon seeing the people, gave a great cry and flew up to heaven. Breaking open the egg, a finally formed, beautiful child emerged … the people called him King Hyŏkkŏse.⁹²

Later rulers too, such as Yi Sŏnggye (1335–1408; 李成桂), the founder of the Chosŏn Dynasty, relied on foundation myths to justify their rise to power. One such story described Yi's powerful relationship with land, the forests and the animals. A prophetic writing discovered in Mt Chiri (智異山), in the southern part of the country, revealed that 'The Son of the Trees [Yi Sŏnggye] rode astride a swine and conquered the land of the Three Hans [the Korean peninsula] (*mokcha sŭngjŏha, pokchŏng samhan'gyŏng*; 木子乘猪下, 復正三韓境)'.⁹³ Mokcha is usually interpreted as a combination of Yi's family name 李. Here, I suggest another, more literal reading of Mokcha (木子), as 'Son of the Trees', suggesting his role of leader over people and command over the wild, much akin to Tan'gun, the prince of the sandalwood tree. His contemporaries understood Yi's origins in the forested north in regions heavily populated with Jurchen

---

⁹¹ Grayson, *Myths and Legends from Korea*, 68. An early fifteenth-century version of the story appears in the *Sillok* in which a she-animal consumes a potion, transforms into a woman and, after procreating with the Son of Heaven, gives birth to Tan'gun. See Grayson, *Myths and Legends from Korea*, 50.
⁹² James Grayson, *Korea: A Religious History* (New York: Routledge Press, 1998), 244–5.
⁹³ *CWS*, 1:20.

tribes. They lauded his hunting and archery skills. Even the apparent location where this mysterious text that prophesised the rise of Yi Sŏnggye to the throne is revealing. With roots in the sparsely populated and heavily forested northeast, far from the agricultural zones and the people with their domesticated animals that included swine, Yi and his supporters justified his rulership by claiming Yi was preordained to lead those in the southern part of the peninsula, where this mysterious writing appeared, in regions once ruled by early Korean dynasties, rather than his northern roots in less civilised lands.

The recording of foundation legends like these reveals the concern of elite writers at a time of national distress. Another way to read such stories is that not only do they highlight the significance of mountains and forested areas to early people on the peninsula, but they also demonstrate a belief that animals and people are one continuum, a strong undercurrent of shamanism, Buddhism and Confucianism. Certainly, in the case of the Tan'gun or Chumong legends, in very much a Buddhist sense, animals wished to be 'reincarnated' as humans, apparently a higher form of life. Implicit here is that predators such as the tiger, the one unable to follow orders and become human, were uncontrollable and untamable and a threat to these early people. In Chinese tradition, the supernatural or animal-related origins of founding rulers was not prominent. Koreans may have adopted Confucian rhetoric, but they maintained a distinctive worldview at the same time. Animals were not only living in close proximity to these early settlers, these stories also suggested that animals were part of the DNA of the early people, especially the royal family, on the peninsula.

* * *

Korean elites wrote about animals and commoners encountered beasts, whether domesticated or wild, in some form or another in their daily lives, and passed down stories about them orally and in works such as the official histories of the dynasties and literary collections of Confucian scholars and Buddhists. Despite the appearance of animals in writings and tales, there is no evidence that these observers were elevating animals for the sake of animal preservation or ecological awareness.[94] Rather, the sources and stories reflect the importance of animals to society and how people used animals to better understand the human condition. The sources are full of the contradictory sentiments the people – especially the elites – held about animals. For

---

[94] This was also the case concerning sixteenth-century Ottoman writings on ecology. See Sam White, *The Climate of Rebellion in the Early Modern Ottoman Empire* (Cambridge: Cambridge University Press, 2011), 50.

instance, while Buddhist doctrine taught the centrality of life, including for animals, adhering to these practices was hard, in the context of social pressure to eat meat. Animals, while sentient beings, offered humans opportunities for enlightenment (by releasing them in Buddhist ceremonies), the pleasures and satisfaction of consumption (by eating them), or the ritual obligation of sacrifice (through Confucian and shamanistic rituals of butchering them and arranging them on altars). The animal hierarchy reflected the hierarchy of human society, from the grandeur of the scholarly elites' dedication to Confucian scholarship and Buddhist dedication to the decrepit lives of slaves and the barbarian Jurchen. Animals were both feared and loved.

As will be seen in the chapters to come, the government began taking animals more into consideration by writing about them, tabulating them, and controlling access to them. Wild beasts were not productive in the sense of the people producing goods from the land. However, they became valuable in other ways, highlighted by the arrival of the Mongols in the late thirteenth century, as the struggle between the scholarly order and the kingship took on new meaning over access to the royal and elite hunts.

2

Koryŏ and the Empire of the Hunt

Beginning with the Mongol era in the late thirteenth century, the royal hunt empowered kings, allowing them to legitimise their authority over non-scholars and Mongol imperial personnel through a Northeast Asian cultural practice that many in powerful positions in the bureaucracy, scholarship and the Buddhist institutions regarded as a threat. Hunting was an occasion for feasting and an activity that brought royalty and non-royalty outside the Confucian bureaucracy together. Because elites often mimicked the practices of their leaders – emulating royal behaviour – hunting became the definition of elite masculine identity, a neo-nomadic ethos, among those connected to the king and other influential politicians. By the fourteenth century, more Korean kings and yangban elites had begun participating in the hunt and gained access to power through their hunting skills. It was while participating in the hunt that royal family members and elites assumed roles that mimicked imperial connections and shared favours between Koryŏ rulers and Mongol emperors.

These issues speak to the complexity of Koryŏ political identity. Koryŏ leaders blended philosophies and belief systems while scholar elites perceived the land as both an empire and a kingdom.[1] Within this complex worldview, the political system constructed in the first half of the Koryŏ Dynasty favoured the bureaucracy and thereby weakened the political legitimacy of central authority.[2]

One challenge of reading sources is that they were written by men not well inclined to document the royal hunt. Confucian scholars were dedicated to recording the history of both the Koryŏ and Chosŏn dynasties.

---

[1] Remco E. Breuker, *Establishing a Pluralistic Society in Medieval Korea, 918–1170* (Boston, MA: Brill, 2010); and John Duncan, 'Maintaining Boundaries: The Military and Civil Branches in the Koryŏ and Early Chosŏn', *Taiwan Journal of East Asian Studies* 8 (2011): 21–50.

[2] John Duncan, *Origins of the Chosŏn Dynasty* (Seattle: University of Washington Press, 2000), 48–51.

Official historical records reflected the Confucian moral objection to hunting, especially when such events involved members of the royal family. This was especially true during the Chosŏn Dynasty with its strong adherence to Confucian philosophies. Chronicling the history of the previous Koryŏ Dynasty in the early fifteenth century, Chosŏn government officials witnessed the world through the Confucian lens of morality, and disdained martial or leisure activities as interfering in scholarship and study, placing the dynasty at risk economically, socially and morally:

> Since ancient times, inferior men have spied a king's favorite things, curried favors through such things and encouraged [these bad practices]. Through flattery, music, feminine allures, hawks and hounds, the imposition of heavy taxes, the construction of extravagant palaces and pavilions, or some other wicked talents (*kisul*; 技術), they all pursued their purposes in providing the king what he enjoyed [thus distracting him].[3]

Kings were not to take part in entertainment that diverted them from their job of governing. Such strong disapproval reveals that the popularity of the hunt had persisted. The constant necessity of reiterating the need for royal abstention illustrated the centrality of the hunt to governing practices, political power, and elite male identity. Rather than a frivolous pastime that distracted kings and other political leaders from state affairs, the hunt strengthened their legitimacy.

It is evident that the royal hunt and scholar official resistance to such events were present during the early Mongol era under King Ch'ungnyŏl (r. 1274–1308). Korea's incorporation into Mongol domains (1230s–1360s), which stretched across the Eurasian continent, inevitably resulted in contact with new political and cultural forces of Mongol governing practices and Neo-Confucian learning in China. The Koryŏ court, and its military government under the Ch'oe family, who had dominated Korean politics since the previous century, initially resisted full submission, and it was not until 1270 when the court finally entered into a close political relationship with the Mongols. Seismic events during this time were the marriages of Koryŏ kings with daughters of Mongol Yuan emperors. These in-law relationships facilitated a transformation away from a Confucian bureaucracy in Korean court culture and governing procedures as the peninsula came under the influence of Northeast Asian practices and semi-nomadic traditions. Within the evolving political landscape of the capital Kaegyŏng (near modern-day Kaesŏng), debates over the

---

[3] *KS*, 3:671a.

royal hunt re-emerged, taking on added meaning. It was then that the clash of political values between the Confucians in the bureaucracy and the royal authority surfaced as the Mongols brought the Koryŏ Dynasty into its empire.

The hunt, as I explain in this chapter, provided kings and elites on the peninsula with means to solidify authority over their realms, but it disappeared from the sources as an activity conducted at the court as Buddhism and Confucianism became more powerful forces for governance from the tenth until the thirteenth centuries. While under Mongol control from the 1230s through the 1360s, the balance of political power tipped in favour of kings and the hunt when elite interaction with beasts of the wild emerge as important indicators of governance and status. In general, the emperor in China supported such dynastic authority, resulting in various power struggles between the kingship and the bureaucracy.[4] Interaction with the Mongol Empire helped transform the political culture of the Koryŏ Dynasty. The 1290 invasion by renegade Mongol leader Qadan (?–1292; Haptan; 哈丹) and his followers, which I discuss later in this chapter, exposed tensions between the Confucian bureaucracy and the re-emergence of a Northeast Asian regional political identity. The latter involved a lifestyle based on uxoriocality, where the wife's household defines authority, and was demonstrated by the hunt, which resulted in different patterns of governance and identity.

An Overview of Hunting: The Korean Court and Beyond

The hunt had been an integral element of elite political identity throughout most of the Eurasian continent since antiquity.[5] On the steppe, hunting was necessary for survival, as it provided additional sustenance in times of hardship while helping preserve nomadic herds – people could hunt and consume wild animals like deer, for instance, instead of slaughtering and eating the precious sheep from their own herds. Where hunting played less of a role for survival and sustenance, the political significance of the royal hunt increased. In Shang Dynasty China (1600–1027 BCE), hunting was a popular activity among leaders, assisting in state formation by imbuing these elites with respect

---

[4] Peter Yun, 'Mongols and Western Asians in the Late Koryŏ Ruling Stratum', *International Journal of Korean History* 3 (2002): 58.

[5] Thomas Allison, *The Royal Hunt in Eurasian History* (Philadelphia: University of Pennsylvania Press, 2006); and Yannis Hamilakis, 'The Sacred Geography of Hunting: Wild Animals, Social Power, and Gender in Early Farming Societies', *British School at Athens Studies* 9 (2003): 239–47.

and authority.⁶ At the imperial court under the Mongols of the thirteenth and fourteenth centuries and other steppe or semi-steppe elite families, the hunt never lost its significance in terms of sustenance or political power.⁷ In medieval Islamic societies, it appears that falcon hunting was a popular sport among elites and non-elites alike.⁸ In Europe, hunting shaped a particular aristocratic, upper-class lifestyle.⁹ During the age of modern imperialism in parts of Africa and India, hunting was an expression of colonial domination.¹⁰ For centuries, hunting has also been construed as an important definer of masculinity and social class.¹¹

Critics of the royal hunt were as widespread as its proponents. For instance, in fourteenth-century Europe, scholars began to condemn the royal hunt 'as mere butchery and hunters as empty-headed, snobbish aristocrats' and a 'complete waste of time'.¹² Sixteenth-century writers in Britain questioned the morality of the hunt, quoting Shakespeare by using hunting as a metaphor for murder and rape. Matt Cartmill argues that as hunting became a focus of class conflict, most likely the attacks came because of the erosion of the power and prestige of the old, landed aristocracy. But ultimately, he concludes that it was the growing scepticism of the religious claim that humans held superiority over animals.¹³ In China, Confucian officials remonstrated against emperors

---

[6] Magnus Fiskesjo, 'Rising from Blood-Stained Fields: Royal Hunting and State Formation in Shang China', *Bulletin of the Museum of Far Eastern Antiquities* 73 (2001): 48–192.
[7] Nancy Shatzman Steinhardt, 'Imperial Architecture along the Mongolian Road to Dadu', *Ars Orientalis* 18 (1988): 59–93.
[8] G. Rex Smith, 'Some Remarks on the Economics of Hunting in Medieval Islam', *Journal of the Economics and Social History of the Orient* 23, nos. 1–2 (April 1980): 205–6.
[9] J. B. Owens, 'Diana at the Bar: Hunting, Aristocrats, and the Law in Renaissance Castile', *The Sixteenth Century Journal* 8, no. 1 (1977): 17–36.
[10] William Beinart, 'Empire, Hunting, and Ecological Change in Southern and Central Africa', *Past & Present* 128 (1990): 162–86; Natasha Nongbri, 'Elephant Hunting in Late Nineteenth-Century North-East India: Mechanisms of Control, Contestation, and Local Reactions', *Economic and Political Weekly* 38, no. 30 (2003): 3189–99; and William K. Storey, 'Big Cats and Imperialism: Lion and Tiger Hunting in Kenya and Northern India, 1898–1930', *Journal of World History* 2 no. 2 (1991): 135–73.
[11] Tina Loo, 'Of Moose and Men: Hunting for Masculinity in British Columbia, 1880–1939', *Western Historical Quarterly* 32, no. 3 (2001): 297–319; Rosalind O'Hanlon, 'Manliness and Imperial Service in Mughal North India', *Journal of the Economic and Social History of the Orient* 42, no. 1 (1999): 47–93; and Joseph Sramek, '"Face Him like a Briton": Tiger Hunting, Imperialism, and British Masculinity in Colonial India, 1800–1875', *Victorian Studies* 48, no. 4 (2006): 659–80.
[12] Matt Cartmill, *A View to a Death in the Morning: Hunting and Nature Through History* (Cambridge, MA: Harvard University Press, 1993).
[13] Cartmill, *A View to a Death in the Morning*, 76–91.

for their hunting practices.[14] Zhou Dynasty (1122–221 BCE) era sources recommend that ministers who did not reprimand leaders for hunting and other forms of entertainment be punished by the state.[15]

By the Three Kingdom's era on the Korean peninsula, hunting had long ceased to be a means of survival, rather it came to shape the political legitimacy of rulers. Even in early Korea, scholarly disapproval of the hunt mirrored some of those critiques in China and elsewhere. Resistance to royal participation in the hunt appeared practical at times. Kings could be injured falling from their horses, assaulted by animals, or fall ill while on the hunt. Buddhist monks too criticised the king hunting, basing their arguments on Buddhist scripture and its prohibition against killing. Buddhist criticism of the royal hunt coincided with Confucian attacks but tapped into religious arguments to justify its suppression. Confucians were concerned with morality and manners as signs of refinement, a means to draw social distinction between the elite and the rest of society.

On the Korean peninsula, even though tribal leaders and kings had long hunted in Northeast Asia, scholarly elites held mixed feelings about the hunt. Some vilified it while others took part in hunts or at least supported hunting when at court. While kings hunted during the Three Kingdoms and Silla eras, and probably in the northern kingdom of Parhae, Koryŏ Dynasty scholars began denigrating hunting practices starting in the second half of the fourteenth century. Ostensibly supporting the hunt for maintaining military skills, these officials began fostering a political culture in which they attempted to regulate the hunt as being a morally deficient activity.

Elites in Korea were familiar with classical Confucian texts from China, the most critical works of which mention hunting. While not central to these texts, Confucian philosophers and scholars used hunting as a foil in their discussions of morality and good governance. Mencius (372–289 BCE; 孟子), for instance, mentions the hunting practices of King Liang Hui (魏惠王), who disrupted the lives of his people, criticising him for taking pleasure in activities his subjects were disallowed to perform. Leaders, according to Mencius, must foster a harmonious society to provide subjects time to enjoy hunting as King Liang Hui does.[16] In another passage, Mencius spoke about the overindulgence in pleasurable activities, criticising those who hunt with 'thousands

---

[14] Howard J. Wechsler, 'The Confucian Impact on Early T'ang Decision-Making', *T'oung Pao* 66, nos. 1–3 (1980): 1–40.

[15] Carrie E. Reed, 'Tattoo in Early China', *Journal of the American Oriental Society* 120, no. 3 (2000): 364.

[16] Yang Boujun and Yang Fengbin, eds, *Meng zi* [Mencius] (Zhangsha: Yue lu shu she, 2019), 8.

of chariots'.¹⁷ The Confucian text, the *Book of Rites* (*Liji*; 禮記), highlights an example of how the Son of Heaven (the emperor of China) conducts a hunt in the fields (*chŏllyŏp*; 田獵) as a way to practise war and capture animals to sacrifice:

> In this month, the Son of Heaven, by means of hunting, teaches how to use the five weapons of war, and the rules for the management of horses. Orders are given to the charioteers and the seven [classes of] grooms to see to the yoking of the several teams, to set up in the carriages the flags and various banners, to assign the carriages according to the rank [of those who were to occupy them], and to arrange and set up the screens outside [the royal tent]. The minister of instruction, with his baton stuck in his girdle, addresses all before him with his face to the north. Then the Son of Heaven, in his martial ornaments, with his bow in one hand, and the arrows under the armpit of the other, proceeds to hunt. [Finally], he gives orders to the superintendent of ritual animal sacrifices [who prepares the animals at the altars], to offer some of the captured game to [the spirits of] the four quarters.¹⁸

Another section of the *Book of Rites* reinforces this connection: 'Let the ceremonial rules be observed ... in the different hunting expeditions and the skills of warfare will be acquired.'¹⁹ The *Garden of Stories* (*Shuo yuan*; 說苑), the *Records of the Grand Historian* (*Siji*; 史記) and other Confucian classical works confirm in clear terms that hunting formed an integral element of kingship.

During the Three Kingdom's era, political elites on the Korean peninsula hunted. The earliest history, as recorded in the *Memorabilia of the Three Kingdoms* (*Samguk yusa*; 三國遺事), compiled at the end of the thirteenth century and based on no-longer extant texts, depicts political leaders as avid hunters. On the one hand, the hunt helped leaders maintain their fighting skills during times of peace, while on the other, it demonstrated the logistical prowess of the king by showcasing his ability to organise expansive hunting parties. Also, the killing of bigger animals, and dangerous game, such as the boar and tiger, provided examples to the citizens of the realm and neighbouring enemies of the martial prowess of the leader. Hunting contributed to diplomacy as early leaders sometimes sent gifts of game to border tribes. King Onjo (r. 18 BCE–28 CE)

---

[17] Yang Boujun and Yang Fengbin, eds., *Meng zi*, 80.
[18] Daisheng an Liu Zhangjiang, *Liji* [Book of rites] (Beijing: Zhong guo gong ren chu ban she, 2016), 82.
[19] Daisheng and Liu Zhangjiang, *Liji*, 3.

of Paekche, for example, is said to have shot a mystical deer and sent it to the people of Mahan to help maintain good relations.[20] The slaying of prey served metaphorical purposes and signalled the leader's ability to control supernatural forces as kings killed animals that appeared otherworldly. The *Memorabilia of the Three Kingdoms* depicts examples of kings killing animals purple or white in appearance, blending secular politics with religious roles. Purple and white are uncommon in the animal kingdom. Encountering and slaying such beasts suggest a connection to and control over animals from a spiritual realm.

Animals and hunting shaped bureaucratic language and institutions. Beginning in the thirteenth century and the integration with the Mongol Empire, variants of the royal hunt are explicit in the numerous terms that refer to the hunt (*yŏp* [獵], *suryŏp* [狩獵], *chŏllyŏp* [佃獵], *yuryŏp* [遊獵]), many of which appear interchangeable in the sources. Whether going out in intimate groups or accompanied by numerous soldiers for protection against bandits and animals, kings rode horses and shot prey from horseback. Excursions included dogs who were trained to flush out prey such as deer, and falcons who searched from above to hunt for small game such as hare. Beginning at least in the thirteenth century, the popularity of royal hunting also produced specific government posts, such as hunting attendants who accompanied the king, falconers (*ŭngsa* [鷹師], *ŭngbang* [鷹房], *ŭnggun* [鷹軍], *pangŭng* [放鷹], *ŭngbang hwan'gwan* [鷹房宦官] and *ŭngbang nangch'ŏng* [鷹坊郎廳]), and an official in charge of hunting parks (*yŏbin* 猎人). More will be said about falconry in Chapter 8. Two specific hunting terms include the 'ring (or circle) hunt' (*t'awi*; 打圍) and the 'fire hunt' (*hwaryŏp*; 火獵). With roots across Eurasia, these two hunting styles used teams to circle areas to scare up game for leaders on the chase. In a ring hunt, foot soldiers would encircle an area and begin moving inward, pressing prey into the middle of the circle where they became easy targets for the king's companions to hit with arrows. In the case of a fire hunt, soldiers set fires to frighten game into the open. Both styles had immediate advantages for the sovereign as game would appear in front of him expediting the kill rather than the king seeking the animals in the wild which was fraught with danger. On the other hand, both of these forms of hunting removed part of the thrill. Fire hunting could lead to devastating environmental consequences if not controlled and such events during the late thirteenth century led to attempts to prohibit it. Regardless, fire hunts were still practised during the Chosŏn Dynasty when a fire destroyed a substantial Buddhist monastery in Ch'ungchŏng Province.[21]

[20] Iryŏn, *Samguk yusa*, 1:14.
[21] *CWS*, 10:66.

The royal hunt displayed the ruler's abilities to organise and control labour, military might and individuals (both humans and animals). Put differently, it was a means to build camaraderie among royal family members, elites and soldiers on the hunt while threatening scholars' roles in society by excluding them from activities that helped bond other elites with the king and military. The hunt touched on status via the question of social hierarchies. The subsequent feasting on game fostered personal relationships between the king, his entourage, foreign envoys and allies. The guest list was also a means to exclude groups out of favour with the political sphere surrounding the king. Those who hunted with the king, understood the hunt, and demonstrated strong horsemanship and archery found royal favour and access to authority, circumventing the normal path to advancement. The royal hunt also served as a means to shut people out, as the king excluded scholars without any hunting prowess from taking part in hunting trips and their celebrations, thus preventing them from building trust with the king.

The Koryŏ Hunt

At the beginning of the Koryŏ Dynasty, hunting was a visible aspect of peninsular cultural and political practices and royal authority. Like earlier elites before him, Wang Kŏn (r. 918–43; 王建), also known as King T'aejo, the founder of the Koryŏ Dynasty, embraced the hunt. With roots in the merchant class, Wang Kŏn rose among the ranks of regional strongmen based on his military skills sharpened by his struggles in the disintegration of the Silla Dynasty. Apart from obvious access to animals for nutrition, warmth and wealth, it offered Wang Kŏn and others opportunities to legitimise their power and as possible avenues for advancement. Participation in the hunt illustrated the potential fluidity of social and political boundaries as well as demonstrated gender hierarchies on the peninsula. On one occasion, in the tenth century, Wang Kŏn bequeathed the surname Kim to a man of lower status whom he admired for his equestrianism and marksmanship with a bow. Once, while on a hunt with a group of soldiers, Wang Kŏn encountered this Kim by the side of a road. The man invited Wang Kŏn to stay in his home for two nights. Inside, the man offered his two daughters to the founder, presumably for sexual companionship. As a consequence of the visit and sexual encounters, the two daughters, apparently with no other options, departed their home to become Buddhist nuns (ni; 尼). Taking pity on them, Wang Kŏn summoned the women to the capital, but they had already taken their religious vows, which were unbreakable. Not to be deterred, Wang Kŏn arranged to have each daughter reside in separate monasteries close by his official residence, keeping them as wives.[22]

The hunt held the potential to shatter hierarchies as can be seen by the bringing together of Kim, clearly of low status as he originally lacked a surname, and Wang Kŏn (King T'aejo), the most powerful man on the peninsula. This example also illustrates the precarious position of women in early Koryŏ society as the two daughters, through the chance encounter of the hunt, were offered to the king. Through marriage to Wang Kŏn, these women became two of his many wives and helped elevate the social status and reputation of their father and themselves. While only one example, these kinds of interactions were possible due to the popularity of hunting.

The Koryŏ court consisted of the king, the royal family, and a bureaucracy of scholar officials trained in Confucian learning. These Confucian scholars staffed the bureaucracy. None of these groups were monolithic, and the nature of political power changed over time. The royal family appeared more united because the small size promoted closeness between the king and other royal family members.[23] The king sat above a government that, while adopted from the Tang and Song models, administered the structure differently based on earlier governing patterns from the previous Silla Dynasty.[24]

Aristocratic families, while not monolithic, shared important features. Living near the capital, men from these families were brought into government posts, some based on the earlier successes of their fathers and grandfathers who had worked in government service, others on having passed the Koryŏ civil service examination.[25] In the first half of Koryŏ, the exam stressed literary culture and proper etiquette and rhetoric and downplayed the Confucian Classics; however, after the adoption of Neo-Confucianism in the late thirteenth century, the Confucian Classics, which taught social transformation and obligation, became integral to the exam.[26] These exams may have contributed to a greater sense of unity in thought among the officials who staffed the bureaucracy. Early bureaucrats may have been less critical of the hunting activities of kings, but this changed with the adoption of Neo-Confucian learning that

---

[22] KS, 3:4a–b.
[23] Myoung-ho Ro, 'The Makeup of Koryŏ Aristocratic Families: Bilateral Kindred', *Korean Studies* 41 (2017), 183.
[24] Jae Woo Park, 'Early Koryŏ Political Institutions', 10–12.
[25] See Kenneth Robinson, 'Pak Tonji and the Vagaries of Government Service in Koryŏ', *Korean Studies* 40 (2016): 79–80.
[26] Hyeon-chul Do, 'Analysis of Recently Discovered Late Koryŏ Civil Service Examination Answer Sheets', *Korean Studies* 41 (2017): 157–8.

became more interested in social transformation and proper conduct. Through their monopoly of the examination system, Confucians dominated the government, including the highest posts that interacted directly with the king. While all of these scholars understood Confucianism, early elites were often equally adept at Buddhism, geomancy, Daoism and shamanism. In the first half of Koryŏ, rather than sharp differences among scholars over these worldviews, greater cultural differences and practices arose between capital elite families and local leaders in the countryside with their strong Buddhist, Daoist and Confucian traditions.[27]

After the founder, hunting, while certainly practised on the peninsula, was not a pastime of kings or other elites in the first centuries of the Koryŏ Dynasty – or it went unrecorded in the official sources. While silence does not mean absence, hunting did not appear to be an activity that many early Koryŏ kings or elites practised after Wang Kŏn, or at least their hunts were not represented in the official histories, such as the *Koryŏsa*. While they may have hunted, later editing of the court histories did not find recording the events a necessary part of official state records, and there are no known extant collections of scholarly writings from this era to shed light on the subject. One exception was King Mokchong (r. 997–1009; 穆宗). King Mokchong was said to have been skilled at horsemanship, archery, hunting and drinking, and 'did not pay attention to political affairs'.[28] The depiction as an immoral leader distracted by hunting justified his deposition and assassination.

However, beginning with King Hyŏnjong (r. 1009–31; 顯宗), the court took greater interest in military matters to strengthen defences against the frequent invasions by the Liao Dynasty (907–1125; 遼朝).[29] This growing royal interest in military issues appears to have begun altering the perceptions of the royal hunt – or at least the need to record it. This growing commitment to the military was summed up by King Chŏngjong's (r. 1034–46; 靖宗) perception of the hunt in 1039:

> Since the age of the ancient kings, many years have passed from the time when they stopped fighting and began cultivating scholarship. Even when the world is safe, do not forget warfare. According to the *Rites of Zhou* (*Zhouli*; 周禮), 'To safeguard the country with the army, you must practice military affairs through hunting.' The *Chronicle of Zuo* (*Zuo zhuan*; 左傳)

---

[27] Jong-ki Park, 'The Characteristics and Origins of Koryŏ's Pluralist Society', *Korean Studies* 41 (2017): 202–3.
[28] KS, 1:84c–d.
[29] See Breuker, *Establishing a Pluralist Society*, 397–8.

says, 'If you take part in a battle with a man who does not conduct training, it is like throwing a person away [you will easily overcome him in combat].'[30]

Basing his arguments on ritual texts, Chŏngjong supported the idea that hunting and national security were intertwined. Time spent killing beasts in the wild sharpened fighting skills. Refusing to hunt doomed the individual soldier in combat and, by extension, the fate of the nation.

While early Koryŏ leaders such as Wang Kŏn, Mokchong and Chŏngjong perfected their military skills by hunting animals, the actions of other leaders represent some of the contradictory nature of early Koryŏ political and religious identity. By the time of King Munjong (r. 1046–83; 文宗), the court went as far as prohibiting the slaughter and hunting of animals.[31] In 1081 on Nabil (臘日), a seasonal hunting celebration held on the first day of the twelfth lunar month (January–February), the king and his officials performed ancestral rites using game presented to the court as gifts.[32] Polo (*kyŏkku*; 擊毬) played a prominent role in court politics too. King Ŭijong (r. 1146–70; 毅宗) used polo to such an extreme he was widely criticised and eventually deposed for his support of the military.[33] By the thirteenth century, roughly 250 years later, officials such as Yi Kok (1298–1351; 李穀) affirmed the growing scholarly prejudice against royal participation in the hunt: 'Hunting in spring prepares you for the military arts, but will it not interrupt farming?'[34] Here, Yi gently criticised the king for his practices, suggesting that the hunt did interfere with rice production and should be ended. Agricultural production benefited the state more than the military hunts, but the involvement of the king in these affairs appeared to be diminishing, compelled by both Buddhist arguments against killing animals and Confucian arguments for limitations on the hunt because it disrupted the economic activities of the people.

The nexus between hunting, animals and political legitimacy took on dramatic new meaning in the thirteenth century in the context of the Mongol

---

[30] KS, 2:777b.
[31] KS, 1:158a-b.
[32] KS, 1:197a-b.
[33] For a study comparing the development of polo in East Asia, see Chŏng Hyŏngho, 'Tong Asia kyŏkku ŭi chŏnsŭng kwa pigyo yŏn'gu' [Transmission mode and comparative study of East Asian polo], *Pigyo minsokhak* 41 (2010): 253–85. For more on King Ŭijong, see Kim Ch'anghyŏn, 'Koryŏ Ŭijong wa kŭ e tamgin kwannyŏm' [King Ŭijong's royal visitations and their meaning in the Koryŏ Dynasty], *Yŏksa wa Hyŏnsil* 53 (2004): 129–60.
[34] Yi Kok, edited by Sŏng Nakhun, *Kajŏngjip* [Collected works of Kajŏng] (Seoul: Tonghwa ch'ulp'an kongsa, 1973), book 10, Soŏ.

Empire. The Mongols first arrived in Korea in late 1218, but the court refused to incorporate into the Mongol order until the late 1250s. The Korean court, the military faction in power, and scholar officials in the central government withdrew to the nearby coastal location of Kanghwa Island, where the court would retreat in times of invasion. From here Koryŏ officials resisted the Mongols as they moved freely throughout the peninsula, trying to subjugate it from horseback from the 1230s until 1270. The gaining of the throne by King Wŏnjong (r. 1259–74; 元宗) ended Koryŏ's official resistance although the court did not return to Kaegyŏng (near present-day city of Kaesŏng) until 1270. The submission of Koryŏ in 1270 included the return of the court from its exile on Kanghwa Island when Korea entered into a tributary relationship with certain economic, military and ritual requirements. One of the major Mongol demands was the dispatch of the crown prince to the Yuan capital Daidu. Crown Prince Ch'ungnyŏl travelled to the Yuan capital, married a daughter of Mongol leader Kublai Khan (1215–94; 忽必烈) and returned to Koryŏ after his father, King Wŏnjong, died.[35] While an alliance of political convenience, intermarriage between the two courts created a rapprochement of Koryŏ–Yuan relations, facilitating Mongol cultural and political influence at the Koryŏ court.[36]

For many scholars and commentators from Chosŏn times to now, the most humiliating aspect of Korean submission to a foreign power was this in-law relationship between the Mongols and Koreans. Korean crown princes married the daughters of Mongol emperors. The children of the union were raised in Daidu in Mongol customs, wearing Mongol clothes and speaking Mongolian. Until they were of age or upon the death of the Koryŏ king (his father), crown princes moved to the Koryŏ capital with their Mongol wives, leaving younger children behind to be raised by a presumably foreign and non-Confucian imperial family. Despite later residence in Koryŏ, the connection to the Mongol family was not severed as the Koryŏ royal family, including crown princes, travelled repeatedly between the two capitals. The marriage alliance represented the ascendancy of Mongol courtly norms and the final submission of Korea to Mongol rule.[37]

---

[35] KS, 1:564a.

[36] For an important study on the matter, including a summary of Korean, Chinese and Japanese secondary sources, see David M. Robinson, *Empire's Twilight: Northeast Asia Under the Mongols* (Cambridge, MA: Harvard University Press, 2009), 98–113. See also Sixiang Wang, 'What Tang Taizong Could Not Do: The Imperial Koryŏ Surrender of 1259 and the Imperial Tradition', *T'uong Pao* 104, 3–4 (2018): 338–83.

[37] Yun Eŭnsuk, 'K'ubillai wa Koryŏ' [Kublai and Koryŏ], *Yŏksa pip'yŏng* 90 (2010): 334–55.

Rather than a humiliating relationship, however, such an alliance illustrated a certain level of trust the emperor held for the Koryŏ royal family. This marriage coincided with the longer Northeast Asian practice of trust building through marriage alliances and was made possible because of a shared set of values and customs held by Mongols and Koreans based partly on uxorilocalism. Korea's uxorilocal family practices have been pointed out by several scholars.[38] However, mostly overlooked today because of the Confucian transformation of the subsequent dynasty, it had been common in Korea among elites since the earliest descriptions of the peninsula by Chinese travellers in the third century CE. In this arrangement, when the husband married, he moved into his wife's home alongside her parents. Women inherited property and were considered economically powerful. She and her parents also exercised authority and influence over the children. These types of marriages could also be polygamous in the homes of the upper classes. While not universal, the Silla and Koryŏ dynasties practised uxorilocalism. Confucians denounced this uxorilocal relationship indirectly from the founding of the Koryŏ and directly following the collapse of Mongol power. Confucians argued that the practice conflicted with Confucian ritual regulations of ancestral worship and wrote uxorilocalism out of family practices in the founding years of the Chosŏn Dynasty. By the seventeenth century, uxorilocalism was not widely practised. Because of the uxorilocal marriages to women of the Mongol court backed by their fathers-in-law the Mongol emperor and his army, Koryŏ kings took advantage of the relationships as a means to tip the balance of power in their favour and against the Korean bureaucracy during the Mongol period.[39] An example of this was when King Ch'ungnyŏl introduced slaves and eunuchs into the court as a 'counterbalance to bureaucratic power'.[40]

This was a formative period in the way capital elites defined themselves. Rather than locating the source of their legitimacy exclusively in lineage clans linked to powerful families in the countryside, these elites began to identify

---

[38] Martina Deuchler, 'The Tradition: Women during the Yi Dynasty', in *Virtues in Conflict: Tradition and the Korean Woman Today*, eds Martina Deuchler and Sandra Mattielli (Seoul: Royal Asiatic Society, Korea Branch Samhwa Publishing Company, 1977), 1–48; Kim Sangjun, ed., *Yugyo ŭi yech'i inyŏm kwa Chosŏn* [Confucian ideology and Chosŏn] (Kŏnggido P'ajusi: Chŏnggye ch'ulp'ansa, 2007); and Yi Chongsŏ, '"Chŏnt'ongjŏk" kyemogwan ŭi hyŏngsŏng kwajŏng kwa kŭ ŭimi' [The formation of traditional views on stepmothers and its meaning], *Yŏksa wa hyŏnsil* 51 (2004): 135–63.

[39] Kim Hyŏlla, 'Koryŏ Ch'ungnyŏl wang tae ŭi Yŏ Wŏn kwan'gye ŭi hyŏngsŏng kwa kŭ t'ŭkching' [The special characteristics and formation of Koryŏ–Yuan relations at the time of King Ch'ungnyŏl], *Chiyŏk kwa yŏksa* 24 (2009): 195–224; and Yun, 'Mongols and Western Asians in the Late Koryŏ Ruling Stratum', 51–69.

[40] Duncan, *Origins of the Chosŏn Dynasty*, 86.

themselves based on connections to family positions held in the government. The dynasty also created new institutions to enhance the power of those the king favoured, helping the palace overcome the power of the bureaucratic elite.[41] These newcomers took over high positions in the government and influenced the king in policymaking. The re-emergence of the royal hunt at this time was indicative of this power shift, which similarly consolidated a non-scholarly support base for the king and allowed the formation of a new cohort of elite.

In theory, the Mongol governing philosophy differed from the Korean or Chinese views.[42] While the Confucians viewed their systems through the Mencian model that elevated the needs of the people, or farmers, above all others, the Mongols embraced social relations through family and clan connections. Non-Mongols could be brought into the governing structure when they offered something tangible to Mongol rule. Subjugated people, who were farmers, were only a concern in that they continued to submit taxes to support Mongol rule, a kind of realpolitik.

When it came to hunting, the Chinese, Koreans and Mongols had more in common. Like classical Confucian theory, the Mongols linked hunting to training for warfare.[43] They carried out what early Chinese leaders and scholars believed should be the purpose of the hunt – to prepare soldiers for battle. However, unlike Confucian critics of the hunt, the Mongols were unconcerned about the hunt disrupting the livelihoods of the people. This was due in part to the fact that the areas where the Mongols and other pastoral nomadic people hunted, such as the steppe or mountainous regions, were sparsely populated – unlike Korea. In such secluded terrain, hunting teams, whether small or large, practised their horseback riding and archery without interference. Recognising the popularity of the hunt to the Mongols and fearing the potential environmental damage of Mongol hunting on the peninsula, the Koryŏ court hoped to convince Kublai Khan, the founder of the Yuan Dynasty, of the unpopularity of hunting on the peninsula, conveying to him that 'the land was small with many mountains, and therefore not an appropriate place for hunting or raising livestock'.[44] They feared that Mongol nobles would exploit the peninsula, converting it into a hunting ground, much like the Yuan did by

---

[41] Duncan, *Origins of the Chosŏn Dynasty*, 20–8.
[42] A. Zhambal, *13–14 zuuny Mongolyn uls toriin setgelgeenii zarim asuudal* [Research on the political thought of the Mongols in the thirteenth and fourteenth centuries] (Ulaanbaatar: Bembi san, 2006).
[43] Timothy May, 'The Training of an Inner Asian Nomad Army in the Pre-Modern Period', *The Journal of Military History* 70, no. 3 (July 2006): 617–35.
[44] KS, 3:666a.

constructing horse ranches on Cheju Island, a large Korean island south of the peninsula.

Despite such excuses to his father-in-law, King Ch'ungnyŏl, Mongol Queen Cheguk (1259–97; 齊國大長公主) and other members of the royal family, including the young crown prince, frequently hunted. There are numerous references to the royal hunt during King Ch'ungnyŏl's reign, which describe the king hunting game such as deer and hare from horseback. At times, he hunted with falcons and participated in fire or ring hunts. Although he hunted at a number of locations, including the P'yŏngju (平州), Myogot (猫串) and Tora (都羅山) mountains, he frequented Mt Maje (馬堤山) located near Tŏksuri, only a day's journey from the capital Kaegyŏng. However, most of their excursions were daytrips. In 1278, early in his reign, King Ch'ungnyŏl built a royal residence on Mt Maje for the crown prince, naming it Sugang Palace (壽康宮), the 'Palace of Longevity and Good Health'. The construction of such sites replicated, on a more modest scale, similar structures in the Mongol Yuan empire, creating a familiar location for the crown prince and his family. Yet, in addition to being pastimes, these projects served as attempts to widen the king's rule, as the construction of hunting pavilions and the expansion of hunting grounds helped the king establish regions where he could build a support base beyond the highly contested politics of the court. When he retired to his hunting palace, King Ch'ungnyŏl was often absent from the factional debates of the court and spent time there with others in his political circle. As the king brought in skilled military soldiers and Mongol *darugachi* (達魯花赤), military officers in charge of administering the country until the late thirteenth century, this earned the ire of Confucian officials who criticised the king indirectly and sometimes unequivocally.[45]

The movement of the royal entourage on these hunting trips permitted those in attendance to affirm their personal connections with the king. When the king chose one military officer, Yi P'yŏng (?–1289; 李玶), to join the royal hunt because of Yi's hunting skills, Yi benefited from this royal patronage. Through the personal bond of trust with the king formed through the hunt, Yi was rewarded with a mission to travel to Daidu, the Yuan capital, where he presented the Mongol emperor with hunting falcons.[46] Other military and non-military elites outside of the capital also endeavoured to benefit from their close proximity to the king by joining along. On one hunt in Ch'ungch'ŏng Province, a regional official presented gifts of rice cakes, while regional magistrates travelled long distances to offer their regards to the king. The central bureaucracy, apparently concerned about the challenge to their power – as

---

[45] For examples of the king hunting with visiting Mongols, see KS, 1:572b.
[46] KS, 1:613d.

gift givers circumvented normal protocol for royal meetings and might lead to royal favours – attempted to prohibit the giving of gifts to the king while he was outside the capital.[47]

Alternately, the absence of the king also provided an opportunity for officials in the capital to act for their own benefit. On one royal hunt at P'yŏngju, where the king and other officials visited the local hot springs, a charge was made against corrupt officials who took advantage of their absence from the capital by 'invad[ing]' and 'trespassing' on farms, while 'plundering' and 'forcing [peasants] into corvée labor'.[48] In the eyes of his Confucian advisors, this abuse of power offered an example of how the absence of the king sitting in the court not only prevented the functioning of the bureaucracy but also empowered officials to act in their own interests even if that meant damaging the lives of the common people. In another incident, King Ch'ungnyŏl and his officials Yi Chijŏ (?–?; 李之氐) and Mun Ch'angyu (?–1285; 文昌裕) joined a hunt at the king's hunting grounds on Mt Maje.

> But their men and horses trampled the fields and paddies, and the people were very angry. Troops informed the people that the forces would leave quickly ... [at first] the king took the domesticated pigeons of the people hoping to give the birds to the imperial court, but Yi Chijŏ and Ch'a Tŭkkyu (?–?; 車得珪) disapproved and finally returned them.[49]

This shows that rather than derelict in his duties as leader, the king grudgingly performed his moral role as leader by compensating farmers for their losses. In another event that also reflected the king's conscientiousness when a fire hunt resulted in scorched farmland – the farmers were compensated.[50] When one such ring fire destroyed crops, an official chastised the king, saying, 'If you put this much effort into hunting, how will the affairs of the country turn out?'[51] Examples like these demonstrate deliberate attempts to single out and attack hunting activities. Framed in terms of abuse of power, they were meant to reign in the actions of the king, as well as establish precedence for future leaders on the proper way to morally govern.

Many military officers joined King Ch'ungnyŏl on his excursions, with General Yi Chŏng (?–?; 李貞) frequently accompanying him. Some of those

[47] KS, 2:863c-d.
[48] KS, 1:613a.
[49] KS, 3:683a-b.
[50] KS, 1:608a.
[51] KS, 3:23c.

invited by the king to join the feasts after the hunt were Mongol *darugachi*.[52] Mun Ch'angyu and Yi Chijŏ also accompanied the king to Mt Maje. General Yi P'yŏng, talented at horsemanship, archery and falconry, reportedly always guided the king on his hunts. Others good at falconry and the use of hunting dogs, such as Chang Kong (?–?; 張公), offered daily instruction to the king.[53] General Pak Ŭi's (?–1321; 朴義) promotion was credited as having been gained through the king's favour of Pak's talents with falcons and dogs.[54] Local clerks (*ajŏn*; 衙前) also sought advance from the king through the hunt. Han Hŭiyu (?–1306; 韓希愈), a local official from Kaju (嘉州), a remote area now located in north P'yŏngan Province, was poorly educated but a talented horseman and archer. Han was also fond of fire hunts, where once he rode his horse into the flames to chase game. He had earlier joined the king on hunts, shot animals from horseback, and was eventually promoted to general.[55] General Yun Su (?–?; 尹秀) accompanied the king when the hunt was conducted in the Mongol Yuan territory, winning the king over with his refined hunting and falconry.[56]

These and other examples demonstrate the benefits individuals outside the civil bureaucracy received by virtue of their proximity to the king and their hunting prowess while the king was participating in the royal hunt. Monetary, political and social advancement through the hunt also extended to experiences in the Mongol Yuan. Taking part in the hunt with the king could not only bring rewards during the Koryŏ Dynasty, but it could also provide an avenue for upward mobility via imperial favours. One Yuan officer named Langgedai (?–?; 郎哥歹) faulted General Pak Ŭi for believing that he could receive favours from Kublai, 'If you present a falcon and fourteen hunting dogs to the emperor, do you think you'll receive some great reward in return?' Proving him wrong, upon travelling to Daidu and presenting [the hunting animals] to the emperor, Park Ŭi was promoted to [the post of] grand general (*taejanggun*; 大將軍) upon the command of the emperor.[57] Han Hŭiyu too benefited from imperial patronage when he received military awards (C. *Shuangzhu jinpai*; 雙珠金牌), directly from the emperor, promoting him.[58] There were opportunities afforded to individual men and women through integration into the Mongol Empire. From

---

[52] *KS*, 1:572c.
[53] The *KS* does not give his position. *KS*, 3:690d.
[54] *KS*, 3:691c-d.
[55] *KS*, 3:298b-d.
[56] *KS*, 3:689a-d.
[57] *KS*, 3:691c–692a.
[58] *KS*, 3:298b-c.

the Mongols, Koryŏ kings learned to give lower social status groups a means to upward mobility, and lower status groups learned how to sidestep the king.

The royal family's Buddhist beliefs apparently conflicted with their engagement in the hunt. While travelling the countryside, the king and queen visited Buddhist temples for religious purposes. One trip to Ch'ŏnsu Monastery (天壽寺) allowed them an opportunity to take part in monastic prayers while also participate in the hunt.[59] Not lost on contemporary observers, Buddhists pointed out the contradictory nature of King Ch'ungnyŏl's fascination with the hunt and his Buddhist beliefs. Criticising the king's actions at his hunting retreat on Mt Maje, Chang Sullung (1255–97; 張舜龍), a Mongol official now serving in Koryŏ, said, 'On the one hand, the king has accepted the Buddha and rings a bell at the time of his meal [he practices the Buddhist prayer ritual], but on the other hand, he hunts, shoots, and kills wild animals with arrows. What kind of virtue is this?'[60] Such critical depictions conveniently overlooked Ch'ungnyŏl's responsiveness to moral concerns such as the peasants losing their livelihoods or excessive hunting. After the monk Yŏm Sŭngik (?–1302; 廉承益) won the king's favour by presenting him with charms to help improve his health, Yŏm advised the king to carry out Buddhist practices, after which Ch'ungnyŏl was said to have hunted less frequently, although he continued to hunt.[61]

Throughout King Ch'ungnyŏl's reign, hunting trips came under intense criticism at the court. The court officials Sim Yang (?–?; 沈諹) and Yi Sŭnghyu (1244–1300; 李承休) were two of the most vocal opponents. In 1280, they submitted a memorial to the throne, reprimanding the king for his actions:

> Today, our country has many problems. There is drought, and it is said that the people are starving, so there is no time to be absorbed in hunting and feasting, but Your Majesty does not assist the people in their affairs and only absorbs himself in hunting.'[62]

Hoping to separate the king from company and the social circle of the hunt, officials suggested an alternative. Recommending that the king act as an observer, a role that did not involve the direct participation of the monarch, revealed their true intentions to isolate the ruler. 'If you cannot forgo hunting, is it no better to order only soldiers to shoot animals on the plains and for you

[59] KS, 1:571d.
[60] KS, 3:687b.
[61] KS, 3:675a.
[62] KS, 3:344b-d.

to ascend a high place and watch?' In 1286, the minister of state petitioned the king to delay the hunt:

> The ancient sages taught [us] to forgo the consumption of wild birds. This is a long period of drought, and the crops decrease. So, this is not a time to seek enjoyment. Not only that, at this time, when the commoners are busy tending their crops, a royal expedition interferes with their agricultural work, stirring anxiety. It is hoped that Your Majesty will wait until the autumn to hunt.

Apparently unconcerned about the criticism, the king simply 'did not listen to [the minister's] words'.[63] The king's silence was rather curious. This underlined again the growing independence from court norms and the embrace of a wider Northeast Asian hunting lifestyle, inspired by the king's close relationship with the Mongol imperial court, but such relationships weakened the king's connections with his advisors.

Attracted by their economic value and indicators of status, it was in the context of empire that wild animals began appearing more often in Koryŏ court records. In the first half of the eleventh century, the leader of the tribal kingdom Tieli (鐵利國) sent Jurchen with horses, sable and red squirrel pelts to the Koryŏ court apparently as tribute.[64] By the second half of the thirteenth century, Koryŏ's growing connection with the Mongols – through the hunt – accelerated interest in beasts. Records note the deer, wild swine, fowl and other animals Korean elites were killing on these hunts. Killing animals marked a level of skill and ability that complemented and even challenged the previous indicators of success: family lineage and scholarly learning. Those with superior archery and horsemanship skills or hunting prowess, such as the killing of deer and wild swine, became public indicators of achievement. Where and how did these people acquire such specialised skills? They could have begun perfecting these new skills, more and better military training may have prepared them well, or existing lifestyles and practices in the countryside may have become more valuable (and visible) in the capital. Most likely, it was a little of all three. Regardless, the killing of animals – or at least the recording of these kills – took on new meaning. As more yangban went into the wild to hunt – much like scenes in the late thirteenth and early fourteenth century painting 'Crossing the River on Horseback' (Figure 2.1) depicting a hunting group crossing a frozen stream on the hunt – encounters increased, resulting in new outcomes for both humans and animals.

---

[63] KS, 1:615b.
[64] For instance, see KS, 1:93b and KS, 1:118d.

Figure 2.1 Presumably Yi Chehyŏn (1287–1367; 李齊賢), *Crossing a River on Horseback* (*Kimadogang to*; 騎馬渡江圖), c. Early 1300s. Silk fabric. Note the frozen landscape and the cautious horses apparently reluctant to traverse the ice. Such frozen scenes became more common in the second half of the fourteenth century.
Courtesy of the National Museum of Korea.

Animals on the Altar

Animals were also sacrificed as Koryŏ conducted religious rites at altars around the capital. Based on Chinese ritual texts and indigenous shamanistic practices, the meat of deer, swine, hare and other game were offered in ceremonial rites to Confucius and royal ancestors suggesting that hunting continued to be an important practice in the countryside, where such game was procured. Implemented at the founding of the dynasty – even some adopted from the earlier Silla Kingdom – the government carried out these rites to appease spirits, calm the sentiment of the people, and protect the state from inauspicious forces. Koryŏ held four types of state rituals. They were categorised as great sacrifices (*taesa*; 大祀), middle sacrifices (*chungsa*; 中祀), minor sacrifices (*sosa*; 小祀) and miscellaneous sacrifices (*chapsa*; 雜祀). The rituals in the great, middle and minor categories were Confucian, reflecting the centrality of Confucianism to the state. While termed 'miscellaneous', rites in this category, many of them with peninsular or Daoist origins, were equally important. In total, the number of state rites carried out throughout the year was thirty-seven. While many mirrored rituals adapted from China, Koryŏ did not simply copy Chinese ritual patterns but instead followed Koryŏ practices to symbolically depict Koryŏ's independence from and equality to China.[65]

As tribute to the state, wild game arrived at the court. Animals were hunted – although the process is lost – killed, extracted from the wild and their bodies cut up, processed, and shipped to the capital as a form of tribute tax. Most likely commoners or slaves hunted and provided their bounty on demand of local officials. Once there, the flesh, in the form of dried or fermented meats, became sacred offerings to the spirits and ancestors. Food prepared and offered during rituals included dried deer jerky (nokp'o; 鹿脯), fermented hare (t'ohae; 兔醢), and fermented venison (nokhae; 鹿醢). At the altar to the God Xiancan (先蠶壇), the deity that brought silk worms to humanity, officials offered fermented and dried venison and the leg of a suckling swine (ton; 豚).[66] The number of wild animals presented to the court for ritual ceremonies is unclear but would have been modest in the Koryŏ era as the number of state rituals that demanded wild animals appears few.

While state rituals demanded only small portions of wild beasts, domesticated animals were included in the ceremonies as religious sacrifice. Three days before sacrificial ceremonies for the god of the wind (p'ungsadan; 風師壇), the ritual halls were to be prepared. One ox and one swine were sacrificed. At the altar for the god of rain (usa dan; 雨師壇), one ox and one swine were sacrificed, the same number at the altar of the spirit stars (yŏngsŏngdan; 靈星壇). According to sacrificial protocol (saŭi; 祀儀), the Grand Provisioner (T'aegwallyŏng; 太官令) led in the official holding the animal – probably either an ox, sheep or swine, one of the sacrificial animals described in the Book of Rites – killed it, sliced it up, and prepared it (halsaeng sup'aeng saeng; 割牲遂烹牲). The remaining blood and fur from these ceremonies were placed on the south side of the burning incense.[67]

The state altar (sajiktan; 社稷壇) demanded two swine annually. Here, as in other animal sacrifices, rules were intimately involved with the methods of human–animal interactions through ritualised killing. The day before the sacrifice, between 3 p.m. and 5 p.m., the officials began preparing. The next

---

[65] For more on Koryŏ ritual, see Kim Anesŭ, 'Koryŏ sidae kaegyŏng iltae myŏngsan taech'ŏn kwa kukka chejang' [Great mountains and streams and national ritual rites in the Koryŏ capital], Yŏksa wa kyŏnggye 82 (2012): 1–45; and Kim Ch'ŏlung, 'Koryŏ kukka chesa ŭi ch'eje was kŭ t'ŭkching' [Organisation and characteristics of Koryŏ state ritual], Han'guksa yŏn'gu 118 (2002): 135–60.
[66] KS, 2:391b.
[67] KS, 2:403b–404c.

day, they gathered at the altar where one official led in the sacrificial animal by hand. The sacrificial officer (*changsaengnyŏng*; 掌牲令) observed the cleansing of the animal. After the animal was cleansed, the animal was led to the great altar, the sacrificial officer approached the animal, raised his hand, and called out, 'Fat and sturdy (*tun* 腯)'. Other attendants examined the animal and said, 'Satisfied (*ch'ung*; 充)'. After this observation ceremony, the animal was led to the sacrificial kitchen (*chu*; 廚). On the evening of the rites, the sacrificial official accompanied the attending officers who killed the animal and butchered it. Any fur or blood remaining were given to the palace kitchen (*ch'anso*; 饌所).[68]

Rituals like these starkly contrasted with the hunt. While animals had the chance of escape in the field – although many hunts involved numerous personnel, beaters, chasers, and even controlled fires to help kill game – domesticated animals, raised in captivity, were restrained and killed in rituals that were very different. Hunts were unpredictable. Ritual sacrifice of domesticated animals at altars were codified into practices and laws, carefully planned, controlled, carried out, and repeated. The end result was always the same – death. Sacrifices were not taken lightly. They were important ways to connect with another world, appease spirits, calm other creatures (i.e. insects that harmed crops), control environmental conditions (i.e. rain and winds), connect with the dead, and help the state govern the people. In the best of times, animals were well treated before sacrifice, and fed in a manner that allowed them to grow and reach a healthy size and weight to pass the ritual inspection at the altar. How this played out in each sacrifice is impossible to uncover. In many ways, without the spilling of animal blood or the offering of wild animal meat at these altars, the dynasty faltered, and the people suffered. Confucian ritual protocols demanded the sacrifice of animals to balance the cosmos, enabling society to function. Humans and animals were intimately entwined.

Hunting animals was a meaningful activity for Koryŏ leaders. Hunting was a large part of the early years of the dynasty: it lapsed in relative importance because of the strengthening of Confucian institutions in the capital and Buddhist beliefs among members of the royal family, and then re-emerged in the late thirteenth century as a result of new political imperatives. Hunting excursions by the founder of Koryŏ appeared to be more private and small scale, and the sources are largely quiet about the hunting practices of royal family members or other elites before the thirteenth century. When the Mongols arrived on the peninsula, new forms of hunting practices appear to have included private hunts, hunts with close members of the royal family, and large-scale

---

[68] KS, 2:405a.

chases with soldiers that hunted around the capital region and well beyond into mountains and forests farther afield. Along with the sacrifices of animals at the state alters, these hunts exemplified how animals affected political rule in Koryŏ.

A Challenge: The Qadan Insurrection, 1289–91

As we have seen, in the wake of Mongol expansion in Northeast Asia, the alignment of the Koryŏ kingship with the Yuan – and its heightened symbolic meaning for Koryŏ – combined with the uxorilocal relationship the king enjoyed with the Mongol political and cultural centre, fostered new patterns of governance and elite identity. A pivotal moment in the late thirteenth century illustrates these shifting trends, alliances and relationships and their consequences on politics and the military broadly, and the hunt specifically. In the final section of this chapter, I focus on how a failed uprising by a Mongol challenger reinforced a martial identity for the Korean kingship. While the hunt may seem marginal to the moment, the actions taken by Koryŏ and Yuan during the uprising, including debates at both courts whether to relocate the Koryŏ capital again, changed the nature of the Korean kingship and the king's involvement with the military for the next two centuries.

In the early 1290s, debates on King Ch'ungnyŏl's political authority, associated with a Northeast Asian lifestyle of hunting and the practice of uxorilocalism, took a new twist. These debates broke out in Daidu and Kaegyŏng following the 1287 Nayan insurrection against Kublai because Kublai's nephew, Nayan (1257–87; 納揚), had risen up against the Mongols, which might potentially upset stability in Northeast Asia.[69] A descendant of either Chinggis Khan's youngest brother, Temuge Ochigin, or of his half-brother, Belgutai, Nayan held domains in the Manchurian region and had the support of other Mongols such as Qadan. Qadan had his powerbase in Manchuria and Eastern Mongolia. Because of the seriousness of the uprising and its threat to the northeastern borders, Kublai, at the age of seventy-two, personally led his army to

---

[69] Peter Golden, '"I will giveth the people unto thee"; The Cinggisid Conquests and Their Aftermath in the Turkic World', *Journal of the Royal Asiatic Society* 10, no. 1 (2000): 21–41; David M. Robinson, *Empire's Twilight*, 17; Yun Eŭnsuk, 'K'ubillai k'an ŭi chung-gang chipkwŏnhwa e taehan tongdo chewangdŭl ŭi taeŭng: 'Naan pallan' ŭl chungsim ŭro' [Kublai Khan's central power in relation to the Eastern princes' response: Focusing on the Nayan rebellion], *Chungang asia yŏn'gu* 8 (2003): 29–50; Yun, 'Mongols and Western Asians in Late Koryŏ Ruling Stratem', 59–60.

Manchuria, defeated Nayan at the Liao River, and had him smothered in felt carpets.[70]

Despite this victory over Nayan, Qadan remained active. King Ch'ungnyŏl intended to travel to Mongolia to celebrate the suppression of the uprising, but his visit was postponed. Kublai instructed him to remain in Koryŏ with his forces to prepare for possible military actions, dispatching Yuan officials to Koryŏ in early 1289 for backup. In late 1289, King Ch'ungnyŏl, the queen and the crown prince travelled to the Yuan. After this, remnants of the Nayan insurrection forces regrouped under the leadership of Qadan in the Liaotong region and then suffered a major defeat in the autumn of 1290 by Yuan forces.[71] Following this, the Yuan assisted Koryŏ troops in preparing soldiers along northern towns.[72] Despite these preparations, in the first month of 1290, Qadan's troops reorganised and penetrated Koryŏ territory.[73] Immediately, the court dispatched the Koryŏ General O Inyŏng (?–?; 吳仁永) to the Yuan capital to report on the incursion while the government sent troops north to confront the invaders. Qadan, perhaps hoping to unite other Mongols against Kublai in order to carve out greater domains in the region, was a potential threat to the Yuan, including Koryŏ. Contemporaries described Qadan's army as numbering in the tens of thousands who killed, plundered, and committed acts of violence against women and children in Korea.[74]

King Ch'ungnyŏl, the queen and the crown prince were still in the Mongol capital when news of the attack reached Daidu.[75] Because he was outside of the country, King Ch'ungnyŏl was unable to hear that the debates on moving the capital from Kaegyŏng to Kanghwa Island had been revived. Rumours broke out about Qadan's attacks across the frontier, touching off great anxiety in the country. Just as the dynasty had resisted full Mongol subjugation

---

[70] Henry H. Howorth, *The Mongols Proper and the Kalmuks* (New York: Franklin, 1964), 178–9. See also Timothy May, *The Mongol Empire* (Edinburgh: Edinburgh University Press, 2018), 203.

[71] *Yüan shi* [History of the Yuan Dynasty], 15 vols (Beijing: Zhong hua shu ju, 1992), 2: 33–40.

[72] *Yüan shi*, 2: 342–43.

[73] *Koryŏsa chŏryo* [Essential History of the Koryŏ Dynasty] (Seoul: Minjok munhwa ch'ujinhoe, 1968), 3: 168–74; 526–28. For a detailed description about the movement of Qadan's troops in Koryŏ territory, see Kim Chinsu, '13-segi mal Haptan'gun ŭi ch'imgong e taehan Koryŏ ŭi taeŭng' [The Koryŏ response to the thirteenth century invasion of Haptan's army], *Kunsa* 77 (2010): 97–107. For a brief summary of the battle in English, see David M. Robinson, *Empire's Twilight*, 37–8.

[74] Yi Chehyŏn, *Kugyŏk Ikchae chip* [Collected works of Ikchae], 2 vols (Seoul: Minjok munhwa ch'uljinhoe, 1997), 2: 123.

[75] *KS*, 1:622b.

for half of the thirteenth century by relocating to Kanghwa, leading officials, such as Hong Chabŏn (1227–1306; 洪子蕃), proposed withdrawing the court anew though former palace structures on Kanghwa had been burned by the Mongols after 1270. Because the king was in the Yuan capital, a faction in the court argued that they did not have the proper authority to act based only on rumours of Qadan's approach. Two senior officials, Hŏ Kong (1234–1291; 許珙) and Ch'oe Yuŏm (1239–1331; 崔有渰), resisted the call to move the capital. 'With the king still in the imperial capital, we cannot believe such groundless rumors, and we cannot transfer the capital as we please.'[76] Hong Chabŏn summoned the senior ministers to discuss the matter. All these officials agreed with Hong that the capital had to be moved. Recognising the majority opinion in favour of the move, Hŏ Kong understood he could not interfere, but announced his decision to defend the capital while awaiting orders from the king. Hŏ returned to his home, demanding that his sons join him and remain in Kaegyŏng.

When news of the impending move reached Daidu, the emperor was enraged. Shortly after this incident, the Mongol official Inhu (1250–1311; 印侯) arrived from the Yuan. 'The Emperor has heard rumors about moving the capital and has said, "If these rumors are true, then arrest the ring leaders and bring them back to me!"' The Mongol emperor threatened those who talked about moving the capital with punishment, earning great praise for Hŏ Kong, especially since he was the head of the faction of officials that believed the capital must not be relocated. Kublai was infuriated with such a premature move, as Qadan's forces had not imperilled areas south.

In response, the emperor had King Ch'ungnyŏl, the queen and the crown prince return to Koryŏ a month later where they could report directly to him. Once they had returned, Kublai issued a decree returning the Eastern Commandery (Tongnyŏngbu; 東寧府), a region the Mongols had held in the northwestern portion of the peninsula for twenty years, to Koryŏ. Abolishing the Eastern Commandery region and returning the territory to Korea not only indicated the warming of relations between the two countries but also may have been granted to win over Koryŏ support at a time when Qadan, a Mongol rebel, disturbed the peace. At any rate, this region, full of animals, was prime hunting grounds for Jurchens, Mongols and Koreans.

When fresh reports in the fifth lunar month 1290 (June–July 1290) of Qadan's attacks reached the Koryŏ capital, the king dispatched General Kim Yŏnsu (?–?; 金延壽) to Mongol lands on the sixteenth of that month to inform Daidu of the war. From Kaegyŏng, King Ch'ungnyŏl asked for Yuan troops and

---

[76] *Koryŏsa chŏryo*, 168.

permission to move the capital. Having heard the royal family reports and the observations of military commanders, Kublai agreed.

While Qadan's forces raided parts of the country at the end of the summer in 1290, King Ch'ungnyŏl, his Mongol queen and the crown prince went hunting and visited monasteries on the Maje and Tora mountains.[77] While the latter may have been to foster Buddhist support for the protection of the dynasty by praying for the country at temples, hunting trips took on a new significance allowing the king to stay abreast of efforts to control Qadan, as his closest military officers would have accompanied him.

In the summer of 1290, the king called together his ministers to discuss a defence strategy against Qadan. Inhu argued that the king should personally travel to the eastern frontier to cut off the route of the enemy. 'If the enemy happened to penetrate into nearby territory, Your Highness can go to Kanghwa Island and your ministers will lead the troops.' Basing his arguments on the protection of his people over his own safety, the king replied,

> The people are the foundation of the country. If I were to retreat first, wouldn't this upset the people's hearts? Even if the enemy rode their horses all the way here, I would become the rearguard of the Three Armies and protect the national shrines.

By the summer of 1290, the state of affairs was reaching a tipping point as Qadan's army overcame Koryŏ defences and approached the capital. With this, the emperor again accepted Koryŏ's demand to relocate the capital. The royal family withdrew, choosing instead to alternate between several different Buddhist sites. Shortly thereafter, the capital was abandoned as wives, the elderly and children of the elite fled to Kanghwa Island and the court issued a general order for villagers to retreat to mountain fortresses or offshore islands. Government archives moved to Kanghwa indicating fear that the capital would be sacked. By the eleventh lunar month 1290, palace staff transferred to Kanghwa Island, taking with them statues of the founder of the dynasty, indicating the seriousness of the attack.[78]

It was impossible for Koryŏ to control the invading forces, and they quickly lost some northern cities to Qadan. His troops appeared as far south as Wŏnju and Haeyang (海陽; present day Kwangju). In the first month of 1291, Qadan and his troops returned to Koryŏ, joined by his son

---

[77] KS, 1:623d.
[78] KS, 1:624a.

Nojŏk (?–?; 老的).⁷⁹ Following this incursion, the crown prince, residing in Daidu, met with the emperor, requesting help to suppress the raiders. To ensure success, the crown prince dispatched an envoy to seek assistance and to secure 13,000 troops.⁸⁰ Kublai resisted. Basing his argument on Korea's history, the emperor contended that the founder of the Tang Dynasty had led expeditions against the peninsula but had failed because of the strength and ingenuity of the Korean states. Insisting that the Mongols had also encountered enormous difficulties in subjugating the peninsula, there was no need for additional troops given Koryŏ's long history of resistance. Despite such rhetorical resolve, however, a few months later, Kublai agreed to dispatch a major force. Temur Oljaitu Khan (r. 1294–1307; 成宗), who would become the second emperor of the Yuan, put down Qadan and pacified Manchuria a month later. Clean up campaigns against remnants of Qadan's forces by Koryŏ and Yuan armies continued into early summer.

The experience of the uprising reveals some contradictions in the newly forming royal cultural legitimacy and the evolving relationship Korea held with the Yuan. The Qadan insurrection was different from previous Mongol invasions because it took place after the full submission of the Koryŏ court. Led by a rebellious faction, there were limited resources for Qadan and his forces to rely upon. Qadan sought political-military benefits from the raid of an in-law state. He may have been hoping to distract Kublai by attacking the in-law Koryŏ kingdom to draw Kublai into a longer battle and provide other areas under Mongol control to the rebels.

But what it touched off had greater consequences for Northeast Asia. Debates over a proper response revealed fissures among powerful scholar officials who were unable to act in unison in the face of a national threat. Instead, the majority of leading officials in the capital sought to take action without the consent of the king or emperor, but an opposing faction resisted calls to decide such a dramatic move. A vocal minority of officials, like Hŏ Kong, recognised that the relationship with the Yuan, and the time the royal family spent in Beijing fostering the connections between the two courts, must not interfere with the regular decision making of the government. They sought to wait until the royal family returned to Koryŏ, arguing that the government should defend the capital from the attacking Mongol invaders rather than abandon it. A majority of the senior officials, however, supported Hong Chabŏn's proposal to move the capital, an implicit critique of the king. Rather than being

---

⁷⁹ KS, 3:300d.
⁸⁰ KS, 1:624a.

present in Koryŏ at a time of national distress, the king was absent celebrating the defeat of the 1287 Nayan insurrection with the emperor even though the danger to Koryŏ seemed imminent. The emperor, infuriated about rumours of a premature move, threatened to punish officials such as Hong for wanting to relocate the capital. As it turned out, the decision was out of the hands of the scholar officials at the court. Of course, within the year, after repeated calls from Koryŏ officials to move the capital, the crown prince personally convinced Kublai to accept the move and to send troops to suppress Qadan. Koryŏ officials had to rely on the imperial support from the king's uxorilocal marriage to the Mongols and the protection of military generals, a move that limited their power further under Mongol rule.

This episode also solidified the image of the king as a powerful military figure. Working closely with top Koryŏ and Yuan officials, King Ch'ungnyŏl demonstrated his leadership skills. No longer was hunting and involvement in military training mere symbolic expressions of power. The Qadan insurrection reminded Koryŏ of the real-life significance of these skills for protecting the country, the outcome of which reverberated through the peninsula for centuries to come.

* * *

The late thirteenth century was pivotal for shaping future discussions over animals and the hunt. Debates over the hunt among late Koryŏ Dynasty officials touched on favouritism, social hierarchies, gender relations, and the definition of court culture. Further, these debates over the role of the royal hunt involved policies of land management and access to game. King Ch'ungnyŏl's marital practices and neo-nomadic ethos, where the ruling family entered into an uxorilocal marriage alliance with the Mongol Yuan court, challenged Confucian norms, revealed through the political turmoil unleashed during the 1290 Qadan insurrection. From the Confucian perspective, this practice was highly disdained because this uxorilocal, female-empowered practice obfuscated ritual and blurred the lines of political and military decision making, and other values – the reason a majority of court officials disdained it. Indeed, as we will see later, in the Chosŏn Dynasty, Confucian codes strictly regulating social bonds and relations between classes, such as the Five Relations between father–son, ruler–minister, husband–wife, senior–junior, and friend–friend, were implemented into law. Part of this process also included regulating access to the king so he could become a sagely ruler, replicating those in ancient Chinese texts of the past. Hunting and other forms of entertainment, including feasts, drinking or music were viewed as contradictory to good governance. Officials criticised all of these activities during King Ch'ungnyŏl's reign, and all of them can be viewed as definers of political legitimacy. Feasting and heavy drinking, for example, were Mongol practices as well, partly as a means to cement social relations, partly because the Mongols had little interest in spending all of their time on the bureaucratic matters of governing. The close relationship developed between the Mongol and Koryŏ courts legitimised Korean kings through the practice of uxorilocalism and the hunt. Uxorilocal marriages made the family relationship between the Koryŏ and Yuan courts amenable, but in the eyes of a majority of Confucians who would write the history of the Koryŏ period, such practices, along with the hunt, were unacceptable.

3
Growth, Transformation and Challenge in the Late Fourteenth and Early Fifteenth Centuries

The preceding chapters describe the natural environment, animals and humans across the Korean peninsula while emphasising the centrality of the chase. By the fourteenth century, hunting acquired new meaning, and more people seemed to participate. In the aftermath of the Qadan attack, King Ch'ungnyŏl's authority as a militarised monarch solidified. The incident set a template for later kings. The attack also reinforced hunting as an important military skill and time spent in the field as a significant definer of rulership and masculinity based on a neo-nomadic ethos where the king held power over the realm including wild beasts. This era also marked a time of transition that reinforced bonds with the Mongol Empire and helped affirm royal control within the dynasty. On his trips to Mongol lands, for instance, King Ch'ungnyŏl occasionally hunted with his father-in-law, the emperor Kublai Khan. These became moments for them to bond and discuss political affairs and the dealings of other royal family members.[1] For later Koryŏ kings, and the men who supported them, authority over the land and wild beasts expressed domination in several ways. Hunting helped them build allegiances outside the bureaucracy to counter the power of civil officials at the court and competing elites in the countryside and navigate the changing dynamics of Northeast Asia.

Korean kings replicated this pattern of male comradery and bonding through the chase. The stories of rulers such as King Sin U (r. 1374–88; 禑) illustrate the centrality of hunting and time spent among the animals of the wild to rulership as it displayed a sense of martial valour and a renewed affinity with the military. Framed within the hunt of the late Koryŏ and wider climate change, this chapter outlines the shifting worldviews and political strategies on the peninsula and in Northeast Asia in the fourteenth and fifteen

---

[1] For instance, KS, 1:639b–640b.

centuries. Some of those forces impacting the peninsula were regional – for instance, the fall of the Mongol Yuan Dynasty in the 1360s and the rise of the Chinese Ming Dynasty (1368–1644) – and unleashed political, religious and cultural shifts throughout the region that I detail below. Other forces came in the form of climate fluctuations and population growth that complicated politics, societies and animal habitats. Korean leaders responded by forming new political bonds of their own both in and beyond the peninsula. All of these international, intellectual, socio-economic, climate and population pressures are relevant for explicating the hunt and the impact of wild animals on the court and state explored in later chapters.

Late Koryŏ Royal Hunting Practices

Beginning with Mongol imperial rule in the 1270s, the frequency of royal and elite hunts increased dramatically – or at least took on more import and were recorded in the official histories the *Koryŏsa* and *Koryŏsa chŏryo*. Kings Ch'unsŏn (r. 1308–13; 忠宣), Ch'ungsuk (r. 1313–30, 1332–39; 忠肅), Ch'unghye (r. 1330–32, 1339–44; 忠惠) and Sin U took part in the chase to various degrees. While these subsequent leaders did not engage in hunting at the same level as King Ch'ungnyŏl, they nonetheless found these expeditions valuable. Even though the hunts were sometimes not annual events, as they had been under Ch'ungnyŏl – most likely because of political struggles inside the country, succession conflicts that replicated struggles in the imperial centre, and the fact that kings often lived outside of Koryŏ in Mongol territory for extended periods of time – they still served as indicators of royal and elite status. Ch'ungnyŏl was tied to the political power of Kublai. After the passing of the emperor, while still potent connections, some of the political capital was lost. Successive emperors did not hold the same political and military prestige as the founding leader of the Yuan.

Benefits from the imperial centre came with other limitations and concerns. While Koryŏ kings and officials often travelled to the Yuan because Korea was part of the Mongol world, one official attempted to protect Korea's wildlands from the Mongol imperial eye. As noted earlier, the envoy Pang Sinu (1267–1343; 方臣祐) told the Yuan Mongol emperor, 'In Koryŏ, the land is narrow and the mountains are so numerous that there are no places to hunt or raise livestock.'[2] His statement, intended to protect the peninsula from Mongol Yuan hunting groups and excessive demands for animal gifts, was far from the truth, as he and other officials understood.

---

[2] KS, 3:666a.

By then, a hunting culture was growing among the elite of the country, driven by the popularity of the hunt at the imperial court in the Mongol capital Daidu and the involvement of Koryŏ kings and the elites close to them. The scholar official Sin Ch'ŏng (1300–?; 申青) was adept at falconry, earning him praise and various government posts from King Ch'ungsuk.[3] Another military official was Yun Su (?–?; 尹秀) who had earned the admiration of King Ch'ungnyŏl because of his mastery of his falcons and hunting dogs. Ch'ungnyŏl insisted Yun join him on his trip to the city of Shenyang and when Yun returned, he was put in charge of the royal birds. Later, when Yun visited Daidu, his talents caught the attention of the emperor who bestowed on him a few hunting falcons, which he kept with him when he returned to Koryŏ.[4]

Yun and other officials received titles and rewards from the Yuan emperors and even the Koryŏ kings were indebted to the practice of hunting for imperial attention. On one visitation, Kublai asked King Ch'ungnyŏl if he were familiar with horseback riding and falconry. Trying to interpret the question for Ch'ungnyŏl, one attending official, General Yi Chŏng (?–?; 李貞), believed the emperor had asked the king to compel Ch'ungnyŏl to hunt more frequently. Yi's sensitivity towards hunting and riding was understandable considering his own background and recognition. Yi Chŏng himself was admired for his physical strength and hunting skills. His horsemanship and archery prowess earned him his promotion to general. Most likely because of Yi's hunting skills and knowledge of animals, King Ch'ungnyŏl enjoyed the hunts that Yi led. Yi also participated in falconry. He held such an affinity for his birds that he trained them to capture their prey alive, after which he killed the feathered game himself, plucked their feathers, chewed their raw meat, and fed it to his hawks. Accustomed to routinely consuming half of a raw bird, after his death, General Yi Chŏng was lauded for his falcon-like qualities and apparently sprouting bumps all over his body like the skin of a bird.[5]

Royal attention could transcend status, age, and even country of origin. Groups of officials, and even their sons, accompanied kings on hunts. On one occasion, Yi Punhŭi (?–1278; 李汾禧), Yun Su and King Ch'ungnyŏl went on a hunt with the Mongol *darugachi* military administrators. Knowing Ch'ungnyŏl's delight in the hunt, Yi Punhŭi, a scholar official, accused Yun and his son of currying favours with the king through falcon hunting. Trying to persuade the king to stop hunting, Yi voiced his disapproval of

---

[3] KS, 3:700a.
[4] KS, 3:689b-c.
[5] KS, 3:690b–691a. These bumps may have represented more than his affinity with birds; they could have been a contagious disease.

the level of violence hunting displayed in front of the royal personage; the king was witness to hawks ripping open the abdomens of the birds they captured.⁶ Other officials, like Pak Ŭi, were recognised by the king for their falconry skills. The official Ch'oe Anto (1294–1340; 崔安道) hunted with King Ch'ungsuk in P'yŏngju (modern Hwanghae Province). On one occasion, a deer jumped out in front of them and sprinted past the king. Ch'oe hit the deer with an arrow, pleasing Ch'ungsuk, who then promoted Ch'oe to garrison commander and conferred a government post on him.⁷ Wŏn Ŭi (?–1358; 元顗), Kyŏng Pokhŭng (?–1380; 慶復興) and Hwang Sang (1328–82; 黃裳) enjoyed falcons and hunting dogs, but it was supposedly a hobby about which they 'blushed in shame'.⁸ While these and other officials received favours from the king for their hunting talents and 'hobbies,' a lack of hunting skills could demonstrate masculine weakness. One official, Yi Chonsŏng (?–1388; 李存性), did not know how to wield a bow and arrow, which angered King Sin U who demoted him.

Subsequently, King Kongmin (r. 1351–74; 恭愍) navigated the political and cultural impacts of the transition from the Mongol Yuan to the Chinese Ming dynasties by adopting a restrained attitude towards the hunt. He attempted to curtail, albeit not abolish, the royal practice. King Kongmin, who advocated a pro-Ming stance after 1369, was praised by his officials for *not* having the character to kill living things and for *not* hunting in ten years.⁹ He pointed out his relationship with animals. 'I raise a falcon, not to hunt, but to admire its courage and integrity.'¹⁰ He saw them more as representations of power and strength and less as items to take into the field to catch and kill other beasts. In the wider context of the Yuan-Ming transition, a shift well recognised in the capital, one official stepped up criticism of the hunt and voiced concern that when all of the king's subordinates follow the ruler and hunt, they end up destroying the crops and harming the livelihoods of the people. 'This is an old evil that comes back to life today, so we hope to abolish it.' King Kongmin agreed with him, in words but not action, as Kongmin continued to hunt.¹¹

As Korea was not isolated from events across the frontier, but well aware of the decline of the Yuan and establishment of the Ming after 1369, perception of the hunt began to shift in the court. Official Yun Sojong (1345–93; 尹紹宗) criticised King Kongmin for harming the people by hunting while travelling

---

⁶ KS, 3:678a-c.
⁷ KS, 3:702c-d.
⁸ These and other biographies can be found in KS, 3:503a.
⁹ KS, 1:817d.
¹⁰ KS, 1:842d.
¹¹ KS, 1:843a.

through the countryside. The king's hunting entourage sparked rumours that, Yun Sojong claimed, reached as far away as China. To avoid such widespread criticism, Yun argued, the monarch should abstain from hunting because when the king travelled to hunt in the spring, his hunting party delayed crop production. Despite such rebukes, King Kongmin did not listen. Instead, he permitted the court to restrain the hunting activities of others through legal means as the central government attempted to prohibit various forms of the chase. In 1351, King Kongmin prohibited the hunt in the capital and adjacent regions, most likely to protect the livelihoods of the farming population. Later, the court extended another hunting and falconry ban in 1372 to include all three state altars, Wŏn'gu (圓丘), Sannŭng (山陵) and Chinsan (鎭山) in order to protect these areas from the damage hunting parties might bring. Under King Kongmin, the government also took actions to prevent fire hunts in the spring.[12] Gauging the efficacy of these decrees is difficult as no follow-up reports seem to exist. However, given that the court had to pass additional laws to fortify existing regulations over the next century, their impact might have been weak.

After the killing of King Kongmin by a factional coup that brought to power a pro-Mongol government under King Sin U, who was barely eleven years old and easily manipulated by pro-Mongol officials, the Censorate Yi Inim (?–1388; 李仁任) chided the young king for letting his interest in the hunt interfere in government decision making.[13] One Confucian official, Cho Chun (1346–1405; 趙浚), faulting the royal hunt, advocated banning all hunting and feasting because not only did the hunt interfere with the farming season and land use, but the people had little to eat. Cho claimed that the government failed 'to meet the needs of the people's health' by 'eliminating the waste of hunting'.[14] The military commander and official Ch'oe Yŏng (1316–88; 崔瑩) broke down in tears when he heard that Sin U wasted his days hunting and returned to the palace late at night. Yet subsequently, Ch'oe attended several hunts with him.[15] Ignoring the advice of important officials close to him, King U's behaviour was indicative of the royal family's desire to rebuild royal authority by looking beyond officials at court for alternate ways of conducting affairs. Koryŏ kings had found success with this pattern through Mongol imperial support. In the absence of real Mongol power in the region, kings such as Sin U struggled to find ways to regain political significance. The

---

[12] KS, 1:756b.
[13] KS, 3:737d–738a and 3:895b.
[14] KS, 3:601c.
[15] KS, 3:490b-c.

hunt offered a lifestyle connected to an earlier era of Mongol power when Koryŏ kings held significant connections beyond the peninsula.

While a young man, Sin U embraced the cultural practice of earlier pro-Mongol kings and officials and grew to become an avid hunter. In 1380, he attended a five-day-long hunt that took place south of the capital, a relatively extended journey when compared to other hunts. On yet another occasion, King Sin U assigned eunuchs Yi Tŭkpun (?–?; 李得芬) and Kim Sil (?–?; 金實) to the ranks of military officials and departed for the adventure with a falcon sitting on his arm along with a bow and a quiver of arrows. In a show of support for the Mongols and a world beyond the peninsula to which the court once so intimately supported, he ordered the eunuchs and other underlings to play 'barbarian songs' and 'barbarian flutes', strum the zither, beat the drums and follow along (*hoga hojŏk t'an'gŭm*; 胡歌胡笛彈琴).[16]

King Sin U's admiration of animals compelled him into the field with all its opportunities and dangers. The king, for instance, practised equestrianism and falconry and grew proficient in hunting by bow and arrow.[17] He explained that he was not fond of hunting at first, but that some of his senior-ranking ministers, who enjoyed the hunt, had turned him onto it.[18] When Sin U went on one hunting expedition to Sŏhae Province, Pan Pokhae (?–1388; 潘福海) journeyed with him. Pan was a trusted confidant of King Sin U. When Sin U struck a boar with an arrow, the injured animal turned and charged him. The king, taken by surprise, fell from his saddle. From horseback, Pan Pokhae hit the boar with a single arrow, saving Sin U. This dangerous hunting encounter solidified the relationship between the king and Pan; Pan received special titles, and his father was promoted. Sin U and Pan themselves were said to have bonded like 'father and son'. This replicated the Mongol practice of promoting the lower social order and foreigners for their abilities and prowess. Later, Sin U was so impressed by Pan's actions, he reminisced in a personal letter to him. In it, the king explained that only in emergencies and in times of disaster do people learn about the true nature of others. Sin U described the moment in the forest:

> When we went hunting in the western district, a large wild boar charged me. At this point, my servants around me cowered and did not know what to do. When my life ran in a flash [in front of my eyes], you came galloping on your horse and struck it in the abdomen with a single arrow. It fell to the

---

[16] KS, 3:895a.
[17] KS, 3:872a and 3:892c-d.
[18] KS, 3:895a.

ground protesting in loud squeals. This is when you inherited my life . . . if it weren't for the loyalty and bravery of heaven in your heart, how could I serve my ancestors and the mountains and streams today?[19]

On another hunt with King U, Pan fell from his horse, and to demonstrate his appreciation for the earlier hunting incident with the wild boar, the king bestowed his own steed to Pan.[20]

Through the end of the fourteenth century, and the push and pull between Koryŏ officials who either supported the Mongol Yuan or the Ming, hunting brought humans and animals together in places far away from the power politics of the capital. Koryŏ royalty and elites navigated the changing power dynamics in Northeast Asia though a number of means. As discussed above, one was by associating with Mongol nomadic cultural practices of movement, hunting and closeness to animals. By adopting these outward expressions, and assuming a Mongol-inspired identity, kings and their supporters sought to dominate the central government and control the countryside by building informal relations outside the capital. In time, even some civil officials hunted. Whether a majority of classically educated civil officials had also come to receive basic training in the use of arms and riding horses as a result of Koryŏ integration with the Mongol Empire is hard to know. The evidence suggests that kings expected their civil officials to command a modicum of martial skills; at least those who did thrived. Animals were the quiet forces that compelled the elite – either as participant, observer or both – to interact in new spaces. The Yuan–Ming transition complicated the popularity of the hunt, however, stirring up competitors with and beyond the capital, all seeking novel ways to legitimise the major political and military decisions they began undertaking at the court and beyond.

Late Koryŏ–Early Chosŏn Transition

Beginning in the 1340s, major socio-political change swept through East Asia.[21] These changes had dramatic consequences for Koryŏ. In the Yuan Dynasty, Mongol power declined in China as widescale domestic rebellions coalesced around the Chinese leader Zhu Yuanzhang (1328–98; 朱元璋),

---

[19] KS, 3:706b–707b.
[20] KS, 3:706b–707b.
[21] For a fascinating study of this era in Northeast Asia, see David M. Robinson, *Korea and the Fall of the Mongol Empire: Alliance, Upheaval, and the Rise of a New East Asian Order* (New York: Cambridge University Press, 2022).

also known as the Hongwu Emperor (r. 1368–98), the founder of the Ming Dynasty. Disorder led to powerful Chinese rebel groups, such as the Red Turbans (religiously inspired Chinese rebels that rose up in the Yuan Dynasty and launched attacks into Korea), attacking Koryŏ in 1359 and 1361. Witnessing the disintegration of the Yuan, Koryŏ ruler King Kongmin dislodged the Mongols by retaking territories in the northwest in 1356. A campaign for political reform and social justice accelerated in Koryŏ, including calls for retribution against Mongol collaboration. During the Yuan Dynasty, the Mongols took control of Jurchen land, present along the northeast coast of Korea. Koryŏ reclaimed this land from the Mongols. After the founding of the Ming in 1368, China began to reclaim areas in northeast Korea. The Ming, desiring this territory, pushed out the remnants of the Yuan state and threatened invasion of the peninsula by the 1380s.

Pressured by the Ming and Mongols to the north, Koryŏ also had to contend with Japanese raiders and gangs that marauded and looted the coasts. In the fourteenth century, Japan was not an integrated state. Instead, it was a divided land with two rival courts and a military leader, or shogun, who held power over his own domain, but did not govern other regions directly. Poorer regions, especially those along the southwest coast, had a habit of piracy. At times, armed ships or armadas of quasi-military forces arrived along the Korean coast and plundered the coastal villages, attacks that continued to trouble Korea until the sixteenth century. As the pirates increased their activities, Korea had difficulty defending against them. However, while still a Koryŏ officer, military leader and founder of Chosŏn, Yi Sŏnggye (King T'aejo, r. 1392–8; 李成桂) successfully contained the Japanese. Yi overcame piracy by combining communication, naval vessels, intelligence, militias and gunpowder weapons. Gunpowder had not yet reached Japan. In the 1380s, Yi sunk numerous Japanese ships, defeating a major force of pirates. His successes against the Japanese subsequently elevated his reputation as a military leader. Holding political ambitions through the 1380s, Yi reached out to many Neo-Confucians – many of whom were ready, capable and ambitious – wanting to gain their support.

In 1388, Ming armies finally reached Manchuria and defeated the Mongols. The Koryŏ court ordered Yi Sŏnggye, then commander of the army, to deal with the Ming and sent him and his army north to attack. This demand led to a split between Yi and the court. When Yi reached the Yalu River with his troops, he commanded them to return and then marched into the capital and overthrew the government. Back in the capital, he set himself up as chief councillor of the state, purged pro-Mongols and corrupt officials, and began passing laws favouring Neo-Confucianism. Yi and his supporters, many of them inspired by Neo-Confucian teachings, passed land reform laws, which converted all of the land around the capital to state property, then reassigned it to merit subjects, those who supported him. Yi and these reformers, who began realising the need for a strong central government to ensure their power, needed each other.[22] Between 1374 and 1380, reformers, supported by the self-appointed Chief Councillor of the State Yi Sŏnggye, argued that Sin U was not the biological son of King Kongmin, but instead was the son of a monk and had to be dethroned. Yi searched through the royal family for someone without any Mongol blood and found a distant descendant who became King Kongyang (r. 1389–92; 恭讓), whom he installed on the throne. Yi purged the royal family, downgraded Buddhist monasteries, built up the army, and brought new 'order' to Koryŏ. Yi also sent diplomatic envoys to China and stressed his desire to maintain a friendly relationship with the Chinese. He conducted these efforts to cleanse the Korean royal family of Mongol connections and to convince the Ming of his sincerity.

From its founding, Koryŏ had favoured Buddhism, and its totalistic approach to life and truth, which heavily dominated society.[23] Although Buddhism was not a state religion, kings and the ruling elites associated themselves with Buddhism, and it played an important spiritual role in protecting the state. This was acknowledged in the phrase 'protect the country' (*hoguk*; 護國) adopted from the well-known Mahayana Buddhist principle that held that the power of the Buddha had been devoted to the preservation of the state. In turn, the state funded religious projects, such as building monasteries, supporting monks through exempting them from taxes and military service, and the re-carving of the *Tripitaka*.

In China, Confucianism went through an intellectual reawakening, transforming into a new form of learning referred to as Neo-Confucianism, from the teachings of the Song Chinese scholar Zhu Xi (1130–1200; 朱熹) and others, to differentiate it from earlier Confucian practices. Earlier Confucianism mainly focused on the family and ancestral rituals and an education in the Chinese Classics. Confucianism had not been philosophically strong and had taken second tier to Buddhism. Neo-Confucianism was considered revolutionary, even in China. Neo-Confucianism went beyond the ideas of the simple filial piety found in earlier Confucian teachings and transformed into a philosophy about human nature, acquiring a metaphysical dimension. There

---

[22] See Duncan, *The Origins of the Chosŏn Dynasty*, 274.
[23] See Jongmyung Kim, 'Kings and Buddhism in Medieval Korea', *Korean Studies* 41 (2017): 128–51.

was an intellectual concern to it, including a new emphasis on ritual that extended into society, focusing on the immediate, deeper philosophical and metaphysical dimensions, which had Buddhist and Daoist origins. Koreans began studying more about Neo-Confucianism in the late thirteenth century. From the 1280s, Neo-Confucian books from China, and from people who went to the Yuan to study, circulated and brought new ideas back to the peninsula. The introduction of Neo-Confucian philosophy encouraged Korean scholarly elites to re-evaluate the role of Buddhism in society and politics. In the middle of the fourteenth century, some Neo-Confucians believed that these monks led licentious lives, ones full of womanising and drinking, rather than studying and meditating. They argued that since Buddhism was old and in decline, the religious institution must be attacked.[24] Neo-Confucianism did not accommodate Buddhism, and Neo-Confucians felt Buddhists needed to retreat from politics and society.

While practised widely and deeply throughout society, one sect of Buddhism (Kyo; 教), as an institution, declined somewhat since the beginning of the period of military house rule in 1170, while another sect (Sŏn; 禪) prospered and expanded significantly. While more complex than commonly argued, as monks themselves attempted reforms in the late thirteenth century, much of this decline has been described in terms of morality and corruption. Many Buddhist monasteries became havens for oppressed peasants. Originally, the state supported Buddhism by providing tax-exempt land to monasteries where monks practised. To evade government conscription and taxes, poor peasants worked for these monasteries. With the assistance of these peasants, monks found support for their farming, but this led to a decline in the number of peasants as Buddhism protected these former tax-paying farmers who no longer paid taxes to the state. The loss of a number of peasants meant a decline in state revenue as they were the ones who worked the land and submitted taxes to the government. Serious arguments and debates broke out among officials in the capital arguing to uproot Buddhism, but the state was still tied to the Buddhist structure and supported the religion.[25] The decline of Buddhism and the rise of Neo-Confucianism among the old Koryŏ elites has also been explained less as an ideological clash and more as a separation

---

[24] While Confucians attacked Buddhism and the Buddhists themselves criticised the actions of monks, Buddhist monasteries and monks were still actively teaching moral precepts. See Sem Vermeersch, 'Views on Buddhist Precepts and Morality in Late Koryŏ', *Journal of Korean Religions* 7, no. 1 (April 2016): 35–65.

[25] For more, see Lewis Lancaster and C. S. Yu, *Buddhism in the Early Chosŏn: Suppression and Transformation* (Fremont: Asian Humanities Press, 2002), xi–xv.

between religion and wealth involving funeral rites.[26] In other words, Neo-Confucians attacked Buddhists not because of their beliefs, but because of the exorbitant costs of the funeral rituals monks demanded for their services.

The Koryŏ–Chosŏn transition involved maintaining the continuity of some of the old forces from the Koryŏ era while blending in new powers of Neo-Confucianism.[27] Allegiances to the old dynasty were strong, as were calls for a break from the past to form something new. The changeover was more than the Neo-Confucian officials merely attacking the forces of Buddhism. By 1392, some Neo-Confucians began calling for a new dynasty and, wanting more power, they convinced former general, Chief Councillor of the State Yi to take control as king. This was not an easy move; he had led the coup but still held loyalty to the old dynasty. The Koryŏ state found itself in a perilous situation with the Mongols in retreat and Ming armies near the northern frontier. Some scholars who embraced Neo-Confucianism supported the overthrow of Koryŏ, while others did not. Those who had supported a new order, including the military, overthrew Koryŏ and founded Chosŏn.

The Chosŏn founder, Yi Sŏnggye, now King T'aejo, was a charismatic and formidable military leader, who relied on the former Koryŏ bureaucratic structure to govern. One of his early decisions was to insert his own comrades as merit subjects. Another was his moving the location of the court away from Kaegyŏng. In 1395, Hanyang, the only sizable city on the peninsula and Koryŏ's southern capital, became the main capital for the new dynasty. At the time of infighting among his sons, the city was badly damaged, and the court moved back to Kaesŏng, but it returned to Hanyang in 1405. Hanyang, centrally located, was a more secure location from invasion from the north. Its position, having better access to food, crafts and animal-based products shipped in from the countryside, also allowed for easier governing of the more populated regions of the south.

Developments in the first century of the Chosŏn Dynasty laid the groundwork for the changes that took place in the dynasty during the second half of Chosŏn.[28] Recent scholarship on the transition between the Koryŏ and

---

[26] See Juhn Ahn, *Buddhas and Ancestors: Religion and Wealth in Fourteenth-Century Korea* (Seattle: University of Seattle Press, 2018), 15, 35.

[27] John Duncan has extensively explored the transition. For an outstanding summary, see John Duncan, 'Confucianism in the Late Koryŏ and Early Chosŏn', *Korean Studies* 18 (1994): 76–102.

[28] As Anders Karlsson points out, while they disagree on the interpretations, scholars across fields have identified the many socio-economic changes that took place earlier in the dynasty that led to developments in the second half of Chosŏn. See Anders Karlsson, 'Confucian Ideology and Legal Developments in Chosŏn Korea: A Methodological Essay', in *The Spirit of Korean Law: Korean Legal History in Context*, ed. Marie Seong-Hak Kim (Boston, MA: Brill, 2016), 84–5.

Chosŏn dynasties identifies continuity, rather than radical change, as being a major condition with the ruling class. Along with this was the effort by lawmakers to create a centralised bureaucratic polity. As John Duncan explains, reform in political institutions was made possible by the overwhelming military control of the new royal family, which only became possible after the founding king had eliminated private armies and had concentrated all of the military under the throne.[29] One of the greatest differences between the Koryŏ and Chosŏn institutions was the expansion of control over the provinces. Reformers replaced weak and low-ranking Koryŏ governorships with senior-ranking officials who exercised a broad range of control over the provinces. Also, reformers began to bring the entire countryside under the influence of the central government, which was important for the state's ability to extract resources from the land, animals and humans.

Once in power, Neo-Confucians began to shape the new dynasty. While not clear from the beginning, the overarching idea of some of these scholar officials was to make Neo-Confucianism the main directive underpinning every aspect of the state's institutions. For example, the Neo-Confucians redesigned the criminal code, which included the violation of filial piety. According to Neo-Confucian philosophy, the Confucian patrilineal, father-to-son, male-heir family system was necessary to conduct ritual and mourning rites. Neo-Confucians insisted on the creation of a patrilineal society and began to uproot uxorilocalism. In uxorilocal society, defining an heir was difficult. In Neo-Confucianism, the male descendant line must be identified and there could only be one primary wife, distinct from other wives. While implemented at the elite level the process took centuries to reach throughout society, as families on the peninsula had been uxorilocal for at least a thousand years. The first three kings of the Chosŏn Dynasty – King T'aejo (r. 1392–98), King Chŏngjong (r. 1398–1400; 定宗) and King T'aejong (r. 1400–18; 太宗) – were raised in uxorilocal households in their mother's homes. During the uprooting of uxorilocal practice, the families of wives lost the rights to their security through their property. This was a major blow to women and their families as many women lost the right to hold and bequeath property, weakening their social leverage and wealth.[30]

As pointed out in previous chapters, during the Koryŏ Dynasty, Confucians were a small minority working as civil officials in the central bureaucracy.

---

[29] For more, see Duncan, *The Origins of the Chosŏn Dynasty*, 266–7.
[30] For more on the complexities of gender, women, and the legal system, see Jisoo Kim, *The Emotions of Justice: Gender, Status, and Legal Performance in Chosŏn Korea* (Seattle: University of Washington Press, 2015), 3–21.

This began to change with the introduction of Neo-Confucianism. Increased interest strengthened the prestige of Confucianism. Those among the elite with political aspirations needed to learn Confucianism and take the Confucian exams. The status structure of society also changed during the Koryŏ–Chosŏn transition. Many rural elites became members of the national elite, a rural to urban process that accelerated early on during the Chosŏn Dynasty. Over the course of one hundred years, many families adopted Neo-Confucian ways, which led to the spread of Confucianism and the creation of even more people with lofty politically inspired aspirations to place sons in high positions of power in the central government. Advancing was impossible according to Neo-Confucianists because of the notion of the hereditary nature of status – those who wished to sit for the examination had to prove elite yangban lineage, all but ensuring that Neo-Confucian learning was tied to birth. This, combined with a strong monarchical tradition alongside a powerful bureaucracy, sparked political and social tension. Chosŏn Dynasty architects wanted to maintain and strengthen Confucianism especially among the elite.

Also, a strong ideological reason anchored these reforms. Confucianism had been eclectic before the introduction of Neo-Confucianism and had existed in parallel with Buddhism. Even during the Buddhist period of the Koryŏ era, officials had been trained in Confucianism. At the founding of the new Chosŏn, the two worldviews sharply separated. From 1392 on Neo-Confucians continued an ideological hostility towards Buddhism based on social, political, ethical and philosophical ideas. Neo-Confucians did not want Buddhist believers involved in politics or visible in the public sphere. Private practice continued to be acceptable, and women were allowed to practise Buddhism, including the wives of the elite *sadaebu*.

Another way to delineate the powerful was the introduction of the study of Chinese classical literature. Neo-Confucianists elevated the knowledge of Chinese to an indicator of elite status. In-depth knowledge of Classical Chinese was necessary for men of power. These elites identified with Kija (1,000 BCE). As noted earlier, Kija of Shang Dynasty China was a legendary, though probably inaccurate, figure who founded a kingdom on the Korean peninsula, bringing Chinese civilisation to Northeast Asia. However, this origin story – that did not involve animals or mystical unions with beasts – centred the beginning of Korean society in China, in contrast to the animal foundation myths of Tan'gun and Chumong discussed in Chapter 1. The story of Kija, which Confucians raised as part of the mythical union between the Korean peninsula and China, connected the two civilisations in the minds of many scholar officials.

Neo-Confucian reforms helped normalise political, commercial and cultural relations with the Chinese Ming leaders. Never too close with Koryŏ, the Ming remained sceptical. The transformative Neo-Confucians in Korea felt China to be an anti-Mongol ally. It took a number of diplomatic missions to the Ming during the late 1300s and the early 1400s to convince China of Korea's friendly intentions.[31] By the first decade of the fifteenth century, diplomacy grew productive as Chosŏn entered into a tributary relationship with the Ming. According to the rules, the emperor in China, as 'the Son of Heaven', was the only ruler. The legitimacy of all other leaders was derived from their recognition of the Chinese emperor. While Korea assumed inferior status vis-à-vis China, this relationship had its advantages by promising stability. In theory, the Son of Heaven in Beijing legitimised the king of Korea and in so doing reduced the potential for coups or political conspiracies at court. After the founding of Chosŏn, political factions that had hoped to replace the Korean king were required to travel to China and ask for recognition. While the Chinese representative ratified new Korean kings, China never chose the Korean king. This relationship existed in the realm of ritual, not actual power. Kings of Korea, through their ambassadors, demonstrated their loyalty to China annually on the Lunar New Year and accepted the graces of the Chinese emperor by kowtowing nine times while hiding their faces. The Chinese reign calendar, based on the name of the current Chinese emperor, was used on all government records and documents in Korea. Travel between the two countries was monitored. Entering Korea without the authority of the emperor was illegal, and Koreans were not permitted to travel freely to China unless on official business. These arrangements ensured a level of mutual security.

Trade was conducted in the context of the tributary system. Korea contributed tribute or gifts, such as ginseng, paper and animal skins from the northern forests, where animals were more plentiful, and presented these items to China. In return, China gave valuable products to Korea, for example silk, tea and other high-value treasures.[32] While on tributary missions, Koreans conducted business with Chinese merchants who purchased items from them. This system provided these elite travellers and the Korean government with some economic opportunities and access to Chinese markets, including the latest books, science and medicine. The Ming also understood that theoretically they had to defend Korea from attack, but the relationship between the two countries grew amicable and stable over time, which provided the new Chosŏn Dynasty with an opportunity to develop institutions of governance and a new identity

---

[31] Kenneth Robinson, 'Pak Tonji and the Vagaries of Government Service in Koryŏ and Chosŏn, 1360–1412', *Korean Studies* 40 (2016): 78–118.

[32] Yuan-kang Wang, *Harmony and War: Confucian Culture and Chinese Power Politics* (New York: Columbia University Press, 2010), 146.

around Neo-Confucianism. By the late fifteenth century, Chosŏn political culture had changed significantly. The civil bureaucracy, in particular, was infused with Neo-Confucian ideals that had come to dominate the government and were increasingly able to dictate court culture and even the royal lifestyle.

Climate and Human Population Pressures

Typical narratives of the Koryŏ–Chosŏn transition highlight such political, religious and ideological developments. However, concurrent with these well-recognised events of the fourteenth and fifteenth centuries were larger forces that often go overlooked. Some of these pressures were manmade (like land-use patterns and demographic shifts), others were beyond the capacity for humans to control (such as the weather) no matter how much they tried through prayers, rituals and offerings to the gods. These two centuries are particularly important to investigate because they straddle what scientists refer to as the Medieval Climate Anomaly (800–1350) and the Little Ice Age (1350–1850), significant climate events present in the Northern Hemisphere, including Korea and Northeast Asia. Also during this era, populations contracted, expanded and shifted because of warfare, empire building and disease. Examining weather conditions and human demographics during this transition between these two climate periods helps us better understand the political and military responses to local, regional, and even global events. Shifting human demographics and the needs of a growing state demanded stronger and more centralised control. As will be seen, weather and demographics impacted terrain, hunting practices and the population of animals in the wild.

A major problem with demographics in the premodern world is the inaccuracy of population figures. Governments did not conduct widescale surveys of the people. Those that attempted to measure demographics often failed to consistently count the population. In East Asia, in places such as the Mongol-Yuan territory, although the government tried to register households, people and livestock, population figures never represented reality. However, general trends are revealing. A consensus of modern scholars believes that during the period of Mongol wars and subsequent expansion into China, population numbers declined from battle deaths and famines, while the movement of armies displaced increasing numbers of refugees south and westward.[33] The

---

[33] For instance, see Li Sha, 'Jin sanshi nianlai Yuan dai renkou yanjiu zonshu' [A summary of population research in the Yuan Dynasty over the past thirty years], *Yindo xuekan* (2007): 43–8; and John Durand, 'The Population Statistics of China, AD 2–1953', *Population Studies* (March 1960): 209–56.

unification of China under the Yuan stabilised society as the Mongols encouraged economic growth, agricultural output and merchant trade, all policies that promoted the eventual recovery and growth of the population by the early fourteenth century.

On the Korean peninsula, people migrated in similar patterns. As I discussed in the Introduction, the arrival of Mongol troops spurred the Korean court and ruling military family to migrate as refugees to the protection of the islands off the west coast, where they lived for decades. The Koryŏ military leader also called on farmers and villagers to abandon the peninsula and flee to coastal islands. Battles with Mongol forces spurred the movement of Koryŏ soldiers to fight in the north or to garrison mountain fortresses. Like in China, war brought death and destruction to Koreans and served as an engine of population movement. But after capitulating to the Mongols in the late thirteenth century, joining the Mongol Empire brought stability to the peninsula. Society stabilised, but populations continued to shift in other ways as royal family members, elites and scholars travelled to and spent time in the Yuan. This migration even included a small number of professional female musicians who moved to the Mongol Yuan.[34]

In the first half of the fifteenth century, however, societies and governments across Eurasia stagnated. Some of this decline was linked to population loss from diseases such as the outbreak of the Black Death, or the plague, in the late 1350s that swept across Eurasia, or from growing warfare that resulted in the decline and collapse of the Mongol Empire. The impact of these events was so widespread that it was not until the latter half of the fifteenth century that economies began to improve as agriculture increased and trade grew after the greater distribution of precious metals, such as copper and silver – China, Southeast Asia and West Africa began to mine again and circulate for regional and international trade – and responses to climate fluctuations.[35]

The Koryŏ and Chosŏn dynasties were no different. Both governments depended on taxes collected from the people, mostly in the form of rice and other grains as well as cash crops like cotton after its introduction to Korea via the Yuan in the 1360s. The decrease in agricultural production due to natural disasters such as flooding and drought impacted tax collection, and the Chosŏn government looked for ways to respond. In the early fifteenth century,

---

[34] Wu Mingwei, 'Gaoli xiang Yuanchao renkou qianyi zhong de yinyue wenhua jiaoliu' [Population migration of Korea and the Yuan dynasty music cultural exchange], *Fujian shifan daxue xuebao* 5 (2015): 104–11.

[35] William S. Atwell, 'Time, Money, and the Weather: Ming China and the "Great Depression" of the Mid-Fifteenth Century', *The Journal of Asian Studies* (February 2002): 83–4.

the government established laws in the National Code for the buying and selling of land as the crops grown on the land was the basis of wealth. As has been well established, most land was privately owned by the yangban, the scholarly and military elite of society, at this time.[36] By the second half of the century, the government had to accept the realities of the private buying and selling of land, while still emphasising policies that promoted agricultural production.

The lack of available land stressed a shifting population.[37] Population trends are hard to estimate during this period because the government did not partake in official census counts. One recent study claims that the population increased after the founding of the Chosŏn Dynasty, rising from 5.7 million to 9.4 million by the year 1500; while other scholars offer a more modest population increase of 4.1 million people on the peninsula by the middle of the sixteenth century, the majority of which farmed the land.[38] Regardless of scale, anecdotal evidence in government sources such as the *Sillok* reinforce these recent studies on population growth and its estimate. Further, even greater population trends are noted in Japan and China during this era. In Japan, the number of people roughly doubled between 1280 and 1450, while in China, the population most likely increased during the Ming Dynasty in the early decades of the fifteenth century.[39]

Another government decision that touched on questions of population growth and taxation was the dynastic expansion into the northeast which extended the Chosŏn border beyond the claims of earlier dynasties (see Map 3.1). In these early decades, Chosŏn was expansionist. Koryŏ territory reached the Yalu River (but not the Tumen), followed the Yalu along its westernmost stretches and then dipped farther and farther below the Yalu as the border moved eastward. In response, Chosŏn shipped people north to strengthen Korean settlements in the region. These areas were not uninhabited, but Korean bureaucrats considered themselves superior to the non-Chinese

---

[36] Gi-Wook Shin, *Peasant Protest and Social Change in Colonial Korea* (Seattle: University of Washington Press, 1996), 22–3.

[37] Yi Kyŏngsik, '16-segi chijuch'ŭng ŭi tonghyang' [Trends of the landlord class in the sixteenth century], *Yŏksa kyoyuk* 4 (1976): 143–4.

[38] See Son Pyŏnggyu, 'Chosŏn wangjo ŭi hojŏk kwa chaejŏng kirok e taehan chaeinsik in'gu wa kajok ŭi kyŏngje sujun ch'ujŏk kwa kwallyŏnhayŏ' [A new understanding of household register and financial records of the Chosŏn dynasty], *Yŏksa hakpo* 234 (June 2017): 160. See also a study by Professor Kim Chaeho, 'Chosŏn sidae ŭi in'gu-changgi pyŏndong' [Population estimates during the Chosŏn era], *Han'guk kyŏngje* 19 (May 2014): 18.

[39] See William Wayne Farris, *Japan's Medieval Population: Famine, Fertility, and Warfare in a Transformative Age* (Honolulu: University of Hawai'i Press, 2006), 94–5; for China, see Durand, 'The Population Statistics of China', 233.

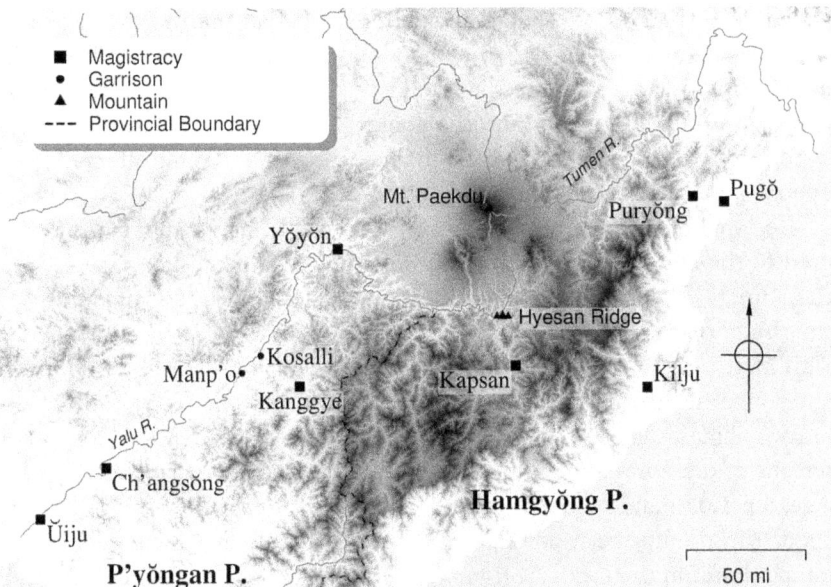

Map 3.1 Northern regions of the Korean peninsula and its topography, fifteenth century.

Jurchen who resided there yet, according to the court, did not have any civilising legitimacy. Chosŏn established firm frontiers along the Yalu and Tumen rivers, increasing the territory of the state. The shortage of arable lands and the increase in population in the south drove government policy to find solutions in the north. The subtle rationale was to make these territories, including the people and animals in them, subjects of the Chosŏn king. This included Jurchen military elites who the court had assigned to military positions in the north.[40] The Jurchens traded with Koreans across the frontier, and Jurchen individuals who had immigrated to the peninsula were exempted from paying taxes for three years.[41] The push north was not only a way to provide greater security – having a border farther away from the capital made it less likely for the court to be in danger from invasion – the inclusion of important agricultural zones also served to stabilise the country's economic decline in the wake of the Mongol collapse. The expansion north to the Yalu and Tumen rivers

---

[40] Kenneth Robinson, 'Residence and Foreign Relations in the Peninsular Northeast during the Fifteenth and Sixteenth Centuries', in *The Northern Region of Korea*, ed. Sun Joo Kim (Seattle: University of Seattle Press, 2010), 19.

[41] Kenneth Robinson, 'Residence and Foreign Relations', 21.

added more than 60,000 square kilometres (23,000 sq. mi.) to the total area of the kingdom, much of it heavily mountainous and forested. While unsuitable for intensive agriculture that could produce high yields because of the expansive mountain ranges and the cooler, continental climate, these areas were dense with wildlife used for fur and medicine, and the land afforded some opportunities for farming.

Regional climate change during the Medieval Climate Anomaly contributed to the abundance of vegetation on the Korean peninsula, especially in the south.[42] However, based on pollen count studies, the decline of forests and the rise of open landscape in central South Korea has been more associated with increased human disturbance of the environment – burning woodlands and converting them to paddy-fields to increase food production – rather than only to climate shifts.[43] After an era of warm temperatures, Korea, like other regions of the Eurasian continent, cooled in what is known as the Little Ice Age, a period that saw the growth of glaciers in alpine regions and dramatic cooling in the northern hemisphere. Climate models suggest the cooling of temperatures in the Pacific region began in the 1300s. East Asia experienced temperatures well below the average global decline.[44] As temperature fluctuations impacted precipitation, the Chosŏn Dynasty witnessed changes in weather and documented such events.[45] However, from 1300, Northeast Asia began experiencing wetter climate conditions, induced by La Niña, as well as solar activities that influenced monsoon patterns; the peninsula also experienced a few dry periods.[46]

Anecdotal evidence from the sources supports these climate models. The winter of 1396 was so cold that it forced the king to implement an evening curfew in the capital.[47] Among the many observations of unusual climate phenomena, one reported in 1397 that heavy rainfall during the month had destroyed 'nearly 10,000 bags' of rice in Kyŏngsang Province, wiping out a

---

[42] Jaesoo Lim, et al., 'Relationship Between Environmental Change on Geoje Island, Southern Coast of Korea, and Regional Monsoon and Temperature Changes during the Late Holocene', *Quaternary International* 344 (2014): 11–16.

[43] Sangheon Yi and Ju-Yong Kim, 'Pollen Analysis at Paju Unjeong, South Korea: Implication of Land-Use Changes since the Late Neolithic', *The Holocene* 22 (2011): 227–34.

[44] Gee Soo Kong, et al., 'Characteristics of the East Asian Summer Monsoon in the South Sea of Korea during the Little Ice Age', *Quaternary International* 286 (2013): 39.

[45] These were the climate models for the age. For instance, see Patrick D. Nunn, 'The AD 1300 Event in the Pacific Basin', *American Geographical Society* 97, no. 1 (January 2007): 4.

[46] Mingming Zhang, et al., 'Hydrological Variation Recorded in a Subalpine Peatland of Northeast Asia since the Little Ice Age and Its Possible Driving Mechanisms', *Science of the Total Environment* 772 (2021): 7.

[47] CWS, 1:89.

considerable amount of food.⁴⁸ A year later, heavy snowfall struck the capital region.⁴⁹ In 1401, 'heavy rain fell and strong winds uprooted trees and destroyed homes'.⁵⁰ While anecdotal, these examples suggest that such extreme weather conditions were worthy of recording. Weather like this was another factor that impacted agriculture, underscoring the needs of the ever-growing population. Examples of the harmful effects of changing weather on the economy appear throughout the *Sillok*. In 1471, the Board of Rites worried about a seemingly never-ending drought during the planting season.⁵¹ The year 1473 seemed to be a particularly bad year for the harvest in Kyŏnggi Province, the region around the capital of Hanyang, made worse by damage sustained a year earlier from high winds.

The period beginning in 1500 saw the greatest frequency of unusual climactic events recorded in the sources.⁵² Temperatures cooled and precipitation decreased.⁵³ There were significant increases in storms that resulted in hail, frost and unseasonably heavy snowfall over the course of approximately seven decades between 1500 and 1570, some of the most dramatic accumulation ever recorded during the Chosŏn Dynasty.⁵⁴ In one example, in the winter of 1506, the court, concerned about the impact of cold temperatures, postponed rebuilding student dormitories at the elite National Confucian Academy (成均館). 'The weather is so cold that repairs will be difficult.'⁵⁵ Within two weeks, temperatures swung to the other extreme. The cold gave way to unusually hot weather. The king even noted, 'The weather was so frigid ... but is now hot, I don't know what's causing it. I worry so deeply about it.'⁵⁶ Other officials noted that 'the winter weather is like the warmth of spring'.⁵⁷ The court rationalised these events in terms of heavenly intervention. Confucian ideology blamed

---

⁴⁸ *CWS*, 1:106.
⁴⁹ *CWS*, 1:115.
⁵⁰ *CWS*, 1:208.
⁵¹ *CWS*, 8:568.
⁵² Yi Taejin, 'Sobinggi (1500–1750) ch'ŏnbyŏnjei yŏn'gu ha *Chosŏn wangjo sillok*" [An interim report of the Little Ice Age (1500–1750) base on the records of the *Veritable Records of the Chosŏn Dynasty*], *Yŏksa hakbo* 149 (March 1996): 213.
⁵³ Yi Chunho, '1623–1800 nyŏn Sŏul chiyŏk ŭi kisanggihu hyangyŏng" [Weather and climatic environment of the Seoul region from 1623–1800], *Han'guk chiyŏk chiri hakhoeji* 22, no. 4 (2016): 870–1.
⁵⁴ Yi Taejin, 'Sobinggi (1500–1750) ch'ŏnbyŏnjei yŏn'gu', 215; and Christopher Lovins, *King Chŏngjo: An Enlightened Despot in Early Modern Korea* (Albany: State University of New York Press, 2019).
⁵⁵ *CWS*, 14:105.
⁵⁶ *CWS*, 14:108.
⁵⁷ *CWS*, 14:112.

these disasters on bad governance, in particular the king's role in conducting sacrificial offerings. Officials deemed the appearance of portents, such as halos around the sun or comets at night, to be messages from heaven, thereby linking weather patterns with the poor leadership of the central government. Along the same line, unease within the spirit world resulted not only in astral phenomena but also in bad weather and disease. According to officials such events must be related to governmental mismanagement and had to be addressed through rites and rituals including the sacrifice of animals. Anecdotes like these, numerous in the sources, reinforce the statistical trends representing the state observing the consequences of climate fluctuations. The hardship of these weather conditions must have been more extreme for those exposed to the elements much more so than elites and royal family members, such as farmers, slaves, hunters and animals.

Some evidence suggests that major climate events contributed to the rise and fall of dynasties in China and Asia, particularly those involving nomadic or semi-nomadic peoples. Warmer temperatures and increased rainfall stimulated the growth of grasslands that animals from pastoral societies, like the Mongols, relied on for food and warfare.[58] Conversely, cooling may have reduced grassland coverage. The fracturing of steppe lands weakened the political and military unity of these semi-nomadic societies, making them more susceptible to challengers. Like these macro-climate events for pastoralists, climactic events may have had profound consequences for the eco-social development of the Korean peninsula. The relative warmth of the climate before 1300 promoted the growth of vegetation and forests and the population of people and animals that lived on the land. A rising human population on the peninsula, security needs in the north, and cooling weather that impacted food production, compelled political and military leaders to look for new solutions – an intersection of climate, land and animals that will be further explored in later chapters.

* * *

Shifts in belief systems, scholarship, governing structures both inside and outside the capital, and the changing nature of the relationship with the Yuan

---

[58] Zhang Shengda, Pei Qing and Zhang David Dian, 'Xiao bingqi sichou zhi lu diqu qihou bianhua yu zhanzheng guanxi de dingliang fenxi' [A quantitative analysis of the relationship between climate change and war along the Silk Road regions during the Little Ice Age], *Di si ji yanjiu* 42 (2022): 250–60; and Aaron Putnam, *et al.*, 'Little Ice Age Wetting of Interior Asian Deserts and the Rise of the Mongol Empire', *Quaternary Science Reviews* 131 (2016): 33–50.

and Ming spurred elites and members of the royal family in Korea to use hunting and wild beasts as a means to control political and economic power. The late fourteenth and fifteenth centuries witnessed a period of gradual social and economic change. Often described as the Confucian transformation of Korea, where the government began adopting Neo-Confucian laws and practices that ultimately transformed Korea into a 'little China', in fact this never was fully realised. Scholars now question the Confucian transformation model. Neo-Confucian laws transformed the centre and elites, yet Chosŏn remained a pluralistic society, at many levels, inherited from the Koryŏ. This was most evident in the identity of the kingship. Connections formed during the Mongol era continued to impact practices, education and philosophies. While the rise of the Ming Dynasty severed direct links to Mongol power, the cultural and political repercussions of those earlier connections lasted well into Chosŏn, including the popularity of hunting and significance of animals. In the unfolding climate challenges of the Little Ice Age, the central government, court officials, elites and the royal family members struggled over land resources including access to the wild beasts in the mountains and forests, putting pressure on animal species. Within these developments, the hunt acquired added symbolism in a growing contestation for power and political control.

4

Confucian Beasts: Human–Animal Relations in Early Chosŏn

This chapter first looks at domination of wild beasts through the hunt, a public symbol of monarchical power in the Koryŏ–Mongol era, as it shifted from the responsibility of the king to the responsibility of the bureaucracy. I argue that along with restraining the actions of kings, the state attempted to transform human–animal relations. Animals grew more plentiful in the expanded domain in the north and were increasingly sacrificed on the altars of both the state and private homes, examined in the second half of this chapter. Ritual sacrifice is an important yet often neglected historical analysis. While based on earlier principles of Confucian rites, these rituals took on added meaning in early Chosŏn. Animals, wild and domestic, helped define Chosŏn identity, becoming the blood and bones of the dynasty's political legitimacy. What may seem like dry descriptions of arcane court ritual were, in fact, inseparably tied to highly contentious issues of political power, economic life, and the fate of the dynasty. This chapter explores the consequences of these newly regulated royal hunts on human and animal interactions within state, political and cultural developments of the fifteenth century.

In 1402, the Ministry of Rites (Yejo; 禮曹) submitted the *Rules of Hunting* to the king. Based on the *Book of Rites*, officials outlined the Confucian structure of royal state hunting for the Chosŏn Dynasty.

> When the Son of Heaven and the feudal lords had no business to attend to, they went on three hunts a year. Not to hunt when there was no special business was irreverent (*pulgyŏng*; 不敬). To hunt without adhering to hunting ritual was said to waste natural resources recklessly (*p'okchin ch'ŏnmul*; 暴殄天物). [The ancient classics] also say, 'There are three kinds of sacrificial animals (*samsaeng*; 三牲). As for hunting, in conveying filial piety [during the sacrifice], domesticated animals are not as plump (*pimi*; 肥美) as animals that live in nature. There are many birds and beasts that

harm the five crops [rice, millet, soybean, sesame and barley]. [Culling animals that harm these crops] is the reason for the practice of military arts.'[1]

These *Rules* effectively co-opted hunting. The hunt was not to be entertainment. Instead, it was a means to protect the dynasty's interests. Animals killed on the hunt were to be presented to the altars as sacrifices to spirits and ancestors in dynastic ceremonies. These sacrifices were a necessary part of the cosmic order. Also, the hunt was to provide valuable military training. The regulations specified the steps necessary for a successful hunt. The guidelines were strict. Based on these rules, the king should hunt three times a year near the capital. Seven days prior to the hunt, the court was to gather everyone at the Ministry of Military Affairs (Pyŏngjo; 兵曹) following the rules of the hunt (*chŏnbŏp*; 田法). The Military High Command determined the hunting location. Before dawn on the day of the hunt, a flag was to be displayed below the hunting grounds in an appropriate location in the suburbs of the capital. The generals and their troops were to gather around the flag and those who arrived after daybreak were to be punished. The Ministry of Military Affairs would divide up the hunting grounds, and when a gong rang out, the hunt was to begin. The troops were to take breaks during the hunts.[2]

Only after the generals planted their flags should the king emerge and enter the hunting ground. When approaching the location of the hunt, soldiers were to encircle the area beating drums, proceeding towards inside the circle, as on a ring hunt. The official in charge of the hunt was to be next to the king when the drums sounded. The people in the southeast were to face west, the people in the southwest were to face east. All of the generals, when the drums were struck, began surrounding the area and moving forward. On the opposite side, mounted troops were to stand by when the king rides his horse south, the attending officer was to follow, and all of the troops were to trail the king's horse, carrying bows and arrows. They were to spread out around the king, and the attending official was to follow them. When the troops drove out an animal next to the king, the first animal to emerge (*ch'oilgu*; 初一驅) was allowed to pass by as the attending official arranged his bow and arrow and to proceed alongside [the king]. When the second animal to emerge (*chaegu*; 再驅) passed by, the soldiers respectfully advanced with their bows and arrows ready. When the third animal to emerge (*samgu*; 三驅) passed by, the king should immediately shoot it from the left

---

[1] For these hunting regulations, see *CWS*, 1:237.
[2] *CWS*, 1:237.

side. Every expelled animal should be more than three of its kind.[3] After the king unleashed his arrow, the soldiers and generals could begin to shoot. Once the king's hunting party had begun, the mounted soldiers on the opposite side were to come to a stop. After the royal hunting party had finished, the government allowed commoners access to the area to hunt.[4]

Animals harvested in the military hunting grounds were to be butchered, the various sections of their carcasses were offered as tribute:

> The left flank to the right shoulder bone [of the deer] is to be offered as tribute. They should be made into offerings as vessels of dried meats (*kŏndu*; 乾豆) and presented to the national shrine. The meat below the left ear should be given to esteemed guests (*pin'gaek*; 賓客). The meat from the left thigh to the left rib is deemed inferior and should be supplied to the kitchen. When plenty of animals chase each other, do not kill them all. If they have already been hit by an arrow, do not shoot at them again. Also, do not shoot at them in the face, do not remove their fur, and do not track animals (*p'yoji*; 標識) that emerge [in other words, do not pursue them beyond the hunting grounds].
>
> When the hunt ends, the Military High Command is to plant a flag in the hunting ground (*chŏnnae*; 田內) and the drums of the various generals and drums of the king are to be beaten loudly. The soldiers are then to call out urgently, and the men who have kills are to present their game to the general below the flag and dedicate the left ears of the beasts [to the king]. Large animals are to be state owned (*taesu kongji*: 大獸公之). Small animals are for private use (*sosu saji*; 小獸私之). A messenger is to inform the court of the animals that were caught, and the game is to be presented as sacrifice at the state temple. Later, guests are to feast in tents and consume three cups of alcohol in celebration [of a successful hunt].[5]

These regulations from 1402, many derived from the *Rites of Zhou*, a well-known text that was more than 1,500 years old, were distinctive and particular to the early Chosŏn.

To co-opt the hunt, these officials now highlighted classical ritual in these regulations. First, the hunt was clearly a military matter to these Confucian officials. Generals and soldiers, led by the king, mustered and assembled as though they were readying for battle in order to engage with the enemy. In

---

[3] CWS, 1:237.
[4] CWS, 1:237.
[5] CWS, 1:157, 1:237 and 5:364.

this case, the enemies were the beasts of the wild. The hunt had its rituals, as did warfare. Next, the Board of Rites wished to set guidelines for the 'fairness' of the hunt. Ring hunts – like the one described above – included massive numbers of soldiers who served as beaters and had the potential of flushing out herds and flocks of game. To control the number of animals killed, the Board of Protocol ritualised the hunt. The designation of the animals that emerged and the demanding of a hierarchy of hunting opportunities – who shot first, who shot second, and so on – acted as checks and balances on the number of animals taken and evened out the chances for the game to survive. For instance, the tracking of animals was not permitted. The board did not want the hunt moving off the designated hunting grounds and recommended against following animals into the brush and instead encouraged the killing of animals during ring hunts. While it could serve as an important hunting technique, tracking animals could result in the king and soldiers straying from the forested hunting grounds. This could potentially harm the crops on adjacent agricultural land or bring the king and his men further into the mountains where hazards, such as dangerous terrain and predators, might injure or kill the members. Finally, following the practices in the Chinese rites, the Korean court determined state ownership of animals was based on size. Larger animals, such as tigers, leopards, large deer such as sika, red deer, elk and moose were more valuable for their size and provided more meat and hides. Small animals, such as roe deer, wild swine and hare were given to the soldiers who hunted them on these royal Kangmu hunts, their meat used as food and their fur used for warmth.

Court recognition of the hunt and its role in society is another important suggestion spotlighted in these early regulations. The royal hunt was a spectacle, an event that demonstrated the power of the king and the state, and as such it attracted commoners from around the area. The board recognised this and decided that after the king, generals and soldiers had hunted, commoners would be permitted to hunt in the area. Commoners hunted the game that the royal hunting party had flushed out or had failed to recover. Access to hunting grounds and determining who would hunt the animals as they were flushed out were based on societal hierarchies. The board and the court did not attempt to ban the common people from taking part, rather they only meant to regulate access.

Regulations for the hunt and interactions like these among kings, ministers, soldiers and commoners in the wild demonstrate the growing importance of animal interactions of the early Chosŏn. The expansion of Confucian ritual at the court involved the extension of control over animals, turning them into ritual items. Another classical work explains,

'Those who are irreverent offer simple sacrifices and poorly treat their visitors and guests. Those who recklessly waste natural resources, surround marshy thickets, or take a whole herd by surprise [while on the spring hunt], take young animals or eggs, and disturb the nests of birds.' Thus, when there are no matters to tend to, then it is not right *not* to hunt. If you do not spare animals when on the hunt, this is also not right. We, your ministers, have consulted the past for the rites of hunting in spring (*susu chiŭi*; 蒐狩之儀) and have outlined them hereafter. Your Majesty should hunt in the surrounding areas, three times a year, and offer up the game you kill as sacrifice to the state, [all of these actions are] to conduct military training.[6]

While many of these ritual practices had roots in China, Chosŏn inherited these rituals from the previous dynasty, systematised them, and strengthened them. In early Chosŏn, several, sometimes overlapping, sometimes conflicting understandings of animals were emblematic of rulership. This chapter sketches out the rich and complex conceptual universe of the domestic–wild animal dyad and of animals as integral elements of lifestyles and rituals.

Hunting and Animals in Early Chosŏn

It was not a coincidence that the strongest kings in the Chosŏn Dynasty hunted. Between 1392 and 1495, kings and royal family members held an enormous amount of power and prestige. Their power provided them with the political capital they required to conduct their affairs, including activities such as the hunt, in the face of an increasingly defiant scholarly bureaucratic order. Kings T'aejo, Chŏngjong (r. 1398–1400), T'aejong (r. 1400–18), Sejong (r. 1418–50; 世宗), Munjong (r. 1450–2; 文宗), Tanjong (r. 1452–5; 端宗) and Sejo (r. 1455–68; 世祖) hunted. In fact, the Chosŏn royal chase has roots in the Koryŏ royal hunt and the more generalised life of military elites (see Map 4.1). King T'aejo had learned to hunt as a member of the military elite in the latter half of the fourteenth century. Early Chosŏn royal hunting resonated strongly with an entire generation or more of military commanders in the Koryŏ–Chosŏn transition. As Donald Baker argues, the display of martial skills was more important than the Mandate of Heaven in helping T'aejo gain legitimacy, true of all founding rulers.[7] This was particularly true of mid-fifteenth century court

[6] CWS, 1:237.
[7] Donald Baker, 'Rhetoric, Ritual, and Political Legitimacy: Justifying Yi Seong-gye's Ascension to the Throne', *Korea Journal* 53, no. 4 (Winter 2013): 141–67.

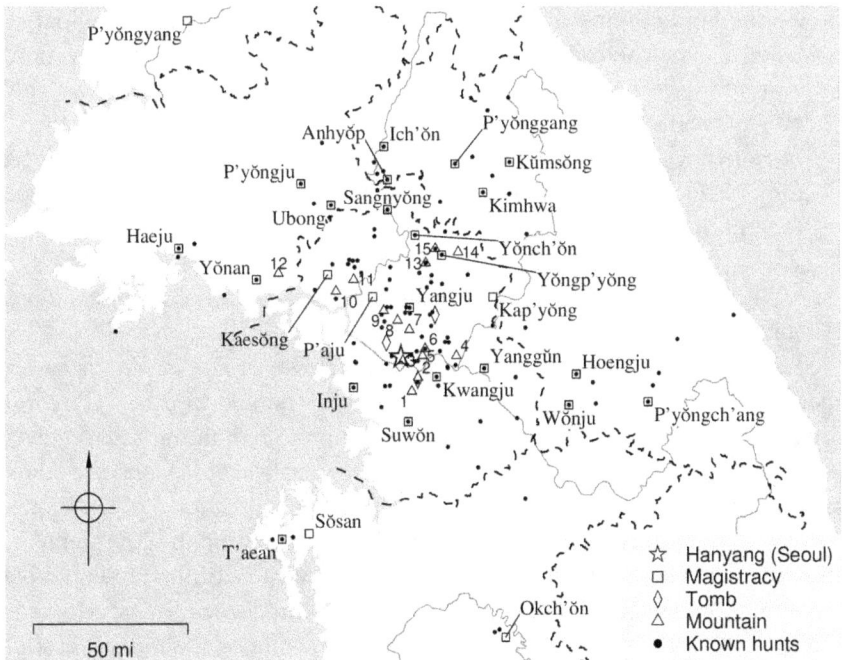

Map 4.1 Locations of known royal hunts from the late Koryŏ and early Chosŏn dynasties. Many additional hunting sites in the *Koryŏsa* and *Sillok* sources have been lost. Number key and mountain name: (1) Mt Chŏnggye; (2) Mt Taemo; (3) Mt Namsan; (4) Mt Chogok; (5) Mt Ach'a; (6) Somangol Mountain Pass; (7) Mt Tobong; (8) Mt Sŏ; (9) Mt Hongbok; (10) Mt Maje; (11) Mt Tora; (12) Mt T'o; (13) Mt Chonghyŏn; (14) Mt Kwanŭm; (15) Mt Pojang; (16) Mt Kwanŭm (close to P'yongyang).

officials who readily played up this dimension of T'aejo's identity as a military commander and dynastic founder. King T'aejo loved to hunt with a bow and arrow. Chŏngjong hunted in places like Haeju (海州; city of South Hwanghae Province), eighty kilometres (50 mi.) west of the royal palace at Kaesŏng, and Wŏnjungp'o (原中浦; South Hwanghae Province), on the road back to the capital, where he found success killing roe deer.[8] In 1400, after being appointed crown prince, T'aejong offered an observant and practical statement about the land and animal resources, views that presaged the conflict to come between elite hunting practices and the state's control over animals. He explained,

---

[8] For instance, see CWS, 1:156. The capital was temporarily moved back to Kaesŏng at this time.

As the land of our country is very small, the hunting fields are all farmlands . . . and there is usually no empty land that is not under cultivation. Hunting necessarily damages the crops. There are about 100 *li* [roughly 60 km or 80 acres] of land south of P'yŏngju, [100 km (60 mi.) northwest of Hanyang]. If we were to build a hunting ground there, people will be forbidden to cut down trees [not allowed to collect firewood or clear space to farm the land].⁹

As politics stabilised during the first decades of the fifteenth century, kings had more time to pay to the hunt.

Regardless of these early concerns of the crown prince and royal family members, the crown prince himself and his father hunted together. The royal family learned about the importance of the chase by hunting as a family.¹⁰ After abdication, the former King T'aejong unofficially met his sons, including his third son King Sejong, to chase game. Under the protection of King Sejong, Sejong's father, the former King T'aejong, enjoyed hunting in his retirement, in particular, the art of falconry. On one occasion in 1419, he presented his son Prince Yangnyŏng (1394–1462; 讓寧大君) with falcons.¹¹ T'aejong went often to Tonggyo (東郊), a hunting and military training ground just east of the capital. King Sejong would travel to Yangju (楊州) city, roughly twenty-five kilometres (15 mi.) north of the capital or the more distant Mt Sŏngsan (城山) in Kangwŏn Province with his retired father.¹² Hunting in rugged lands like these, where game was plentiful, offered the men a chance to spend more time together and to bond with their companions. King Sejong hunted with his oldest son, the future King Munjong, at the hunting sites reserved for royal family members or at times the crown prince observed hunts at Tonggyo. These locations were on the outskirts of the capital which the king could reach on horseback or palanquin.¹³

As in late Koryŏ, falconry was practised during early Chosŏn royal hunts. King Sejong went falcon hunting frequently with his sons, Yi Yŏm (1434–67; 李琰), Yi Ku (1420–69; 李璆) and Yi Yu (1426–57; 李瑜). The king advised his sons not to ride horseback when working with falcons because of the risk of falling from their horses and injuring themselves. He defined the act of injury in Confucian terms as an affront to the bodies their parents had bestowed on

⁹ *CWS*, 1:176.
¹⁰ For instance, see *CWS*, 1:167.
¹¹ *CWS*, 2:300.
¹² *CWS*, 2:375.
¹³ Some examples include *CWS*, 5:111 and 7:55.

them. Sejong insisted on using Confucian descriptions of loyalty and filiality to one's parents juxtaposed against the fleeting pleasure of shooting a few deer.[14] While the king advised his sons on the dangers of the hunt, he did not admonish them for their hunting habits. Instead, he provided them with specific advice while hunting with falcons, in essence, it was wise to focus on the bird and refrain from riding a horse at the same time. He also extended this caution to deer hunting with bows and arrows. He wished to shield his sons from potential harm but encouraged them to hunt. This suggested that a reconciliation of the royal hunt and Confucian lifeways was entirely possible. Neo-Confucians chose interpretations of Neo-Confucianism that foregrounded incompatibility of the two, hence it was not an ideological inevitability.

Such fatherly recommendations were an integral part of Chosŏn family traditions, not just state matters. King Sejong and his sons frequented such areas as Mt Pojang (寶藏山) in P'och'ŏnhyŏn (抱川縣), a mountainous region fifty kilometres (30 mi.) northeast of the royal palace, where they preferred to hunt and kill wild boar.[15] In 1422, King Sejong travelled with his father, the former King T'aejong, and brother Prince Yangnyŏng (1394–1462; 讓寧大君) to Mt Pojang where they hunted and bagged both sika and river deer and wild boar. On this occasion, they ventured far into Poŭmi on Mt Kŭmjang (甫音伊 金藏山) – a mountain in North Kyŏngsang Province, 230 kilometres (145 mi.) southeast of the capital, with peaks reaching 850 metres (2,700 ft) – where his father, the former King T'aejong, killed three deer with arrows. Later that night, they stayed in Yŏngp'yŏng, a village in north central Kyŏnggi Province, and celebrated by drinking alcohol with military officer Ch'oe Pu (1370–1452; 崔府).[16] On the same trip, King Sejong and his father hunted in Sinjŏndong on Mt Chonghyŏn (鍾懸山), 106 kilometres (66 mi.) south of the capital, where they downed deer and wild boar.[17] Hunting in lands like these, more distant from the capital, allowed the king and his party access to more game than was found in frequently hunted areas. No evidence in the sources indicate that these distant places had seen substantial royal hunts before and, unlike other locations, allowed the king to expand his symbolic domination of the land and animals on it. Unlike hunting in the popular locations his royal ancestors had gone to on the chase (where such events were more common), pursuing game in areas more distant from the capital not only gave him access to new hunting grounds but also helped spread the king's reputation as a strong leader.

[14] CWS, 7:56.
[15] For instance, see CWS, 2: 427.
[16] CWS, 2:477.
[17] CWS, 2:478.

Much like his grandfather, King Tanjong too hunted. Coming to the throne at a young age, older royal family members continued to hunt with other officials of the court during Tanjong's reign.[18] However, beginning in 1454 at the age of thirteen, he began attending hunts regularly, like other members of his family, even to the point where the Office of Censor General (Saganwŏn; 司諫院) chastised him. 'Your highness is now young, so frequently hunting is not right. Now, you are going to Mt Ach'a to take part in hunting, but it hasn't been long since you last observed a hunt ... please cancel it.'[19]

Despite such pleas, recognising the royal fondness for the hunt, other scholars and officials joined kings at times. In 1419, Han Hwak (1400–56; 韓確) was one of a host of officials who accompanied King Sejong on a large military hunt training excursion to Kangwŏn Province. They went falcon hunting at P'yŏngguyŏk and took the animals they had caught, presumably hare, squirrels and other prey, south of Namju to hold a feast. They hunted again south of Yongjin and drank and ate heavily.[20] Military men also recognised the importance of these military hunting grounds. One such officer, Hong Yak (?–?; 洪約), insisted that Yich'ŏn (伊川), a mountain region in North Kangwŏn Province roughly 120 kilometres (75 mi.) north of the capital, was a more suitable location for the king to hunt. 'Yich'ŏn was farther away from the capital, so there are more beasts there. It is more natural for the king to go.'[21] The officials, upset at Hong for making this suggestion, accused him of being unlearned and talentless. The only reason the king liked him, they wrote, was because of his hunting skills.[22] King Sejong agreed with Hong. The king went on to ready his hunting party and ordered that he would travel and hunt there for only four or five days because of the great distance. Sending the king farther into the wilderness provided these men with more access to the king.

Like other members of his family, King Sejong was Buddhist, but this did not change the fact that he enjoyed hunting.[23] Despite their faith, these men saw no conflict of interest between their desire to hunt and kill animals and the Buddhist precepts against killing. Their Buddhist beliefs did not conflict, in their minds, with their hunting practices.

[18] For instance, Yi Yong (1418–53; 李瑢), the oldest son of King Sejong, continued to hunt. See CWS, 6:621 and 6:646. This also included the eventual King T'aejo. CWS, 6:680.
[19] CWS, 6:710.
[20] CWS, 2:344.
[21] CWS, 4:313.
[22] CWS, 4:313.
[23] CWS, 12:256.

Hunting was a pastime, but it was also a means for them to gain legitimacy in the eyes of their people. They inherited the hunting practices of their fathers who had, in turn, found inspiration in the habits of their fathers and grandfathers and other leaders with roots in the late fourteenth century. Based on a lifestyle of the rugged northeast, his family home, King T'aejo adopted hunting practices used during the earlier century, when Koryŏ was under Mongol rule, as a means to elevate his status. As mentioned in the previous chapter, Mongols used religion to rule over their vast territory and people different from themselves. The Mongolian leadership had mostly maintained their beliefs in Mongol shamanistic practices, and hunting did not conflict with their worldview. In fact, their religious beliefs, that their leader owned everything under the sky, including the land and animals, confirmed their right to hunt. Koryŏ kings under Mongol rulership adopted the importance of the hunt to politics as a governing practice. To them, the hunt displayed military might, royal regalia and their ability to control both the people and the wild beasts of the land.

As a deeply hierarchical society, the new Chosŏn government had maintained strict social division between societal groups. Beginning in the Chosŏn Dynasty, if not earlier, lists of animals captured on the hunt depicted the importance of some animals over others. Although not common on these hunts, when captured, tigers were always listed first followed by two types of deer, roe and sika, whereas, other animals killed on the hunt were generally categorised under miscellaneous animals (*chapsu*; 雜獸). To Confucians, tigers were considered fearful or wicked, violent animals (*aksu*; 惡獸), most likely because they posed a danger to people. They were also referred to as ferocious beasts (*maengsu*; 猛獸). In the past, the government permitted commoners, slaves and elites to collect tiger pelts, which was a sign of successfully reducing the number of dangerous animals that might harm the people. In addition, there was a reward for killing tigers.[24] By 1471, the Ministry of War announced that soldiers who killed tigers and leopards would receive more auspicious titles depending on the size of the animal.[25]

With an understanding of tigers as wicked beasts, the central government developed plans to control the tiger population, while hunting and killing

---

[24] Kim Tongjin, '17 segi huban 18 seigi ch'o hosokmok hyŏkp'i wa chejŏng unyŏng ŭi pyŏnhwa saengt'ae hwan'gyŏng kwa kukche chŏngse pyŏnhwa rŭl chungsim ŭro' [Impact of the changing environmental and international situation during the late seventeenth and early eighteenth centuries, focusing on the abolition of the tiger skin penalty], *Saengt'ae hwan'gyŏng kwa yŏksa* 1 (December 2015): 50.

[25] CWS, 8:546.

tigers brought advancement to some and restrictions for others. Military men and others were encouraged to hunt them, but it appears that Chosŏn kings were not.[26] In 1476, the Chosŏn government constructed screens to teach Confucian morality. The screens were painted with images that detailed stories from Chinese classical Confucian legends, such as Duke Zhou, and were meant to dissuade the king from hunting certain types of animals. Duke Zhou was known to have loved the hunt. But a screen told a different story: 'A diviner stated that Duke Zhou did not hunt dragons, hornless dragons, bears, or tigers, but [it] is that [not hunting dangerous animals] which helps the rulers (*wangja chibo*; 王者之輔).'[27] Scholars taught kings to avoid pursuing animals that could potentially cause them bodily harm. Hoping that Korean kings would emulate these practices, they taught that sage rulers of the distant past naturally understood the limits of their own hunting skills.

The culmination of such teaching was to persuade kings that wild animals lay outside the royal realm. With all of this hunting, especially at the elite level, a powerful and growing bureaucracy strove to check the ambitions of the king and others who joined him on the hunt. While not using specific terms, the state increasingly described wild animals as natural resources for the government to use. Wildlife, like rice and other crops produced on the land, while not explicitly expressed in government documents, was another form of national wealth. Much of the new region of Chosŏn along the Tumen and Yalu rivers was mountainous where agriculture was difficult to carry out, and animal populations were greater. In the southern part of the peninsula, mountainous regions were vast along the east coast. The extension into these territories expanded the resources, such as lumber, ginseng and animals, available to the state.

To officials, animals were exploitable and divided into two categories, domesticated and wild. Domesticated animals (*kach'uk*; 家畜) provided practical labour, military security and protein for the state and for its people. In Chosŏn, the most significant domesticated animal was the horse. Horses were kept and maintained for strategic purposes – for war, agricultural production and communication. Governments across the Asian continent considered horses essential to the state, society and security.[28] Because of their significance

---

[26] CWS, 9:369.
[27] CWS, 9:387.
[28] For instance, see Mitsutaka Tani, 'A Study on Horse Administration in the Ming Period', *Acta Asiatica* 21 (1971): 73–97; Henry Serruys, 'Sino-Mongol Relations during the Ming (III) Trade Relations: The Horse Fairs (1400–1600)', *Melanges chinoises at bouddhiques* 17 (1975): 9–275; and Alan Mikhail, 'War and Charisma: Horses and Elephants in the Indian Ocean Economy', in *Asia Inside Out: Connected Places*, vol. 1, eds Eric Tagliacozzo, Helen Siu and Peter Perdue (Cambridge, MA: Harvard University Press, 2015), 128–68.

for transportation, diplomacy and war, many officials paid great attention to breeding and training them. Horses were an integral part of Ming–Chosŏn diplomatic trade relations. Korea imported some of the strongest breeds of horses from Manchuria.[29] Fourteenth-century raids by Red Turbans resulted in the theft of many animals, including horses, and convinced officials in the new Chosŏn government to ban the killing of horses for food. Horses were kept by the upper classes and were too expensive for commoners to maintain. Other domesticated animals included swine and poultry. Some commoners owned oxen that assisted in tending the fields and raised pigs and chickens for food.

Wild animals (*kŭmsu*; 禽獸) were different. They existed within an amorphous region of nature just beyond the control of human society. Some were exploitable, like deer and hare, while others, such as wild boar, were a nuisance to farms. Others were feared – bears, tigers, leopards and wolves – and potentially harmful to commoners who formed the agricultural foundation of the country. Wild beasts thrived in the mountains and lived along the edges of human settlements. Crows, ducks, geese and cranes preferred the fields and lived among and above homes and agricultural lands sometimes 'raiding' them for food. Land use impacted these wild animals. Unlike its many policies regulating agriculture, the Chosŏn court did not have a grand policy to control wildlife. Few governments around the world, if any, had separate laws regulating wild animals.

Animals and their habitats fuelled debates over the nature of rulership and governance. Animals forced the government to think more deeply about how wildlife was to be incorporated into an expanding state. On the one hand, this was a struggle over natural resources, which included animals as the part of the transition from Koryŏ to Chosŏn that is often framed in terms of agricultural wealth. As demonstrated throughout this book, wild animals were more than just passive resources, fought over by groups of elites. Wildlife, their comings and goings, habitats and natural patterns of life, influenced how people thought of themselves in society and shaped how they lived, farmed, found livelihoods, hunted, worshipped and interacted with the spirit world. As Sarah Cockram and Andrew Wells put it, 'In these

---

[29] For instance, see Yi Hongdu, 'Chosŏn ch'ogi Suwŏn tohobu ŭi mamokchang sŏlch'i yŏn'gu' [Research on the installation of horse ranches in Suwŏn tohobu during the early Chosŏn], *Kunsa* 106 (March 2018): 329–59; and Yi Hongdu, 'Homa ŭi chŏllae wa Chosŏn sidae homa mokchang ŭi sŏlch'i [The importation of Manchurian horses and the installation of Manchurian horse ranches during the Chosŏn dynasty], *Kunsa* 99 (June 2016): 113–44.

centuries of intellectual ferment, political upheaval, and dramatic social change, animals were a perennial topic of interest.'[30] Indeed, like those that kings, royal family members and other elites hunted, animals – wild and domestic – shaped Chosŏn politics and identities.

The Ritualisation of Human–Animal Affairs

The ritual butchering of animals for sacrifice at altars was practised on the peninsula from at least the Three Kingdoms era or earlier. Shamans conducted some of these rites on mountains, while other rituals' origins can be traced to Confucian beliefs. Whether performed by an individual shaman, head of a family or village, or a king, the rites were vital, religious–political practices that helped identify leaders of families, villages and regions on the peninsula. With wildlife plentiful throughout the peninsula's many mountains, valleys, forests and plains, the availability of ritual offerings easily satisfied the frequency of these rituals. Beginning in the Koryŏ era, if not earlier, and as the types of animals deemed suitable for the sacrifices evolved, demand for animals began to outpace the ready availability of beasts that could be used as state altar sacrifices. As the dynasty integrated these long-standing patterns, the supply-and-demand equilibrium for these animals pushed the late Koryŏ and early Chosŏn officials into rethinking how they should deal with animals and their habitats.

To procure ritual animals, the dynasties bureaucratised access to animals, both wild and domestic. These steps accelerated in the fifteenth century as the Chosŏn state codified Confucian rituals as important definers of state identity and began demanding yangban families follow certain rituals, practices that included greater numbers of meat offerings. Demands such as these spoke to the interest in animals and human affairs.[31] In 1411, the Chosŏn Board of

---

[30] Sarah Cockram and Andrew Wells, 'Introduction: Action, Reaction, Interaction in Historical Animal Studies', in *Interspecies Interactions: Animals and Humans in the Middle Ages and Modernity*, eds Sarah Cockram and Andrew Wells (New York: Routledge, 2018), 7.

[31] There is a large body of literature on Confucian rites in Korean. For a representative sample, see Kim Sangjun, ed., *Yugyo ŭi yech'i inyŏm kwa Chosŏn* [Confucian ideology and Chosŏn] (Kŏnggido P'ajusi: Chŏnggye ch'ulp'ansa, 2007); Pak Chongch'ŏng, 'Sangjeryeŭi Han'gukjŏk chŏn'gae wa yugyo ŭi yeŭi munhwajŏk yŏnghyang' [Historical change of funerary and ancestral rites and cultural influence of Confucianism], *Kuk'ak yŏn'gu* 17 (December 2010): 365–96; and Yi Hyesun, *Chosŏn chunggi yehak sasang kwa ilsang munhwa: Chuja Karye rŭl chungsim ŭro* [Mid-Chosŏn study of rites and Zhu Xi's Family Rituals] (Seoul: Ehwa yŏja taehakkyo ch'ulp'anbu, 2006). In English, see Martina

Rites discussed the royal regulations with respect to sacrifices and the use of six animals considered important by the Zhou Dynasty: bull, horse, sheep, pig, dog and chicken. Many of these animals and their sacrifice rituals had been adopted from the Royal Regulations (Wang Zhi; 王制) in the *Book of Rites*.

The government post in charge of ritual animals was the animal tender (mogin; 牧人). He was responsible for raising the animals and preparing them for state sacrifice at altars in the capital. Suppliers (ch'ungin; 充人) also raised animals to be used in sacrifice. The sacrifices should be offered in the third lunar month (March to April). Minor sacrifices (sosa; 小祀) would be kept for ten days at the Transit Authorisation Bureau (Samun; 司門). The king was to select a bull from among those raised (yang; 養) for sacrifice. Upon selection, the animal was removed from the other animals and covered with fabric, making it auspicious. As for bulls sacrificed to heaven and earth, they should be very young, 'their horns . . . not to be larger than a cocoon or a chestnut'. The bulls used in the ancestral temple (chongmyo; 宗廟) would be 'small enough to grasp by the hands'. Calves should be used for guests to feast on and should be smaller. The board emphasised the *Book of Rites* and that the animals used for great sacrificial ceremonies (taesa; 大祀) should be cultivated for ninety days (yeyang kusun; 預養九旬). Those sacrificed in second tier ceremonies should be cultivated for thirty days, and those for minor sacrifices should be cultivated for ten days. 'This is to pay respect to the spirits.' Two officials went to the Ceremonial Stable Bureau (Chŏn'gusŏ; 典廄署), inspected the fur and horns of the bulls, and selected them.[32] If rain fell during the sacrificial rites to the Lord on High (Sangje; 上帝), then the animals should be returned.[33] Sacrifice meant selecting these animals, preparing them ritually, taking them to the altar, killing them the day before the ceremony, and then dressing and laying out their bodies on the altar.

Based on Chinese precedence for the *Book of Rites*, early Chosŏn planners recognised the shortcomings of the ritual guidelines and altered them to fit the political needs of the court. Rather than demand the king himself select an ox for sacrifice, for instance, two officials assumed this responsibility. This allowed the men to gain knowledge of the animals they observed and select

---

Deuchler, 'Rites in Early Chosŏn', in *King Sejong the Great: The Light of Fifteenth Century Korea*, ed. Young-Key Kim-Renaud (Washington, DC: International Circle of Korean Linguistics, 1992), 35–40; and Spencer J. Palmer, *Confucian Rituals in Korea* (Berkeley: Asia Humanities Press, 1992). For general studies on ritual, see Serpell, 'Animals to Edible', 46–63; and Perlo, *Kinship and Killing*.

[32] *CWS*, 1:582.
[33] *CWS*, 2:684.

the appropriate ones based on the guidelines in the *Book of Rites*. These two officials walked to the Ceremonial Stable Bureau, fields just beyond the south entrance of the capital walls, and interacted with the government employed slaves who had raised the animals that were used for sacrifice. During the first decades of the fifteenth century, the Board of Rites deployed Confucian morals to argue the court's control over animals. They borrowed an expression from Mencius, 'If the chickens, pigs, and dogs breed in the appropriate season, then even a seventy-year-old man can consume meat.'[34] In other words, raising animals responsibly ensured the consumption of meat which helped people stay alive. The Board of Rites was concerned about the availability of animals that could be used in sacrificial rites to honour seniors, as part of the Confucian respect for one's elders, and for consumption. While this may have worked well for China, a country with an abundance of wealth and animals, the official notes that chickens and pigs were not common in the homes of the Chosŏn country folk. Concerning the use of animals in rites, current Chosŏn practices differed from the rituals of *Family Rites of Zhu Xi* (*Wengong*; Wengongguli; 文公家禮). By 1425, to make up for the shortage of pigs, the board took 580 of its sows (*chajŏ*; 雌猪), which the board found too great a number, and chose 300 of the biggest and fattest to be left behind, probably to bear young and be slaughtered. The remaining pigs were distributed to households around the capital to raise to ensure that the rural people had animals to use for sacrificial rites at home and meat to offer to their elders.[35] While only a tiny proportion of the total households, it is difficult to know who exactly received the pigs.

In addition to swine, the Board of Rites raised sheep, chickens, wild geese and Chinese geese (*tangan*; 唐雁) in the vicinity of the town of Suwŏn and Inghwa Island (south of the Han River).[36] In 1421, the board, concerned that the sheep and pigs had suffered from a shortage of food, hoped to move them to places with better supplies of water and grass.[37] By 1457, the board outlined the types and the numbers of animals to be used in sacrificial ceremonies.[38] To the Lord on High, one calf was to be sacrificed. The animals in one of the sacrificial vessels (*tu*; 豆) were to include deer, swine, hare and oxen. A stand for the sacrificial food (*cho*; 俎) was to hold a box with a variety of sacrificial

---

[34] CWS, 2:666.
[35] CWS, 2:666.
[36] Known as Hongjewŏn, this location was along a transportation route northwest of the capital that has since disappeared. The scale of this area and the number of animals involved are lost.
[37] CWS, 2:422.
[38] Lists of these items can be found in CWS, 7:165.

animal meat (*saengyukkap*; 牲肉匣) and sacrificial animal heads (*saengsugap*; 牲首匣). Another stand held fresh intestines (*pisŏk*; 脾析), stomach and lungs in small boxes, while another stand would hold the same animal parts that had been cooked. 'Animal sacrifice to the sun spirit (*taemyŏng*; 大明) shall include one calf, a vessel that includes dried venison [smoked over firewood], and a vessel filled with hare, venison, and pork along with intestines.' Another vessel contained duck blood curds (*mohyŏl*; 毛血), while another held a sizable soup made of meat stock (*taegaeng chayukchŭp*; 大羹煮肉汁). 'Sacrifices to the imperial earth spirit (*hwangjiji*; 皇地祇) require one calf. Another calf is to be sacrificed for King T'aejo.' The most sacrifices were offered to the wind, clouds, thunder and rain (*p'ungun roeu*; 風雲雷雨): five sheep, five pigs, as well as a number of different vessels were to be set out including venison, pickled meats, duck blood curds and stews.[39]

The Chosŏn court based many of these ritual requirements on a late fourteenth-century Ming document, the *Encyclopedia of Government Posts* (*husi zhizang*; 諸司職掌); they adopted other ritual protocols from Koryŏ and early Chosŏn dynasty practices.[40] A different set of guidelines applied to game. Roe deer (*chang*; 獐), sika or red deer (*nok*; 鹿), and pheasants (*ch'i*; 雉) taken during a hunt were to be used in sacrificial offerings, and oxen (*so*; 牛), as well as domesticated animals, sheep (*yang*; 羊) and pigs (*si*; 豕), were to be offered for the remaining services. Earlier, Koryŏ used raw pheasant meat (*saengch'i*; 生雉) on Cold Food Festival Day (*Hansik*; 寒食), but the Board of Rites banned the use of pheasants in the ceremony.[41] Perhaps this move was made because of the difficulty and time involved with capturing pheasants, an animal often hunted in falconry. In the winter of 1429, venison was widely available in markets. The king noted that Kyŏnggi was the only region with such a high concentration of large deer (*changnok*; 獐鹿), probably sika or red deer.[42] Animals like these made their way to the capital for sacrifices.

The Ceremonial Stable Bureau was in charge of raising domesticated livestock for the government. This system sustained the animals until they were sacrificed during rituals. Dating to the beginning of the eleventh century, the Ceremonial Stable Bureau had been a small institution staffed by only three officials. Reorganised in 1308 under King Ch'ungnyŏl, the bureau expanded

---

[39] CWS, 7:165.
[40] CWS, 7:165. For more on the adoption of *Encyclopedia of Government Posts*, see Kim Kyŏngnok, 'Hongmuyŏn'gan Myŏng ŭi pongjŏn chŏngbi wa Cho-Myŏng kwan'gye' [Ming–Chosŏn relations and preparations of the conferral ceremony during the years of the Ming Hongwu Emperor], *Chungguksa yŏn'gu* 106 (February 2017): 59–94.
[41] CWS, 2:304.
[42] CWS, 3:169.

to six personnel, and the king ordered it be attached to the Office for Ceremonies (Chŏnŭisi; 典儀寺), which was in charge of state ritual.⁴³ At the founding of the Chosŏn Dynasty, the bureau joined other institutions and moved from the old capital to the new capital outside the Great South Gate (Namdaemun), in what is now central Seoul (in the district of Hoamdong, Yongsangun). The office had one first rank (yŏngil; 令一), grade seven official of the scholarly order and two second tier (sŭngi; 丞二), grade eight officials. In 1407, the court elevated the rank and importance of these officials to grade six.⁴⁴ The bureau raised a variety of animals, such as oxen, chickens and pigs. At one point, the bureau tried to raise wild ducks but failed to breed them in captivity.⁴⁵ Hearing of this, King T'aejong, believing that the official assigned to the bureau was incapable of performing his job, requested that the Border Defence Council (Ŭijŏngbu; 議政府) reappoint him. The council agreed that the stable official was not adept at breeding animals and such animals should be bred by slaves working in the granaries (ch'anggo nobi; 倉庫奴婢), based on the Ming Dynasty custom at Shanglin Park (Shanglin Yuan; 上林苑).⁴⁶ This differed from the Ming practice because China did not employ slaves to breed its animals. The state changed the name of the Ceremonial Stable Bureau to the Ceremonial Animal Office (Chŏnsaengsŏ; 典牲署) in 1460. These structural changes and rank upgrades attest to the growing responsibilities of this office for fulfilling ritual demands and providing sacrificial animals to the Chosŏn state.

Under King Sejong, the court began reimagining dynastic Confucian ritual practices and implemented what is referred to as the Five Rites, many of which Koryŏ adopted from the *Rites of Zhou* and Chosŏn revised. Among these rites were state ceremonies to pray to the ancestral shrine, sacrifices for mournings and funerals, the arrival of foreign envoys, and the worship of China as senior to Korea, as well as a host of marriage and court ceremonies.⁴⁷ At this time, the government reconsidered both land and animal resources to fit the state's economic needs around ritual requirements. The government had to compensate for deficiencies in animal management, animal shortages, and the competing demands for animals from other groups in society, such as hunters who killed them for food and fur, or people catching and killing animals to use

---

⁴³ *Kyŏngguk taejŏn* [Administrative code of the Chosŏn Dynasty] (Seoul: Han'guk pŏpche yŏn'guwŏn, 1993): ch. 1; and KS, 2:678b-d.
⁴⁴ CWS, 1:23 and 1:419.
⁴⁵ CWS, 1:585.
⁴⁶ CWS, 1:588.
⁴⁷ Sook Ja Kang [Kang Sukcha], 'The Role of King Sejong in Establishing the Confucian Ritual Code', *The Review of Korean Studies* 9, no. 3 (2006): 79.

as ingredients in medicine. All kinds of animals were included in sacrifices, whether they came from the land, lakes, rivers or the sea.⁴⁸

The number and diversity of animals necessary for rituals prompted the state to find new sources. There were at least twenty-four different types of state rituals that demanded animal sacrifice. These ranged from the most significant ceremonies such as those conducted at the altar of earth and grain (*sajik*; 社稷) and the ancestral shrine, to that of minor offerings to the famous mountain and great river (*myŏngsan taech'ŏn*; 名山大川) spirits, which were responsible for the protection from heavy rain (*yŏngje*; 榮祭) and pestilent insects (*p'oje*; 酺祭). The state was to carry out these sacrifices annually. The number of animals sacrificed at these state altars and for various other ceremonies roughly amounted to one calf, nine bulls, thirty-one sheep, and fifty-one pigs a year. In bad years, such as in times of famine or other hardships, the number of sacrifices decreased. Despite this, as the dynasty progressed, the total offered at the ancestral shrine grew in accordance with the rising number of royal ancestors, thus demanding more animal products over time. The National Ritual Code (Kukcho oryeŭi; 國朝五禮儀) completed in 1474 by Kang Hŭimaeng (1424–83; 姜希孟) systemised these ritual offerings. Most likely all of these rituals were practised before they became standardised.⁴⁹

Ceremonial Animal Office personnel handled the animals sacrificed at these ceremonies.⁵⁰ They began by collecting the animals from various regions of the country. The bulls used in these particular rituals, for instance, appear to be of a stock raised on Cheju Island.⁵¹ The Cheju black-coloured bulls differed from the average beige oxen relied upon on the mainland for agricultural power. Local Cheju officials presented these black bulls to the central government as a means to pay their tribute tax. The breed of sheep that were sacrificed originated from China. In 1419, perhaps as a diplomatic gesture of friendship, the Ming gave more than a thousand head of sheep to Chosŏn. These sheep that the emperor granted the country were distributed to various government offices, probably in the capital region, which had been tasked

---

[48] Only land animals will be examined here. To examine the relationship between people and fish is beyond the scope of this study.

[49] For an excellent study on early Chosŏn ritual, see Han Myŏngju, 'The Establishment of National Rites and Royal Authority during Early Chosŏn', *International Journal of Korean History* 9 (December 2005): 89–131.

[50] Another expression for sacrificial animals was *t'aeroe* (C. *tailao*; 太牢).

[51] For more, see Han Hyŏngju, 'Chosŏn sidae kukka chesa esŏŭi hŭisaeng sayong kwa kŭ unyŏng' [Use and operation of sacrifices of Chosŏn period national rites], *Yŏksa minsokhak* 52 (June 2017): 47–75.

to raise them.⁵² In addition to sheep, the Ming emperor offered other gifts of animals to Chosŏn envoys, including goats and horses.⁵³ The Chosŏn Border Defence Command wanted people travelling to the Liaodong peninsula to purchase goats and pigs there and, after returning with them, inform the Office of Protocol (Punye pinsi; 分禮賓寺). The office hoped that these breeds, originating from China where they were also used for ritual, would reproduce with Korean breeds. As it turned out, the Chinese breeds were smaller and thinner and while they were suitable for consumption, they were deemed inappropriate for use in sacrificial ritual.⁵⁴ In 1473, official Yi Sungwŏn (1428–91; 李承元) believed that one pig could sire eighty or more piglets in a year, and that they should all be transported to the Office of Sacrificial Animals (Sach'uksŏ; 司畜所).⁵⁵ The ritual altars (cheso [祭所] and tanso [壇所]) in the capital, where sacrifices were carried out, were themselves difficult to maintain. Originally constructed of soil, they collapsed easily, especially in heavy rain. They lacked barriers to protect them from people. Most of all, the bulls, sheep, dogs and pigs sacrificed at the altars were filthy. Ritual sacrifice of animals, including dogs, have been found in gravesites dating back to the Silla Dynasty and the Three Kingdoms period.⁵⁶ The lack of barriers protecting people and animals interacting resulted in altars that were continually unclean (pulgyŏl; 不潔), both literally and ritually, and the areas around the altar narrow and congested because the animals and people were together in a tight space. In other words, it seems as though altars were not cleaned on a regular basis, which interfered with the efficacy of the rites. Called to complete a difficult task, King Sejong repaired the national shrine and the earth and grain altar. The people who maintained the altars (sudan chiin; 守壇之人) in the capital did not cleanse them. There were accusations that not only were the altars in disarray but that bulls, sheep and pigs also wandered freely around the altars.⁵⁷ Other critics derided the poor condition of these shrines that these sacrificial animals had trampled and soiled.⁵⁸ Court officials expressed these complaints a number of times beginning in the 1430s.⁵⁹ Unlike the king and

⁵² CWS, 2:333 and 2:334.
⁵³ For other examples, see CWS, 2:134 and 2:299.
⁵⁴ CWS, 4:604.
⁵⁵ CWS, 9:78.
⁵⁶ Ko Ŭnbyŏl, 'Han'guk kodae tongmul hŭsaeng ŭirye ŭi t'ŭkching Samguk sidae Silla punmyojŏk ŭl chungsim ŭ ro' [Animal sacrifice rituals in ancient Korea centring on Silla tombs of the Three Kingdoms], Haebu saengmul illyuhak 33, no. 2 (2020): 69–77.
⁵⁷ CWS, 3:216.
⁵⁸ CWS, 3:627.
⁵⁹ For instance, see CWS, 4:172 and 6:319.

various court officials, the State Council was not concerned about the conditions of the altars.[60] However, despite initial repairs, by 1450, the court had deemed around seven or eight of the minor sacrifice altars in bad condition. While some discussion took place in the court about the benefits of using stone rather than soil, it was decided the 'correct' way, to construct the altars, according to the Book of Rites, was to build up a soil platform rather than stacking up stones. Basing his argument on the precedence of earlier generations, rather than on the Book of Rites, King Sejong ordered the shrines be reconstructed with stone despite the heavy effort stone demanded.

Officials who did care presented suggestions to the court to help improve the conditions of the sacrificial shrines in other ways. One idea was to systematise the number and types of people who took care of the shrines, suggesting that no fewer than two slaves (noja iho; 奴子二戶) from two separate households clean and arrange each site. To provide for them, the government granted the slaves two kyŏl each of land (enough land to feed themselves and their families), including the rice it produced, and exempted them from other services.[61]

In a state with a sizeable number of designated official positions, the fact that the people taking care of the altars had no status in the government is striking. Slave status designated the low social level of these posts and implied that the people tasked with this work were socially unimportant. This contrasts sharply with the national importance placed on these shrines. The persons who tended these altars not only dealt with the animals, they also prepared them for ritual and cleansed the area after killing them at the altars. Yangban did not want to deal with any physical labour, let alone work that involved dead animals or blood. Also of importance was the fear of pollution from the death of the animals. Butchers, for instance, were lowborn because of the pollution that arises from the slaughter of animals, a shamanistic and folk belief. Instead, the most vulnerable segment of the social hierarchy shared control of the most sacred affairs of the state. Dealing with animals, alive and dead, slaves worked alongside government officials in charge of these state rituals. Certainly, the government rewarded slaves for their actions – by providing them with land to grow food on and exempting them from having to complete other work. While these humans and animals were often mistreated, here they are both well cared for.

King Sejong's reign (1418–50) was the period when the government began structuring land and animal resources to fit government economic needs

[60] CWS, 6:319.
[61] CWS, 3:216.

around ritual requirements. The Ceremonial Stable Bureau and the Ritual Guest Agency and Palace Catering Service Office (Yebinsi; 禮賓寺) required fodder for a growing number of sheep and pigs. Hence, the court established agricultural fields in Koyanghyŏn county just northwest of the capital. Lands like these were sometimes brought under cultivation from central government decree – simply seizing land and turning it into taxable agricultural fields – or through the initiative of individuals petitioning the government, and working with tax officials, to survey and open land.[62] The court was also worried about the cost of the seeds and fieldworker labour. Further, since the people living in the village were unable to transport sufficient quantities of grain, the court collected additional levies so that the government could purchase what it needed to make up for the deficiency. The court's solution was to exempt village farmers and have local government office slaves carry the harvest to the capital.[63]

In 1421, the Board of Rites provided the Ritual Guest and Palace Catering Service Office with ten bags (sŏk) of rice to feed the sacrificial pigs, geese and ducks.[64] A year later, the office petitioned the Board of Rites that the stench of the meat produced from the chickens, pigs and fish was unbearable and the area filthy. In essence, the sacrificial ceremonies and offerings were unsuitable. By 1425, the Board of Rites explained the importance of rites both great and small to the country and that the sacred place where these animals were sacrificed must be cleansed ritually. The board decided that walls and doors had to be built to prevent the various animals from mixing together. This also allowed them to remain cleansed and to fatten up. It was also determined that when sacrificing animals, loading their carcasses on oxen or on people was especially ritually unclean, a practice that would compromise the efficacy of a ceremony. Once cleansed, animals had to remain prepared for the ritual slaughter. The board asked the court to request that the Directorate for Construction (Sŏn'gonggam; 繕工監) produce carts with sidewalls (sangch'a; 廂車) so that apart from oxen, sacrificial sheep and pigs (chŏ 猪) could be loaded aboard and presented.[65]

Chosŏn officials consulted each other over proper animal sacrifice protocol. One discussion concerned neutered and unneutered animals. In 1424, Ch'oe Yangsŏn (?–?; 崔揚善) asked if the sacrificial animals used to honour the deceased kings T'aejo and Chŏngjong had to be neutered sheep and pigs.

---

[62] For instance, see Pak Kyŏngan, 'Sŏnch'o kadae ŭi chŏlgŭp e kwanhayŏ' [Distribution of public lands from residence sites in the early Chosŏn Dynasty], Yŏksa wa hyŏnsil 69 (2008): 225–54.
[63] CWS, 2:689.
[64] CWS, 2:433.
[65] CWS, 2:666.

State Councillor Hwang Hŭi (1363–1452; 黃喜) pondered why only neutered animals were permissible. Ch'oe Yangsŏn believed that, apart from oxen, all other male sacrificial animals (unsaeng; 雄牲) should be castrated. Soon after, the Board of Rites determined that castrated sheep and pigs should be used in all sacrifices. Decisions like these were based on the *Family Rites of Wengong* (*Wengong jiali*; 文公家禮) that discusses the appropriate usage of animal meat after sacrificial rituals.[66] Here, the board was attempting to 'correct' Chosŏn practices by relying upon the advice of low-level officials and Song Dynasty era texts. Diseased animals also concerned the Board of Rites. In 1428, the chickens, pigs and goats at the Office of Protocol displayed sickness (*yubyŏng kyedon'goyang*; 有病雞豚羔羊). The board relied on the government slaves from the Office of Protocol to administer medicine to cure them. There were no details about the disease or remedies. As punishment for not keeping the sacrificial beasts alive, the board removed two officials from the Office for Raising Animals (Kanyang pyŏlgam; 看養別監).[67]

All of the officials working in the Office of Protocol appear to be part of the military order and members of the yangban class and had slaves to assist them tend the animals. While these appointments may seem to have been low-ranking positions – yangban status did not ensure access to the highest positions in the government – they were more important than the rank suggests. Having military officers in charge of the Office of Protocol may have been necessary because many of the envoys arriving from the Ming were military men themselves. A familiarity with feasting and the ability to display one's prowess with hunting bows and keeping up a conversation on military affairs helped strengthen diplomacy. Rewards, such as promotions to a higher rank or a new position, were possible for these staff members. Office of Protocol personnel received houses, land and slaves, as well as elevated ranks.[68]

The central government wanted to raise animals in the countryside, most likely in areas with more space to increase the number of animals available to the state. Perhaps based on the needs of the central government and the realities of demanding families to raise these animals, it set minimum and maximum numbers of animals to be produced and criminalised failure. In 1449, the Border Defence Command ordered each village (*kwan*; 官) to divide up its

---

[66] CWS, 2:617. The *Family Rites of Wengong* was also called the *Family Rituals of Master Zhu*. See Song-Chong Lee, ed., *The Role of Meaning of Religion for Korean Society*, Internet Resource, 113n11. https://www.mdpi.com/books/pdfview/book/1266.
[67] CWS, 3:107.
[68] CWS, 8:201.

sheep and raise them based on the example of raising horses on pasture land (*mokchang*; 牧場). It was declared that each ewe should produce between five and ten offspring. If the people raising the sheep were unable to reach five offspring, they were classified as criminals.[69] Details about the actual implementation or effectiveness of this system were not explained.

The central government expanded the responsibilities of the agencies accountable for animals. The Office of Sacrificial Animals, a bureau under the Ministry of Rites, was originally established as part of the Ritual Guest and Palace Catering Service Office in 1392. The Place of Meat Carving (Saryŏnso; 司饔所) existed as early as 1400 and was the location where initially oxen and horses were raised for use by the state (*kugyong*; 國用). The Ministry of Rites was also referring to the Office of Protocol by 1428. By 1434, with access to animals raised in the region, the office had the capacity to mobilise as many as 700 pigs to the capital a year.[70] In 1460, the court combined the Office of Protocol with the Place of Meat Carving.[71] The number of animals the state came to manage created other opportunities for officials and commoners to take advantage of the growing system for personal gain to the detriment of the country. Having so many animals in one place, the government worried that the people would steal from it.[72]

Continuing the restructuring, as it did with other agencies, the court changed the name of the Office of Protocol to the Office of Sacrificial Animals as part of a massive reorganisation of bureaus and offices throughout the government in 1466.[73] From its inception, the Office of Sacrificial Animals was responsible for the procurement, transportation and preparation of animals such as chickens, pigs, goats and oxen for use in state rituals and official welcoming events.[74] Raising pigs appeared to be the most pressing issue for the office. Pork was a major ingredient in consumption rituals. Some of the animals included wild boar captured in the provinces and submitted to the government as part of the tribute payment.[75] In 1469, the court was concerned about the growing expenses for the central government of raising pigs

---

[69] CWS, 5:127.
[70] CWS, 3:563.
[71] CWS, 7:396.
[72] CWS, 1:167.
[73] CWS, 8:2.
[74] See *Sach'uksŏ samok* [Guidelines for Office of Sacrificial Animals] early Chosŏn Dynasty, original document, Kyujanggak Library, Seoul National University.
[75] For example, in 1459, the Office of Protocol received fifty wild pigs from Kangwŏn Province. Other animals included 'thin pigs' or those considered too lean. The pigs sent from some villages in Kyŏnggi were difficult to transport. CWS, 7:347.

for sacrifice. Criticising the cost to raise swine, the Minister of Works Yang Sŏngji (1415–82; 梁誠之) pointed out that 'the Office of Sacrificial Animals raises hundreds of swine a year ... So the cost of raising one swine in a year is each about ten *p'il*, but is the original cost of a pig about ten *p'il*? [It is not.] Sheep actually cost this much, and chickens are even costlier.'[76] In other words, officials inflate prices to turn a profit. Despite trying to expand the availability of animals for the state, the apparent expenses of these new measures were higher than market value and costly to the government.

The Office of Protocol served as an extension of government control over animal husbandry and the diplomatic rituals between Chosŏn and international visitors, including those with the Ming and adjoining countries (*in'guk*; 隣國), such as Jurchens and Japanese. Acquiring this meat for the sacrificial ceremonies and court banquets for domestic and foreign guests was the responsibility of the Office of Protocol, as animals as gifts played a role in diplomatic relations with Chosŏn's neighbours. The Board of Rites wanted to give venison (*chang nokyuk*; 獐鹿肉) to Ming diplomats. Arguing such a gift was difficult – perhaps because such game was hard to find that year or reserved for other occasions – the Office of Sacrificial Animals recommended preparing chickens and pigs for the Ming ahead of time.[77] In 1419, a year after taking over the throne, King Sejong provided his brother Prince Yangnyŏng with live Chinese pig (*tangch'a*; 唐猪), wild geese (*am*; 雁), ducks (*ap*; 鴨) and falcons (*ŭng*; 鷹). Korean envoys also transported living animals back to the peninsula after trips abroad. In 1425, the magistrate of P'yŏngan Province sent an urgent message to the capital. The Chosŏn envoy Kim Man (?–?; 金滿) was returning from China with ten Ming envoys and had crates full of sheep, dogs, chickens and geese from Beijing. The envoy was to arrive at Ŭiju (義州), a border town, in a few days.[78] Ming envoys arriving from China were treated to food and alcohol. At times, the Office of Sacrificial Animals deployed meat, medicine and gifts from the central storehouses or the provinces to entertain these diplomatic guests.[79] The office also passed along appeals from Ming envoys to the court. These appeals, in addition to game requests, sometimes referred to decorative hunting bows. The office provided these hunting bows on the request of the king and other military officials.[80] In 1468, Ming official Wang Heng (?–?)

---

[76] CWS, 8:393.
[77] CWS, 3:170.
[78] CWS, 2:666.
[79] For instance, see the order by the Border Defence Command (Ŭijŏngbu) directing the Office of Protocol to procure 150 swine from all of the other provinces if the numbers are insufficient around Kyŏnggi. CWS, 4:157.
[80] CWS, 8:186.

requested fifteen such bows.⁸¹ In 1470, King Sŏngjong ordered that officials be sent to Mt Kŏmdan in Kwangju to hold a fire ring hunt and cull deer to be later presented to the visiting Ming envoy. This site was selected because rain had been coming down too heavily near the capital, most likely preventing a hunt closer to the court from taking place.⁸²

Chosŏn was also well aware of the Jurchen, Korea's most immediate neighbours along the frontier, and their customs. One official reported that 'the summer season is a time the steppe grows thick with grass, the horses grow plump, and the barbarians hunt'.⁸³ Another complained that 'when the vegetation is thick, they [the Jurchen] always come [to Chosŏn] to hunt'.⁸⁴ Jurchen envoys who occasionally travelled to Korea on diplomatic missions discussed deer and other game. At the Hall of Northern Peace (Pukp'yŏnggwan; 北平館), where the Jurchen envoys gathered, one Jurchen official discussed the population, geography and economy of his homeland. In addition, he extolled the quality of the venison and fish his people consumed.⁸⁵ The Jurchen envoys expected Chosŏn audiences to understand and appreciate their experiences, and officials recoded their words with care.

The Jurchen envoys told stories of plentiful animals in the north, perhaps to the interest of the central government for more than just simple curiosity. As will be discussed in future chapters, the supply of animals was growing uncertain because of discreet events that raised anxieties. The state was constantly concerned about access to animals, a matter that heightened in urgency over the fifteenth century. The Ministry of Military Affairs expressed unease with the commanders from each province and whether they had properly recorded the presentation of deer and wild boar to the state.⁸⁶ At a feast held in Masan, a local magistrate requested one hundred chickens and fifty-two pigs. This was considered a high number and the request was further complicated because the game taken in the hunt was to be used in ritual sacrifices not for feasting.⁸⁷ Another time, a shortage of swine elicited concern among relevant officials of the court. For example, Chief State Councillor Sin Sukchu (1417–75; 申叔舟) was satisfied with substituting dried slices of pork

---

⁸¹ The court declined Wang Heng's request. See CWS, 8:182.
⁸² CWS, 8:490.
⁸³ CWS, 9:212.
⁸⁴ CWS, 12:171.
⁸⁵ CWS, 4:180.
⁸⁶ CWS, 2:663.
⁸⁷ CWS, 2:625.

from wild boar until more pigs were bred for a ceremony. After breeding the swine, it was declared, more generous amounts of fresh pork would be used.[88]

This shortage extended to meat used in rituals and in state ceremonies held in the capital. In 1470, the Queen Dowager Insu (Taewang taebi; 大王大妃) ordered that, since precedence called for meat to be offered in sacrificial burial ceremonies, hunting of animals before the ceremony should be carried out in the capital region and adjacent provinces.[89] It was also determined that dried meats were to be used for ancestral rites (chep'o; 祭脯). Game originated from the villages. Local magistrates selected commoners to hunt for game as a means to pay their taxes. If the amount of game was insufficient, the people had to make up the difference monetarily. In 1475, the senior meritorious advisor (wŏnsang; 院相) Chŏng Ch'angson (1402–87; 鄭昌孫) lamented that domesticated animals were now scare at royal banquets. He stressed that game would not provide a sufficient amount of food compared to domesticated animals. The court begrudgingly accepted this substitution. 'Using domesticated animals,' Chŏng Ch'angson said, 'would be more convenient.' The king appeared hesitant to fully give up using game at the banquets, which were held for merit subjects and attended by the three most senior female members of the royal family (samjŏn; 三殿) – the grandmother of King Sŏngjong, Queen Chŏnghŭi wanghu; the mother of King Sŏngjong, Queen Dowager Insu Sohye wanghu; and the wife of the former king, Queen Ansu wanghu. These gatherings, often accompanied by music and dance, reinforced relationships among those who attended, and food was a major aspect.[90] Instead, the king insisted that it should be domesticated animals that be used to make up the difference, 'if there were insufficient amounts of hunted animals'.[91]

A decade later, in 1486, the court recognised that at the beginning of the dynasty every village was supposed to prepare dried venison for ancestral sacrifice. The local magistrates, having a great deal of control over the lives of the people, selected commoners during the agricultural seasons to hunt for the game that was used for the dried meat. If the amount the commoners hunted was insufficient, then the magistrate forced them to pay the difference. This 'unfairly burdened the people'. The court abolished the practice and ordered the army commanders to mobilise soldiers during the farming season and to hunt only for two or three days. The court concluded of this situation:

[88] CWS, 9:78.
[89] CWS, 8:459.
[90] Kim Jong Su, 'Royal Banquets and Uigwe during the Late Joseon Period', *Korea Journal* 48, no. 2 (2008): 111–35.
[91] CWS, 9:251.

When Chŏng Nanjong (1433–89; 鄭蘭宗) became the military commander of P'yŏngan Province, the number of animals he killed on the hunt was fewer than a thousand. He did not divide up his troops. Instead, they were all sent out to the various villages to produce dried meats. They each had a fixed amount to make. The local magistrate wished to make up the amount. Some supplemented the jerky with lamb or suckling swine. The whole province scorned this.[92]

Statements like this demonstrate the changing needs of an expanding state, well beyond the resources of local military commanders trying to brainstorm temporary fixes. Put differently, the acceptance of domesticated animals, in lieu of wild game, was a slow but necessary process.

* * *

Korean kings and royal family members wanted to hunt. They found enjoyment not only in killing animals but also in spending time with family members, reinforcing bonds among themselves and their peers, and displaying their martial identities. Officials, drawing on centuries-old, deeply established precedent, sought to regulate access to animals by turning them into ritual items. While ritual animal sacrifice is not unique to the Korean experience, the protocols Korean states adopted, initially from Chinese ritual procedure and indigenous shamanistic practices, took on new and added meaning in the fifteenth century as the state expanded control over the animals and land where they were raised and hunted. Kings and other elites were to follow strict rules when entering places where wild animals resided. Hunting should be for the state, not personal enjoyment – a perennial issue in neighbouring China. Paradoxically, with hunting guidelines in place, these officials almost immediately attempted to weaken the hunting rituals they established in the beginning of the dynasty by suppressing hunts, partly understood as the military preparation of the dynasty and the display of royal authority through the pomp and circumstance of the hunt. Policies that promoted population growth and attempts to regulate interactions between people and animals complicated the Chosŏn court's relationship with hunting and wildlife. As outlined in the previous chapter, the government dealt with growing populations and the expansion of agriculture during the economic recovery of the fifteenth century when wildlife populations began to collide with people. One way to govern this increasing interaction was to

[92] CWS, 11:117.

rationalise the use of wild and domesticated animals and categorise them as state resources. Confucian ritual sacrifices required more animals, both wild and domestic, and more personnel involved in handling them or locating them in the countryside. Managing resources such as animals became an ecological strategy for early Chosŏn.

5
Stalking the Forests: The Military on the Chase in the Mid-Fifteenth Century

In 1393, well-known scholar official Chŏng Tojŏn (1342–98; 鄭道傳) dedicated the *Pictures of Hunting Scenes in the Four Seasons* (*Sasi susudo*; 四時蒐狩圖) to the throne. This gift was greatly appreciated by the founder of the Chosŏn Dynasty, Yi Sŏnggye (King T'aejo). Two years later, the Chosŏn Dynasty's Three Army Command (*Samgunjinmuso*; 三軍鎭撫所) circulated the screen, apparently among military commanders and other military officials throughout the country. By 1397, the army studied another work Chŏng produced, the *Diagram on the Five Army Formations* (*Ojinto*; 五陣圖) and distributed it throughout the country.[1]

The gift of the *Pictures of Hunting Scenes in the Four Seasons* screen expressed Chŏng Tojŏn's personal relationship with King T'aejo. What background did Chŏng have that would have given him the knowledge to advise the king of military hunting strategies? As the leading reformer for the state, Chŏng was deeply familiar with all of the aspects of Neo-Confucian teachings, including the hunt and ritual sacrifice. The king asked Chŏng, 'In ancient times, hunting from the spring and winter, animals were sacrificed at the ancestral shrines, but today, only when I catch an animal in the spring hunt, I first consider offering it as sacrifice to the ancestral shrines. What do you think of this?' Chŏng replied, 'As for the ceremony of animal sacrifice (*hŏn'gŭm chiye*; 獻禽之禮), it is truly appropriate. The great sacrifice (*taehyang*; 大享) has already passed [in other words it had already been carried out], but [since you are unable to attend the rituals in person] please offer sacrifice by watching from afar [rather than attending each ritual personally].'[2]

---

[1] CWS, 1:107. These hunting screens and handbooks are no longer extant.
[2] CWS, 1:48. In other words, Chŏng informs the king that he does not personally have to attend each sacrifice. Instead, the king could turn to the direction of the sacrifice to display reverence for the ritual. The hunting screen is no longer extant.

In the first century of the Chosŏn Dynasty, two forms of royal hunting practices emerged. The first and grandest, led by the king, was the royal military Kangmu hunt, explored here and in Chapter 6. The *Pictures of Hunting Scenes in the Four Seasons* presented guidelines for royal military Kangmu hunts (講武). These hunts were large-scale annual events encompassing sometimes thousands of soldiers with a formal set of rules for engaging animals to help build military skills. The second was the smaller and more intimate, personal hunting event, when the king hunted with a small entourage, the subject of later chapters. While both differed in scale and frequency, the large-scale royal military Kangmu expeditions and the smaller private hunting practices occasionally overlapped. For instance, at times, an early Chosŏn king participated in the royal Kangmu hunt, either by wielding a bow himself and travelling alongside his army or by observing hunts conducted by his troops. Kings also joined smaller hunting parties while on these bigger Kangmu expeditions. Kangmu hunts were more visible representations of the king's power and the needs of the dynasty related to the military and security. Private hunts were intimate occasions when the king bonded with close royal family members and like-minded officials. However, both forms of the chase were integral components to state building as the government extended its dominance over the land and beasts of the wild.

This chapter begins by exploring military developments of the early Chosŏn in the context of wider Eurasian history. Viewing these developments with a broader lens helps us locate the struggles Koreans and others on the borders of the empire experienced during the collapse of Mongol control and the rise of other powerful states. Next, it examines the royal military Kangmu hunts. The Kangmu hunts were meaningful activities, producing important bonds that transcended the violence directed at the animals that kings and soldiers hunted. These relationships mattered. On the one hand, as pointed out in the previous chapter, the state promoted the killing of wild and domestic animals for ritual sacrifice. On the other, as will be seen in this chapter, it sought to set boundaries for hunting and killing them. While seemingly contradictory policies, I argue that the conservation of resources was less about ethical questions over killing animals – the humane treatment of another sentient life – and more of a dispute over using animals as a way to perfect human society. Finally, this chapter analyses borderland dynamics to tease out the complicated relationships between the Kangmu, military preparedness and national security. Hunting in general held significance for military readiness. Not only was it a way for the country to sharpen the skills of the military to prepare for war but the hunting for wild beasts also brought outside groups to the peninsula, threatening the peace. As soldiers, officials and commoners moved north and into coastal regions, their encounters with non-Chosŏn peoples in contested hunting grounds challenged ideas of civilisation and displayed the limits of central authority, heightened by the effects of a cooling climate.

Early Chosŏn Military Structure

Sweeping military and political developments throughout Eurasia began in the late fourteenth century as the Mongol Empire crumbled.[3] Sometimes characterised as a 'military revolution', this century's changes in tactics and the scale of war impacted societies in new ways. The Mongol collapse had immediate consequences in some regions, especially where the Mongols held direct power; in others, especially more distant lands or locations where they indirectly ruled, developments unfolded over the next century. Europe was entrenched in warfare between England and France during the first half of the century, while the expansion of firearms technology unleashed new levels of violence.[4] In western Eurasia, successful military reforms, such as the formation of the Ottoman Janissary army and the exchange of land grants for military service, helped propel the Ottoman Empire into power after the capture of Constantinople in 1453 and their expansion into Eastern Europe.[5] In other parts of Eurasia, the Mongol Yuan decline brought new challenges and opportunities. Russian armies adopted the military practices of their enemy – mounted warrior horsemen – helping Russian princes consolidate and challenge Mongol rule, leading to greater military and political centralisation later in the century.[6] In eastern Eurasia, the disintegration of the Yuan energised the rebels who had coalesced around Chinese leadership as the Ming unified the Chinese mainland and maintained formidable standing armies.[7] On the edges of empires, politics adapted and prospered.

---

[3] Richard Eaton and Philip Wagoner, 'Warfare on the Deccan Plateau, 1450–1600: A Military Revolution in Early Modern India?' *Journal of World History* 25, no. 1 (March 2014): 6. Interpreting these changes as a military revolution, with the slow and piecemeal adoption of firearm technology, has been challenged by other historians. For an overview of the debate, see Gabor Agoston, 'Firearms and Military Adaptation: The Ottomans and the European Military Revolution, 1450–1800', *Journal of World History* 25, no. 1 (March 2014): 85–124.
[4] Jeremy Black, *Military Power and the Fate of the Continents, 1450–2000* (New Haven: Yale University Press, 1998), 18–20.
[5] Kaya Sahin, 'The Ottoman Empire in the Long Sixteenth Century', *Renaissance Quarterly* 70, no. 1 (2017): 222.
[6] Michael Paul, 'Military Revolution in Russia, 1550–1682', *The Journal of Military History* 68, no. 1 (January 2004): 9, 13–14.
[7] See David M. Robinson, 'Why Military Institutions Matter for Ming History', *Journal of Chinese History* 1, no. 2 (July 2017): 297–327.

For Korea, the Mongol collapse held both immediate and long-term military consequences. The Korean military, responding to the shift in power relations in Northeast Asia, replicated Eurasian patterns after the calming of the political order in Hanyang. As in other parts of Eurasia, the Chosŏn Dynasty responded to shifts in empire from the Yuan to the Ming and took steps to secure its borders through deep political and military reforms. The military transformation from the late Koryŏ to the early Chosŏn dynasties was closely related to Neo-Confucian political and social reform movements. What ensued was a legal and social system that relegated the military to lower positions in terms of status, privilege and authority. Following an unsure beginning with the Ming, the peace of the fifteenth century allowed Confucian bureaucrats to centralise their authority, struggles that transpired in the wake of massive political and military shifts in East Asia and beyond.

At the beginning of the fifteenth century, the military was decentralised and complex, a structure inherited from Koryŏ. Private armies (*kapsa*; 甲士) – families with wealth that hired mercenaries to protect them – dominated, an arrangement established under King T'aejo.[8] These armed forces evolved from a pre-Koryŏ tradition in which regional leaders formed regional armies. While earlier dynasties, such as Silla and Koryŏ, had attempted to restrain private armies at various times, each had failed. This was especially true in 1170 when a military coup against the civil branch led to a period of military domination of the government.[9] Under Mongol Yuan rule, the Mongols and Koryŏ elevated officers in the military, but it was not until after 1351 that the court attempted to place the military under direct control. Greater military reform began in 1400 when the bureaucracy outlawed private armies. King T'aejo's personal soldiers became the primary force within the capital that protected the king. His soldiers were then absorbed into the fold of the state. The Capitol Command and what would later become the Three Army Command included troops with the most loyalty to the founder.

Reforms unfolded over the next several decades. Until the 1450s, the state restructured the military by introducing several initiatives. One of the architects of early Chosŏn military policy was the scholar official Chŏng Tojŏn. Chŏng, well known as an influential Neo-Confucian adviser in the late Koryŏ

---

[8] My discussion here is gleaned from Ch'a Munsŏp's thorough study of the early Chosŏn military. Ch'a Munsŏp, *Chosŏn sidae kunje yŏn'gu* [Research into the Chosŏn military structure] (Seoul: Tan'guk taehakkyo ch'ulp'anbu, 1973), 26–51. For English, see Duncan, *The Origins of the Chosŏn Dynasty*, 227–8.

[9] Kim Chongsu, 'Imjin waeran chŏnhu chungan'gunje ŭi pyŏnhwa' [Changes to the command system of the central army after the Imjin War], *Kunsa* 84 (September 2012): 88–90.

and supporter of the new dynasty, composed a number of books and designed several screens, including the *Pictures of Hunting Scenes in the Four Seasons*, introduced at the beginning of this chapter, and *Diagram of Military Formations* (*Chinbŏp*; 陣法) that outlined tactics and strategies, which he gifted to King T'aejo.[10] Along with officials such as Nam Eŭn (1354–98; 南誾) and Sim Hyosaeng (1349–98; 沈孝生), Chŏng became known for his concern about the military preparation of the country. These Neo-Confucian scholar officials were part of the king's inner circle. The reforms that began at the start of the dynasty significantly changed and centralised the command system to avoid the distribution of military power. King T'aejong had accelerated military reform because changes across the state and social system had to be enacted at the same time. This was very different from Chŏng Tojŏn's ideas of reform.[11] The changes the king adhered to were structural, while Chŏng's suggestions were more tactical and strategic. Restructuring was mostly completed by the 1450s when the court established the Military Command Headquarters (Wido ch'ongbu; 衛都摠府), which had absorbed the earlier structure of the Three Army Command. In 1457, the government formed the Five Military Commands (*owi*; 五衛). Armies from the Five Military Commands protected different regions of the country. The Ŭihŭng Commandery (Ŭihŭngwi; 義興衛) guard was the most important as it was responsible for the capital and Kyŏnggi, Kangwŏn, Ch'ungch'ŏng and Hwanghae provinces.[12] All of these changes placed the army under direct control of the throne.

Size mattered too. The number of troops composing the central army amounted to several thousand and this number expanded over the century. Troop numbers doubled during King Sejong's reign to 7,500. The size of the professional army doubled again by the end of King Sŏngjong's reign, reaching 14,800. King Sejo established provincial armies during his reign in 1456. King Sejo first combined the armies defending the north with the soldiers from the south. Each province organised their militaries around subunits while simultaneously establishing naval commands. Professional soldiers who took the military examination were the main force of the Five Military Commands. Each command consisted of progressively smaller military units. Commoners constituted part of the army as well. The government conscripted many more able-bodied men between the age of sixteen and sixty to serve as unprofessional soldiers.

---

[10] Min Sŭnggi, *Chosŏn ŭi mugi was kabot* [Weapons and military uniforms of Chosŏn] (Seoul: Karam kihoek, 2004), 27.

[11] Yun Hunp'yo, *Yŏmal Sŏnch'o kunje kaehyŏk* [Military system reform in the late Koryŏ and early Chosŏn], (Seoul: Hyean, 2000), 323–4.

[12] Pyŏn T'aesŏp, *Han'guk t'ongsa* [Outline of Korean history] (Seoul: Samyŏnsa, 2000), 288–90.

However, it was the highly trained elite who comprised the core of the military. With additional expansion, there were roughly 6,000 army chief commanders and 6,000 naval chief commanders distributed throughout the provinces.[13]

The transformation of the military, especially regarding personal armies, was not an easy task as it grew into an elaborate, unwieldy system that was not prepared to protect the country from war. Putting into place new organisations and procedures for management, while evaluating military members for promotion, proved difficult.[14] Over time, this new bureaucratic system promoted a clear distinction between military and civil branches – previously, military men could serve in bureaucratic posts – a reorganisation that helped the bureaucracy extend its control over the military.[15] The end of the personal army system, where private troops were no longer directly loyal to a single military leader, along with the growth of an army having been restrained by the bureaucracy and reliant on unprofessional soldiers – conscripted farmers – in turn, diluted the military strength of the dynasty.[16] On the other hand, this extension not only helped the bureaucracy and kingship acquire power over the military, it also helped the bureaucracy rein in the king.

Animals as the Enemy: The Military Hunt

Royal Kangmu hunts were expansive military excursions where the king would gather his generals and soldiers at predesignated sites across the land and perform a series of hunting events.[17] Chosŏn leaders linked the Kangmu hunts to ancient Chinese practices. The leaders of the Chinese states would practise their hunting techniques four times a year during the spring, summer, autumn and winter seasons. Chosŏn was different. By recommendation of the Office of the Censor General, Chosŏn held hunting sessions during the agricultural off-seasons, what were referred to as 'the spring and autumn hunts' (*usŏn*; 蒐獮).

---

[13] Pyŏn T'aesŏp, *Han'guk t'ongsa*, 290.
[14] Yun Hunp'yo, 'Chosŏn ch'ogi kapsa ŭi t'ongsol ch'egye' [The private army command system of the early Chosŏn], *Yŏksa wa sirhak* 17 (January 2000): 8–9.
[15] Eugene Y. Park, *Between Dreams and Reality: The Military Examination in Late Chosŏn Korea, 1600–1894* (Cambridge, MA: Harvard University Press, 2007), 19.
[16] Kim Chongsu calls this a 'public army system' (*kongbyŏngje*). See Kim Chongsu, 'Imjini waeran chŏnhu chungan'gunje ŭi pyŏnhwa', 88.
[17] Other military exercises included *sŭpchin* (習陣), *sŭpsa* (習射) and *taeayŏl* (大閱). *CWS*, 4:108. Some works on these include Yi Hyŏnsu, 'Chosŏn ch'ogi Kangmu sihaeng sarye wa kunsajŏk kinŭng' [The military function and practices of the Kangmu in the early Chosŏn], *Kunsa* 45 (2002 April), 235–7; and Kwak Nakhyŏn, 'Chosŏn chŏn'gi sŭpchin kwa kunsa hullyŏn' [Military training methods in the early Chosŏn], *Tongyang kojŏn yŏn'gu* 35 (2009): 359–84.

This was done in order to avoid damaging crops in the spring or taking men away from the fields and endangering the soldiers and their horses before the weather turned cold in the winter.[18]

Rooted in the royal chases of the previous century, royal Kangmu hunts emerged in 1385 under the leadership of the Koryŏ ruler, Sin U. On one occasion, Sin U visited Maam (馬巖), roughly 140 kilometres (85 mi.) southeast of the Koryŏ capital, where he not only observed the festivities but also took part by riding his horse, shooting arrows and consuming alcohol.[19] Five years later, in 1390, scholars told King Kongyang (r. 1389–92) that the royal Kangmu hunt was an institution of antiquity (kojije; 古之制), arguing the significance of the Kangmu hunts were based on Chinese and Korean precedent.[20] At the founding of Chosŏn, King T'aejo (1392–8) promulgated the Kangmu royal hunt in 1398.[21] After that, the dynasty held these royal spectacles extensively throughout the fifteenth century, particularly during the reigns of kings from T'aejong (r. 1400–18), King Sejong's reign (r. 1418–50) – who was particularly interested in Kangmu events – through to Sejo (r. 1455–68) and again during King Sŏngjong's reign from 1469 to 1494.[22] King T'aejong went on twenty-three Kangmu expeditions whereas King Sejong went on no fewer than thirty.[23] The expansion of the Kangm hunt during these eras reflected the military interests of these early rulers who found legitimacy in this hunting technique.

Over the fifteenth century, the Kangmu hunts, as one variety of royal hunts, evolved with the needs of rulership. Initially, they were highly formal affairs which the king led and took part in. Later, by the end of the fifteenth century, the king's participation in these hunts diminished as he took on more of an observant role. But unchanged over the century was the military aspect and the rationale for holding them. At first, the state considered these large-scale hunts an important means for training the army.[24] In the eyes of these officials, building military skills and hunting were two sides of the same coin. These hunting expeditions were enormous and formidable. Some Kangmu hunts involved mobilising 25,000 professional and non-professional soldiers.[25] On one occasion, 136 officers and their aides gathered in the palace grounds

[18] For instance, see CWS, 11:519 and 11:632.
[19] KS, 3:922b.
[20] KS, 1:875d.
[21] Yi Hyŏnsu, 'Chosŏn ch'ogi Kangmu sihaeng sarye wa kunsajŏk kinŭng', 237–8.
[22] Yi Hyŏnsu, 'Chosŏn ch'ogi Kangmu sihaeng sarye wa kunsajŏk kinŭng', 237–8.
[23] For a list of royal military Kangmu dates and locations during these periods, see Yi Hyŏnsu, 'Chosŏn ch'ogi Kangmu sihaeng sarye wa kunsajŏk kinŭng', 239 and 243.
[24] CWS, 9:254.
[25] See CWS, 11:498.

to prepare for the Kangmu.[26] Numbers like these evoke the scale and spectacle of such events. Officers set up military banners and mobilised their troops. Others shot arrows at targets while teams of armed men sparred with each other, re-enacting battles. Soldiers were at the ready. They sat down, stood up, marched forward and back, and advanced quickly or slowly when ordered by their superiors. When it was time to hunt, drummers beat their drums and banged wooden sticks together producing loud sounds while they advanced to flush out animals. When the game startled into view, the men unleashed a volley of arrows. Most of the animals hunted and captured during the Kangmu were non-predatory, such as roe deer, sika and musk deer, hare and pheasants. Wild boar made an appearance at times. On these expeditions, King T'aejo preferred hunting small game with his royal guard.[27] For the most part, the animals that kings and other elites hunted during the Kangmu, and when in the smaller hunting parties like their Koryŏ predecessors, were not dangerous. However, dangerous predators did live on the peninsula at this time and when necessary, soldiers would be responsible for clearing the hunting grounds and surrounding areas of predators, including tigers. As pointed out previously, doing so not only protected those participating in the royal Kangmu hunts but it also safeguarded the lives of commoners and facilitated farming nearby, by ridding the area of predators and other formidable animals including boar, elk and moose, which were often the culprits responsible for missing livestock and people or destroying rice and other grain fields.[28]

While these practices became an important way to maintain and sharpen military skills, especially during times of peace, they also provided military elites and common soldiers access to scarce state resources such as food and clothing, royal interaction and mobility. The recruitment of soldiers for the Kangmu was nationwide and began including men from the northern provinces in the first half of the fifteenth century. Planning began one or two months before the start of the expeditions. Soldiers mobilised for the Kangmu hunts were garrison forces and troops that were off their rotational duties. In addition to the royal military, the troops and military officers of the province where the hunt took place were identified and mobilised. Soldiers travelled to Hanyang with their weapons, armour, raingear and food supplies for both the troops and their horses. For the cavalry, additional horses were provided by provincial sources. For one such expedition, the soldiers gathered at the

[26] CWS, 11:534.
[27] See CWS, 9:139.
[28] Kim Tongjin, 'Chosŏn chŏnjŏn'gi Kangmu ŭi silhaeng kwa p'oho chŏngch'aek' [Operation of Kangmu and tiger hunting policies in the early Chosŏn], *Chosŏn sidaesa hakpo* 40 (March 2007): 93–4.

village of Salgot, just outside the capital, a week before the start of a royal Kangmu hunt where the king reviewed the troops. In total, these soldiers were on hunting duty for about a month.[29] This gave the troops sufficient time to learn about new places and people beyond their hometowns, while interacting with the court.

Participation by troops from around the peninsula fostered companionship among those who would not normally interact due to geography and status. By spending time together with the court and with other soldiers from beyond their villages, these men fostered a sense of shared values and ideas, an important contribution to the unification of the dynasty as this experience must have changed thousands of people. The Kangmu hunts were reminiscent of travelling monarchs and their courts, when many members of the bureaucracy, military and royal family would travel together with the king and interact with the people they encountered along the way.

Early in the fifteenth century, Kangmu hunting grounds (*Kangmujang*; 講武場), locations where kings, elites and soldiers practised their military hunting skills, were widespread throughout the southern half of the peninsula. As one general put it, these grounds were 'places where soldiers became comfortable with shooting arrows and riding their horses' by hunting animals.[30] Lands throughout the southern provinces, from nearby Kyŏnggi in the capital region to distant Kyŏngsang Province in the southeast or North Chŏlla Province in the southwest, held designated Kangmu sites. Only a few appear to be in the north. For example, King Sejong conducted military practice by hunting in P'yŏngyang (平康) where he hit a deer in the neck with seven arrows.[31] On another outing, he travelled to Kangmu grounds in North Kyŏngsang Province staying overnight in Kangwŏn Province. With its rugged mountains and high animal density, the Kangwŏn region, along the eastern edge of the peninsula, was an attractive place for the Kangmu hunt. The Army Command presented an extensive list of forty-nine Kangmu hunting sites, all of them located in the mountains of Kyonggi Province – far away from agricultural production zones of the south.[32] This distance ensured these excursions would not interrupt the production of grain and cotton by trampling the fields. In the late 1420s, the Ministry of Military Affairs, apparently wary of the frequency and distance of these hunts from the capital, reduced the number of Kangmu hunting grounds outside of the capital province and

---

[29] Yi Hyŏnsu, 'Chosŏn ch'ogi Kangmu sihaeng sarye wa kunsajŏk kinŭng', 255–6.
[30] *CWS*, 3:169 and 3:372.
[31] *CWS*, 7:55.
[32] *CWS*, 5:107.

removed them from the list of sites where kings could hunt.³³ Beginning with the second half of the fifteenth century, the Ministry of War promoted the land around the capital as ideal Kangmu sites, where most – but not all – of the Kangmu grounds were located at the time. The government hinted at the reason behind changing the location of the Kangmu hunts – the king should not travel far from the palace and the distant Kangmu hunting grounds should be converted to farmland to allow farmers to 'plow and plant'.³⁴ At any rate, these demands placed additional restrictions on the king and the military to limit access to wild animals.

By the 1470s, these government policies on hunting ground locations collided with the realities of the dynasty's growing human population. As examined in earlier chapters, the expansion and shifting of human settlements in the south – some statistics reporting as high as four million people by the end of the century – and the government's policies heavily promoting agriculture reduced the amount of forested land where wildlife thrived. Humans were now living in closer proximity to these wildlife ranges in the south. This shift impacted animal populations. With Kangmu hunting grounds now located around the capital, overhunting took a toll on the number of animals available. In some areas, prohibiting the hunt in former Kangmu grounds adjacent to farmlands – as well as the decline in the number of predators (including tigers) and wildlife habitat – adversely affected farming as unchecked animal populations damaged crops and consumed grain.³⁵ In other areas, the court took note of the decline in wild animal encounters. More will be said about the decline of animals in later chapters. Mindful of these developments, the court and King Sŏngjong contemplated allowing Kangmu hunting grounds in the north. By 1487, the government expressed its concern about the human population, the expansion of farmlands and the falling animal population. One report noted, 'The commoners say that there are not many birds and beasts in the area, not like there used to be.'³⁶ To compensate for this decline in game, some officials pushed to open up Kangmu hunting grounds in places like Hwanghae Province, northwest of the capital region, where game was plentiful.³⁷ The court noted that traditionally the Kangmu hunts took place only in the three southern provinces, not the north, although earlier officials recognised that the northern part of the dynasty – Hwanghae, P'yŏngan and

---

33 CWS, 3:99.
34 See CWS, 7:431.
35 See CWS, 6:541.
36 CWS, 11:232.
37 CWS, 11:232.

Hamgil (Hamgyŏng, in the northeast) – were 'provinces where wild beasts thrive'.[38] These developments suggest the tug-of-war between the king and officials at the court.

Debates over land and animal access for the military and the royal family extended from discussions about non-elite hunting. Early on in the Chosŏn Dynasty, the court outlawed private hunting on royal lands.[39] This restriction not only reserved the rights to game, it also extended to the culling of trees for firewood and the clearing of grass to make way for agricultural fields.[40] These prohibitions must have been hard to enforce. In 1431, for instance, noting that there were no provisions in the national code to punish poachers (*saryŏp chijoe*; 私獵之罪) on Kangmu lands, the government declared hunting in forbidden parks (*kŭmwŏn*; 禁苑) illegal and a crime punishable with one hundred lashes.[41] However, as the number of Kangmu hunting grounds diminished during the second half of the fifteenth century, the grounds that remained became important instruments of government land policy. During times of hardship, for example, the court permitted commoners access to most of these lands – an exception being the limited number of grounds near the capital, for example the forests of Mt Ach'a, still reserved for the king – to hunt animals and search for firewood.[42] In this way, such government policies served as a check on the Kangmu hunting grounds. The policymakers would open up the lands when necessary to help non-elites during times of hardship and then restrict access to allow the wildlife and wildlands time to recover.

The Kangmu experience varied and often proved challenging for all those involved. While these hunts were sometimes rewarding experiences and vital for military preparation as some argued, they were also potentially dangerous. Horses died and soldiers suffered from the extreme cold – most likely succumbing to hyperthermia and frostbite – sickness and other injuries.[43] Other times, the extra financial costs that soldiers or the state might incur sparked heated debates at the court, often regarding the food required to feed the soldiers and horses; as peasants still had to pay taxes even if the king and troops trampled through the fields, such arguments sometimes resulted in the postponement of an upcoming hunt. At other times the king cancelled the hunt on his own blaming bad weather or a poor harvest as the food provided to the

---

[38] *CWS*, 5:111.
[39] See *CWS*, 1:625.
[40] *CWS*, 3:196.
[41] The king was concerned that this law was too narrow and applied only to palace gardens. See *CWS*, 3:287.
[42] For instance, see *CWS*, 10:261 and 10:322.
[43] For instance, see *CWS*, 11:649.

horses and men increased hunger and hardship on the people. While these matters forced the court to defer the Kangmu from time to time, overlooked was the irony that hardships like these were also an aspect of warfare and prepared the army and taught the leaders and their men to be resourceful. If military and civil officials were aware of these problems, they remained silent or their concerns were unrecorded, throwing into question whether those in power believed the Kangmu hunt really trained for war.

These royal military hunting expeditions on Kangmu lands, with their colourful banners, thousands of troops, hundreds of horses, archers, falconers and boisterous festivities, were visible displays of royal authority and state power that extended from the capital to the boundaries of the peninsula. Kangmu hunting grounds in nearby Kyŏnggi Province were easier for the king to reach and offered quick access to game – the wildlife there had not been overhunted yet – but these areas were also places where *sadaebu* families and merit subjects held land, and it was groups like these that the king most sought to hold in check. Other hunts were farther away. On one Kangmu excursion, King Sŏngjong and a number of soldiers performed several hunts in numerous locations as they moved in and around the capital region, and to other provinces, all of which communicated his royal authority by organising and leading these large gatherings.[44] Hunting grounds were often inundated with military soldiers and personnel from the government. Some of these Kangmu hunts were extensive with thousands of people while others were smaller affairs. Regardless of size, the royal pageantry and display of military force must have intimidated and awed the people who observed it. These Kangmu hunting events were some of the only times commoners and local yangban in these regions interacted with central authority and the kingship. After a Kangmu hunt ended and the officials and the army withdrew, traces of these events remained behind in the Kangmu grounds, such as fewer wild animals after a successful hunt, and in the popular consciousness of those who witnessed them.[45]

In essence, Kangmu lands were the places where the kings and his soldiers went to 'battle' against wild animals. Animals served as moving targets for members of the royal family, his officers and soldiers, which proved more challenging to hit than stationary targets. Strategically flushing out and killing fleeing animals established coordination among units and encouraged soldiers to follow military orders. Of course, this was a one-sided battle,

---

[44] For instance, see CWS, 11:503.
[45] While these royal hunts were impressive spectacles, little if anything is left behind in the popular consciousness about them. One reason for the lack of songs, poetry or fables about these events may be because the state successfully eliminated the hunts early on, and they receded from popular memory.

as the wild animals rarely fought back. They did not typically charge soldiers, nor would they ever regroup, single out and kill leaders, or have any other strategy other than survival. Tactical strategies on the Kangmu hunting grounds were nothing like those the Chosŏn army faced against human enemies. The animals instead became an imaginary, ritualistic enemy, prey carefully depicted in hunting screens such as the *Pictures of Hunting Scenes in the Four Seasons*, created at the beginning of the dynasty.

As did other forms of the royal hunt explored in earlier chapters, the hunting of animals at Kangmu sites shaped a particular kind of masculinity and royal authority. Leaders spent time side by side in the fields with their men, searching for animals, killing them, and then celebrating their kills while transporting and then dressing the carcasses. Bonding this way represented a masculine ideal among all those who took part. The king portrayed the role of a military commander experiencing the hardship of a seemingly formalised battle with his officers and infantry men who, along with the king, 'risked' their lives in this illusionary confrontation against a symbolic enemy. For most of these men, this was the closest to war they would come to for generations. Animals shaped how royalty, elites and common soldiers spent time and saw themselves as protectors of the dynasty.

Rather than arbitrary matters of mere entertainment, the royal Kangmu hunts were serious affairs, as they were for other powers across Eurasia.[46] King T'aejo adopted them, and his sons and grandsons followed his example by continuing the tradition during their subsequent reigns. Through the Kangmu, the king displayed his command over the military. By calling for, planning and holding a Kangmu hunt, the king demonstrated the skills necessary to muster troops, command an army and organise offences, powerful images that reinforced loyalty to him and buttressed the idea that the king was the centre of national security. A king's power extended to animals of the realm. The Kangmu reinforced notions that the king was intimately associated with state ritual as some of the animals killed on these hunts were presented as sacrifices at Confucian state altars. His command of the land, people and animals stretched from the provinces where troops had been mobilised to the capital, where the king, the court and the military leaders gathered. The king also commanded the roads along the way to the Kangmu grounds, the villages and towns the Kangmu troops passed through, and the military training grounds where the Kangmu took place. The king was one of the most visible spectacles

---

[46] Thomas Allison, *The Royal Hunt in Eurasian History* (Philadelphia: University of Pennsylvania Press, 2006), 209–13. For hunts in Ming Dynasty China, see David M. Robinson, *Martial Spectacles of the Ming Court* (Cambridge, MA: Harvard University Press, 2013).

of the Kangmu, but the soldiers, dogs, hawks and horses would have also been an awe-inspiring sight.

Military Encounters on the Hunt: Borders and Barbarians

The prevalence of the royal Kangmu hunts in the fifteenth century paralleled the growing military and ideological needs of an expansionist state. Among other military and political changes to the dynasty in this period, the government sent officials, soldiers and commoners to regions that were sparsely populated or contested by non-Chosŏn people (Jurchen, Chinese and Japanese) that brought Koreans into conflict with foreigners over access to animals in hunting grounds. The expansion of the Chosŏn frontier northward and along the coast and islands of the peninsula began solidifying state control over these lands, yet this development generated tensions over food, territory and other resources.[47] On top of these, the cooling of the Little Ice Age and shifting climate patterns discussed in Chapter 3 created additional challenges in the northern regions of the peninsula because of its high altitude, less predictable growing season, and many rivers and streams that served as demarcation between Chosŏn and non-Chosŏn lands had begun to freeze over or run dry.

The habitats in these peripheral spaces offered ample opportunities to hunt game. The northern forests and mountains had diverse ecosystems that supported a wide variety of animal species, including large ungulates such as elk and moose. Since farming was a marginal practice at best in these northern regions, food was scarce relative to the south. That was especially true during the winter months. The region was well known then and now for its harsh climate and heavy snowfall.[48] Temperatures often drop well below freezing for several months during the year. People new to these areas, such as Chosŏn soldiers and farmers who had moved in from the south, or criminals and their

---

[47] Access to ginseng, for instance, concerned the Chosŏn and the Ming. See Soyoung Suh, *Naming the Local: Medicine, Language, and Identity in Korea since the Fifteenth Century* (Cambridge, MA: Harvard University Press, 2017).

[48] This region is well known for its extremely cold winters and high wind chill factors. During the Korean War, Korean, Chinese, US and UN military troops suffered from frostbite and hypothermia during the winters of 1950 and 1951. For the US experience, see Andrew Hall, Kendrix Evans and Shea Pribyl, 'Cold Injuries in the United States Military Population: Current Trends and Comparison with Past Conflicts', *Journal of Surgical Education* 67, no. 2 (2010): 61–5. For more on the casualties from the harsh weather, see Richard Peters and Xiaobing Li, *Voices from the Korean War: Personal Stories of American, Korean, and Chinese Soldiers* (Lexington: University of Kentucky Press, 2014), 117–24.

families forcibly settled here, must have experienced hardships. *Ondol*, wood-fed heated floors, originated in the area and remained a vital custom to help overcome the frigid winters. Animal furs, including deer, fox and sable, were important attire. Firewood for the *ondol* heating system and animals for meat and clothing came from the surrounding mountains. Coastal islands along the southern part of the peninsula and coastal mountain ranges isolated from farming villages were generally more difficult to reach and subsequently were places where wildlife thrived. Yet, these peripheral regions were also dangerous. They became sites of conflict between hunters. When groups travelled to these places to hunt, they encountered each other and fought over resources. Animals were the catalyst that brought together opposing groups. Drawn to these areas because of the high density of deer or sable, many people travelled to hunt. These hunting parties took great risks entering wilderness areas for potential food and profit. The risk was great, but the chance of reward was just as high.

Hunting in these extreme conditions demanded new tactics and techniques. Whether Chosŏn or Jurchen, hunts in these regions appear well organised. They included numerous people, sometimes Chosŏn military squads or Jurchen hunting parties. Regardless of size, parties with more hunters held greater advantage over smaller units, pairs or individual hunters, whether over animals or other humans. A group of hunters would work together as a team of both beaters and archers, some would flush out game while others would ready their bows for a clear shot. A bigger group ensured a wider range of hunting talent among the party – but could also produce more noise and scare away the chase. Some, like the Jurchen in the north, were skilled hunters and were familiar with the terrain. These skills and experience promised a greater kill ratio. Hunting together in groups also guaranteed assistance for hauling game to the camp. All parts of the deer were most likely used, so the entire carcass – sometimes too heavy for one individual to carry – could be moved quickly with help of several men. Transporting game quickly from the kill sites was vital, for instance when hunting in buffer zones or territories that were contested. Hunting in the outer edges of the Chosŏn frontier risked assaults by the Jurchen and the Japanese; predators, such as tigers, were a threat when the distance was great and the load heavy. Groups could collect and transport game more efficiently and ensure success. Of all the animals hunted in these regions, ungulates were the most vital. Venison offered the highest amount of protein. A harvested elk from Mt Paekdu could feed a family throughout the winter. Animals killed in the cooler climates of the north could be processed before bacterial growth spoiled the meat.[49] Under these winter-like conditions, game could be processed slowly once carried back to camp. Given these payoffs, it is understandable why humans ventured far into the field.

Throughout these contested areas, the state grew more anxious over encounters with Japanese raiders in the south and Jurchen tribes in the north. King Sejong's 1419 military attack on Tsushima Island suppressed Japanese piracy for the most part, but some marauders continued to appear along Korea's southern shores and islands. Many of these Japanese were hunting the same game as Korean soldiers. Along the islands and coasts of the peninsula, areas with high animal density, the risk of unfriendly encounters was great. In one incident, local Chosŏn troops were illegally hunting in Chŏlla Province for several days after which they stumbled upon a group of Japanese raiders (*waejŏk*; 倭賊) who killed one Chosŏn soldier. The Chŏlla naval commander punished his troops.[50] A report from Cheju Island in 1478 describes an incident when another group of Chosŏn soldiers sent to hunt on a nearby island were ambushed by Japanese pirates. Many of the soldiers were killed.[51] In the spring of 1486, a group of Japanese marauders clashed with a dozen soldiers hunting on Haedo Island.[52] Officials complained that despite the government forces, these Japanese were able to fish and hunt freely in places like Mijo harbour (彌助項鎭) located on the southern tip of Namhae county.[53]

These types of encounters were more frequent and more dangerous in the north given the terrain, weather, distance from the capital and the number of Chosŏn (those who spoke Korean) and non-Chosŏn people who moved around the region. In the early decades of the fifteenth century, the dynasty secured lands in the north that had been under direct Mongol control. As pointed out earlier, the Mongol retreat opened up competition among groups in Manchuria and northern Korea, a region the Jurchen tribes still occupied. From the perspective of Chosŏn, these tribes threatened control of the north as the Jurchen conducted frequent raids across the new frontier. The Chosŏn policy was to overpower the Jurchen with troops or quiet them with bribes and merit titles. Some officials even asked them to resettle in Chosŏn. During the 1440s, after moving Korean settlers from the south into the area, the central government, under King Sejong, launched a number of military strikes along

---

[49] Temperatures below 10°Celsius (50°F) are ideal. The cold temperature and high elevation of the north delay the spoilage of the kill. See Dennis Austin, *Mule Deer* (Logan: Utah State University Press, 2010).
[50] *CWS*, 8:515 and 8:538.
[51] *CWS*, 9:564.
[52] *CWS*, 11:157.
[53] *CWS*, 11:333.

the frontier to control the violent incursions across the Yalu River, hoping to repeat the successes Korea had had against the Japanese earlier by attacking Tsushima. Partly successful, Chosŏn established garrisons in the region and below the Tumen River to protect these new northern expansions.[54] To further defend the new frontier and demarcate the line between Chosŏn and non-Chosŏn, the dynasty linked these forts to form defences.[55] Hand in hand with the military presence, the court's policy was to open land to cultivation where possible. By 1485, three islands in the Yalu River were under cultivation by Chosŏn commoners from nearby Ŭiju. Though the court had recognised the difficulty defending the peasants on the islands, some officials insisted that these islands had been cleared of woodlands and under cultivation since the founding of the dynasty, and hence demanded they be reinforced with fortresses.[56]

Chosŏn expansion north encroached upon Jurchen traditional hunting grounds and Jurchen tribes that had lived in the region for generations but now fell nominally under Korean control. Rather than uninhabited, these islands in the Yalu River and lands in the north were places where Jurchen frequented. Unlike the Chosŏn settlers, the Jurchen had been born and raised in the northern climate and its lifestyle and moved around the area freely, especially in the autumn and winter when the streams and rivers begin to freeze over, making it easier to track animals and find firewood along long-established foraging zones. Some of these tribal groups did not recognise the 'frontiers' of the expanding Chosŏn state. The encroachment of central authority into the north, and the Chosŏn people who resettled into the region, competed with these tribes for game, firewood, ginseng and other resources of the forests and mountains. Sending people and troops north was a tactic meant to dominate these distant areas and bring their people, and the animals of the land, under dynastic authority.

Considering the abundant wildlife in the region, hunting was an attractive activity for everyone involved. This was apparent in many of the court discussions about the region. The court and military voiced their concerns

---

[54] For more on the northeast border, see Kenneth Robinson, 'Residence and Foreign Relations', 18–36.

[55] For more on the Chosŏn Dynasty's northern expansion and relations with the Jurchen, see Ki-baek Yi, *A New History of Korea*, trans. Edward Wagner (Seoul: Ilchokok, 1988); Kenneth Robinson, 'Organizing Japanese and Jurchens in Tribute Systems in Early Chosŏn Korea', *Journal of East Asian Studies* 13, no. 2 (May–August 2013): 337–60; and Adam Bohnet, *Turning toward Edification: Foreigners in Chosŏn Korea* (Honolulu: University of Hawai'i Press, 2020), 24–53.

[56] CWS, 11:67.

about troops spending their time hunting in the north. The army commander of the western P'yŏngan Province Ha Sukpu (?–1501; 河叔溥) left behind a list of orders for the troops responsible for protecting the three-island region of the border town of Ŭiju before he withdrew from his post. Included in his list were orders to stop drinking and hunting and instead remain vigilant and alert at all times of the day. Another demand he listed was to fortify the military in the area.[57] Senior-level military officers such as Ha Sukpu were apprehensive about hunting in areas that were militarily sensitive, most likely because of the fear that hunting distracted soldiers or that they may be injured on hunts or ambushed by the enemy. Another example of the central government trying to curtail the frequency of hunting was the enactment of an important decree in 1476 that stated that the chief military commander was to order all generals to disclose anyone who drank or hunted while on duty.[58]

Moving Chosŏn soldiers and commoners north understandably sparked tensions with Jurchen tribes. In 1472, the border inspector (sunch'alsa; 巡察使) of the remote Yŏngan Province reported a clash with tribal 'thieves' over the governing of people and animals of the region. Chosŏn officials attempted to bribe the Jurchen with horses and animal pelts, which offended them. These groups demanded that the Chosŏn officials return their people and livestock that had, according to the Jurchen, been stolen.[59] In 1473, army commander of western P'yŏngan Province Ha Sukpu held an audience with King Sŏngjong and informed him that the barbarians (yain; 野人) frequently crossed the river with their dogs to hunt. Finding these hunting incursions troublesome, the king demanded that the frontier be prepared to protect the security of the country.[60] Ha Sukpu worried that these foreigners (p'iin; 彼人) crossing the border to hunt might someday invade the dynasty.[61] One envoy returning from the Liaodong Peninsula believed that the enemy had used the excuse of the hunt to spy on conditions south of the frontier.[62]

Most Jurchen groups appear to have been small at first. The P'yŏngan commander reported a group of ten barbarians frequently crossing the border on horseback to hunt.[63] In 1477, a report from the Board of Rites described an encounter with a group of Jurchens in P'yŏngan Province. Fighting over a

---

[57] CWS, 8: 468.
[58] CWS, 9:384.
[59] CWS, 8:683.
[60] CWS, 9:66.
[61] CWS, 9:112.
[62] CWS, 9:222.
[63] CWS, 9:380.

deer that that they had managed to kill by hunting together as a team, a man who was most likely Jurchen from the Uryangkhad (Wuliangha; 兀良哈) tribe shot and killed another from the Sohŏ (C. Suoxu; 所虛) region.[64] At other times, groups of hunters numbering as many as 600 were reported.[65] Such sizeable numbers of armed men constituted a threat to the northern region. In 1480, Governor of P'yŏngan Province Kim Kyo (1428–80; 金嶠) and the Military Commander Sim Han (1436–82; 沈澣) reported to the throne about an incursion of 500 mounted Jurchen from Jianzhou that had crossed the river. The group had claimed they were on a hunting expedition (yuryŏp; 遊獵). The court was very disturbed by this development. King Sŏngjong called on important officials, senior ministers and the Ministry of War to discuss the matter with him. A number of these officials reported details to the king.

> The barbarians say that they are only on a hunting expedition. However, it is possible that they want to look around our country at what is good and bad and take advantage of us. We should fortify the defences of the frontier and dispatch important officials in support . . . to uncover the strength of the enemy.

The king dispatched three officials to the border to learn more about the situation.[66]

In the eyes of the Korean court, these fears appeared justified. In 1482, the court began hearings about the bands of 'barbarians' crossing the Yalu River at the city of Manp'o (滿浦). On one occasion, a group of Korean commoners hunting along the river encountered Jurchen hunters. Both sides exchanged arrows, which resulted in the killing of a few Jurchen men. A number of court reports followed when one of the Jurchen leaders, Shenazhiyingke (Simajiŭngga; 沈阿之應可), sent a message to the court to inquire about the death of his son and injuries of two of his people.[67] His letter (sŏgye; 書契) warned Koreans to stay away. 'You, Koryŏ people, don't come rampaging around our hunting grounds (C. wotianlie zhidi; 我畋獵之地).'[68] Army commander of P'yŏngan Province Yi Kŭkkyun (1437–1504; 李克均) hoped that the king would clarify the government policies about the issue along the border out of concern for

---

[64] *CWS*, 9:553 and 12:37. Uryangkhad was the name of a Jurchen tribe appearing throughout the *CWS*.
[65] *CWS*, 9:401.
[66] *CWS*, 10:159.
[67] *CWS*, 10:382.
[68] *CWS*, 10:403.

national security.⁶⁹ A year later, the Ministry of War addressed the matter of Jurchens crossing the river to hunt. It insisted that they not be allowed to hunt when they come across the river.⁷⁰ The fear was that the Jurchen people coming from across the border could not be trusted. Court officials maintained that 'those people hunt recklessly, and we are afraid they will end up stealing'.⁷¹

Others at the court were more nuanced in their understanding of the nature of these incursions and searched for compromise. The senior scholar official No Sasin (1427–98; 盧思愼) pointed out that hunting animals was necessary for the livelihood of these 'barbarians'. He indicated that their land was not productive for farming, so they crossed the river in search of sustenance.⁷² When one winter was brutal and their farming failed because of bad weather, a group of farmers turned huntsmen crossed the frozen river and camped on the other side to hunt for food.⁷³ Some of these people included the Jurchen leader Choushengyingju (K. Susŭngŭnggŏ; 愁升應巨) who traversed the river to hunt and interacted with Chosŏn officials.⁷⁴ In other words, the northern frontier could be a shared space where people from multiple civilisations might cohabitate, communicate and co-exist.

No Sasin was a lone voice, however, as more called for a zone of exclusion. In 1489, the military commander of Yŏngan Province reported that Jurchen leaders had constructed wooden forts (sisŏng; 柴城) in the Yunch'ong and Hyesan mountains where they were living and hunting. The men had informed the commander that they were living on their own lands. 'We would rather die than be forced to leave,' these Jurchen retorted. Some officials, including Yun P'ilsang (1427–1504; 尹弼商), argued that troops should be mobilised to remove them: 'If they refuse, they should be annihilated.' Whereas Hong Ŭng (1428–92) pointed out that Jurchen hunters had appeared at the same location in the past and had been convinced to relocate to Kangwŏn Province. Officials continued to worry about Jurchen soldiers encroaching into the area under the excuse that they were 'hunting'.⁷⁵

These fears intensified in 1490 when bands of Jurchen continued crossing into territory that Chosŏn had claimed to hold hunting expeditions around the village of Manp'o. To curtail these movements, Chosŏn troops stationed at Manp'o crossed the river to the north and launched a night-time raid,

---

⁶⁹ CWS, 10:403.
⁷⁰ CWS, 10:455.
⁷¹ CWS, 10:461.
⁷² CWS, 10:622.
⁷³ CWS, 10:631.
⁷⁴ CWS, 10:622.
⁷⁵ CWS, 11:484.

without the consent of Hanyang, killing several Jurchen. Disturbed by the potential fallout of the incident, the court considered punishing the soldiers. The king believed that it was not an arbitrary decision by a few men, but rather a policy planned by the military and civilian leaders of the province. He felt that news of the attack had been leaked by people who had not taken part in the matter.[76] Here, the problem was not just the threat of possible Jurchen retaliation, but equally as problematic was the breakdown of discipline and control demonstrated by local Chosŏn commanders and their soldiers. Military action should not be taken without the approval of the king.

In the discussion that followed the event, officials reiterated that at the time of King Sejo, magistrate of the town of Ŭiju U Kong (1415–73; 禹貢) and two military officers led a group north across the Yalu River to hunt illegally. Because the soldiers they led were captured by Jurchens, these military officials were imprisoned, interrogated and set to be executed. King Sejo intervened and reduced their sentences. The two men went on to help suppress rebellions in Hamgyŏng Province in 1467 and 1470 led by Yi Siae (?–1467; 李施愛), a local military commander who rose up against the central government, thus atoning for their crimes of violating the ban against searching for animals across the border. But this time, Magistrate Chŏn Hyosang (?–?; 全孝常) reported that the Jurchen had crossed the river and sacked the defensive fortress. Some court officials went on to argue that the commanders must be executed, not for the river crossing but because of their negligence in protecting the fortress from the Jurchens.[77]

The situation escalated. In the spring of 1491, the court received word that roughly 1,500 Jurchen soldiers led by several Jurchen leaders were gathering across the Yalu River in what appeared to be a military strike against Manp'o. Under the pretense of hunting, 300 troops were making their way south along the river. Some of these 'raiders', officials speculated, might besiege Manp'o's fortress, while others might move south to assault the village of Kanggye (江界). A defensive strategy included the movement of troops over frozen rivers. Officials feared that many Jurchen soldiers could move around P'yŏngan Province easily because the rivers had begun freezing over, but they believed the Chosŏn troops could also use this to their advantage and destroy the enemy. Other officials argued that 100 'brave troops' must be quickly mobilised and dispatched along three different routes.[78] This strategy was likely suggested as a means to reinforce local garrisons. Some of the troops attempted to cross to

[76] CWS, 11:683.
[77] CWS, 12:15.
[78] CWS, 11:693 and 12:59.

the south, but the river had not frozen over. The local commander Kim Yunje (?–?; 金允濟) was therefore unable to force the Jurchen hunting party out of the area.[79]

The court debated this issue over a number of days in the autumn of 1491. The military commander of P'yŏngan Province O Sun (?–?; 吳純) wrote that the country had not specifically prohibited hunting along the frontier. However, 'these people were akin to groups of dogs and rats (*kusŏ chido*; 狗鼠之徒) and because they take advantage of the king, they and their livestock should be killed and plundered'. He urgently advised the king to dispatch troops to interrogate the Jurchen for their crimes. The king supported these and other measures against the Jurchen.[80] Rumours of an imminent Jurchen raid reached the court within days.

One of the Jurchen leaders, Wudiha (Ulchŏkhap; 兀狄哈), and 150 of his men were hunting when some were killed by a person from Chosŏn. They all moved to a mountain encampment, along with their wives and children. The Jurchen mobilised 3,000 soldiers in an effort to kidnap the Chosŏn envoy travelling to Ming territory to pay respects on New Year's Day. There were also rumours that the Jurchen leader Buhuatu (K. Pokhwatok; 卜花禿) and three others were gathering 1,000 men and horses to invade Chosŏn.

To counter this attack, the military commander of the northwestern territory (*sŏbungmyŏn towŏnsu*; 西北面都元帥) Yi Kŭkyun (1437–1504; 李克均) called for the rapid deployment of 1,500 troops to punish and kill them.[81] Some of the reports also originated from Ming Chinese officials who had travelled to P'yŏngan Province to warn the military commander about a planned Jurchen raid on the village of Ŭiji. They also informed Yi that they were going to intercept the Jurchen. The Ming officer relayed that the Jurchen leader had hinted that the reason for the raid was because Chosŏn soldiers had murdered 'our innocent hunters' (*amujoe chŏllyŏbin*; 我無罪田獵人).[82] The court and the commanders termed this a 'punitive northern strike' (*pukchŏn*; 北征). After the attack, the court initially received a report that the general had fared poorly and that there were many casualties on the Korean side. However, the Chosŏn commander reported that there had been no casualties from fighting in the Jurchen territory, but rather only the occasional death caused from an outbreak of disease inside the country.[83]

---

[79] CWS, 12:4.
[80] CWS, 12:102.
[81] CWS, 12:106.
[82] CWS, 12:119.
[83] CWS, 12:176.

These punitive strikes against the Jurchen, however, found some success. By 1493, some of the Jurchen leaders along the disputed frontier had been captured and beheaded at Kosalli (高山里), south of P'yŏngyang. Pressed by these Chosŏn victories, Jurchen leadership performed a ritual over a slain ox, promising, 'We will not be the cause of another dispute with Chosŏn, and we eternally pledge allegiance to you.' The military commander of P'yŏngan Province believed this resolved the dispute over the Jurchen crossing the Yalu River to hunt in Chosŏn territory. The king, however, seemed mindful of an immediate Jurchen assault after he inquired about the water level of the Yalu, wondering if they could cross the river over the ice. In response, the court ordered that wooden barricades be constructed along the river to prevent future Jurchen incursions. All of these efforts to fortify the frontier pleased the king.[84]

The border issue was still under discussion in the spring; hunting ground access in exchange for Jurchen allegiance in the lands located south of the Yalu River was now the subject of debate. Jurchens who travelled to Manp'o spoke of the murder of other Jurchens. They felt unsure as to whether they could accept the formally declared allegiance or having to send their envoy to the capital Hanyang. In his discussion with the king, the scholar official Yun P'ilsang insisted that the Jurchen not be allowed to cross the mountain frontier to hunt. Anxiety once again permeated the court when officials repeated their concerns that the Jurchen were not hunting but rather sending scouts into Chosŏn to probe the area and learn military information. Others thought that by allowing them into the Sandan Island (山丹) area to hunt was unavoidable. The Jurchen homeland was only a day's journey away from Sandan, across the Yalu River, where they appeared desperate to seek permission to hunt. They should be told to 'accept their surrender and allegiance (*kwisun*; 歸順) in order to receive permission'. Only then could both sides sincerely trust each other. The king supported this view.[85]

For those Jurchen permitted into the peninsula, court officials pondered what to do with the Jurchen hunters who appeared along the shore with 'bows and arrows', who apparently intended to travel onward to Hanyang for diplomacy. Considering their hunting lifestyle, should they be allowed to carry their bows and arrows? Officials declared that, while a Jurchen custom, these hunters could not display their weapons in the country based on Korean precedent.[86] Only soldiers were permitted to carry weapons, not hunters. The

---

[84] *CWS*, 12:284.
[85] *CWS*, 12:298.
[86] *CWS*, 12:592.

outward displays of Jurchen identity, in this case their hunting weapons, also conflicted with official laws that regulated the display of weapons.

Why did the court spend so much time and energy on the issue of hunting in the north? Many concerned officials, including those from China, considered hunting along the frontiers a matter of national security. In 1494, the court received a report about Ming Chief Military Officer Luo Xiong (?–?; 羅雄) via an envoy returning from Ming land. 'The people of your country from upstream frequently hunt outside the river. The land across the river is all our territory.' In other words, the Ming were laying claim to the side of the Yalu River on which people from Chosŏn were hunting. Similar to how Chosŏn officials had accused the Jurchens of trespassing, the Ming were doing the same to Korea. Further, Luo wanted all Koreans who were captured while hunting by the Jurchens returned but was not sure how to assist the Chosŏn soldiers. Luo called for the Chosŏn king to order the dispatch of a senior-level official to deal with Koreans trespassing on land the Ming claimed. This angered King Sŏngjong and he pointed to the U Kong incident when two Chosŏn officers went hunting on the three islands where they encountered Jurchen 'hunters' and defeated them. Sŏngjong argued that the military situation of Chosŏn had not changed since the event. He called for the county magistrate to be interrogated about this issue regarding Luo and his accusation of Chosŏn people hunting on Ming lands.[87] The king was angry that Luo's report disparaged Chosŏn by assuming the dynasty's military was incapable of defending the country against Jurchen hunting parties. The court took the report about the situation along the Yalu River under advisement but wanted to gather more information about the accusation of illegal hunting across the river from Luo Xiong's reports before taking action. They hoped they could prevent hunting along the river because the rules were strict. The law codes of the country held a section on forbidden activities (*kŭmjang*; 禁章) that included hunting along the river frontiers. As such, if someone were to hunt there, they would be subject to punishment. But after hearing of Luo's experience, the court learned that sometimes people were sidestepping these laws and crossing the river anyway.[88]

Other elite and non-elite Koreans were captured too. The Magistrate of Ŭiju Ku Kyŏm (?–?; 具謙) and the five soldiers who accompanied him were interrogated for crossing over the Yalu River, but they refused to confess to hunting.[89] The court believed that Luo Xiong held a grudge against the

---

[87] *CWS*, 12:578 and 12:587.
[88] *CWS*, 12:587.
[89] *CWS*, 12:601.

people of Chosŏn hunting and fishing in the region.[90] Because of this resentment, some felt that the investigation and punishment of those involved were enough to placate Luo. Senior scholar official No Sasin, again displaying a nuanced interpretation of the borderland, argued that the Ming had voiced their want to treat Chosŏn as one family, so there was nothing peculiar about someone from Chosŏn crossing the river to hunt. No Sasin maintained that Chosŏn should have the freedom to cross the river to monitor the Jurchen. Of course, crossing the river into lands outside of Chosŏn boundaries was a serious offence in the eyes of the central government. Crossing the river in rare situations – such as in pursuit of a tiger – was inevitable, Luo and the Korean court agreed, but in most cases, there was no justification for stepping outside of Chosŏn lands. In reality, however it appears that border crossings in search of game were a frequent activity for people throughout the region. Chosŏn soldiers, waiting to meet Chinese envoys, occasionally encountered Chinese-speaking people hunting in the area on the other side of the river. It seems like all sides hunted in illegal territories. The king wished to put aside the situation and passed another decree banning local hunters from crossing the river.[91] Like many decrees before, these prohibitions, promulgated from the distant capital, appeared to have little immediate impact.

* * *

The fifteenth-century Chosŏn push northward into regions with a small but diverse population of people ignited debates at many levels of the government over how to respond to the new challenges this push unleashed. Borderlands in the north were contested spaces where the protein and fur of animals brought people from different regions, languages and lifestyles together. This became significantly truer in the fifteenth century when the Little Ice Age induced climate change in Northeast Asia. Rainfall patterns shifted, drying up watersheds along the frontier at times and causing earlier and more frequent freezing of rivers and streams from late autumn into early spring. Shorter growing seasons destabilised agriculture in the north, pushing Jurchens south across these frozen waters to hunt, many Jurchens colliding with Chosŏn people also trying to survive in the north. These locations, at the limits of central authority, were too distant from the capital and were never considered for royal military Kangmu hunting sites. Nor were local soldiers encouraged to hunt in the mountains and forests because of the dangers such

[90] CWS, 12:592.
[91] CWS, 12:601.

unfamiliar landscapes held from predators and Jurchen hunters who knew the terrain much better and who pursued the same game. Military reforms of the century, including a heightened interest in the royal military Kangmu hunt, appear to have succeeded. They provided the government with the logistical and tactical knowledge it needed to calm the borderland frontiers, even if momentarily. Through a balance of diplomacy, trade and military affairs, the Chosŏn people engaged with Jurchens and even the Japanese who frequented the Korean peninsula to hunt for animals.

6
Challenges to the Royal Military Kangmu Hunt

A herd of deer grazed in a rugged forest in north central Kangwŏn Province in the middle of the peninsula. Within the herd was a single white stag. This was a rare experience in the fifteenth century as it is now.[1] While striking in appearance, appreciated for their beauty, and awed for their near-mystical appearance, this colour aberration put at risk animals like this one. Most likely these deer experienced a form of piebaldism or leucism. Piebaldism, or the absence of pigmentation, produces a patchy white fur, while leucism, a more extreme form of piebaldism produces a total lack of pigmentation, turning the animal pure white. Both conditions leave the eyes and noses black. Another possibility was albinism, a much rarer condition, which results in a lack of pigmentation throughout the entire body including the skin and fur as well as the eyes, ears and nose. Piebald and albino deer have shorter lifespans. They experience genetic deformities, such as shortened appendages, that could place them at a disadvantage, and they sometimes suffer rejection from the herd or potential mates.[2] Lacking camouflage, they are unable to blend into the forest and stand out, becoming easier prey. To underscore this, a single arrow shot through the air from above, struck the deer, downing it, as the others in the herd darted away, escaping into the forest.

It was in 1442 when a white stag was slain on a royal military Kangmu hunt. King Sejong had travelled to P'yŏnggang, Kangwŏn Province to participate in

---

[1] The number of white deer recorded in the *Sillok* expanded during the late fifteenth century, most likely as more human-animal encounters occurred and the state became more adept at extracting wild animals from the northern provinces. Their numbers rapidly declined after the 1520s. This was probably due to over hunting which, in turn, reduced or eliminated deer with piebald or albinism from the gene pool.

[2] For more, see Anil Mahabal, *et al.*, 'Colour Aberrations in Indian Mammals: A Review from 1886–2017', *Journal of Threatened Taxa* 11, no. 6 (2019): 13690–719.

this Kangmu hunt. He had spotted the white stag (*paengnok*; 白鹿) in a herd of deer. His royal relatives (*chongch'in*; 宗親) and the soldiers had seen the deer too. Everyone wanted to be the one to capture the magical beast.

Sejong's son, Prince Chinyang (1417–68; 晉陽大君), the future King Sejo, told the official in charge of the royal palanquin, 'Even though a hundred men desire it, it will only die by my hand. Just keep your eyes on me!' From an elevated area, Prince Chinyang (King Sejo), true to his word, unleashed arrows, striking and killing the deer. That evening, King Sejong commented to the soldiers,

'With one whip of his horse, [my second son and future King Sejo] Prince Chinyang can kill ten beasts. Yi Im (1427–45; 平原大君 李琳) – Prince P'yŏngwŏn – and Prince Kŭmsŏng (錦城) Yi Yu (1426–57; 李瑜) – can kill five or six. [Whereas] it takes the hands of three men to bring down one of the animals inside the hunting range (*winae chisu*; 圍內之獸). The purpose of training the soldiers on the military hunt is to make them unleash their arrows at these [animals], isn't it?'[3]

Everyone present said, 'The troops cross the many mountains and streams and the sound of the beating drums (*kŭmko*; 金鼓) gather them together: these are what the royal military Kangmu hunt mean. There are ferocious beasts and fleeing deer (*illok*; 逸鹿). Why do we worry about not carrying out the Kangmu?' While travelling with them, the Mongol envoy Tongluo Songjie (童羅松介) observed Prince Chinyang [King Sejo]'s divine martial prowess (*sinmu*; 神武), knelt before him, and exclaimed, 'Indeed, our Noyan (Nayan; 那衍), our Great Lord![4] If you, Prince, were in our lands, then you would truly be Batu Khan (拔都) [The great khan of the Golden Horde 1205–55; in other words, a powerful ruler and uniter].'

Prince Chinyang [King Sejo] simply smiled and asked, 'You have already heard of me?' Tongluo Songjie replied, 'Among the people of our lands, who does not know you?' Upon this, the barbarian praised the prince, 'You, Prince Chinyang, are a great tiger (*taeho*; 大虎)!' Tongluo Songjie gingerly picked up the prince's bow and tried to pull back the string. He was unable to do it and greatly admired the prince. The people who saw the hunting party returning to the capital [Hanyang] said certainly, '[Prince Chinyang (King Sejo)] is but only one man (*ilin ii*; 一人而已)! He will always be called "Batu Khan".'

---

[3] CWS, 7:56.
[4] An in-text reference in the *Sillok* notes that 'Nayan' is a Mongolian expression for commander-in-chief. CWS, 7:56.

Later, King Sejong bestowed his son [Prince Chinyang (King Sejo)] with two powerful bows. Because Pak Sŏngnyang (?–?; 朴成良) was the only soldier strong enough to draw these bows on his own, the weapons were humorously coined 'Useless great antlers!' (muyong taegak; 無用大角) [the bows were sizable, curved like antlers, and difficult to handle easily]. Prince Chinyang always shot his bow from horseback. One day, Prince Chinyang mistakenly used an inferior bow and shot an arrow, his brother Prince Kwangp'yŏng Yi Ŏ (1425–44; 廣平 李璵) saw him, and sighed in admiration: 'That bow is no good, so why is the arrow so fast?' Prince Chinyang smiled and replied,

'Those who are good at books do not select the brush. Those who are good at the bow do not select the flute. [In other words, people have unique talents, some are made for study, others for calligraphy or music, and then there are those who are talented at hunting] Those good at instructions are not choosy about people. A Confucian gentleman (kunja; 君子) acts with benevolence regardless of the place. Determined ministers act with loyalty regardless of the time.'[5]

Prince Kwangp'yŏng simply replied, this is 'good indeed'.

Stories like these are telling in several ways. Beasts such as the white stag and other animals drew Korean royalty and soldiers to royal military Kangmu hunting grounds where kings spent time in the wilderness bonding with family members and non-scholar class soldiers. Through the comings and goings of the royal military Kangmu hunts, elites, such as the future King Sejo, impressed all those watching when he drew his huge, transcendent bow. The Kangmu hunt, sometimes attended by foreign soldiers and officials, served as a means to strengthen the northern borders. Inviting Mongol and Jurchen envoys to witness and, at times, participate in these events allowed the Chosŏn elites to impress the outsiders with the martial skills of Chosŏn kings, their kin and their soldiers. This appears to have been done with the purpose of pacifying these northern neighbours. To the Mongols and Jurchen, the Prince (King Sejo) was equal to Batu Khan, the great khan of the Golden Horde from the Mongol Empire, a leader who required the utmost respect, and this must have curried favour with the Korean court. Strengthening this relationship was another way to prevent – or at least keep an eye on – potential threats from across the northern frontier. Ostensibly used to train the soldiers, royalty also used the Kangmu as a stage upon which to boast about their martial skills and brag over the number of their kills. Upper body and hand strength, which

[5] CWS, 7:56.

is necessary to pull back powerful bows, and the dexterity needed to properly handle them while riding on horseback – represented the masculine ideal, one that intimidated some officials excluded from these trips.

This chapter examines the rising challenges and obstacles to the royal military Kangmu hunts in the fifteenth century. As will be seen, some of these obstacles were climate related, but others were a backlash to the very successes of the Kangmu. The royal military Kangmu hunts fostered the power of masculinity where hunting acumen and physical strength dominated the enemy and animals. Here too were moments when the royal family tapped into a Chinggisid legacy (connected to the family of Chinggis Khan), and legitimised their rulership in the present over domestic control and foreign relations. However, such ideals clashed with the ideological rhetoric of officials around the king who began negotiating the boundaries of royal authority. A rising number of voices inside the government believed that the proximity to animals, domestic and wild, was incompatible with rulership. Neo-Confucian officials did not understand animals, nor were they privy to the training necessary to kill them. This lack of authority over the hunt and wildlife bothered them and, as I argue in this chapter, they wished to limit royal access to wildlife.

Contesting the Royal Military Hunt in the Late Fifteenth Century

The struggle over the involvement of the kingship in the royal military hunt was, on one level, a struggle over power and legitimacy. The successful involvement of kings in the Kangmu, as demonstrated above with King Sejong and his sons, drove bureaucratic resistance. As the generations of kings who held direct connections to the dynasty's founder and later kings passed away, subsequent generations pursued ways to solidify their royal authority. Harnessing the power and prestige of the Kangmu hunt and the royal involvement with the military proved effective. To the kings of the fifteenth century, participation in the Kangmu was a vital part of royal and elite identity that harkened back to a past glory when hunting displayed wealth, power and masculinity.

As discussed in earlier chapters, over the thirteenth century and into the fifteenth century, kings battled for legitimacy in multiple ways, and the hunt became one of the significant displays in which these Korean leaders sought to secure their places in power. This form of validation started around the 1270s, when Koryŏ kings began to depend on the spectacle of hunting as an important symbol of their political legitimacy. When members of the royal family reached their teen years, they were allowed to join in the hunts. As we have seen, with the decline of Mongol power in China during the 1350s, Koryŏ rulers reasserted their royal authority over an increasingly aggressive Confucian bureaucracy by utilising the visual and material power of the hunt.

Like rulers elsewhere, Korean kings did not go unchallenged.[6] Competing interests in the court tried to curtail the ability of kings to make decisions independent of the bureaucracy. This happened in one of two ways: remonstration by officials or, in extreme cases, bureaucrats would authorise the ousting and banishment or even the assassination of kings. At the beginning of the Chosŏn Dynasty, ruling elites in the court introduced laws that set in motion a struggle over power. Maintaining balance with the king allowed these elites to acquire and remain in positions of political and economic import for themselves and their clans.[7]

Challenges from the court officials over the royal military Kangmu grew more acute in the mid-fifteenth century because of institutional reforms in the central government, especially regarding the kingship. A major part of this institutional control over the king was the royal lecture. In these lectures, tutors and top officials of the central government sat with the king and held conversations with him on the classics, history and current events. By the end of the century, these lectures were sometimes held multiple times a day and instructed the king on the ethics of good governance. The impact of these royal lectures waxed and waned over the century, but reforms under King Sejong strengthened the lectures.[8] In many ways, these royal lectures balanced political power with the king. Through remonstrations and royal lectures, officials sought to restrict the king's actions by offering him advice and criticism. Lectures and other audiences with the king at court mirrored the royal military hunt – both were forums where participants interacted with the king and often influenced his behaviour. However, they obviously differed in the types of experiences and lessons learned and, even more, the royal Kangmu hunts empowered the king to directly rule a wider number of people. By isolating the king and holding his ear throughout the day, court bureaucrats endeavoured to correct what they considered inappropriate behaviour.

---

[6] 'The fifteenth-century [English] king was not free to rule as he chose.' Michael Hicks, *English Political Culture in the Fifteenth Century* (London: Routledge, 2002), 36.

[7] While scholars understandably accuse kings such as Sejo and Yŏnsan'gun of being 'despotic' or 'disastrous', I argue that they were pushing back against the Confucian officials' attempt to delegitimise royal authority. See Deuchler, *The Confucian Transformation of Korea*, 249, 299.

[8] Yŏnung Kwŏn, 'The Royal Lecture and Confucian Politics in early Yi Korea', *Korean Studies* 6 (1982): 44–5, 55.

For many, but not all, of these officials, this meant a kingship stripped of a direct military engagement. Authority and prestige were derived from learning and Neo-Confucian morality and ethics not through martial skills. In 1455, for instance, scholar official Yang Sŏngji (1415–82; 梁誠之) submitted a petition demanding the disbandment of the Kangmu hunting grounds in Kangwŏn Province. Quoting examples from China's past, he feared hunting would lead to the downfall of the state. In antiquity, Yang argued, the Liao Dynasty (916–1125) had collapsed because of the royal family's use of falcons and hunting dogs (*ŭnggyŏn*; 鷹犬). In other words, the leaders had spent too much of their time away from the court entertaining themselves with the hunt rather than tending to the affairs of the country. When a ruler behaved in ways court officials found to undermine their authority, officials would cite examples from the ancient sage kings of Chinese antiquity and pick and choose precedence from Koryŏ and early Chosŏn rulers to 'correct' the king's behaviour. The downgrading of the Kangmu was not inevitable. While many voices among these concerned officials hoped to remove the king from the Kangmu hunt, as will be seen, not all of them supported this move. Others argued for a dual role of the kingship where legitimacy would be also derived from the king's participation in both martial and scholarly matters.

In the late fifteenth century, conflict over the royal Kangmu hunts remained unresolved during the reign of King Sŏngjong. In King Sŏngjong's epitaph composed following his death, Confucian officials extolled the moral nature of his rulership. 'King Sŏngjong read Confucian books in the evenings. He knew only two things: the brush and the arrow. He enjoyed his falcons and hounds, but he did not believe they were frivolous entertainment.'[9] In this hagiographic re-imagining of Sŏngjong's values, activities such as hunting are aptly noted, yet writers felt compelled to defend Sŏngjong's penchant for hunting not as entertainment but as equal to his scholarly endeavours. This was a misrepresentation. In the spirit of his ancestors, Sŏngjong was an avid hunter who frequently took part in all kinds of hunting expeditions great and small, including royal military Kangmu hunts.

King Sŏngjong was only twelve years old when he took the throne and was too young to rule. As noted earlier, in his stead, Queen Chŏnghŭi wanghu – Sŏngjong's grandmother who selected Sŏngjong as king – and Queen Dowager Insu Sohye wanghu – Sŏngjong's mother and wife of the former Prince Tŏkchong (1438–57; 德宗), Sŏngjong's father [Prince Tŏkchong was the grandson of King Sejong and son of King Sejo] – governed Chosŏn from 1469 until 1476 when Sŏngjong turned nineteen and came of age.

[9] *CWS*, 12:262.

Queen Chŏnghŭi and Queen Dowager Insu, during Sŏngjong's early years, made important state decisions for the young king, including those involving animals. The tensions between Confucian sacrificial protocol and Queen Dowager Insu's personal Buddhist beliefs collided during her rule. Unlike the Mongol era, when the Mongol queen, Queen Cheguk, of the first Koryŏ king, King Ch'ungnyŏl (who married into the Yuan imperial family) took part in the hunt, these Chosŏn women who obtained power through their sons and grandsons, which happened on occasion in Korea, had to balance their personal views on faith (here, the killing of animals) with the need to carry out state ritual and tax policies.

This clash demonstrates the contradiction present at the time in Confucian policies. While fully engaged in politics and governance, the senior women of the royal court held power during a time when the male Confucian bureaucracy adopted Neo-Confucian laws and family practices that reduced the economic and social abilities for elite women in the dynasty. However, the most senior females of the court served as regents for young kings when the new kings were deemed too young to rule, a demonstration of matrilineal power, a holdover from traditional Korean and Northeast Asian practices that remained policy until the end of the Chosŏn Dynasty in 1910. These women, like King Sŏngjong's royal Confucian advisers, hoped to convince their young charge of the improprieties present in the act of hunting. Conversations Sŏngjong had with his mother and grandmother over his involvement in hunting have been lost. But these senior females, now the most powerful women in the country, were navigating the affairs of a Confucian state that sanctified the killing of animals.

Sŏngjong planned and attended a number of military Kangmu hunts. In 1475, he postponed one previous Kangmu circle hunt because of heavy rain. He expressed concern about the hunt and wished to cancel it the following day. However, Sŏngjong worried that if a military campaign broke out, the troops would be unprepared because they had not honed their skills during the Kangmu. Calling on the precedence of King T'aejo, the court officials respectfully pointed out that the founder had never postponed a spring or autumn hunting exercise. However, the officials agreed with King Sŏngjong that the hunt should be delayed.[10] Division Commander of the Right (Usang taejang; 右廂大將) Yi Ch'ŏlkyŏn (1435–96; 李鐵堅) questioned the appropriateness of the location for the event. The circle Kangmu hunt was to be held at Mt Sŏnjang (仙場山) where 20,000 or 30,000 troops were to be

---

[10] CWS, 9:275.

mobilised in order to take part. The animals, hearing the sounds of the beating drums and horns, had scattered. Because of this, Yi argued, there would be no game to hunt. He suggested that the hunt be moved to Mt Hyoil (曉日山), roughly thirty kilometres (20 mi.) southeast of the royal palace, instead. The king reminded Yi that the purpose of the expedition was for military training and 'not for hunting'. The distance to Mt Sŏnjang made a return trip there to the field camp (*p'aoda*; 波吾達), roughly twenty kilometres (13 mi.) southeast of the royal palace, easier. Military commander Yi Ch'ŏlkyŏn emphasised the hunting aspect of the trip. While King Sŏngjong enjoyed hunting, he appeared to be more mindful of time spent away from the capital and appreciated the ease of transportation to the Kangmu hunting grounds for himself and other royal family members who joined him.

On the autumn campaign, the king wished to hold the expedition near the gravesite burial mound of Yi Yong (1418–53; 安平大君 李瑢), Prince Anp'yŏng (King Sejong's third son). While there, they bagged twenty-two roe deer (*chang*), sika or other deer (*nok*), and other miscellaneous animals.[11] The next day, while hunting on the Sŏnjang and Hyoil mountains, one tiger and thirty-six roe deer, sika deer, and other miscellaneous animals were collected.[12]

Kangmu such as these highlighted the clash between military and Confucian customs. King Sŏngjong insisted on hunting at the royal tombs (Kwangnŭng), but Inspector Kim Chesin (1438–99; 金悌臣) protested, 'This is inappropriate for a monarch, so please stop hunting.' Kim went on to argue that the distance was too far to traverse before dark. The king, confused, looked around and pondered, 'In the past, Emperor Wu of the Han Dynasty is said to have gone on processions at night. The gatekeeper did not let him in [in other words, the emperor did not return in time before the city gate was locked]. This was because of hunting. I am not trying to do this [spend all my time and nights outside the capital hunting]. I intend to drive out wicked animals and return.'[13] Kim Kukwang (1415–80; 金國光) and Yun Chaun (1415–78; 尹子雲) argued that going out at night to perform ancestral rites was the same as going out at night to hunt.

Demonstrating that not all scholar officials were unified over the issue of the king's involvement in the royal military Kangmu, two officials challenged Inspector Kim Chesin on behalf of the king: 'It would be the same if you [the king] tried to go out at night to conduct ancestral worship at a tomb. What harm can come from riding out at night and hunting? Send the mounted

---

[11] CWS, 9:275.
[12] CWS, 9:275.
[13] CWS, 9:490.

horsemen to flush out the game (*kugun*; 驅軍) and observe the men from the foot of the mountain. After conducting ancestral rituals, join them.' Censor An Ch'im (1445–1515; 安琛) supported them. 'Duke Yin went into the area of the capital to observe the capture of animals. Zang Xibo of the Lu remonstrated him. As for now, going out at night and catching animals in places meant for ancestral worship is not a very prudent thing. Dispatching the generals to go out and capture them [instead of the king] will be a great fortune.' Officials repeated the words of the king to criticise his love of the hunt. 'It is not about catching animals. Rather, it is about training the troops.'

King Sŏngjong declined to listen. Inspector Kim Chesin went further and argued for the dismissal of the scholar official Hyŏn Sŏkkyu (1430–80; 玄碩圭), but the king refused, insisting that Hyŏn had not committed a crime. Kim argued that 'he [Hyŏn] is someone who is not respectable'.[14] Hyŏn had been the one who remonstrated against Prince Yangnyŏng earlier that year for engaging in a hunting trip outside the palace walls. To win Hyŏn over, King Sŏngjong invited him on a hunting tour (*yujŏn*; 遊畋), a gesture for which Hyŏn felt deeply moved.[15] Despite this invitation, Hyŏn submitted his letter of resignation two days later most likely because he did not agree with the king's actions and wanted to display a sense of moral integrity. Perhaps to reward Hyŏn for this unwillingness to compromise his beliefs, the king offered to elevate Hyŏn's government status, but Hyŏn refused expressing his unworthiness for both the offer to travel with the king to hunt and for elevated status.[16] As seen in these debates, the royal military Kangmu hunts offer a particularly revealing perception on the control of political patronage, status and socio-economic interests. Ideology – the embrace of a certain interpretation of Neo-Confucianism that sought to isolate the king from the wild – was one key factor in tensions between the king and the civil bureaucracy.

By 1475, a concentrated effort by senior-level officials sought to curtail military training via Kangmu hunting practice. This was in response to one of the most spectacular royal Kangmu hunts to date. That year, King Sŏngjong organised a Kangmu with more than 28,000 soldiers. In response, a joint petition, submitted by a number of scholars, recognised the importance of the hunt for military preparedness. However, the appeal also critiqued such excursions. It criticised these large spectacles for interfering with the assignments of conscript troops, soldiers who would be sent to the central army.[17]

[14] CWS, 9:490.
[15] CWS, 9:493.
[16] CWS, 9:494.
[17] CWS, 9:254.

One scholar official, the proofreader from the Office of Diplomatic Correspondence, Cho Chisŏ (1454–1504; 趙之瑞), submitted a petition calling for an end to the Kangmu system. He criticised the hardships the Kangmu had on the local communities. Over the years, famine and other disasters (ch'ŏnjae; 天災) had occurred, he argued, causing great suffering. During such disasters, King Sŏngjong hunted hares and foxes over a period of ten days. He suggested now was the time to focus on governing, not hunting. To alleviate the suffering the king and his men had magnified, Cho Chisŏ called for a postponement of the Kangmu. Following his report, a number of officials stepped in to defend the Kangmu, advocating that these hunts were an essential institution. 'The poor harvest has not been a disaster for the whole country this year. The Kangmu cannot end.'[18] Even within the ranks of civil officials, tensions flared.

These extraordinary royal hunts continued despite the critiques. In 1479, as part of one Kangmu excursion, King Sŏngjong went on an extended trip. He and his party hunted on a mountain at the village of Kaju (加注), in nearby Kyŏnggi Province, where he slept in a tent (ch'a; 次) and the next day continued to hunt on Mt Ch'ŏngsong (青松山). Following this expedition, several senior officials submitted petitions to the king, demanding the removal of other bureaucrats, accusing them of trying to curry favours with Sŏngjong by supporting his desire to spend time outside the capital on the Kangmu. In these petitions, the Censor General Kim Yanggyŏng (?–?; 金良璥) reprimanded the king for spending nights in the deep, dark mountains. King Sŏngjong, perhaps concerned that officials would use these apparent improprieties to further their arguments against the king's involvement in the Kangmu, apologised for displaying apparently preferential treatment to certain officials while on these hunts and promised not to replicate such behaviour in the future.[19] Undeterred, the king continued to organise and participate in Kangmu hunts, which included hunting with hawks. After these hunts he would hold feasts with senior-ranking generals and even low-level lieutenants, such as Yu Kyŏng (?–?; 柳涇) and Yi Undal (?–?; 李雲達).

These conflicts over the royal military Kangmu hunts were reoccurring, based on specific allusions and specific phrases from the Chinese classical texts that were well-known to all. In fact, much of the rhetorical impact derives from familiarity. The key point was that the issue was never fully resolved on a permanent basis. Instead, it was revisited by every generation, some more frequently than others. This repetition does not make the debates

[18] CWS, 9:497.
[19] CWS, 10:58.

and arguments any less important but they do underscore the seriousness of the issue of the king's involvement in the royal Kangmu hunt.

After the king assisted Lieutenant Chŏng Hoea (?–?; 鄭懷雅) in a royal military Kangmu circle hunt on Mt Kwanŭm (觀音山), officials criticised the excursion and held an extended conversation at the royal lecture with the king, where Neo-Confucian tutors instructed him in issues of moral governance and Confucian studies. In their criticism, they drew on the *Zhou Commentary* (*Zuo zhuan*; 左傳), a text that warns of the harm of military training on the common people. The king recognized the clear disdain for Kangmu festivities and the hunt, responding, 'It seems that the Censorate does not want me to undertake these [Kangmu].'[20] A week later, the king insisted that the circle hunt was not a simple divertissement (*hŭisa*; 戲事). He associated the Kangmu with the military training necessary to prepare for war with an enemy. This was a matter, he insisted, where the army spent days in hard terrain and in harsh weather conditions. 'Even a minor mistake can lead to the fall of the country.' It was also important, he argued, to share wine and music with his generals while on the royal Kangmu hunts as a way to demonstrate his appreciation for their service.[21]

In the midst of these debates on the hunt, a report arrived from Ch'ungch'ŏng Province Army Commander Kim Sŏhyŏng (?–?; 金瑞衡). Kim was hunting around Mt Sŏsan (瑞山) in South Ch'ungch'ŏng Province, roughly 135 kilometres (80 mi.) southwest of the capital. It was there that he started a fire for a 'fire hunt' in a prohibited area of the mountain. In his haste, he lost control and the subsequent blaze burned down the trees used for timber in the area and destroyed Kaesim Monastery (開心寺).[22] The fire caused troops to disobey orders and spurred criticism of Kim. The court deliberated over Kim and ultimately decided not to punish him, partially because of his astounding archery skills and other talents he presented during Kangmu hunts.[23] Here, his achievements at the Kangmu protected him from punishment. However, Censor General Pak Ansŏng (?–?; 朴安性) took up the question of Kim's episode with this fire hunt. After listing Kim's faults as a leader, the censor general waited to hear more from King Sŏngjong about a verdict, but the king did not offer any specific recommendations on punishment, ostensibly dismissing any actions against Kim.[24] Protected by the throne, Kim remained in favour at the court and occupied a number of positions until Sŏngjong's death.

[20] *CWS*, 10:60.
[21] *CWS*, 10:62.
[22] *CWS*, 9:233.
[23] *CWS*, 10:66.
[24] *CWS*, 10:67.

Whenever King Sŏngjong went on a military Kangmu hunt, he recruited troops on reserve he had previously employed. It was thought that having the king request their services was an honour, and many were quite flattered by it.[25] However, Inspector General Ch'oe Kwan (?–?; 崔灌) feared that recruiting off-duty soldiers from nearby villages for the king's hunt would exhaust these troops because they would be unable to rest. To the contrary, the king expressed his concern that the inspection of troops having long been abolished would mean that the soldiers would no longer be prepared for these moments. Now King Sŏngjong wanted to requisition them to train them. Scholar officials pushed back further, even expressing displeasure for the reviewing of troops, a simple level of training that called for the mustering of soldiers in formations for the king to inspect. However, not everyone supported their view. Consul (Yŏngsa 領事) Yun P'ilsang agreed with the king about the importance of troop mobilisation. Requisitioning troops once or twice annually for the spring and autumn hunts was not harmful, Yun argued. Such moments could garner attacks by those who opposed the Kangmu. Officials recording this encounter criticised Yun P'ilsang, claiming that he always attempted to curry favour with the king through flattery and agreement.[26]

In this way, the Kangmu was a system that measured the military skills of those involved and tested the morality of others. The court promoted those with outstanding hunting skills, such as those good at archery. Sanctions were levied against others, such as officials and soldiers in distant parts of the dynasty, who profited from their positions for personal gain. Taking advantage of the importance of the Kangmu hunts, district magistrates insisted that untrained, miscellaneous troops submit game to them. The court called for these magistrates to stop taking advantage of men in their charge.[27] One instance involved an official, Chŏng Kwan (?–?; 鄭寬), in Puan, a small county in North Chŏlla Province. The court described Kwan as an uneducated and ignorant man who kept many dogs and horses and hunted with them daily. Along with the local military officer, the soldiers under Kwan's command were weak and lacked discipline. In response to this, the court dismissed both low-level officers.[28] In the eyes of many civil officials, the Kangmu promoted corruption at all levels.

---

[25] *CWS*, 11:146.
[26] *CWS*, 11:147.
[27] *CWS*, 12:440.
[28] *CWS*, 12:472.

Climate, the Environment and the Military Question

While the bureaucracy and court quibbled over the hunt and where it should be allowed in the provinces, the royal military Kangmu hunts continued unabated. But officials found other ways to undermine the royal hunts. One argument used the weather and harsh environment as a pretext for cancelling them. Rain frequently disrupted Kangmu hunts. At other times, officials used the dangerous terrain of the mountains as an excuse to try to convince the king not to go hunting. In 1481, court officials argued that the royal inspection of the troops, as they made their way across the Han River, should be cancelled because of frigid autumn weather and the threat of natural disaster or upheaval (*ch'ŏnbyŏn*; 天變). 'Crossing the river will be difficult, not only for the royal palanquin, but also for the soldiers and horses.' They argued that in the past, King T'aejong prepared for a day's provisions when he crossed the river and went hunting. 'An old saying goes,' they concluded, 'It's dangerous to ride a boat, yet it's safe to cross a bridge.'[29] Despite their appeals, Sŏngjong refused to listen and continued to plan his trip to Mt Ch'ŏnggye. After lecturing the king, advisors pressed him on the difficulties of preparing for an overnight excursion and suggested alternative locations. 'If Your Majesty intends to go through with the Kangmu, perhaps it would be better to hold it at Sŏsan or P'ungyang [nearby mountains roughly twenty-three kilometres (15 mi.) northeast of the royal palace in Kyŏnggi Province]?'[30] The king demanded further discussion about the matter and expressed his concern that the hunt may harm the commoners; such an excursion would draw on local reserves and excessive amounts of food would be necessary to feed his men and their horses and dogs.

In the fall of 1481, debate over the role the hunt played in the economy, politics and society erupted at the court. The many members of the civil officials at the court argued that the Kangmu harmed the people because the hunts intruded upon agricultural land. The king pushed back and claimed that the Kangmu hunts were important, and that they helped the people. 'When we do not hold Kangmu in years of bad harvest, over a number of years, the animals [multiply and] cause greater damage because they consume the grain.' The solution, the king proposed, was to grant the commoners permission to undertake private hunts (*hŏmin saryŏp hayŏ*; 許民私獵何如). A long conversation with a number of officials ensued. The fourth minister, consul, and the royal secretariate discussed the matter with the king. Yi Kŭkchŭng (1431–94; 李克增), the fourth minister, agreed with King Sŏngjong, saying,

---

[29] CWS, 10:269.
[30] CWS, 10:270.

'Ancient people used to say, "In the garden of the country, there are those who go there to cut down trees and there are those who go there to catch pheasants and hare."'[31] The quote from Mencius discusses the size of hunting parks monitored by King Xuan and the law against hunting deer in them; the punishment for killing deer was the same as the punishment for killing people. King Xuan shared the parks with the people for the purpose of hunting pheasants and hare, but not deer. Council (Yŏngsa; 領事) Sim Hoe (1418–93; 沈澮) countered, 'If you do not prohibit these completely, how can you hunt in the future? It is better to put a limit on hunting.' The king appeared to be moved by Sim's argument.[32]

As noted, not all officials at the court supported these attacks on the Kangmu. Some pushed back at times and defended the king arguing that scholars (yusaeng; 儒生) knew nothing about military arts.[33] The powerful meritorious subject, veteran of conflict that brought King Sejo to the throne, and father-in-law to the current king, Han Myŏnghoe (1415–87; 韓明澮) defended the royal military Kangmu and hunting in general.[34] While of the civil order, Han served in many top posts including those for the military. Han observed that an overabundance of animals on mountains such as Kwangnŭng (光陵) damaged crops and requested that competent military leaders, capable of conducting the royal Kangmu hunts without ravaging the fields, be put in charge. King Sŏngjong wholeheartedly supported his father-in-law's observations and approval.[35] He ordered the Ministry of War to take actions concerning the hunt and the economy and insisted that hunting was an essential activity that helped remove harm from the people.

The lands that had been used for Kangmu hunting events since the beginning of the dynasty had signs posted in them forbidding commoners to hunt. The Board wrote,

> During periods of cold weather, kings personally inspected the army and learned the arts of war (武事). Recently, the Kangmu have been abolished because of a year of bad weather. The people still fear the prohibition against hunting, and they are unable to collect firewood. Because of this, the birds and the animals have multiplied (inch'a kŭmsu ikpŏn; 因此禽獸益繁), and these animals have consumed the crops of the people. This is against the motive of the Kangmu.

[31] This is a quote from *Mencius*.
[32] CWS, 10:260.
[33] For instance, see Yun P'ilsang criticising his fellow colleagues in 1489. CWS, 11:524.
[34] CWS, 11:150.
[35] CWS, 11:150.

The king echoed the words of Fourth Minister Yi Kŭkchŭng, 'Ancient people used to say, "In the garden of the country, there are those who go there to cut down trees and there are those who go there to catch pheasants and hare."' He ordered that 'from now on, all bans on the Kangmu hunting grounds will be lifted. The people will be allowed to burn firewood and hunt on them.' Sŏngjong, worried that local magistrates would not follow his orders and try to prevent the people from hunting and collecting firewood, declared, 'Report this to all the hunting parks (*wŏnyu*; 苑囿) in all the villages.'[36]

The conflict over the royal military hunt went unresolved. In another discussion, one secretary of the Office of Royal Confucian Lectures, An Yunson (1450–1520; 安潤孫), attempted to shame King Sŏngjong over his hunting practices. 'In the early days of Your Majesty's ascension,' An told him, 'you put great effort into your work, you did away with falconry and stopped hunting. But now you pass down a message requesting hunting dogs (*talgu*; 獵狗). The *Book of Songs* (*Shijing*; 詩經) says, "Everyone starts, but few are able to finish." I am worried about Your Majesty.' Backing him up, Left Assistant Royal Secretariate Kim Kyech'ang (?–1481; 金季昌) insisted on putting an end to the Kangmu being conducted throughout the provinces.[37]

Despite these arguments, the king refused to end the Kangmu. He continued to carry them out in such places as the Tobong and Ch'ŏnggye mountains. When heavy rain interfered with the royal hunt, the king nevertheless wished to find another location to hold it. Some officials sided with the king and reiterated the belief that the Kangmu was an important ritual of the country (*kukchi taesa*; 國之大事). This may have been paying lip service to the hunt, while others pushed back and tried to offer reasons to cancel them by returning to the argument of poor harvests. Insect damage to crops was yet another discussion held at the court in the summer of 1477; such destruction limited the harvest and made it difficult for farmers to have enough food for themselves, let alone enough for the thousands of soldiers and hundreds of horses present in a Kangmu hunt.[38] By the winter of 1481, Chief Censor Kang Chap'yŏng (1430–86; 姜子平) insisted that the hunt be discontinued because of the hardship it brought to the troops. Inspector General Ku Ch'igon (?–?; 丘致崐) agreed with Kang. In a year of bad harvest, Ku argued, with famine from spring until autumn, the farmlands lay in ruins. Soldiers around the capital experienced food shortages, and horses had little fodder. Ku pointed to the harsh weather, the cold and rain, that seemed like a 'natural disaster'.

[36] *CWS*, 10:261.
[37] *CWS*, 9:698.
[38] *CWS*, 9:471.

Another minister, Yun Ho (1424–96; 尹壕), followed. 'The military must prepare defenses,' Yun insisted, 'but canceling a small-scale Kangmu would not interfere in these preparations.'[39]

Rather than maintain military preparedness, these officials suggested forgoing the military hunt and only conducting the ritual element – the military review – a ceremony meant to access the troops. In reality this did little to provide the men with real military skill experiences. The king reiterated the importance of training the military, stating, 'They are to prevent the enemy from invading.' He connected his argument to the annual harvest by arguing that in good years, soldiers had been recruited and compensated for their work with food from all of the provinces. (But pulling away commoners from the lands resulted in a lack of farmers during the harvest.) The harvest had been bad during the current year (1481), and the king understood this fact. In such hard times, even if the king did not hold a smaller Kangmu, letting the military relax was a mistake. Hunting helped the commoners (*hwangsu sujigŏ wiminjehae*; 況蒐狩之舉, 爲民除害), presumably by eradicating agricultural pests and by providing animals to sacrifice at the state altars to assist in the governing of the state.[40] Nothing should stop it. Even cold weather must not interfere in undertaking military training.

Within a day, the king diminished the size of the hunt at Ch'ŏnjŏm and by midday, he called it off. 'Suddenly rain is beginning to fall,' he grudgingly agreed. 'How can we go through with it?' Consul Chŏng Ch'angson and Right State Councillor Hong Ŭng (1428–9; 洪應) reminded the king that the soldiers had been unable to bring raingear. 'If it rains, it will be difficult to hunt.' To these and other scholar officials, there never seemed to be a good time to hold a royal Kangmu hunt. Consul No Sasin and Director of the Royal House Administration Yun Ho (1424–96; 尹壕) were not so sure. 'The intensity of the rain is not that severe. Why don't we wait just a little longer?' General on the Right Ŏ Yuso (1434–89; 魚有沼) and Deputy Director Yi Kŭkchŭng (1431–94; 李克增) tempted the king into following through with the hunt. 'Even though it has only been a short while, there are so many deer.' The king, however, felt very sorry for the soldiers getting wet in windswept rain without catching a single animal. 'I did not see any game for days,' he lamented. As a way to warm and cheer up the troops, the king offered them alcohol.[41] While certain officials argued that hunts should be cancelled because of bad weather, the king sometimes postponed them unexpectedly. Despite these cancellations,

---

[39] CWS, 10:271.
[40] CWS, 10:271.
[41] CWS, 10:272.

Sŏngjong understood the importance of practising the art of hunting in challenging terrain and harsh weather, because the experience improved the level of training for the soldiers.

One particularly sensitive area on which to hold Kangmu hunts was the land surrounding the royal tombs. These were lands outside of the capital where former kings, queens and royal family members had been buried and where ancestral rituals were performed. The question arose at the court: how appropriate was it to hunt on these lands? Officials tried to persuade the king not to go through with a hunt on Mt Namsan. The king refused to listen, insisting that since the founder of the dynasty hunted on mountains with royal tombs and had sent soldiers to flush out animals in these areas, he had a right to do so as well.[42] Yun Ho, now at the Office of Royal Relatives, suggested that the king should pay respects (*pae*; 拜) at the gravesites on the mountain if he were going to hunt there, but the king refused stating that there was no rationale for conducting such rituals. King Sŏngjong saw no difficulty holding a Kangmu or chasing animals near royal burial mounds.[43] However, as the king pointed out in 1486, it was inappropriate to trample these gravesites.[44] The question went unresolved.

Invoking the illustrious years of King Sejong, Consul Chŏng Ch'angson pointed out that Sejong had suspended the Kangmu in years of bad harvest, and as such it would be best for King Sŏngjong to follow his ancestor's lead and hold a smaller Kangmu. The meritorious advisor Han Myŏnghoe countered that the Kangmu was an important ceremony (*mujungsa*; 武重事), while Hong Ŭng called it a 'state ritual' (*taerye*; 大禮), 'It was abolished long ago because it caused national anxiety (*kukyul*; 國恤).'[45] The hunt was implicated in this hardship of anxiety not over a lack of defences to protect the country but over the timing and resources these large-scale military hunts demanded that took people away from their normal agricultural lives. 'It is not just that the troops and the people do not know the ritual of hunting animals (*susujiye*; 蒐狩之禮), but they are also poor at martial skills.' Critics pointed out that the four- or five-day Kangmu and the training it provided to troops from nearby the capital was insufficient. No Sasin added, 'The ritual of hunting animals was foremost for ritual offering (*kŏndu*; 乾豆) and lesser for martial affairs. The ritual [of the Kangmu] has been canceled for several years because of bad harvests. If the harvest is abundant this year, perhaps it [the hunt] cannot

[42] CWS, 10:270.
[43] CWS, 10:271.
[44] CWS, 11:150.
[45] CWS, 11:165.

be stopped.' No Sasin suggested that if the people fall into debt because of a bad harvest, then the court should recruit wealthier soldiers to take part in the Kangmu. Another official worried about the impact the Kangmu had on agricultural production, suggesting it be held in autumn after the crops had been harvested. The king simply espoused that the Kangmu could not be abolished.[46] In previous years, soldiers taking part in the Kangmu had been conscripted from the northern provinces where agricultural production was poor.[47] Because soldiers lacked military discipline, other officials, such as the general in charge of ring hunts, argued with the king that the Kangmu was necessary to train his men and must not be abolished (*pugap'ye*; 不可廢).[48]

By the summer of 1487, the provincial military commanders petitioned the king to move the Kangmu that had been planned to occur in the lands surrounding the capital, to either Hwanghae or Kangwŏn Province because there had reportedly been a lack of game in Kyŏnggi Province around the capital. The Chief State Councillor Yun P'ilsang suggested that the king dispatch someone to investigate the hunting conditions of the three provinces. The official Hong Ŭng heard that game was scarce in the Ch'ŏrwŏn region located in the centre of the peninsula. A discussion broke out about the best place to hold the Kangmu. No Sasin argued that Hwanghae Province had plenty of game, but harmful air conditions had produced sickness among the people, while Kangwŏn Province had few animals but was a better location for the Kangmu because of its proximity and terrain. Also, there was no place for the king to lodge in Hwanghae. The two Kangmu hunting grounds in Hwanghae had been abolished in the 1420s.[49] Undeterred, the king decided to hunt in Hwanghae.[50] He planned to hunt for twenty days, a considerable amount of time. The king decided to conduct the hunt based on the availability of wild game rather than comfort. Hwanghae Province was further away and a more arduous part of the country to reach but had a healthier population of beasts.

Court officials pushed back against the king's decision to hold the Kangmu in Hwanghae Province. Distant regions like these were described in negative terms. Inspector General Kim Sŭnggyŏng (1430–93; 金升卿), for instance, argued that Hwanghae Province was a place of evil infectious gases (*changdok*; 瘴毒). People who stayed there for a long time grew sick with a cough (*haesu chibyŏng*; 咳嗽之疾). 'If you cannot cancel the hunt, then we request

---

[46] CWS, 11:165.
[47] CWS, 11:166.
[48] CWS, 11:166.
[49] CWS, 2:622 and 3:99.
[50] CWS, 11:232.

that you go hunting in Kangwŏn Province. Since ancient times, the Kangmu has been held in the main provinces (*ponto*; 本道). Royal processions have never gone to Hwanghae Province.' Kim pushed the king to decide hastily because the government had to begin preparations. Kim added that the king had only gone out for four or five days at a time to places like Mt P'yŏngsan, Mt Kangŭm and Mt T'osan. Turning the argument to issues of Confucian piety, he noted how difficult it would be for the king to pay a visit to the residence where the two former queen dowagers lived (*yangjŏn*; 兩殿). Compared to other Kangmu hunts, the mountains and forests in Hwanghae Province were remote and dangerous because the animals congregated en mass (*kŭmsu soch'wi*; 禽獸所聚) and the air was harmful (*p'unggi uak*; 風氣尤惡). In other words, it was not proper for the king to sleep in the mountains and the fields.

King Sŏngjong threw their words back in Kim's face. Sŏngjong recognised that the length of one's life and the timing of one's death were determined by heaven. He argued that when Confucius wandered the lands he was not concerned about the weather. Further, Sŏngjong insisted he would visit the two queen dowagers when he returned. Kim pushed back disputing that he had witnessed diseased people from the areas and the king would be unable to prevent himself from growing ill. Hwanghae Province and Mt Kangŭm were dangerous locations. 'If Your Highness does not believe me, please dispatch someone there to learn more about it and report back.' Kim's criticisms hardened Sŏngjong's determination to hold the hunt in Hwanghae. He ordered that officials 'communicate to the Office of the Inspector General about getting to work on holding the Kangmu in Hwanghae Province'. To allay the anger of his advisers, Sŏngjong announced that all of the animals killed in the hunt would be sacrificed at the state altars, and that he would pay a visit to the queen dowager mothers.[51]

Petitions in the autumn of 1487 asked for Sŏngjong to postpone the upcoming royal military Kangmu. But Sŏngjong saw contradictions in their arguments. On the one hand, scholars argued that the hunt should be dissolved. On the other, they recognised that the Kangmu was a major event for the dynasty that helped ready defences in case of attack. Others wanted to compromise, suggesting that the number of days on the Kangmu be reduced. Hong Ŭng wrote that 'hunting was not a long-established state ritual. It had only been nine years since a hunting ceremony has been conducted.' Since the Kangmu was inconveniencing the people, Hong requested that the king temporarily postpone the hunt. Others, like Right Minister Son Sunhyo (1427–97; 孫舜孝), agreed with Hong, while officials such as Ŏ Yuso, Hŏ Chong and Yi Ch'ŏlkyŏn

---

[51] CWS, 11:233.

argued the contrary. They insisted that the Kangmu be preserved and that the king should conduct the festivities. Even reducing the number of days to seven was unacceptable, they believed. 'The Kangmu is a major event of the country. At the time of King Sejo, it took place frequently. Cancelling such an important military exercise was unacceptable.' Sŏngjong weighed in, arguing that the number of people calling for the cancellation of the Kangmu was fewer than those who advocated for maintaining it.

The ongoing debate over the location really concerned the king's participation. A year later, in 1489, Sŏngjong reconsidered Hwanghae Province for the autumn Kangmu. Again, anxiety peeked at the court about the inclement weather there. Official Kwŏn Pin (?–?; 權瑨) was uneasy about the condition of post stations (yŏngno; 驛路), government operated depots where couriers relayed messages on horseback. Constantly busy, these posts had withered and wasted away because of the comings and goings of Chinese envoys. Kwon pleaded with Sŏngjong to hold the Kangmu in another province. 'Even if you were a normal person, you can't go to this land. How could Your Majesty go?' Travelling there was difficult and lengthy. Another official added that 'six hundred households' had been relocated into the area, attesting to the rugged and peripheral nature of the region as still sparsely settled lands. The movement of these people from the south into the north was part of the government strategy to consolidate control over the land and tap into its resources. Some officials argued that the people who had moved into the north were often criminals and their families. Some commoners had volunteered, while others had been coerced into relocating by the government. Hence, they declared that the area was too dangerous, and the king should not go.

The advantages potentially outweighed the dangers. Sŏngjong insisted that his travelling to Hwanghae Province for the autumn Kangmu was not only to observe military preparations, it was also about securing wild game for Confucian state rituals (ch'ŏn'gŭm; 薦禽).[52] The illustrious scholar official Yi Kŭkpae (1422–95; 李克培) reiterated that the air in Hwanghae Province was full of pestilence. The leading official No Sasin supported Yi's argument against holding the Kangmu in Hwanghae Province, but believed the final decision rested with the king. 'Rulers from kings T'aejong to Sejong all went on royal Kangmu hunts in Hwanghae Province. It is up to Your Majesty to decide.' While familiar about the animal population in Hwanghae Province, No was unsure about their numbers in Kangwŏn, 'I will write a letter to find out more.'[53] Depending on such letters was telling on its own. Rather than

[52] CWS, 11:485 and 11:36.
[53] CWS, 11:485.

using his direct experience or the knowledge of those around him, the king now had to rely on indirect information filtered through advisors who controlled the flow of knowledge to him. For advisors around the king, letters like these appear to have been delaying tactics. Officials may have wanted to leave the final decision to Sŏngjong. However, it is easy to surmise that some of them hoped the king would decide on his own to cancel it.

* * *

The king's participation in the royal military Kangmu hunt was a powerful example of rulership. They were events where he demonstrated his masculine strength and dominated the people, animals and lands of the dynasty, and even beyond by laying claim to a Chinggisid past. The royal Kangmu hunts involved military preparation, but they were more than mere rehearsals. They also acted to reinforce the idea of the ruler as a strong military leader. Simultaneously, these hunts regulated access to wild animals. Game was consumed at feasts held during the Kangmu and offered as sacrifice in Confucian state rituals, traditions that were repeatedly encouraged during King Sŏngjong's reign. Officials frequently spoke of the Kangmu 'as a major event (*taesa*; 大事)' for the dynasty. While on the surface, these words convey the significance of the Kangmu to the state, underneath, they imply a harsher critique. As the hunts were formidable occasions, these critiques also denoted the immensity of the event and argued that they were sizeable affairs that depleted the precious resources of the kingdom. This drain on the government system caused great consternation among civil officials who argued over the frequency of hunts, locations, number of days, and how the troops would be supplied. Many levels of the government were drawn into the planning of the hunts and carrying them out. Royal family members and elites from both branches of the government participated. Local soldiers took part, and even those who did not join in the festivities directly – such as the common people living on the farms the soldiers marched through – were impacted by the sheer number of men, horses, dogs and equipment moving through their fields. Farmers – the agricultural economic base of the dynasty – were certainly on the minds of government officials who critiqued the Kangmu. Many of these civil officials looked wearily on the king's direct involvement in military affairs that involved wild animals. Like the awe-inspiring piebald deer felled by King Sejong's son, many civil officials, alerted to the commanding presence of his Kangmu hunts, took aim at his royal participation and sought to kill it.

7

Public Animals, Private Hunts and Royal Authority in the Fifteenth Century

In the quiet of the forest, two sable emerged from the brush. The edge of the forest had hidden their presence, their dark fur helping them blend in perfectly with the terrain. A nearby stream offered additional camouflage as well as a source of water from which to drink and search for food. Sable, small, slender animals no more than sixty-five centimetres (25 in.) long and weighing on average less than a kilogramme (about 2 lb), are fast and nimble and spend most of their time catching and consuming rodents. Because of their agility and speed, they are able to elude wolves, leopards and tigers. This part of the forest, with very little human presence, was ideal habitat for sable. Nearby, a pack of them – twenty to thirty, probably mostly smaller females – foraged around the forest floor. As the pair of sable neared the stream's edge, suddenly one fell, struck by an arrow. Before responding, the other dropped, felled in one try. By afternoon, twenty more sable, most of the group, fell alongside these two, killed by the apex predator of the peninsula, King T'aejo.[1]

This story is part of a fable told of King T'aejo hunting alone in the deep forest. As he was washing himself in a mountain stream, he spotted two sables (*milgu*; 蜜狗) wandering nearby. The king quickly, with no more than his bow and quiver, readied himself and fired two arrows striking them both. Twenty more sables emerged. He hit them all, his arrows thought to have been touched by the divine (*sinmyo*; 神妙).[2] While hagiographic, this tale suggests some of the elements important to rulership. Spending time hunting alone in the wilderness and having the reflexive, most powerful ability to suddenly draw a weapon when most vulnerable – in the case of King T'aejo being absent his royal garb after taking a bath – all while commanding spiritual forces through the use of the mystical arrows, represent the characteristics necessary for leadership. Here

---

[1] *CWS*, 1:3.
[2] *CWS*, 1:3.

too is the religious aspect: after a ritual cleansing in a mountain stream, the king possessed divine powers over his weapons.

Heroic episodes like this emerged from a different type of hunting event, the private, personal hunts. Kings, royal family members and their supporters held small-scale, intimate hunts much like King Taejo's experience with the sable. Like the formidable royal military Kangmu explored in previous chapters, these smaller hunting events defined the fifteenth century. These smaller, intimate hunting events differed from the Kangmu hunts not only in their size but also in their planning, duration and intent. By the 1480s, the number of both Kangmu events and more intimate and personal hunting outings increased, and the number of government positions related to hunting also expanded. Based on classical references to limit the king's access to the wild, officials responded negatively to the growing prominence of the hunts both large and small. However, the pattern of escalation was not just an ideological conflict, but was also driven by other factors, most notably the economic and practical needs of an expanding state.

How could tales of personal bravery and military acumen, developed after attending small, personal hunts, continue to legitimise rulership as the needs of the central government changed over the fifteenth century? In short, they could not. To tease out a more nuanced answer to this question, I first consider the extension of dynastic control over the peninsula by examining the centrality of animal products as tribute items. Along with other items, pelts, meat, blood and other animal by-products were submitted to the central government as part of the tax obligation of the countryside. Replicating this pattern on the peninsula, Korea submitted animals (some alive, some dead) to the Mongols and Ming as parts of its tribute obligations and traded other forms of animals with Jurchens along the frontier. Including animal tribute in the story is vital. By considering animals as tribute, we can better understand the growing limitation of royal authority over the century. In the rest of this chapter, and extending into Chapter 8, I examine the small, personal hunts, detailing debates at the court over King Sŏngjong's participation. This final section highlights the clash with his officials over private hunting and state ritual, echoing arguments we have seen in previous chapters over his involvement in the Kangmu royal military hunts, but differing in their intent. I argue that controlling small-scale hunts, including those of the king, were important economic and symbolic steps towards the consolidation of central power. Through this process, royal authority was given material shape in the form of animal products that tied local areas to the centre, as well as Chosŏn to the region.

Animals and the State

No later than 1400, heroic tales of personal and intimate hunts, like the founder's sable killing, contributed to the building of dynastic legitimacy and buttressed the authority of the throne. An extreme example of the importance of hunting for the creation of myths of rulership (stories told by this and future generations about the might and ability of such powerful leaders), this story and others like it convey some of the traits important to royal and elite identity at the time. The legitimate founder had no fear of the wilderness and had an ability to dominate wild animals while hunting alone or in small groups on personal hunts. The king hunting alone, as described in this story, is a dangerous endeavour and most likely was not attempted often, given the uncertainties involved with hunting. Yet the story helps build an image of the founder as a man skilled at survival and comfortable with the wilderness. The sable characters in this story are also revealing. Difficult targets to hit because of their size and agility, killing twenty-two on this single outing – during what is described as a chance encounter – further reinforced the heavenly military hunting skills of King T'aejo.

The creation myths and legends of dynastic founders from earlier times on the peninsula reveal a partnership with nature and in some cases a product of divine animal births, such as the founder Chumong, of the ancient state of Koguryŏ, and his emergence from an egg, a tale the state borrowed from Puyŏ people of the north after conquering them, the celestial egg birth of Pak Hyŏkkŏse of Silla, or the divine procreation with a bear to produce Korea's mythical founder Tan'gun. Unlike these creation myths, however, tales such as King T'aejo's encounter with the sable imply his mystical nature, while simultaneously grounding him in the practical concerns of the state. The sable story is a fitting description of human and animal relations during a period that was witness to increasing encounters between humans and wildlife. Such accounts echo stories in the famous *Songs of Flying Dragons* (*Yongbi ŏch'ŏn'ga*; 龍飛御天歌). Compiled between 1445 and 1447, this eulogy to King T'aejo describes the origins and rise to power of the founder through stories of his military abilities and, even more importantly I argue, his mystical hunting prowess as he readily slays animals great and small.[3] Through stories like these that reflect the ethos of the late fourteenth and early fifteenth centuries, King T'aejo was able to secure domination and state control over all wild creatures.

---

[3] For examples of King T'aejo's hunts, including his struggles with a tiger, see Peter Lee, trans., *Songs of Flying Dragon* (Cambridge, MA: Harvard University Press, 1975), 209, 210, 216 and 236.

Animals contributed to the myth building of early kings and to the more practical needs of the country. Collection of animals is one facet of the larger story of Chosŏn state expansion to secure grain, materials and labour from the peninsula. In the fifteenth century, the state wrote wild animals into the tax system in ways that were stronger than in previous times. Korean elites and non-elites hunted, trapped, dismembered and submitted these beasts to the state. Hunters presented many species of wild animals as tribute (kongsang; 供上). Tribute was a type of tax system that demanded specialised products and animal goods from various regions across the peninsula be sent to the central government in Hanyang. These were items the government felt were necessary for the function of state operations. A more diluted system with less tribute and fewer rules and people in leadership roles functioned during the Koryŏ era. However, the transportation system that was responsible for bringing tribute goods into the capital Kaegyŏng had been attacked by the Red Turbans and faltered to accomplish its duties in the middle of the fourteenth century. Overland and waterborne transportation of tribute, some carried by people, some shipped on boats, remained poor until reforms improved conditions in the 1420s under King Sejong. During the Chosŏn Dynasty, tax revenues came from three sources: land, corvée labour and tribute. Grain was the most important tribute contribution because it was traded as cash to cover the expenses of the state. Local magistrates collected these products from their people. Tribute was then carried overland and moved by waterways on the rivers or seas to Hanyang where it was stored in warehouses. Products originating from along the coasts, such as from the Ch'ŭngch'ŏng and Chŏlla provinces, were shipped mainly by boat. This was faster and less damaging. Items from the interior were transported overland, which took time and impacted the quality of some of the items. For example, ceramic wares carried this way over mountain ranges to Hanyang often broke because of the rugged terrain.[4]

These connections between the centre and periphery, even extending to foreign lands, over the supply of animal products and access to hunting knowledge, hint at imperial arrangements as ways to hold regions in check, rather than allow the regions to accrue wealth or withhold information about animals and hunting from the court. On a smaller scale, the relationship between the centre and the outer regions emulated the relationship Korean dynasties

---

[4] For more on the transportation of tribute, see Pak Kyŏngja, '15 segi kongmul ŭi unsung pangbŏp kwa punch'ŏng sagi myŏngmun ŭi chiyŏkbyŏl t'ŭkching' [Transportation methods of tribute items to the central government and the different regional properties of letter markings in the fifteenth century], Yŏksa wa tamnon 47 (September 2007): 215–54.

had with powerful neighbouring states, such as the Mongols and the Ming. Both empires demanded tribute products from Korea, some of it consisting of animals or their by-products. As we recall, Koryŏ resistance to Mongol submission enraged Mongol leadership. To extract revenge, the Mongols placed a heavy tribute burden on Korea. In addition to people, grain and gold, early demands included thousands of horses and wild animal skins annually. Later, after the relationship had settled into an in-law pattern, Mongol demands eased. The Korean court and officials were livid at the tribute demands. After the transition from Mongols to the Ming, and the uncertainty of Koryŏ and the newly formed Chosŏn sentiment, the Ming also demanded an onerous amount of yearly tribute. That meant that products, including animals caught and processed throughout a variety of regions in Korea, especially in the north, were sent across the border as part of Korea's international relationships – animals became part of Korea's connection to the Ming empire. Just like the court's concern with Korean tributary demands to the Ming, within Korea the demand for regional products was similarly onerous and the pressure unsettled local populations. In a way, the transfer of animal products – and other forms of wealth, including local, regional knowledge unique to that area – to the capital ensured centralisation and stability by discouraging the rise of competing power centres on the peninsula. The sable trade with the Jurchen, for instance, having been regulated by the state, held in check any chance of the accumulation of wealth in the hands of military leaders or other local leadership in the north. Similar to local officials, sable were small and at times elusive, but they, like all wild animals, proved to be both a threat and an opportunity to the state.

Government records confirm the centrality of animal tribute for the expanding Chosŏn Dynasty. Local magistrates shipped wild animal products, as tribute items, directly from the counties of origin, many of them from mountainous regions. Except for Kyŏnggi Province around the capital, all of the provinces submitted animal tribute items (*kwŏlgong*; 厥貢). Two provinces with some of the greatest concentration of wild animals provided the state with a significant array of animal parts. In the middle of the fifteenth century, Hamgil (Hamgyŏng) Province submitted leopard furs, golden bear furs (*kŭmungp'i*; 金熊皮), *ayang* deer hides (*ayang nokp'i*; 阿羊鹿皮), roe deer hides (*changp'i*; 獐皮), lynx (*ip'i*; 狸皮) and fox furs (*hop'i*; 狐皮) and leopard hides (*p'yomi*; 豹尾), and fox tails (*homi*; 狐尾), antelope horns (*nokgak*; 鹿角), *ayang* deer antlers (*ayang nokgak*; 阿羊鹿角), and pork or boar jerky (*kŏnjŏ*; 乾猪). Animal products used as medicine included bear gallbladder (*ungdam*; 熊膽), young deer velvet antlers (*nogyong*; 鹿茸), scent sacks of musk deer (*sahyang*; 麝香), ox bezoar (*uhwang*; 牛黃) – undigested material harvested from the stomach – and tiger tibias (*hogyŏnggol*; 虎脛骨).⁵ P'yŏngan Province, also in the north, submitted a similar list, including domesticated and wild animals. Ox and horse hair (*somamo*; 牛馬毛), dog hides (*kup'i*; 狗皮), leopard, fox, lynx, otter (*sudal*; 水獺), sable (*ch'o*; 貂) and flying squirrel (*ch'ŏngsŏ*; 青鼠) furs, sika or water deer and roe deer hides, wild boar skins (*chŏp'i*; 猪皮), sika or red deer, roe deer, pork and male musk deer (*chŏnghyangp'o*; 丁香脯) jerky, antelope horns (*yŏngyanggak*; 羚羊角), and wild pig and hedgehog gallbladder (*widam*; 猬膽). Medicinal items included such things as bear gall bladder, velvet antler resin or gelatin (*nokgakgyo*; 鹿角膠) harvested from dropped antlers and killed deer, musk deer and tiger tibias.⁶ These items were used as ingredients for medicines.

While farmers submitted grain to the state – a back breaking task with its own hardships and uncertainties because of government promotion of agriculture, the centrality of grain to the state economy, and shifting climactic conditions – products of the mountains and forests, such as specialised wood, ginseng, medicinal herbs and wild animals, were collected while traversing dangerous forested mountainous terrain, jobs that demanded their own levels of specialisation. The story of King T'aejo and the sable suggest the difficulty in catching one of the most sought-after animals on the peninsula. Sable and fox furs, used in both luxury and practical items such as clothes and hats, were about twice as valuable as flying squirrel pelts.⁷ Sable furs were so sought after that a triangular trade occurred with the Jurchen. Chosŏn would trade with the Jurchen and the Jurchen would, in turn, trade the furs with the Ming.⁸ Exceptionally skilled hunters, those familiar with the terrain of these areas, entered the forests to collect game.⁹ Sable hunters (*p'och'o sŏja*; 捕貂鼠者) lived deep in such wilderness areas as Kilju Stream (吉州) and Mt Kapsan (甲山), a heavily forested mountain region in northern Hamgyŏng Province with peaks reaching more than 2,000 metres (6,800 ft). Because of the northern proximity to Manchuria, the region is known for its extreme remoteness and bitter winters dropping to minus eighteen Celsius (below zero degrees Fahrenheit). Hunters would collect and skin sable and then submit their pelts to the state as tribute.

---

⁵ *Sejong sillok chiriji*, found in CWS, 5:593.
⁶ *Sejong sillok chiriji*, CWS, 5:682.
⁷ Sable and fox pelts exchanged for about 20 to 25 *p'il* of cloth, a considerable sum. CWS, 2:653.
⁸ Han Sŏngju, 'Chosŏn kwa yŏjin ŭi ch'op'i kyoyŏk sŏnghaeng kwa kŭ yŏnghyang' [The sable trade between Chosŏn and Jurchen and its impact], *Manju yŏn'gu* 25 (2018): 9–42.
⁹ CWS, 4:462.

How effective was it for animal products to be shipped from the interior of the country and peripheral zones to the capital? Animal products were packed up and most likely walked out of wilderness areas on A-frames strapped to the backs of workers (probably public slaves). Meat, mostly cured in advance, did not appear to have been perishable and seems to have survived even distant journeys.[10]

Animal parts were used in many products and medicines during the Chosŏn Dynasty. Animal skins, both the fur and the leather, were made into clothing. Furs were decorative yet also practical, helping to retain warmth. Fox pelts were used for the lining of boots, deer hide for gloves and mittens. Animals and their meat and various parts were vital to the health of the country. Some were consumed for medicinal purposes by the elite and the few commoners who could afford these remedies, while the court rewarded Chosŏn officials with animal skins.

The bureaucracy would present some of these animals, once converted into Chinese medicine or hides, to foreign envoys as gifts.[11] For example, some of the animals taken during private hunts and those killed during the royal military Kangmu hunts were offered as gifts to Ming Chinese envoys. These included dried roebuck and venison (*napchangnok*; 臘獐鹿). Villagers from the southern provinces provided many of the same items.[12]

This was also the case for Chosŏn diplomats travelling to foreign lands. In 1476, Kim Chajŏng (?–?; 金自貞), the envoy to Tsushima Island, reported to the court about his visit. One day, the governor of Tsushima had invited Kim and his group to observe a circle hunt on a mountain. Kim noted that the leader used straw clothing and bows and arrows, which seemed to differ from those used in Chosŏn. A diplomatic gesture, a troop of nearly 400, armed with swords and gongs, did not locate any animals. The governor apologised to the Chosŏn diplomat. 'In this heat and humidity, I'm embarrassed that we were unable to take even a single beast. Let us enjoy a cup of rice wine despite not having any side dishes.'[13]

King Sŏngjong was particularly interested in the hunt on Tsushima. When the Chosŏn envoy returned and reported his trip to the king, Sŏngjong inquired

---

[10] Dried horsemeat came from as far away as Cheju Island. The process for drying meat is unclear.
[11] For instance, see the many products given to the envoy from Japan in 1457 and 1470. CWS, 7:200 and 8:518. Gifts of flying squirrel and hare hides were given to Ming officials. CWS, 3:185.
[12] See CWS, 12:152.
[13] CWS, 9:362.

about the island's hunting area (yŏpch'ŏ; 獵處). Kim Chajŏng explained that it was located twenty *li* (approximately 11 km/7 mi.) away from the headquarters of the island authorities.

> All of the soldiers marched through small canyons and valleys and along a narrow stone path. Even those who were not close family members rode horses, but all of the islanders warned, 'Please be careful where you walk because there are many venomous snakes.' We did not kill a single beast all day long. The king inquired about the military skills of the troops on Tsushima. Kim explained that they could not handle bows so could not shoot arrows well.[14]

This line of questioning highlights the link between hunting and military skills. Sŏngjong inquired about the kinds of hunting locations Kim had observed and learned that these areas were not easily accessible. He went on to follow-up with a question about the Tsushima troops' military expertise. To the king, soldiers without good locations to hunt would have limited opportunity to practise and hone their military abilities.[15]

In addition to the regular tribute of animal products, the court asked for special tribute items. These came in many forms throughout the year. Hunting items submitted as tribute came from as far away as Cheju Island. On one occasion, a rare white stag was presented to the court from the island while another time the island magistrate submitted deer tail and tongue.[16] The court used tigers, leopards and deer, that had been taken during the spring and autumn military Kangmu training exercises and not presented as tribute to the central government, as gifts.[17] For instance, early in the reign of King Sŏngjong, the court proclaimed that local magistrates (*suryŏng*; 守令) must submit all of the hides of the deer they had hunted as tribute. Recognising the hardship commoners had endured from fulfilling local tribute quotas, the king contended that local magistrates should, instead of relying on the commoners, be submitting the game they themselves catch.[18] More voices from Hanyang called for the game coming from the countryside to be presented to the government. These arguments, many based on morality, pressed local officials

---

[14] CWS, 9:367.
[15] Another instance is an occasion when the court inquired about the experience of Cheju fishermen who had drifted to the Ryukyu Kingdom. The king was particularly interested in the hunting skills of the Ryukyu people. See CWS, 10:25.
[16] CWS, 7:607 and 15:26.
[17] CWS, 10:12.
[18] See CWS, 8:458.

into surrendering their hunting prizes to help the common people – this would prevent local officials from burdening the peasants by demanding they stop agricultural work and go into the mountains to catch game to meet the quota.

Animals and the Personal Hunt

The dynasty's effort to secure animal products from the countryside represented one way in which the central authorities tried to extend control over the resources of the country. A strategy in support of this goal was to curtail private hunting practices, including those of the royal family. However, doing so was difficult. King T'aejo's solitary excursions into the wilderness might have been rare, but that did not change the fact that he shared a passion for small-scale hunting excursions with other kings, royal family members and like-minded aristocracy across Eurasia.[19] The royal military Kangmu hunts, the state's mustering of thousands of soldiers that, led by the king, practised military training through the hunting of animals on designated hunting grounds, displayed and fortified grand images of royal authority and power. Smaller, intimate, more personal hunts, many of the kind early kings such as T'aejo and Sŏngjong attended during the fifteenth century, were also important demonstrations of leadership and masculinity. Much smaller than the royal Kangmu hunts, personal hunting events – either small parties or those with a limited military escort – replicated the Kangmu on a more modest scale and did not require advanced preparation. Kings, royal family members and other elites could enter the forest or mountains without planning or approval, and usually near the capital, to spend time together in the field, collecting animals and reinforcing connections among those in attendance. While much like the Kangmu, these smaller, private hunts involved close family members, supportive officials, or even a handful of soldiers, thereby lending themselves to more intimacy.

This conflict over small hunting excursions erupted at the court in a few cases. Chief Royal Secretariat (tosŭngji; 都承旨) Yi Kŭkchŭng petitioned the court over the tribute sent from local magistrates. He believed that these magistrates had caught a plentiful amount of the roe and red or sika deer and that the quantity of deer hides was sufficient to fulfil tribute demand. Hence, it was determined that commoners did not have to submit tribute. Yi expressed

---

[19] European aristocracy turned to the hunt and politics as their military importance declined. See, Kate Mertes, 'Aristocracy', in *Fifteenth-Century Attitudes: Perceptions of Society in Late Medieval England*, ed. Rosemary Horrox (New York: Cambridge University Press, 1994), 53–4.

his concern that these local magistrates had been keeping the deer hides for themselves and that this was inappropriate. Queen Dowager Insu, making the decisions for the young king at the time, agreed.[20] Deeply Buddhist, she wanted to minimise the number of animals needed for sacrifice to the state. In 1470, when Queen Insu Sohye went into mourning after the death of her husband, she understood that precedence demanded the serving of meat after ritual wailing (*cholgok*; 卒哭), a custom when attendants cried and wailed in mourning for deceased relatives as an expression of their loss and Confucian loyalty. Such a ritual meant that many animals would be killed while on the hunt (*yŏpsalsaeng*; 獵殺生) in the Kyŏnggi area and nearby provinces, which saddened her. Meritorious advisor (*wŏnsang*; 院相) Han Myŏnghoe reminded the queen that, in the Chosŏn court, not as much meat was to be consumed after ritual wailing, as had been done in the past.[21] On another occasion, in 1472, Queen Dowager Insu demanded the capture of an animal without killing it, instructing Chief Royal Secretariat Chŏng Hyosang (1432–81; 鄭孝常) to seize a white stag that lived in Hwanghae Province and relocate it to the capital forest (*sallim*; 山林). Such a beast most likely offered good omens. However, transporting it to the capital had injured it somehow. 'The animal's leg is hurt and I'm afraid it will bring misfortune to the other animals. Let's keep it temporarily in the palace gardens (*huwŏn*; 後苑) and wait a while before we release it.' She insisted this directive was her own command and not the order of the king and said that she had already informed the chief royal secretariat (*sŭngjŏngwŏn*; 承政院) to carry out her orders.[22] This move was unusual. With a pond and trees, the rear garden of the palace was a sanctuary for the royal family and not designed as a menagerie. Attracted to the apparent symbolism of the animal, and knowing of its rarity, in 1474, another white stag was brought to the palace gardens to be released on Paegan (白岳), a mountain area behind the royal palace at Mt Pugak.[23]

Like his predecessors, extending back two centuries to the royal families of the Koryŏ–Mongol era, King Sŏngjong partook in personal hunts. Sŏngjong's penchant for hunting was well known among his officials, but the king's interest in hunting began slowly. From 1470 until 1474, while under the regency of the two former queens, Sŏngjong mostly spoke against the hunt agreeing with the Confucian arguments his advisors used to attack it as harmful to the people. In 1471, he asked Country Magistrate Yu Chongsu (?–?; 柳宗琇) if he

[20] CWS, 8:458.
[21] CWS, 8:459.
[22] CWS, 8:663.
[23] CWS, 9:108.

enjoyed hunting. Yu simply replied that he did not hunt.[24] Other members of the court discouraged the young king from such hunting. General Inspector Han Ch'ihyŏng (1434–1502; 韓致亨) composed a seventeen-point petition with the intention to improve the central government and assist the lives of the masses. The first, and most important, point was the recommendation that the way to rule righteously was to reduce expenses and that doing such would help the people, arguments that echoed those against the larger Kangmu hunts; in other words, the king should reject hunting.[25] More advisors attempted to guide the young king away from the apparently harmful practices such as music, Buddhism, Daoism and hunting.[26]

The first record of King Sŏngjong attending a hunt was in the second lunar month (March) of 1472 when he was fourteen and a half years old. To prepare for this hunt, he donned a military uniform and travelled to the village of T'owŏn (兎院), twenty-five kilometres (16 mi.) northeast of the royal palace, where he met his mother Queen Dowager Insu. As noted at the beginning of the book, on this trip, the young King Sŏngjong encountered an old man by the side of the road with quail pinned to his clothing and, to reward him for his catch, the young king bestowed one set of clothes on the elder man.[27]

Immediately after this hunt, several advisors and teachers instructed the young king to avoid hunting and did so by lumping hunting together with the acts of womanising and drinking. Apparently influenced by the Buddhist beliefs of his mother and grandmother as a boy, Sŏngjong displayed strong views against killing animals. He even went so far, after attending his first hunt, as to warn the provincial governor departing for Cheju Island not to enjoy the hunt.[28] Advisors and scholar officials continued to warn the king about the dangers and improprieties present with hunting. When the topic of hunting appeared in the records, it was part of the conversations with military and scholar officials informing the king about encounters with Jurchen, Japanese and the Chinese 'hunting' along the borders. In 1472, two officials, Yi Maenghyŏn (1436–87; 李孟賢) and Kim Chesin (1438–99; 金悌臣), questioned the private hunting practices of King Sŏngjong. Deploying the arguments against the large-scale royal military Kangmu, both officials recognised that hunting during the agricultural off-season was a way to practise military skills, and that this activity had been conducted since antiquity. Preparing

[24] CWS, 8:576.
[25] CWS, 8:576.
[26] CWS, 8:587.
[27] CWS, 8: 638.
[28] CWS, 8:643.

the military during the off-season lessened the harm levelled at the people by reducing the destruction of agricultural lands; such timing also had the added benefit of producing game for ritual sacrifices.[29] However, Yi and Kim claimed that the 1472 harvest had been severely limited in the capital region because of excessive flooding, droughts and damage caused by high winds. They hoped that the king would take these issues into consideration and forbid hunting in the capital province. The young king did take notice of their concerns and forbid hunting there that year.[30]

Private hunts like these promoted foreign diplomacy. In 1472, King Sŏngjong hunted in the woodlands surrounding P'ungyang Mountain Fortress, roughly twenty-five kilometres (15 mi.) northeast of the royal palace, while accompanied by a number of foreigners. Foreign diplomats included the military commander Tonga Wangha (?–?; 童阿亡哈), probably a Jurchen given a military title to help win him over, and twelve other Jurchens, as well as Hikonsaimo (?–?; 皮昆灑毛) and three other Japanese. On this occasion, the group stayed at Yŏnbok Monastery and hunted many birds together. The king provided the Jurchen visitor Tonga Wangha with bows and arrows.[31] Small-scale hunting promoted personal connections with people outside the peninsula who otherwise did not share the same political allegiances or even languages.

Encouraged by such encounters on small-scale hunts with foreigners, in the autumn of that year, Sŏngjong noted that, during his Confucian lectures, he had learned more about hunting and how it served as a way to practise the military arts. In other words, they prepared for more violent encounters with foreigners. P'ungyang Mountain Fortress, he told his advisors, was easy to reach and a good place to perhaps practice. Slightly troubled by this request, the court officials convinced him to select Mt Hongbok instead, an even closer location. Sŏngjong's Confucian lecturers pushed back. They humbly agreed with the young king that because hunting had been conducted quarterly in ancient times, it was necessary to continue this practice in order to properly train the military. However, the men insisted, calamities in the Kyŏnggi region produced a poor harvest and the hardships on the commoners were too great.[32] This conversation apparently worked. Sŏngjong cancelled his hunt and did not talk about hunting again at the court for a year.

---

[29] Early Chinese Buddhist and Indian monasteries insisted that animals should not be used for sacrifice, unlike Confucian and Brahmanical practices. Chen, 'A Buddhist Classification of Animals and Plants in Early Tang Times', 40.

[30] CWS, 8:690.

[31] CWS, 8:689.

[32] CWS, 8:690.

Not until the ninth lunar month (October) of 1473 at the age of sixteen did Sŏngjong begin to express a growing interest in hunting after he viewed a ring hunt at Mt Ach'a, eleven kilometres (7 mi.) east of the royal palace. The distance to Mt Ach'a forced the king to hold his meal at Chungnyangp'o (中良浦), an area on the northeast outskirts of the capital. A year later, he stayed again at Mt Ach'a. The time to travel to this location was too great for him to return the same day and forced him to spend the night at a royal encampment (*chujangso*; 晝停所) on his way back and hold a feast with royal family members and others.[33] He also used this opportunity to order a drinking party. The royal family members and others accompanying Sŏngjong on the hunt attended.[34] While the scale of these hunts is impossible to know, they were most likely small as they did not mobilise troops or demand additional horses. In 1473, King Sŏngjong journeyed to P'ungyang, about fifty kilometres (30 mi.) north of the palace, a mountain region along the Imjin River, where he went more than once to conduct military exercises. His party once again stayed at T'owŏn, sixteen kilometres (10 mi.) northeast of the capital and hunted nearby at a location called Chuŭltong (注乙洞), where streams meet the mountains. He forwarded the birds his party killed to the official Yi Yegyŏn (?–?; 李禮堅) for ancestral rituals at the temple. After the hunt he retired to P'ungyang Palace (豐壤宮) for the evening. Upon his return to the palace, Sŏngjong presented the game to his mother, Queen Dowager Insu.[35] After spending time in the wild interacting with animals, apparently it was imperative for him to return to the civilising power of the royal residence by night and demonstrate his Confucian filial obligations.

As we have seen in earlier chapters, at the founding of Chosŏn, officials attempted to establish hunting regulations. One hunting category, termed 'personal hunting' (*saryŏp*; 私獵), appeared most often during the first half of the fifteenth century, was deemed illegal. Personal hunting seems to have been referring to individual or small group trips into the fields, forests and mountains. Even so, the government recognised seasoned hunters (*uin*; 虞人) and the royal park (*wŏnyu*; 園囿) attendants, who had cared for animals similar to Queen Insu's white stag. There was also another group of hunters present, during the late fifteenth century at least, that the government had titled 'talented people' (*chaein*; 才人). Much like the hunter in the 'Heavenly Maiden and the Woodcutter' tale, these were lowborn (*ch'ŏnmin*; 賤民), who had been trained in various arts or had talent, or in some cases earned a living by selling products

---

[33] CWS, 9:90.
[34] CWS, 9:62.
[35] CWS, 9:67.

they had crafted from the animals they had hunted.[36] Magistrates from every province had erected traps and had hunters equipped with bows and crossbows (*kungno*; 弓弩) at the ready to capture and kill tigers and leopards, but these devices and preparations appear to have been largely for the protection of the local population and not for food, fur or tribute.[37] The laws put into place could get officials into trouble if they went hunting. Members of the Privy Council (Top'yŏng ŭisasa; 都評議使司) wrote that capital officials sent to the provinces directly by the king (*pongmyŏng sain*; 奉命使人) and local magistrates (*sunyŏng*; 守令) would be prohibited from hunting privately.[38] The court was also concerned about local magistrates taking advantage of commoners on the island of Cheju, after they received a report that officials had commandeered some horses to go on a private hunt.[39] In another case, a herd of elk (*taeryuk*; 大鹿) was reported in P'yŏngan Province. The local magistrate requested they be hunted, and their hides be used for ceremonial rituals and submitted as tribute. However, weary of magistrates taking direction of small hunts like this and fearing corruption, abuse of the local population or overhunting, the Minister of Taxation, Chŏng Nanjong (1433–89; 鄭蘭宗), suggested instead that two villages work together to acquire enough tribute and present it to the court. Chŏng believed that there were not enough deer for more than three annual rituals.[40] The sharing of tribute might further help dilute the power of this magistrate as well as contribute to animal conservation. Such laws indicate that officials working for the court also participated in small, personal hunts when beyond the immediate gaze of central authority.

As with the royal military Kangmu, a growing number of civil officials, those pushing a particular interpretation of Neo-Confucianism, loudly expressed their disdain for these small-scale hunts. The bureaucracy sought to punish those who engaged in personal hunting. This extended to controlling access to the hunt by members of their own class. Yet, it is clear that not all civil officials viewed the issue monolithically. In 1471, a number of officials were called out for hunting and fishing with *kisaeng*, female entertainers for the upper class, on National Memorial Day (*kukül*; 國忌日), when the king and queen conducted state ancestral rites. Not only caught while hunting, they were also entertaining women. The court dismissed one and demoted two others for their actions.[41] For other elites, even members of the royal family, personal hunting collided

[36] *CWS*, 9:214.
[37] *CWS*, 8:462.
[38] *CWS*, 1:31.
[39] *CWS*, 11:663.
[40] *CWS*, 11:267.
[41] *CWS*, 8:602.

with the demands of the state. The court begrudgingly tolerated personal hunting by royal family members early in the century but over time this activity became increasingly contested. As has been seen, hunting was a defining element of royal identity passed down from generation to generation. Those who sought to regulate the hunting practices of royal family members did so for a multiplicity of reasons from ideological, practical and economic. The debate was over access to power or potential power. The participation of relatives in personal hunts could challenge the royal authority of the king.

King Sŏngjong's older brother was an early target of the crackdown. Prince Yi Chŏng (1454–88; 李婷), also known as Prince Wŏlsan, was a great-grandson of King Sejong, the grandson of King Sejo, and older brother of King Sŏngjong. The throne should have been passed onto him, the oldest living son of the former king: however, Prince Wŏlsan is thought to have been too ill to take over the throne. Referred to as simple and not prone to anger, Wŏlsan was an avid writer who loved poetry and wine; court scribes described him as a clean-living man uninterested in the three vices: music, women, and hawks or hounds. The metaphorical 'hunting' he did was 'cursory hunting' (sŏmnyŏp; 涉獵), in other words he skimmed texts each day 'hunting' for meaning behind the words. He and his younger brother, the king, had a good rapport, and Wŏlsan also shared a loving relationship with his mother, Queen Dowager Insu. When Wŏlsan's health took a turn for the worst, his mother provided him with medicine – some of it most likely drugs made of animals – but it did not help. Wŏlsan succumbed to his illness at the age of thirty-five.[42] Like Wŏlsan's story, many people were sick at this time from the outbreak of disease. While unable to nurse him back to health, royal family members and other elites in the capital tapped into the animals of the peninsula to try to help their closest family members recover.[43]

Descriptions of Prince Wŏlsan's personality, as described in the *Sillok*, are contradictory. It appears that Wŏlsan did indeed enjoy small-scale hunting before he grew too ill but was forced by the court to give up his personal hunting expeditions that did not involve the king. Prince Wŏlsan is known to have hunted in the area surrounding the capital with hunting falcons (*yangŭng*; 良鷹) and in 1475, he partook in a hunt in the suburbs of the capital with a small number of falconers who had four or five exemplary birds.[44] Six days later, an argument broke out at the court over the propriety of royal

---

[42] For a description of Prince Wŏlsan, see CWS, 11:422. Apparently as a sign of appreciation, in 1487 King Sŏngjong gave his older brother a horse from the Inner Palace Stable. CWS, 11:198.

[43] More will be said about disease in Chapter 9.

[44] CWS, 9:280.

family members taking part in this kind of hunt. The censor from the Office of Censors, Pak Sungjil (?–1507; 朴崇質), criticised the prince for leaving through the palace gate (kwŏlmun; 闕門) and accused him of taking advantage of the king and country. 'This action does not represent the morality of a prince.' The king was angered by this criticism. 'Prince Wŏlsan is my brother,' Sŏngjong insisted. 'How could leaving through the gate on this one occasion violate the law?'[45] He then demanded an inquiry into those who criticised his brother.

The next day, Pak softened his criticism but repeated the accusations against Prince Wŏlsan.

> In general, human emotions are degraded by hunting falcons, hunting dogs, wine, and women. It is easy to see that this happens and to say this is true. In the end, surely [your brother's act] subverts the laws of the country and shows that the prince is losing his way. As for morality, is this [your displeasure with my concern] a means to welcome and accept [the act of hunting]?

Pak ends his argument by asking, 'If the Censorate impeaches him [Prince Wŏlsan], will this bring stability?' The king was not convinced Wŏlsan had done anything wrong. He questioned whether Pak had mistaken Wŏlsan for someone else and asked again who had subverted the law and lived a life of debauchery. The king questioned if Pak were referring to Prince Yangnyŏng (1394–1462; 讓寧大君). The king argued that when former Prince Yangnyŏng became the crown prince, he had not lost his morality because of his hunting falcons and dogs. Like Wŏlsan, the former Crown Prince Yangnyŏng renounced his position as crown prince to allow his younger brother, Sejong, to become king. Like Yangnyŏng's relationship with his younger brother King Sejong, Wŏlsan and Sŏngjong were close.

Left Assistant Royal Secretariate Han Sŏkkyu (1430–80; 玄碩圭), concerned that Pak Sungjil had angered the king and would die for his remarks, defended him. Han wondered if a crown prince, being unable to leave the palace gate to hunt, were akin to someone imprisoned. When former Prince Yangnyŏng had been exiled from the royal palace in 1418, the former King Sejong continued to hold an audience with Yangnyŏng and had bestowed him with falcons and hunting dogs. King Sŏngjong relied on this familiar historical evidence to argue against Pak Sungjil. 'The prince is one of my brothers,' the king insisted. 'He goes outside the palace gate once, and the Censorate

---

[45] CWS, 9:281.

is ready to impeach him ... and make him feel regretful.' Sŏngjong did not believe that what his brother had done was considered a crime. He wanted public discussion about it to cease and warned officials to ignore the criticism brought by Pak Sungjil. Han Sŏkkyu hinted that he wished that it was possible to keep the prince and other royal family members from leaving palace grounds to hunt. Even though he had been criticised for hunting, Prince Wŏlsan, as one of the king's trusted companions, accompanied his younger brother and other royal family members on a number of hunts outside the capital grounds.[46]

Similar to his older brother, King Sŏngjong came under increased criticism during the regency of the queen mothers. Criticism coalesced around the young king's participation in all kinds of hunts. Officials who disdained his hunting practices used much of the same language they used to critique the royal military Kangmu hunt. The following year, in 1474, King Sŏngjong planned to travel to Mt Ch'ŏnggye, twenty kilometres (12 mi.) south of the royal palace, to hunt, but the officials in the Office of the Censor General expressed concern that the weather was too cold and the path up the mountain too treacherous. Taking their concerns into consideration, the king cancelled his trip.[47] Sŏng Hyŏn (1439–1504; 成俔), an official from the Office of the Inspector General, believed that drastic measures had to be taken to curtail the strange weather conditions in the country. Confucian and shaman ideas assumed that the appropriate religious rituals or changing misguided government policy could return balance to the cosmic order. Two senior officials, Hong Yunsŏng (1425–75; 洪允成) and Yun Chaun (1414–78; 尹子雲), dismissed the idea of eliminating the hunt as a way to appease heavenly aberrations (ch'ŏnbyŏn; 天變).[48]

Like debates around the Kangmu, court discussion and subsequent conflict related to hunting also revolved around preserving the sanctity of ancestral lands. In 1474, King Sŏngjong proposed restricting the type of stone altars used for the grave markers of the *sadaebu* elite. He stated that he did not care for nor want statues of people or horses placed at the tombs – these were tombstone-like steles erected at burial mound sites of the elite. Senior scholar official Hong Yunsŏng rebutted that he had never seen a tomb with an altar of a stone horse. Generally, these graves were placed on hills in the countryside. Hong went on to relate a historical moment that touched on the

---

[46] CWS, 9:282. Despite these criticisms, Prince Wŏlsan accompanied his younger brother and others on hunts outside the capital. See CWS, 10:314, 10:322, 10:429 and 11:154.
[47] CWS, 9:80.
[48] CWS, 9:88.

clash over hunting practices at the graves of the *sadaebu* elite and fortified his belief that the markers should stay. According to the story, King T'aejong, an avid hunter, once went hunting at Ch'ŏrwŏn (鐵原), a mountainous region in north central Kangwŏn Province, where he commanded an experienced hunter with him to ignite a fire and begin the hunt. The hunter hesitated and pointed out that the forested area was once the old capital of King Kungye (r. 901–18; 弓裔), a former member of the Silla aristocracy who had broken away and temporarily established his own kingdom during the disintegration of Silla in the early tenth century. The area of the fire hunt held tombs of the *sadaebu* elites from those times. The hunter with T'aejong warned the king that igniting the fire for the hunt would also destroy the stone monuments. The king presumably agreed, and the hunt was cancelled. From this story, Hong concluded, the use of stone monuments for the *sadaebu* had been long established.[49] Here, Hong countered the king's desire to put hunting practices before the needs of the *sadaebu* and Confucian burial rituals. By protecting these stone monuments – themselves a display of elite central authority and Confucianism in areas that were not heavily populated – the court had subtly placed restraints on the locations for destructive fire hunts. Stone steles with inscriptions like these related the lives of local yangban leaders, often extolling their Confucian virtues and morality. These steles were reminders to those residing in the countryside of *sadaebu* authority and the state's civilising force over the environment.

The intersection of personal hunts, ritual, moral governance and land access are represented in one extended discussion at the court. When King Sŏngjong assumed full control of the government in 1476, he continued to participate in these small-scale, personal hunts on numerous mountains surrounding the capital. In one particular incident at Changgyŏngnŭng (昌敬陵), the location of tomb mounds, a tiger had killed and consumed a horse.[50] In its response, the court once again recognised the dangers that can occur when the environments of people and wild animals overlap. The king stated, 'There were no differences' between the places where people and 'wicked animals' live and die. While the king recognised the risk co-habitation zones posed, he was specifically concerned with military horses intruding onto areas of the royal tombs (*nŭngch'im*; 陵寢). Such animals might potentially trample the gravesites. These tombs were most often located in the countryside, often on mountains, bringing those who visited them into contact with wild beasts. He thought it was necessary to rid the people of these wicked animals and that

[49] CWS, 9:84.
[50] The location of the Changgyŏngnŭng tomb mounds has been lost.

doing so would bring the army and their horses onto these lands, but that was a necessary evil.

Sŏngjong's answer to these interactions was a straightforward display of his power and authority. By clearing away the 'wicked' wildlife and flushing out a tiger after he had conducted worship at the tombs of his ancestors, Sŏngjong would further solidify his legacy and bring power back to the throne. Fourth Inspector Yi Ubo (?–?; 李祐甫) surmised as such and suggested that the king himself wanted to hunt the tiger. Yi tried to dissuade the king by insisting that the king would be dressed for conducting the rites and would not have the appropriate clothing for a hunt. He also insisted that the king would be too weak to engage in such activities after participating in the necessary fasting ritual (*chaegye*; 齋戒). 'What I mean is that Your Majesty should permanently give up hunting on days when you conduct ancestral rites.' Third Censor An Ch'im noted, 'The path to the tomb is a quiet and reverential thing . . . and we should be concerned that the spirits will not be comforted.'

Fourth Inspector Yi suggested that the king's soldiers go to the mountain in his stead because the common people did not expect to see the king himself hunting. Third Censor An Ch'im continued, 'Even if foot soldiers pursued the animal, they would be extremely loud and disruptive. Is hunting the correct thing?' An Ch'im feared sending the king to a place with 'wicked animals' and suggested dispatching professional soldiers in lieu of the king to pursue and kill the tiger after the king had conducted ancestral worship. An went on to remind Sŏngjong that the king himself had said that many animals inhabit Kwangnŭng (光陵). Kwangnŭng is a mountain roughly twenty-five kilometres (16 mi.) northeast of the capital and the location of the tomb mounds for King Sejo and where Queen Dowager Chŏnghŭi would later be interred in 1483. Since the king expressed the desire to alleviate harming the commoners, An argued, the king should refrain from hunting. An insisted that the king would damage the fields (*chŏn'gok*; 田穀) if he entered the area even if it turned out there were no animals present. The senior meritorious advisor and Chief State Councillor Chŏng Ch'angson (1402–87; 鄭昌孫) stepped into the debate. He insisted that the wicked animals in tomb gardens (*nŭngwŏn*; 陵園) should not be pursued; presumably he was referring to the king. Instead, excluding mounted soldiers that might damage the area, fires should be set, horns blown and foot soldiers sent in to flush them out (*mabyŏngbanghwajwigak yŏngbobyŏngguch'uk*; 馬兵放火吹角,令步兵驅逐).[51]

Sŏngjong replied to this criticism. He concluded that conducting sacrifices was not the same as pursuing wild animals. The king understood that

---

[51] *CWS*, 9:496.

at other times the agricultural needs of the commoners should be taken into consideration, and he specifically ordered those on the hunt not to damage rice fields.[52] In other words, according to the king, hunting animals, ancestral rituals and assisting commoners' livelihoods were separate matters that need not be discussed together. While An Ch'im and Yi Ubo conveniently conflated these issues to try to convince the king to give up hunting, in Sŏngjong's mind the issues were unrelated and their argument unconvincing. 'After conducting ancestral rites, what is the harm in chasing [the tiger]?' Angered by the revolving argument, the king shouted, 'You, Confucians (yuja; 儒者), are abstruse in all matters (uŏsajŏng; 迂於事情)!'

What should be done about the tiger roaming the gravesites of the royal tombs? The next day, following the royal lecture (kyŏngyŏn; 經筵), Third Inspector Yi Chip (1438–1509; 李諿) reported Chŏng Ch'angson's decision that tigers should not be pursued in tomb gardens. Feeling empowered by the support, An Ch'im continued his argument. Tapping into classical precedence, he discussed the tale of Emperor Wen, a leader who enjoyed galloping on a tall horse, but when Minister Yuan Ang (袁盎) denounced him for it, the emperor gave up riding horses. 'As for Your Highness personally flushing out wicked beasts, this is a dangerous path and puts Your Highness in the proximity of wicked beasts (ch'in'guaksu ch'awido; 親驅惡獸, 此危道),' An Ch'im insisted. The king pushed back declaring he did not attend processions or learn to shoot arrows because of 'wicked beasts', implying that he was the leader of a military not a hunting party.

An Ch'im brought the discussion back to the question of ritual.

> The day of ancestral sacrifices is a solemn occasion. It was written ages ago that this 'Is a day of weeping and there should be no music.' Matters like hunting are mere games (hŭisa; 戲事). If Your Highness carries these out together [hunting and ritual], what kind of things will people hear [from the spread of rumors]?'

King Sŏngjong agreed, 'Ritual days must be solemn.' However, following the ceremony, the sacrificial purification (chaegye; 齋戒) should conclude as well. 'Both sacrifice and the pursuit of wicked animals comfort the departed spirits (sŏllyŏng; 先靈). Say nothing more!'[53]

Days later, after this discussion, King Sŏngjong scheduled a time to conduct rites at Kyŏngnyŭng (敬陵) – the burial mound of Prince Tŏkchong,

---

[52] CWS, 11:198.
[53] CWS, 9:496. More debates continue into CWS, 9:497.

Sŏngjong's father – and Ch'angnŭng (昌陵) – the burial mound of King Yejong (r. 1468–69; 睿宗), Sŏngjong's uncle – the locations of some of the most important ancestral tombs to the king. Minister of Rites Hŏ Chong (1434–94; 許琮) inquired as to the king's intent.

> Today Your Majesty dons memorial service robes (tambok; 淡服) and will bow to the ancestral tombs. If Your Majesty is not extremely sorrowful, it will be inappropriate to engage in a personal hunt (ch'illyŏp; 親獵). If a wicked beast appears [a tiger], it will not have a chance to injure anyone. How can Your Majesty take part in such a hunt personally?

King Sŏngjong replied,

> If what you say is correct … I will not hunt. If there is a fierce tiger (maengho; 猛虎) in the area of the royal tombs, we will be unable to drive it off. After much discussion with the State Council, it was determined that the observations of the State Council agreed with mine. If someone discusses this matter in future generations, perhaps there will be someone [with opinions] like yours or perhaps there will be someone [with opinions] like [those of] the State Council. You must reconsider this![54]

When Hŏ Chong attempted to bring this issue up again with the king, Sŏngjong refused to listen. He brushed aside Hŏ's concerns and proceeded to hold the hunt elsewhere. The king changed out of his ritual garbs and into his martial uniform (yungbok; 戎服) and travelled with his hunting party to a location called Paksŏkhyŏn (薄石峴), only six kilometres (4 mi.) northwest of the royal palace, where he hunted deer and hare. Perhaps out of fear of royal reprisal, other ministers stepped forward, after the king had left, to defend Hŏ Chong as an upright and competent minister.[55]

Later in the week, when the king had returned, Minister of Rites Hŏ Chong reiterated his plea. 'From now onward, I beg Your Highness, please do not take part in the circle hunt on days you conduct ritual sacrifice at ancestral tombs.' King Sŏngjong defended himself by saying that such a hunt was necessary and that he did not enjoy it. 'It was just for flushing out the fierce tiger roaming near the royal tombs. I won't do it again if it's not the right thing to do.' In the king's defence, his distant royal relative and senior advisor Yi Simwŏn (1454–1504; 李深源) stepped into the discussion, adding,

[54] CWS, 9:498.
[55] CWS, 9:498.

'It is recorded in the Great Law Code (Taejŏn; 大典) that improper ritual behavior (ŭmsa; 淫祀) is prohibited [used often to refer to shaman practices or other violations of ritual protocol]. If you abolish the law, it will not have any impact. Customs do not change.' King Sŏngjong agreed with Yi Simwŏn arguing that the law had begun with the founder of the dynasty. Yi Simwŏn went on,

> The court has established that we must pray for a king's long life on his birthday. Thus, the ministers cannot say anything about it [this ceremony calling for the king's longevity]. But in the past, they would say, 'Let's not pray for the king's good health.' They also would say, 'It is flattering to hold a memorial service even if it is not for my spirit.' If the king conducts the affairs of state benevolently, the foundation [of the state] is firm and the country is at ease. Without a doubt, the king will have a long life. [In other words, the king being alive did not require prayers, rather it is necessary to show proper respect to the ancestors and govern the state through sagely principles of moral governance.] Within heterodoxy (sado; 邪道) [outside accepted practices], can good fortune be found?

Another official, Yun Chaun, interjected arguing that offering prayer for the king's long life on this birthday was an obligation to the king. 'Even if it were not orthodoxy, it would be hard to quickly alter it.' While ostensibly a discussion about praying for the king's longevity, underneath the debate, officials critiqued the king's role in the personal hunts, especially at the royal tomb mounds, implying that the king should cease them before such hunts become acceptable ceremonies, like the prayers for the ruler.[56] Regardless of the eloquence of these arguments, Sŏngjong resisted. Supported by other officials – as well as the practices of many on the peninsula – he continued to conduct personal hunts.

The overlapping of human–animal geographies is depicted in the 'intrusion' of tigers onto lands claimed by the state and where important ancestral rituals were conducted. The appearance of the tiger on these ritually significant lands spurred debates over what a good leader should and should not do. This was an ideological debate on one level about the appropriateness of the king going into the fields to hunt tigers. These areas were on mountains, sparsely populated, and ideal locations for wildlife to thrive. But the conversation at the court was also a debate over the nature of good leadership.

---

[56] CWS, 9:505.

Probably not lost on Sŏngjong was that ministers tried to prevent him from hunting on lands that held royal tombs of his ancestors who themselves had been avid hunters. With the number of Kangmu hunting grounds on the peninsula reduced, the lands for the royal tombs offered an alternative location to hunt privately in small groups. Unlike Kangmu lands, the government did not reduce their number. Rather, these lands multiplied over time as generations of royal family members passed away. As they were his direct ancestors, he would have had full access to these lands to conduct himself as he desires. Restrictions on private hunting should not extend to these lands, he argued, especially if he performed the necessary rites. Kingship stories of personal bravery in the field and his mastery of one of the most dangerous animals on the peninsula were as equally important to him as depictions of his filiality, morality and sagely rulership.

* * *

It is easy to imagine a hunting encounter between King Sŏngjong and a tiger stalking the royal tombs spun into a story much like that of King T'aejo and the sable. Yet no such stories are known to exist. By the 1470s, defining royal authority through such heroic hunting displays grew increasingly difficult if not impossible. In the wake of succession disputes and the changing needs of the state, animals took on new meaning for royal legitimacy. Officials in the central government haggled over elite and non-elite access to animals and the king's access to animals on ancestral burial mounds. Royal domination of beasts took the form of animal tribute submitted to the central government in the king's name. To maximise the animals available for tribute to the central government, the dynasty attempted to micromanage small-scale animal encounters through policies that reduced the number of people, even those with elite or royal status, who were allowed to hunt privately. Encounters between rulers and beasts challenged this model of reform.

To a growing number in the bureaucracy, private, personal hunts were much more dangerous than the royal military Kangmu hunts, literally and figuratively. Needing only a few troops, if any, to accompany him, a king could organise these hunts with royal family members and agreeable civil officials at a moment's notice, bypassing the months of planning needed for the Kangmu, time disapproving officials often spent to dissuade the king from taking part. These smaller outings skirted the ritual regulations of formalised hunts where the king served as the head of the military and conducted the hunt based on classical texts from ancient China. Experiences on these smaller hunts were spontaneous, even chaotic.

They were also dangerous because these hunts potentially contributed to the creation of stories about the king, his royal family members and those who accompanied him. Sometimes those stories demonstrated his skilful mastery over animals, such as those involving King T'aejo, or undermined the authority of the king and central leaders, as with private hunts of royal family members. As we will see in the next chapter, without court scribes along to record these small-scale hunts, those who took part could tell fantastical tales that reinforced the king's control over the land and animals. On personal hunts like these under debate, kings and others often appeared free from state demands to surrender captured game for ritual or tribute when they culled animals. Sometimes hunters surrendered their kills to the state as ritual sacrifice or as tribute, but often hunting parties kept them, feasted on them, and spun these animal encounters into humorous and frightening stories. Some animals, such as the white stag, were captured alive and penned in royal parks as personal displays of ownership. As we will see in the next chapter, other captured animals, such as hawks, had their natural instincts bent to benefit their human captors and were trained to hunt for the amusement of the royal family as well as elite and non-elite alike for personal, private hunts. Through trade and gifts and a shared cultural tradition, falconry also connected Korea to a wider Northeast Asian world.

8

Release the Falcons: A King in a Confucian Court

Falconry, another form of the private hunt, was woven into the cultural and political landscape of early Korea and Northeast Asia. A body of knowledge on falconry, some inspired from Chinese texts, and more from native Korean practices – shaped by political, geographical and cultural beliefs – helped inform those involved in the sport and circulated even to the Japanese islands. *New and Augmented Methods for Falconry* (*Sinjŭng ŭnggol pang*; 新增鷹鶻方), a birding manuscript, suggests the level of awareness Koreans and others held about birds of prey.

> All living things are born. Those that have feathers, fly. They are called birds. To begin, the birds of prey are called the following: goshawk (*haech'ŏng*; 海青), great and small peregrine falcons (*taeso apkol*; 大小鴨鶻), sparrow hawks (*nongt'al*; 籠奪), great and small hare hawks (*taeso t'ogol*; 大小兔鶻), Yŏn sparrow hawks (*yŏn'gol*; 燕鶻), and Chŏn sparrow hawks (*chŏn*; 鸇) – these are all types of hawks (*kolsok*; 鶻屬). The falcon (*ŭng*; 鷹), the white-tailed falcons (*paegŭng*; 白鷹), the mountain falcon (*kagŭng*; 角鷹), another type of sparrow hawk (*yo*; 鷂) – all of these are raptors. There are all types of falcons (*ungsok*; 鷹屬) ... Vultures (*ch'wi*; 鷲) are called *chŏgang* (*chŏgang*; 低強), nightjars (*sinp'ung*; 晨風), and black kite (*yŏn*; 鳶) – these are all types of vultures. Hawks and vultures have claws and talons that are [shiny] blue-green, and their eyes are black, they have yellow legs ... The category of birds that are vultures are well known for being untrainable.[1]

---

[1] Here and subsequent quotes are from *Sinjŭng ŭnggol pang* [New and augmented methods for falconry], 1 vol. Shinpei ogura [Showa 1930 edition], 10–11, hereafter cited as SUP. Although the dates of publication are hard to determine, they were produced in early Chosŏn. Kim Pangul argues that *Falconry Methods* was written in the late Chosŏn while the *New and Augmented Methods for Falconry*, under discussion here, dates earlier.

According to the manuscript, nine species had the temperament that allowed them to be trained as hunting companions. Like other migratory birds, these raptors nested on the peninsula in the warmer months. Included was a description of where to encounter them. 'The time for catching migrating hawks is the beginning of the seventh lunar month [late summer]. There are many birds in the interior of the country and few over the frontier. From the beginning of the eighth lunar month until the end of the month, the falcons from over the frontier arrive.'[2] While birds were plentiful, not all were suitable for training. 'It is best to catch those that are young', probably eyas, or nestlings, and branchers, which were more responsive to training than the haggards, or adults.

The guidebook goes on to explain that those involved in reclaiming, or thoroughly training, raptors invested a great deal of time with these birds. Different species demanded specific quarry for training.

> Peregrine falcons learn by using wild geese, ducks, crows, and magpies; hare falcons learn by hares and ringed pheasants; dragon snatchers (*yongt'al*; 龍奪) [perhaps a large eagle], learn by using quail and orioles, sparrow hawks are trained by using quail and sparrows; swifts are taught by using quail and sparrows; hawks, white falcons, and mountain hawks are taught by using ringed pheasants, hare, and ducks; one kind of sparrow hawk learns by quail and magpie . . . if it is a goshawk falcon, without geese, crane, or male hares, they cannot be taught.[3]

Because falconers captured and raised their birds in regions with abundant wild prey, most likely the quarry was unbagged during training – that is, they probably captured prey and let it loose for training.

Falcons were considered meticulously clean birds that bathed frequently. Because of this, they required a constant supply of water, such as a water basin

---

Falconry Methods became well known in Japan, Kim argues, as part of the Chosŏn-Tokugawa thawing of relations. Tokukawa Iyeyasu was an avid falcon hunter and appreciated falcons from the peninsula. See Kim Pangul, 'Maesayuk kwa maesanyang ŭi wihan chich'imsŏ *Ŭnggolbang ŭi yŏjŏng*' [The journey of the *Guidebook on Falconry*], *Muhyŏng yusan* 8 (2020): 161–84.

[2] SUP, 10–11. Breeding takes place from March to mid-June. The post-fledgling period begins with summer. The Korean peninsula experiences a migration of falcons in spring and autumn because of the location of the peninsula in the temperate zone. See Chang-Yong Choi and Hyun-Young Nam, 'Diet of Peregrine Falcons (*Falco peregrinus*) in Korea: Food Items and Seasonal Changes', *Journal of Raptor Research* 49, no. 4 (December 2015): 376–88.

[3] SUP, 11.

to bathe in. They were always thirsty and falconers had to remain vigilant about bowsing, or drinking. 'When hawks fly with open beaks . . . they are certainly fond of drinking water [presumably because their mouths dry out], but if they are still afraid of people, even if they see a water source, they will not drink from it.'[4] If a falcon required casting, or restraining, then water needed to be provided to it with a ladle. 'Those birds that have no choice but to be bound up, must be spoon-fed water, and water poured into their mouths several times', but care was taken so the animal did not choke. The bird needed to bowse before being carried into the field. 'When it is time for the hunt, it is thirsty and will heat up.'[5]

After water came food. 'Half of the time is spent feeding it.' Falcons, 'released to hunt all day, will certainly use a lot of energy and grow very hot'. When they return to their block, they should be fed 'warm-blooded meat', including sparrows, mice and quail, chickens, ringed pheasants, wild geese and ducks. However, 'they are afraid of aggressive roosters'. Care had to be taken with prepared meat. The fear was not too little food but too much: 'Falcons . . . will certainly be injured by overeating.' Bechins, or morsels, were fed to them throughout the day because 'they are constantly hungry'. Also, eyas, or young falcons, also called screamers, 'fearing people, they are permanently baiting, fluttering, or cowering (simyŏl sangjon; 心熱常存), one should be especially vigilant and cautious with them'. They had to remain superior (in good condition for flight). 'You raise them and feed them water and food. You want them neither too thin nor too fat.'[6]

One strategy was called 'water feeding' (susik; 水食).[7] This involved cutting up the meat into pieces – the skin was sliced from the bones, and the fat was removed. The meat was then soaked in water. In the winter, 'there was no harm raising the falcon inside an enclosure and feeding it warm pieces of meat [recently killed], but water feeding was necessary in the spring and autumn'. After preparing the sliced meat in water, 'the meat is laid out on the tree trunks where the bird is weathered [in the open air]'. Amounts depended on the size of the bird: 'Huge hawks should have large ringed pheasants, and small hawks [should] have small ringed pheasants.'[8] Tendons and muscles

---

[4] SUP, 14.
[5] SUP, 15.
[6] SUP, 22.
[7] Water feeding is much like 'washed meat', meat that is soaked in water and dried. This removes nutrients as a means to keep the bird hungry after feeding and ready to hunt. See Lee Eberly, 'Glossary of Falconry Terms', *Raptor Research News* 3, no. 3 (July 1969): 66.
[8] SUP, 16.

from these pheasants were fed to the birds, but 'for internal organs, they are soaked in the urine of people and fed to the animal' (*naerulch'ik innyo ch'imsa*; 內陋則人尿浸飼).[9] Another feeding strategy was 'field feeding' (*yasa*; 野飼). This involved simply providing food to the bird when on hunts. The only fear was low temperatures in winter months, perhaps because of frostbite. 'In extreme cold, do not try field feeding. If one is feeding in the field, then the food should be placed in pouches to reduce the chance of the meat freezing.'[10] It was also suggested that to keep the bird sharp – set and ready to hunt – one should not supply food to the animal while in the field – 'At sunset return home and feed it.' Regardless of the technique, because of the handling of dead animals to feed the birds, it was proper to 'wash your hands and clean the knife and cutting board'.[11]

Falconry techniques differed slightly between the north and the south. One difference was the length of time a falconer carried the new falcon during training. 'Northern people always carry eyasses, or nesting falcons on their arms.' This slight difference in technique elicited criticism from the writer. '[Because of this], they do not do corvée labor or other duties.'[12] In other words, falcon trainers from the northern regions – where many of these raptors originated – took advantage of their falconry skills to gain exemption from government labour. Carrying birds throughout the day may have shortened the time needed to train them, perhaps raising the value of northern eyasses and making them easier to handle. The critique of northern practices is also telling because it suggests that at least some commoners – the class required to do corvée labour – used their knowledge of hawking to gain privilege. While it was a sport of the elite, commoners and slaves took part in falconry – some owned falcons and hawks of their own – while others were hired by the elite to catch, train and tend their birds. Falconry may have displayed status – its popularity also expressed in paintings by royal family members (see Figure 8.1) – but people from all classes appear involved.

---

[9] *SUP*, 16. Urine-soaked meat is much like 'tiring', when birds are fed portions of the quarry that are hard to digest, such as tendons. Pecking and pulling at the food allows the hawk to exercise and feed, but the meat does not offer much nourishment keeping them hungry and ready to hunt. Elberly, 'Glossary of Falconry Terms', 66. While this Korean falconry manual does not explain why it was used, human urine may have helped attract the bird to the meat as they have a strong sense of smell and the urine may have killed parasites.

[10] *SUP*, 16.

[11] *SUP*, 16.

[12] *SUP*, 17.

Figure 8.1 Attributed to Yi Am (1499–?; 李巖). *Goshawk Standing on a Perch* (*Kaŭng to*; 架鷹圖), c. 1499 – after 1546. Ink, colour and gold on silk. Yi Am was a distant royal family member but a well-known and respected artist. While the painting itself was prized for its artistic qualities, Yi Am also produced this at a time when falcon hunting began to wane in popularity at the court. Thus, the subject matter of a well-trained bird of prey may have struck a chord with royal and elite viewers.
Reproduced by permission from the William Sturgis Bigelow Collection, Museum of Fine Arts, Boston.

This chapter first considers the re-emergence of private, personal hunts by the king and his supporters in the 1480s. The second half extends this debate to the moral economy of falconry. The intricate and intense discussions over falconry at the court, one of the most extravagant forms of the personal, private hunt, illuminate important aspects of national and international politics and identity of the kingship and dynasty vis-à-vis contact with other empires and people around the peninsula. I argue that the beliefs of a martial kingship that early leaders represented – vestiges of Northeast Asian cultural practices that took on new meaning in the Mongol period – survived into the late fifteenth century. For kings, falconry was an extension of royal authority that conflicted with the changing bureaucratic, economic and moral needs of the dynasty.

Refining a Martial Legacy

By the 1480s, it was clear that despite the criticism against the private hunt, these practices continued, empowered by a king and supporters who hunted with him. They hunted for a number of reasons, including for pleasure, as it was one of the few physical activities that they experienced outside the capital. While a growing number of personnel at the court attacked these practices, at the same time, other elites took part.

Much like in the days of late Koryŏ kings, pursuing animals in the wilds brought men together to trade stories. Sometimes they recounted hunts of previous kings. Yi Kŭkpae (1422–95; 李克培) reminisced about a tiger hunt he attended with King Sejo, Sŏngjong's grandfather. According to Yi, on one memorable hunt a ferocious tiger thrashed about so much in the hunting enclosure (winae; 圍內) that one official scampered up a tree in fear, while another quickly ran away. The sight entertained King Sejo. The retelling also amused King Sŏngjong and the others.[13] Yun P'ilsang told his own story about Yi Kŭkpae, hunting once with the former King Sejo. Elderly officials reminisced, telling stories about their younger selves and the experiences they had had with King Sŏngjong's predecessors. On these hunting excursions, these men – many of whom witnessed the significance of the hunt to earlier rulers, thus understood Sŏngjong's passion for it – strengthened their bonds with each other and the king. Storytelling also reinforced the centrality of the hunt as being a means for the king to connect the past with the present, by underscoring the king's role in them. Hunting was not only about teaching skills but also about transferring important information from older to younger and from the experienced to the inexperienced; it reinforced the importance of listening to elders.

King Sŏngjong, particularly in view of his young age, found hunting a means to bond with older-generation officials (merit subjects, royal family members, military men and civil officials who did not oppose the hunt). He appears unique among the kings, wanting to hunt and bond with older men who may have represented mentors to him outside of the small but vocal minority of Neo-Confucian tutors at the court. One private hunting party in the autumn of 1486 demonstrates this dynamic. The outing involved Prince Wŏlsan Yi Chŏng, the older brother of King Sŏngjong, who frequently attended the hunts with Sŏngjong. Only three years the king's senior, Yi Chŏng was a close hunting companion of the king. Other members of the party included senior statesmen who rotated in the most powerful positions

---

[13] *CWS*, 11:154.

in the government, such as Yi Kŭkpae, No Sasin, Hong Sang (1457–1513; 洪常), Yim Kwangjae (?–?; 任光載), and Yun P'ilsang, a top official who had distinguished himself by suppressing rebellions in the north in 1467.[14] A number of these officials were in their sixties when they attended this hunt. Royal secretaries were also in attendance to document the event.

Officials in the central government wielded harsh words to criticise others who loved the hunt, such as Han Myŏnghoe, the meritorious subject and veteran of the coup that brought King Sejo to the throne. Officials criticised Han for indulging the king in his love of the hunt. Hunting was 'wrong for the affairs of the state', unnamed ministers wrote. The king, they insisted, indulged in hunting (kŭmhwang chijak; 禽荒之作) and neglected the advice of his officials. Court scribes and other ministers who opposed the hunt continued to attack Han as a minister who agreed with the king only to flatter him (ch'ŏmyu chisin; 諂諛之臣).[15]

When officials accompanied the king on hunts, some tried to deter him from hunting. On one expedition to hunting grounds near the village of Yŏngp'yŏng in Kyŏnggi Province, forty kilometres (25 mi.) northeast of the royal palace, Consul Hong Ŭng and No Sasin flooded the discussion with many excuses, from fear of heavy rain to the denseness of the forest, to dissuade King Sŏngjong from hunting on the hunting grounds (sajang; 射場). They brought up their fear that the king may encounter Japanese pirates (waein; 倭人) and 'barbarians' from the north. The king questioned why such fear was valid considering the presence of Chosŏn soldiers with him on this hunting trip.[16]

As was the case with the large-scale royal military Kangmu hunts, small-scale hunting excursions were a chance for kings to interact with the local population. King Sŏngjong travelled to Hŏllŭng (獻陵), the location of the royal tombs of King T'aejong (1367–1422) and Queen Wŏn'gyŏng (1365–1420) where he watched soldiers hold a circle hunt. Many of the animals escaped having been struck with arrows. Attending the king, Minister of Personnel Kang Hŭimaeng ordered the animals pursued. King Sŏngjong declared that the game be given to those living in the area. 'If the commoners catch them and eat them, these will be granted to them by the king.'[17] On one early hunt in 1472, King Sŏngjong

---

[14] Milan Hejtmanek, 'The Elusive Path to Sagehood: Origins of the Confucian Academy System in Chosŏn Korea', *Seoul Journal of Korean Studies* 26, no. 2 (December 2013): 241 n108.
[15] CWS, 11:150.
[16] CWS, 11:522.
[17] CWS, 9:516.

provided clothes to a man he found weeping on the side of the road because thieves had stolen them during the night.[18] On another, the king ordered that alcohol be shared with the commoners.[19] Other reports indicated that when King Sŏngjong travelled outside the capital to hunt and encountered destitute people, he took pity on them and exempted them from corvèe labour for a year.[20] These trips out of the capital were moments when royal family members and other capital elites interacted with people beyond officials of the court.

These could also be occasions for the king to build ties with distant royal family members, further diluting the court's power. In early 1481, Minister Yu Chi (?–?; 柳輊) expressed his worry again about another royal hunt, this time a circle hunt at Chungnyangp'o, roughly ten kilometres (6 mi.) east of the royal palace. While on the hunt, King Sŏngjong decided to spend the night at the home of Prince Yi Hyŏn (1466–1525; 李珆), his cousin and the son of his uncle, the former King Yejong.[21] On another royal hunt in the winter, King Sŏngjong travelled to the mountains at Chuŭltong, roughly fifty kilometres (30 mi.) north of the capital, a distant journey that called on him to stay with an esteemed huntsman Hong Sang (1457–1513; 洪常). Hong Sang was a master of the bow and arrow, the sword and horsemanship.[22]

In contesting their activities, the central government sought multiple approaches to claim the animals on the land as its own. When rulers believed they had complete access to the mountains and valleys where they could escape the capital with close relatives and supporters, many voices at the court heard the message that rulers should not have that level of personal mobility or unrestricted access to the wealth of the peninsula. How should we frame this discussion? We cannot overlook the role of Neo-Confucianism in shaping debates over the personal hunt and falconry, as the strongest detractors argued intensely often by citing classical allusions. However, we have to be careful of simple reductionism. Neo-Confucianism was not the only source of resistance. Other factors, such as shifting concepts of identity, power sharing with the king, and the economic needs of a growing bureaucratic state were equally – if not more – important.

[18] *CWS*, 8:689.
[19] *CWS*, 9:211.
[20] *CWS*, 10:603.
[21] *CWS*, 10:192. Queen Chŏnghŭi, the wife of former King Sejo and mother of King Yejong, selected the young Sŏngjong as ruler, over Prince Yi Hyŏn, who was seen as too meek. Most likely, other court intrigues and power struggles acted out behind the scenes shaping the selection. Regardless, Sŏngjong and Prince Yi Hyŏn seemed to have an amicable relationship based on the *CWS*.
[22] *CWS*, 14:653.

One issue in the ongoing debate centred on the record-keeping protocol of dynastic history. After one evening royal lecture, an official from the Office of the Royal Lectures, Kwŏn Kyŏngu (?–?; 權景祐), held an audience with the king. 'Concerning tomorrow's circle hunt, both the royal secretaries and official historians have made the order that they will not attend. The royal secretaries record royal orders and write down all that the king does and says.' Kwŏn, in his statement, implied that because there would be no official record of the hunt, the king must not participate. King Sŏngjong understood Kwŏn's concerns but countered, 'The official historians have to write down everything they hear and see. But is there anything for them to record out in the field (*sajang*; 射場)? Furthermore, there are a lot of people in the field, animals fleeing and escaping – this is what it's like [there is no need for officials].' Kwŏn's response was forceful, arguing that every action and movement of the king must be recorded. He linked the king's frequent small-scale hunts with the Kangmu system.

> The hunt this time is a Kangmu. The Kangmu system is an important affair for this country. But is it not correct for the officials to attend? When I became an official in 1475, I followed Your Highness on the Kangmu. Two royal secretaries and a royal historian attended the Kangmu. Following this precedent would be suitable.

The king consented but still planned to hunt at Mt A'cha ten days later.[23]

In the field, due to the seeming chaos of huntsmen, horses, dogs and falcons pursuing prey, scribes were unable to appropriately record the words and actions of the king. Arguing that there was nothing to see of importance while hunting, the king disagreed. Hunting was a physical action, people moving around, animals fleeing and being chased, there was nothing to record. This absence of a record frightened court officials. By setting the precedence of insisting that scribes be present at all royal affairs, officials began to curtail royal habits, such as hunting. Having court recorders present on the hunt was one step towards further controlling the king. What was recorded in the field could be scrutinised later by officials who were not present. Knowing that his actions and behaviour were being recorded was likely to indirectly influence royal conduct. By insisting that hunting events be officially recorded, bureaucrats attempted to insert themselves into areas and events located outside the court from which they had been excluded.

Another factor was the pressure put on the land and animals by the growing number of hunts. In 1488, for instance, the superintendents of hunting

---

[23] CWS, 9:657 and 9:659.

parks (*wŏnyu chejo*; 苑囿提調) – active from 1449 through 1626, and one of many new government posts for hunting – proposed a number of reforms that would directly impact personal hunting parties and the Kangmu. The superintendents noted that there were many hills that were good for hunting outside the prohibited mountains. Thus, hunting opportunities were not scarce. They proposed expanding the hunting restrictions and notifying potential hunters through the placement of signboards. They also declared that the royal Kangmu hunting grounds, established in the first half of the fifteenth century, should not permit those carrying bows and arrows or leading hunting dogs, saying nothing about traps or snares. By issuing these proclamations, the superintendents hoped to increase local administration over the Kangmu hunting grounds. Officials believed the superintendents had brought to the court some good suggestions, but they worried about the ability of the government to successfully regulate hunting in remote mountain village regions. Instead, several civil officials maintained that these regulations should only apply to the Kangmu lands, while others agreed with the superintendents that additional areas should be included. Grudgingly, King Sŏngjong supported these suggestions. While apparently administrative decisions about access to hunting grounds, they reflected the growing concern of the pressure private hunts were having on animal populations.[24]

Valuable Birds

As shown above, people at all levels of society relied on animals for a variety of economic, political, and lifestyle reasons. However, no other animal demonstrates these interspecies interactions in Korea more perfectly than raptors. Hunting with birds of prey has a long and well-documented history on the peninsula, dating back to at least the Three Kingdom's period but probably much earlier. While early Koryŏ leaders hunted with hawks, falconry re-emerged as an important elite hunting practice during the Mongol–Koryŏ period of the late thirteenth century beginning with King Ch'ungnyŏl. Trained birds and their austringers (those who flew them) attended the hunt with the king and other elites, including Mongol dignitaries. The birds hunted small game, such as hare, pheasant and quail, returning to the austringer with the kill. In the fifteenth century, falconry enjoyed a resurgence in popularity. Falconry manuals from the Chosŏn Dynasty include *Falconry Methods* (*Ŭnggol pang*; 鷹鶻方) and

[24] CWS, 11:357.

New and Augmented Methods for Falconry. Kings T'aejong and Sejong participated in numerous falconry events, the frequency of their trips rivalling the kings of the late Koryŏ.[25] Unlike 'wicked' beasts such as tigers, Chosŏn Dynasty officials considered raptors valuable birds (*chin'gŭm*; 珍禽). The early Chosŏn state was unsure what to do with falconry. In 1395, the court discouraged the giving of these trained birds as tribute.[26] By 1403, concerned about expenses and favouritism, the court promulgated a decree outlawing the ownership of falcons and personal falcon hunting.[27] These laws failed to curtail the popularity of owning and training falcons. For instance, on one occasion when the military commanders of the northern provinces attempted to offer a reindeer to King Sejong, Sejong refused the gift, equating such animals to hawks. The state, he reminded the military officer, anxious about valuable birds and rare beasts, did not encourage the presentation of such tribute to the court.[28]

Granted, hawking was expensive and time consuming. Hunting with birds of prey required an elaborate network of people, breeding, hunting areas and birds to guarantee success. Many hawk chicks, or eyas, mostly from the northern provinces, were obtained from the wild. After capture, falconers carefully transported the chicks, when young enough to imprint on the falconer, to the capital region where the trainers worked with the birds for numerous hours every day, over a period of years, before the bird was geared up for hunting.[29] The Chosŏn Dynasty also raised their own kettles of birds in a falcon captive breeding centre (*ŭngbang*; 鷹坊) located on the banks of the Han River.[30] When ready, austringers (falconers trained to work with goshawks) accompanied royalty and elites on hunts.

Birds of prey symbolised national wealth. The cost to train and manage these animals was high. Empires including the Ming and the Yuan, that were well-versed in falconry, demanded the birds be submitted as tribute, which proved to be costly for the dynasty. Raptors provided a means for Korea to

---

[25] For more on falcon hunting, see Sim Sŭnggu, Im Changhyŏk, Chŏng Yŏnhak and Cho Taesŏp, *Sanyang ŭro pon sam kwa munhwa* [Seeing life and culture through the hunt] (Seoul: Kyŏngin munhwasa, 2011); and Kim Kwangŏn, *Han Il tong Siberia ŭi sanyang: suryŏp munhwa pigyoji*.

[26] CWS, 1:86.

[27] CWS, 1:272.

[28] CWS, 3:260.

[29] Some birds have long lifespans. For instance, red-tailed hawks (*Buteo jamaicensis*) can live for up to twenty-five years.

[30] CWS, 1:76. Once set up, King T'aejo visited this breeding centre a number of times to see the falcons.

connect to a larger world. Similar to the trade in game and various animal parts with neighbouring countries, raptors were strapped to foreign diplomacy. Understood by the courts of Koryŏ and early Chosŏn, falconry, even though it produced game on a smaller scale, echoed ancient traditions and established ties with neighbouring continental empires.

These and other hawking practices transformed wild birds into animals that assisted humans in the hunt. If men from a variety of social groups practised falconry, its greatest and most visible supporters were senior officials in the provinces, the king, his royal family members and foreign diplomats. The resources involved in catching, training and maintaining birds of prey awed some, especially foreign dignitaries, and disturbed others, particularly frugal officials at the court. Several bureaucrats believed that falconry served no real military purpose on the battlefield, only symbolic power, and were uncomfortable spending so much money on birds that were not very helpful. To them it displayed an individual's social status and domination over the natural world. Also, hawking as an art appeared in the falconry texts as poetry and on scrolls as paintings (see Figure 8.2). These multiple social, political, economic and artistic relevancies help partly explain its popularity and support among the most powerful, such as late Koryŏ and early Chosŏn kings, including King Sŏngjong.

Given the elaborate history of falconry among royalty and elites, especially among the most powerful kings of early Chosŏn, that King Sŏngjong grew fascinated with raptors once he was older is understandable. His interest reflects a long pattern of royal and elite falconry practices, especially those established under Kings T'aejong, Sejong and, to a certain extent, Sejo. As mentioned in previous chapters, when Sŏngjong was too young to rule, the Queen Dowager Chŏnghŭi and Queen Dowager Insu made all governing decisions in his name until he came of age in 1476. While the *Sillok* reflects these decisions as his own, they really represent much of their priorities and understanding of the significance of falconry to the earlier courts. In the beginning of King Sŏngjong's reign, the court tried to regulate which birds were submitted to the court. In 1470, recognising that there was no one occupying the Office of Inner Palace falconer (*naeŭngsa*; 內鷹師) position, Queen Dowager Chŏnghŭi prohibited officials from eliminating the post despite it not being filled.[31] Most likely she made the decision understanding the symbolism of hawks to the courts of King Sejong (her deceased father-in-law) and King Sejo (her deceased husband), and feared that the officials would eliminate the position if it remained unfilled. In honour of the king, the provincial governors

---

[31] CWS, 8:490.

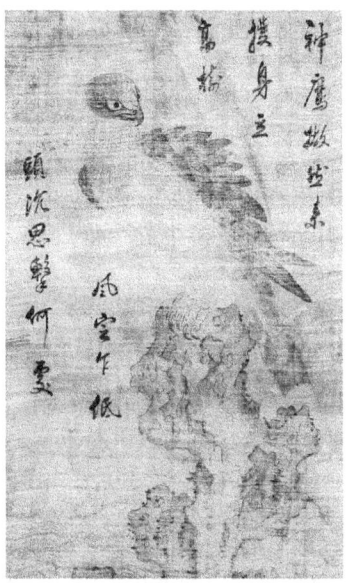

Figure 8.2 Prince Anp'yŏng (1418–53; 安平大君), *Painting of a Falcon*, c. 1450. Silk fabric, hemp fabric. Prince Anp'yŏng was the son of King Sejong and younger brother of King Sejo. This painting, one of several extant prints of falcons, suggests the popularity of falconry at the court in premodern Korea. Courtesy of the National Museum of Korea.

from Kangwŏn, Hwanghae, P'yŏngan and Yŏngan provinces intended to send young falcons (*sinŭngap*; 新雁鴨) to the capital as tribute.[32]

However, through the Queen Dowagers, the king banned the submission of these birds because 'the falconry already had many birds'.[33] The headmaster of the Royal Academy suggested that all the young falcons submitted as tribute from around the country could only be submitted to the court if they were bred in the same province. 'Now the people ... are purchasing them [falcons] and offering them as tribute from around the country. From now on, how about [a new policy that] falcons bred outside [one] province cannot be submitted as tribute [from a different province]?' The throne agreed.[34] In 1471, the court outlawed the submission of all birds of prey because of famine in Kyŏnggi, Kyŏngsang and Chŏlla provinces, apparently to relieve the

---

[32] CWS, 8:517.
[33] CWS, 8:519.
[34] CWS, 8:543.

local population from the hardship of catching, training and maintaining birds of prey to submit to the court.[35]

While his interest in hunting grew gradually, King Sŏngjong, along with the Queen Dowagers, appears to have sat over a court of officials who hoped to degrade the practice of falconry; scholar officials had begun dismantling the institutions necessary for the sport in 1470. Within two years, Sŏngjong began to observe the birds hunting (*pangŭng*; 放鷹). In 1472, governor of Kyŏnggi province Yi Ch'ŏlkyŏn (1435–96; 李鐵堅) was surprised when the king requested a falcon. Sŏngjong replied that it was not for him. 'The falcon is not for my entertainment. It was caught for the Queen Dowager.'[36] Then the military falconer (*ŭngdop'ae*; 鷹都牌) Yu Su (1415–81; 柳洙) informed the king that a peregrine falcon (*songgol*; 松鶻) was already trained. 'Swans are gathering at nearby Salgoji, so please attend and watch the training [the falcon catching the swans].' The king declined, insisting that he had already gone out on a Kangmu hunt recently. 'Going too frequently is not right', he insisted.[37] That same year, Sŏngjong attended falconry hunts, when he was fifteen years old.[38] However, officials still worried about these birds.

Over the next twenty years, a drawn-out debate ensued over the moral economy of falconry, and officials sought to regulate it administratively. In the same year, 1472, the court dissolved the position of falconer (*chwau ŭngbang*; 左右鷹防).[39] Although the government abolished the position for the military official heading the falcon programme, the man continued to raise goshawk falcons in his home, something scholars at the court found unacceptable.[40] Each province had a quota to fulfil and submitted a set number of hawks; however, concern in the court grew about the number of hawks being submitted from the southern provinces. Censor Yi Kŭkki (?–1489; 李克基) pondered about the number of hawks (*ŭng*; 鷹) available in each province. There were enough in Yŏngan and Hwanghae provinces, he insisted, but finding hawks in Ch'ungch'ŏng, Kyŏngsang and Chŏlla was proving difficult. He insisted that this was distressing numerous people. 'Why don't we reduce the number of birds required?'[41] Yi Kŭkki argued that the number was too high for the southern provinces, known for their agricultural fields, and lobbied for the number of birds to be reduced because the burden of finding and transporting these

---

[35] *CWS*, 8:558.
[36] *CWS*, 8:634.
[37] *CWS*, 8:634.
[38] *CWS*, 8:638.
[39] *CWS*, 8:638.
[40] *CWS*, 9:136.
[41] *CWS*, 9:697.

animals was too heavy. Goshawks, in particular, would have migrated north to breed and were easier to locate in the northern provinces. Such discussion coincided with the overall government policy promoting agriculture and human population growth by encouraging the expansion of farming lands and helping the commoners, who made up at least 40 per cent of Chosŏn, overcome famine and other hardships from climate fluctuations.

By the winter of 1482, an official from the Office of the Censor General, Kang Chap'yŏng (1430–86; 姜子平), admonished the king for his love of goshawk falcons and praised the king for apparently abstaining from falconry, comparing him to the former kings who did not raise such precious birds or rare beasts. In his discussion, Kang pointed out a disturbing order that Sŏngjong had re-established the position of falconer to carry out ancestral worship, presumably using the game the birds brought back as part of the ritual. According to Kang, the king had returned to raising goshawks, and he worried that the king's orders concerning the collection of these birds had gone out to the northern provinces. Kang also suggested the possibility that the king's desire for these birds may indicate a decline in the king's brilliance. He ended with these words, 'The biographies say, "rare objects agitate a person's mind", while the *Book of Songs* (*Shijing*) says, "To begin well is common, to end well is rare indeed." I hope Your Majesty releases [frees] the falcons.'

King Sŏngjong pushed back against these accusations. He insisted there was no difference between what a hawk (*haech'ŏng*; 海青) or a sparrowhawk (*najin*; 那進) consume, arguing that they are both just birds, hence no difference in how much they cost to maintain. He defended himself by saying he had asked for only one or two birds to be delivered from the governors of the northern provinces.

> I do not like rare animals or birds (*chin'gŭm kisu*; 珍禽奇獸). You are not the only one who knows this. All the people in the country know this. Hawks are not rare animals or birds. They are used for ancestral rituals (*chesa*; 祭祀) and performing ceremonies (*pongyang*; 奉養) [presumably by hunting and capturing animals sacrificed in the rituals]. Hence, they are raised for the benefit of the country. These birds are also used to train our troops for the military arts.

He concluded by insisting, 'It is not that I am hungry for hunting or playing around.'[42]

A few days later, Inspector General Kim Sŭnggyŏng returned to the issue of the hawks. He was saddened to learn that the king had men raising hawks and

---

[42] *CWS*, 10:297.

admonished him to 'be cautious about pleasure items'. This angered the king who raised his voice, shouting, 'Am I ignoring the countless administrative details of the country and only speaking about falcons? Does hunting with a few falcons during one's spare time disturb matters of the state?' Consul Hong Ŭng responded first, attempting to pivot the conversation to more important matters in the south. The king turned the topic back to that of hunting with birds of prey. 'In the words of the censor, hunting with falcons (pangŭng; 放鷹) is wrong. But what is the harm of falcon hunting from time to time? Shall I go falcon hunting in the rear garden after my evening Confucian lectures?'[43] To officials, this must have been seen as a threat as this act of hunting in the backyard of the court symbolised the power of the king. His statement directly opposed the requests by senior government officials.

Within days, Inspector General Kim Sŭnggyŏng issued a brief memorandum detailing King Songjŏng's order. 'The king has commanded,' he wrote, 'that the rear garden be stocked with animals for the king, himself, to hunt.' The king also intended to go out hunting with his falcons each day following his Confucian lectures. Alongside this note, Kim expressed his concern that having the ruler spend his time hunting in the back garden conflicted with the king's Confucian studies. Kim went on to imply that the order the king had issued, which dictated that government falconers raise falcons collected from the north, was simply for pleasure. Kim was insistent that in a time of famine, in both the capital region and in other areas – a disaster that was upsetting families and society at large – the king should not have any leisure time and instead should be diligently attending to matters of the state. 'I implore you to give up things of leisure like frequently hunting with falcons and live up to the expectations of the subjects of the kingdom.' Underneath these arguments was the concern that falcons, as direct animal tribute to the king from elites in the countryside, placed unnecessary burdens on the country.

Songjŏng was firm in his dismissal of these matters.

> It is not that I am not concerned about the hunger of the people or that I enjoy hunting and neglect governing. If this was so, then your advice would be helpful. However, I must review and inspect the military, how [exactly] does hunting by falcons damage the country's political affairs?[44]

The king's symbolic power over and economic access to animals was dangerous to these officials. Bureaucrats implied that hunting with birds was

[43] CWS, 10:299.
[44] CWS, 10:301.

leisurely, but the freedom from restraint kings gained from leaving the royal palace, interacting with military men and people from different social statuses and regions (like the examples discussed in the previous section) undermined the power of these officials.

Deputy Chief of the Office of Special Advisors Kwŏn Kŏn (1458–1501; 權健) invoked the image of Emperor Shun, the sage king of ancient China, and the wise King Cheng of Zhou. These were great kings, Kwŏn argued, because they were not distracted from governing. Juxtaposed to them, he argued, was the Duke of Shao who enjoyed the pleasures of various things and lost his purpose. Kwŏn quoted *The Song of the Five Brothers* (*Wuzi zhige*; 五子之歌), 'When the palace is obsessed with lust, the country is obsessed with hunting.' This quote, Kwŏn reiterates, is derived from the *Book of History* (*Shujing*; 書經). Put simply, if the king continues in this manner, disaster will befall the country. Kwŏn stressed how the two falcons presented to the court by the governor of Yŏngan Province Chŏng Munhyŏng (1427–1501; 鄭文炯) were frivolous pleasures. 'Officials like [Governor] Chŏng Munhyŏng are only wanting to curry favours with the king.' Kwŏn declared that if the court does not punish Chŏng there would be others who would attempt to even further corrupt the king and echoed the earlier refrains made by other officials, namely that King Sŏngjong had retracted his earlier promise to forgo falcon hunting and was now demanding falcons be returned to the capital. 'This fact [that the king agreed to forgo hunting with birds of prey] is clearly written in the records. But now you are continuing to hunt with falcons, and it is written that you are ordering the tribute of falcons to the court.' These arguments angered the king. 'All you officials of the Classics mat lecture are aware of my intentions, you make your brushes fly around [on paper, writing up rules], fool around with books, and you hope to intimidate the sovereign. Even though I am ignorant, why would I not consider these [things you do]?'[45]

Undeterred, the king went to Toyo Pond (都要淵), outside the city walls in the eastern part of the capital near Salgoji, a pond where water fowl gather, to observe a falcon hunt the next day. On his return to the palace, he held a military inspection of the troops. Senior scholar officials, frustrated by the king's continued dismissal of their warnings, reiterated their plea for him to give up hunting. They selectively chose a passage from Confucian teachings, in an attempt to persuade the king, reiterating the argument about the fall of Duke of Shao and how the duke spent his time with entertainment rather than the affairs of state to the detriment of his people and country, 'Put differently, don't

[45] *CWS*, 10:301.

do anything that is not beneficial to governing. The hounds of Lu (Yŏo; 旅獒) and goshawks (haech'ŏng; 海青) are precious birds and strange beasts [indulging in precious and strange animals and items was a distraction from governing and revealed poor judgment] . . . It seems now that Your Highness likes falcons.' Fearing that the king was pushing aside royal Confucian ceremony, they requested that the king falcon hunt on the outskirts of the capital to indicate to the common people that he does not enjoy frivolous entertainment.[46]

Days later, by the end of the second lunar month (March) of 1482, following another royal lecture, other officials commented that many scholar officials had pointed out the inappropriateness of raising falcons and falcon hunting, but that the king continued to disagree. Yi Chongyun (1431–90; 李從允), an official from the Office of Inspector General, and Ku Sukson (?–?; 丘夙孫), the headmaster of the Royal Academy, spoke,

> In the early days of your enthronement, Your Highness ceased falcon hunting and released deer (pangminok; 放麋鹿) [as a Buddhist ritual], and [by doing so] attained the heights of virtue. Now you have returned to falcon hunting, so how can you acquire sagely virtue? In those early days, the governor of Yŏngan Province, Chŏng Nanjung (1433–89; 鄭蘭宗), presented Your Highness with a falcon. [At that time], Your Majesty criminalized these acts and declared that in the future falcons should not be presented. But this time, Your Highness has ordered the presentation and training of these falcons so you may hunt with them again. How can the beginning and end be different?

The economic relationship between Korea and China partly fuelled the debate over falcon hunting. Confucian Lecturer Cho Wi (1454–1503; 曺偉) brought up Jin Xing (?–?; 金興), the Chinese envoy who visited P'yŏngan Province and inquired about a painting of a peregrine falcon (kol; 鶻) he saw hanging on a wall. 'Is this [falcon] from your country?' the Chinese envoy asked. Cho replied, 'In the past, our country used to provide China with these [falcons] as tribute. But they are difficult to capture. Thus, they are not offered as tribute because there are no more remaining.' Cho pointed out that if the country began raising falcons again, then China might hear of them and begin demanding they be submitted as tribute, which would be very costly for the dynasty.

This argument by Cho, that foreign interests may insist on tribute of falcons, concerned the king. King Songjŏng inquired whether the Ming

---

[46] CWS, 10:301.

representative Zheng Tong (?–?; 鄭同) would hear of the falcons he hoped to raise. Zheng was originally from the Korean peninsula and had been sent to China to become a eunuch for the Ming court. He travelled frequently to Chosŏn during King Sŏngjong's reign. The king expressed his concern that someone would inform one of Zheng's relatives in Chosŏn about the falcons. Another official from the Royal Lectures Office, Song Chil (1454–1520; 宋軼), replied that if China learned about the falcons, the court could not deny their existence. To prevent this situation, he told the king: 'Why not let the birds go?'[47] The king's desire to falcon hunt required the raising of falcons. This threatened to draw Ming attention, which might require additional resources to fulfil Ming tribute demands; such requests would not only depopulate Korean falcons it would cause greater economic burden on the people.

The court intensified its attacks. Several more senior officials implored the king to give up falcon hunting. On the twenty-fifth day of the second lunar month (March) of 1482, they repeated earlier arguments based on Chinese identification of falcon hunting as a frivolous leisure activity, one that distracted the king from more pressing matters of state. Officials then began including the hunt in general in their criticism of falcon hunting. A third official from the Royal Lectures Office, Kim Hŭn (1448–?; 金訢), concluded by saying, 'All of the words of your officials are ignorant and stupid [this expression displayed self-deprecation, spoken out of humility and respect for the king], but if Your Majesty accepts them, then you will follow admonition as a natural flow. You will benefit from virtue by not raising precious and rare creatures (chin'gŭm; 珍禽).' Others, such as An Yunson, stressed again how the king had already declared that he had lost interest in falconry earlier in his tenure and there was no need to return to it. An went on to say that doing so would satisfy the expectations of many.

Inspector General Kim Sŭnggyŏng brought up the memory of King Sejo. When the former king travelled to Mohwagwan (慕華館), the royal guesthouse, to inspect the military – just beyond the western gate of the capital walls where Chosŏn officials had met envoys from the Ming – he released his falcons. 'You have not yet gone so far as to do this [release the falcons].' King Sŏngjong was familiar with this story and replied,

> Sometimes he [King Sejo] hunted in the back palace grounds (huwŏn; 後苑) and other times he hunted on the outskirts of the capital (kyooe; 郊外). I have made it illegal [for others] to hunt there, however I still

[47] CWS, 10:302.

do these things. If these small affairs were not possible, then the monarch would spend all of his time deep inside the palace. These days it has reached the point where people declare military training exercises should not be carried out at all. What is the meaning of this?

The king argued that military drills in general (*sŭpchin*; 習陣) were necessary and was part of the moral rules and laws of the state (*kigang*; 紀綱). Inspector General Kim Sŭnggyŏng (1430–93; 金升卿) delicately debated that military practices were not part of the moral rules and laws and that action should be taken to strengthen them only if they had been abandoned for a long time. Another senior official from the Office of Inspector General Kang Chap'yŏng (1430–86; 姜子平) sided with the king and reminded the court of the importance of inspecting the military. 'It [military preparedness] is an important matter of the state, so how can we abandon it?' But was it not the remonstrations of the ministers in the previous year that compelled the king not to cross the Han River (because of cold weather conditions) and to cancel military training and inspections. Consul Han Myŏnghoe pointed out that kings T'aejo, T'aejong, Sejong and Songjŏng's grandfather Sejo had all raised falcons. He summarised the main point of the conversation. 'It has come to my attention that the censors [Kim Sŭnggyŏng and Kang Chap'yŏng] say they are worried that Your Majesty is uncertain about abandoning the practice [of falconry] or continuing it.' The Royal House Administrator Yi Kŭkchŭng (1431–94; 李克增) added, 'They say that they worry Your Highness's frivolous pastimes are growing worse.' Kim Sŭnggyŏng followed, favouring the king's argument, 'Now [it is true that] King Sejong is considered a sage king, and he raised falcons. As you achieve sagely virtue, if Your Majesty does not give up falcon hunting, then future kings will follow your example [in other words, by not giving up falcon hunting, you now establish a bad precedent for future rulers].'[48]

Three days later, on the twenty-eighth day, senior officials from the Office of Inspector General and the Royal Lectures petitioned the king and submitted a brief statement that the king raising (and presenting) falcons was simply not possible. King Sŏngjong replied that living things (*saengmul*; 生物) had been and therefore could be presented to the court.

> The official [and the position he holds] who attends the falcons (*chwaup'ae*; 左右牌) cannot be abolished. If he can't be abolished, then what is the harm of having one or two falcons? These goshawks were not

[48] CWS, 10:302.

rare things (*imul*; 異物). But now, based on your words and the words of others, why should I do away with the falconry attendants (*chwaup'ae chiŭng*; 左右牌之鷹)? I have already deliberated over this [and decided not to give up falconry], so why are you talking about it so passionately?

The fourth censor from the Office of Inspector General Yun Sŏkpo (?–1505; 尹碩輔) continued to worry that the king wanted to raise falcons and hunt with them at Salgot, an area due east of the Han River and east of the capital where many geese gathered, a plan that worried these top officials. Yun concluded, 'People in ancient times used to say, "A galloping horse gradually slides into the middle." [In other words, a horse that begins quickly in the lead runs out of energy and falls behind at the end and loses.] If Your Highness does not stop this, then we cannot know how this will end.' The scholar official Min Sagŏn (?–?; 閔師騫) reiterated that the king had already agreed to prohibit the presentation of falcons to the court. 'The officials recorded it [the decision to prohibit the birds].' However, he suggested that the king had changed his mind. Sŏngjong requested falcons be presented to him, which the 'officials have also recorded'. These two requests, the officials maintained, would confuse people in the future as to whether the king enjoyed hunting with falcons or not. Rephrasing Yun Sŏkpo's advice, Min Sagŏn concluded, 'People in ancient times used to say, "Be as careful as you were at the beginning as you are in the end." The king must be prudent.'[49]

Again touching on the record-keeping demands of the bureaucratic state, King Sŏngjong, however, pointed out that the scribes had to write down whatever was happening regardless if they thought it was good or bad. The king worried about the subjective nature of this record keeping. 'Will scribes write that immoral people like me (*iyŏ pudŏk*; 以予不德) are good? How can scribes give a straightforward honest account?'[50] The king's rebuttal quieted the conversation about falcons. Officials had strongly presented their opinions to the king about falconry and, by extension, all forms of royal hunting practices. The king resisted their objections and countered that he recogniszed his apparent immorality, but he was not as worried about his legacy as the officials that surrounded him.

Within a month, the king was ready once again to resume his hunting practices. The spring hunt brought an announcement by the Privy Council of Sŏngjong and his group to Mt Ch'ŏnggye where they held a circle hunt.[51] The king declined to take part in the hunt; instead, he called for the military to

---

[49] *CWS*, 10:303.
[50] *CWS*, 10:303.
[51] *CWS*, 10:310.

practice exercises in nearby Chŏn'got (Salgot), the location where he wished to establish his falcon grounds. While there, he announced his intention to view a falcon hunt. In fact, the king used these grounds at Chŏn'got frequently. Three weeks later, his hunting entourage consisted of several officials and members of the royal family, all of whom travelled to the fields of Pojewŏn to view a falcon hunt at Chŏn'got. At least ten people and various attendants took part. This particular excursion included a feast and drinking.[52]

Despite the sustained attacks on his hunting practices and fascination with falcons, King Sŏngjong continued to hunt. In the spring of 1482, he travelled to Mt Ach'a. As soon as he departed the gate of the capital, he ordered a hunt with two different kinds of hawks, the goshawk (*haech'ŏng*; 海青) and the sparrowhawk (*najin*; 那進). On this hunt, they caught crow (*ogol*; 烏鶻). The hunting party was significant and included several royal family members including: Sŏngjong's brother, Prince Wŏlsan Yi Chŏng, his uncle Prince Tŏgwŏn'gun Yi Sŏ (1449–98; 德源君 李曙), and another uncle who was a secondary son and not the offspring from the primary wife of King Sejo Prince Ch'angwŏn'gun Yi Sŏng (1457–84; 昌原君 李晟). Twelve named officials and court scribes also accompanied the king and his royal party to the hunting grounds (*sajang*; 射場). Some of these officials were elderly. The eldest, State Chief Councillor Chŏng Ch'angson was eighty years old. Several of the attendees including top dynastic officials such as Han Myŏnghoe, Sim Hoe and Yi Kŭkpae were in their sixties. These scholar officials, as examples of those who appreciated the hunt, watched as the king ordered military officers such as Kim Sejŏk (?–1490; 金世勣) and Yang Ch'an (1443–96; 梁瓚) to aim their bows at animals to the left and right of the camp. They killed roe deer and sika or river deer and presented them to the senior queen dowagers (*samjŏn*; 三殿) as tribute. On their way back to Waunhyŏn (瓦雲峴), a hill area that is now lost, they hunted with falcons and took several ducks.[53] Falconry appeared interwoven at this time with personal hunts, necessary components of these excursions.

After this hunt, pressure on the king built. A tutor from the Royal Lectures Office, Kim Hŭn warned Sŏngjong that playing with Songgol falcons (松鶻) was a mistake. He reported what the king had previously claimed: 'Sparrowhawks (*najin*; 那進) are not the same as Songgol falcons (松鶻). It is wrong not to remonstrate against sparrowhawks and only criticize Songgol falcons.' The implication is that smaller birds of prey, like sparrowhawks, were less expensive to maintain and less threatening to officials. Kim insisted that his concerns demonstrated that the king enjoyed hunting with falcons and

---

[52] CWS, 10:314.
[53] CWS, 10:322.

dogs, a form of entertainment that Sŏngjong must be very careful about. The king again pushed back, 'The people of the country know that I do not enjoy hunting.'⁵⁴

The king organised another sizable hunt in the first lunar month (February) of 1483. The king and his party travelled once again to Chŏn'got (Salgot), where they viewed falconers hunting with their birds. From there, they travelled to Mt Ach'a for a circle hunt. On this occasion, at least fourteen officials and royal family members were present. Out on the hunting field, royal family members Prince Wŏlsan Yi Chŏng and Prince Tŏgwŏn'gun Yi Sŏ joined the king and his attendants. The men split up into two teams, left and right 'friends' (chwabung; 左朋/ubung; 右朋). They took turns hitting small targets. The left team won the competition, and the king awarded them each with leopard skins (p'yop'i; 豹皮). These friendly competitions reinforced loyalty between the members within the group and with the king, while such affairs excluded officials who had to remain behind in the capital.⁵⁵

By late 1485, officials again attacked the financial burden of the king's hunting practices. When officials learned that the king intended to re-establish the position of falconer (ŭngbang; 鷹坊), they worried that this was a mistake given the famine taking place that year. The government had decreased the amount of grain given to officials and students of the Royal Confucian Academies due to the terrible harvest, causing even the elite to be affected. Adding the position of falconer, officials warned, would even further weaken government finances. 'Falcons and hunting dogs muddy the excellent virtue of Your Majesty', two tutors from the Office of Royal Lectures Yi Kyun (1452–1501; 李均) and Yi Kŏ (?–1502; 李琚) explained. King Sŏngjong agreed with their observations but chose to continue his argument. He reminded his officials that the falconer's expenses were to be paid out of the funds for ancestral food ceremonies (ch'ŏnsin; 薦新) and that had been allocated to the Queen Dowager Chŏngŭi and the Queen Mother Insu. According to the king, abolishing the position would harm the commoners because commoners raised and hunted with falcons, and they were hard workers. If these positions related to falconry were dissolved, the workers would lose their wages and have no rice. Officials rebuked the king's argument, insisting that falconry would drain state resources (kugyong; 國用).⁵⁶ They contended that if falconers (ŭngsa; 鷹師) were allowed, the king could wander in and out of the palace nightly with his guards to hunt. The soldiers would then have to

---

⁵⁴ CWS, 10:409.
⁵⁵ CWS, 10:429.
⁵⁶ CWS, 11:83.

be fed with grain from the warehouse. The officials worried that this would further deplete the food supply during a year of famine. '[Famine is causing great damage] what damage is done to the country with the loss of one falcon?' one inspector from the Inspector General's Office Pan Uhyŏng (?–?; 潘佑亨) questioned.[57] It was clear that Sŏngjong's actions deeply troubled his Confucian advisors and the court censors.

The king was unmoved. These falcons, he declared, were not simple animals that could be easily obtained. Finally, he insisted that he had only taken the birds out once and that he was not spending all his time practising falconry.[58] Officials repeated the earlier warning that if the Ming learned of the falcons, China would demand them as tribute. State Councillor Yi Kŭkpae told the king, 'All the former kings raised falcons. The censor's intense remonstrations is because Your Majesty's [actions] might create a bird shortage.'[59]

The king did not agree and claimed that there was nothing wrong with going on a hunt for ten days. He ended his rebuttal with 'Where is the harm in letting the falconer hunt?' A reader from the Office of Royal Lectures Cho Chisŏ disagreed and suggested that letting the falconers run around damaged the crops. 'This [letting falconers loose on grounds that could be used for agriculture] is wrong,' he contended. Once again, the king questioned how one falcon could be so damaging. Cho answered, 'It may be only one falcon, but there are many people who chase it. Won't this harm the crops?' To clarify his point, Cho proceeded to tell Songjŏng a story.

> Yesterday, while walking along the road, I wondered why I was seeing a man carrying a birdcage (*chorong*; 鳥籠), who later went inside the palace [implying that falcons were being delivered to the king] ... Last year, the people had no way to make a living. There were frequent natural disasters. This year, we do not know if there will be a sufficient harvest. Your Majesty plays around with entertainment [falcons] and [it looks as if Your Majesty] does not show any compassion for the concerns of the people. Is this correct? It appears you will not let the falcon go, does this then mean that you value small things and treat the people with little regard.[60]

The king shouted a retort, 'I know that trifling over small details destroys the will (*wanmul sangji*; 玩物喪志)! ... The people are the foundation of the state,' he added. Cho Chosŏ's suggestion that the king was less worried about

---

[57] CWS, 11:95.
[58] CWS, 11:95.
[59] CWS, 11:114.
[60] CWS, 11:119.

damaging the crops and harming the people than he was about hunting with his falcons also angered Sŏngjong.⁶¹

If questions of morality were unconvincing, officials tried another approach. In 1486, Censor General Kim Suson (?–?; 金首孫) argued for the reduction of royal support for falconry based on bureaucratic redundancy. He presented that there were both falconers who bred and trained falcons inside the palace (*naeŭngsa*; 內鷹師) and outside the palace (*oeŭngsa*; 外鷹師). It was further discovered that promotions for these two positions differed. All falconers served out their duties in three rotations. Falconers located outside the palace served a total of 327 days before they could be promoted. Inside the palace, falconers were required to serve longer before promotion. Falconers working inside the palace served 436 days before the court raised their ranks. The court suggested resolving these inconsistencies by eliminating the position of the inner court falconer, the position closest to the king. This may have been a reason why they wished to eradicate it.⁶²

Going even farther, two officials, Cho Chisŏ and Sin Chongho (1456–97; 申從濩), wrote a petition to the king calling for the complete end of falcon hunting. The king, recognising their petition, agreed to release his own falcons as they had proposed.⁶³ Bad weather had brought about drought in recent years, so he had kept the number of his birds at a minimum. Drought had made raising falcons tenuous, and he was apparently concerned about the heavy burden falconry placed on the people of the peninsula.⁶⁴ But the steady rainfall had ended the drought throughout the country and now that the weather had improved, he was determined to continue falconry and called on the court to send out edicts to the provinces with falcon nests to send him falcons.

Given the economic and moral implications above, it is hardly a surprise that frugal Neo-Confucian tutors and advisors of the central government attacked falconry without hesitation. Weather patterns had made harvest yields unpredictable. When rice production faltered, so too did the government finances to pay for such extravagant displays of royal authority. Even though state support of falconry was marked by disapproval among central officials, royalty, provincial elites, and even commoners and slaves throughout the peninsula, especially in the north, continued to practise it.

* * *

---

⁶¹ *CWS*, 11:119.
⁶² *CWS*, 11:153 and 12:341.
⁶³ This petition was not recorded in the *Sillok*, only a reference to it. See *CWS*, 11:226.
⁶⁴ *CWS*, 11:226.

What can we conclude from this chapter about human–animal relations in the late fifteenth century? It should be clear that the constant voices against the hunt from a vocal minority of officials attests to the ongoing popularity of small, private encounters with animals by others who resisted change. While hard to generalise, sometimes support for falconry and the hunt was generational (those who had witnessed the royal hunts of the first half of the fifteenth century), determined by branch order (military or scholarly) or military experience, or shaped by regional experience (especially spending time in the northern provinces). Next, there was no single agreement on how to deal with human–animal encounters. Not even the king could decide, on his own, how to engage animals. This is best demonstrated by falconry. Falconry, a long-established tradition on the Korean peninsula and Northeast Asia, is one of the best documented examples of interspecies interactions in premodern times. Falcons, raised in the wild and trained in captivity, hunted other wild beasts for the enjoyment of their handlers. They were rare and beautiful creatures depicted in the written and visual sources of the peninsula. They differed from the dead animal parts submitted to the central government as tribute. As living tribute, birds of prey were visual reminders to the capital elites of the king's contacts, influence and power over the country. Kings, royal family members and elites found pleasure and meaning owning these birds, taking care of them, and hunting with them for a multiplicity of reasons. But ownership was costly in terms of time, money and opposition from those who disagreed. Officials who opposed the practice saw little or no benefit in falconry. The practice did not contribute to the military preparedness of the dynasty, unlike the royal military Kangmu hunts.

Debates about falconry lack compassion for the animals themselves, either on the part of those who hunted them or those who wished them released. If Buddhist teachings about releasing them as a means to display salvation of another sentient being informed one debate, these thoughts were not reflected in most of the arguments. The morality of hawking centred not on the birds themselves but on the direct and indirect harm brought to non-elites who supported the expenses of government falconry as well as the moral judgement of a ruler spending time on non-government affairs. The debate was human rather than animal centred. There were no questions about the ethics of capturing young fledglings in the wild and removing them from their nests and parents and nothing about releasing a partially domesticated animal back into the wild that had its instincts shaped by close intimate contact with humans, or about the survivability of such captured birds once released. The debate reduced the birds and their handlers to objects of the administration. However, the close bonds these creatures developed with people reveal an intimacy between species, as we have seen in such works as *New and Augmented Methods for Falconry*. Finally, the king's inability to silence the voices of those civil officials who opposed falconry suggests the limits of the power of the throne.

In the midst of these discussions about private hunts, the morality of falconry, rulership, and scholarly and martial identities, King Sŏngjong died suddenly in 1494, leaving many of these issues open and unresolved. During these debates over the private hunts of the king and the intense pressure to abolish falconry at the court, the bureaucracy transitioned to a new king with even more uncertainty about the direction of the state or resolving the question of the hunt. Sŏngjong's eldest son, King Yŏnsan'gun (r. 1494–1506), came to the throne at the age of eighteen. Called a dissolute, immoral and erratic leader by many Chosŏn-era writers, Yŏnsan'gun soon revealed to officials that he was also an avid hunter, one who pushed the boundaries of acceptance by bringing hunting dogs and falcons into the palace and further enraging the officials at the court.[65]

[65] *CWS*, 14:67.

9
Taming Wild Animals and Beastly Monarchs

> Yŏnsan'gun established falconry runs inside the palace garden. There was not a hawk, dog, rare beast, or bird that he did not raise.
> – *Geographical Reference to Korea* (*Tonguk yŏji pigo*), late Chosŏn Dynasty

In 1501, the powerful Inspector General Sŏng Hyŏn submitted a six-point petition regarding the governance of King Yŏnsan'gun. The final section of the petition criticised the king's fondness of animals:

> Wu Wang [?–1043 BC; 武王, the first ruler of the Zhou Dynasty (China), 1046–256 BCE] received a gift of a mastiff (*o*; 獒). Shao Gong (?–1000 BC; 召公) [a senior minister] told him to exercise caution [a warning against overindulging in entertainment and lavish items, such as a rare dog breed]. Zhou Dynasty Wu Wang and Tang Dynasty China (618–907) Emperor Taizong (r. 624–49) prized hawks and hounds, and the statesman Wei Zheng (580–643; 魏徵) wrote a ten-point petition [suggesting the emperor was neglecting politics because he was too involved in raising dogs]. Wu Wang of the Zhou Dynasty and Emperor Taizong of the Tang were sagely rulers and certainly were not reckless or harmful. As for the boundary between Shao Gong and Wei Zheng, they both said if you don't behave in delicate ways, then trouble (*nu*; 累) appears.
>
> [Our former] King Sŏngjong established the position of falconer (*ŭngbang*; 鷹坊). He did not pay any attention to the scholarly remonstrations to stop this. He was only concerned about [raising hawks]. The only things absent were the *Book of Songs* and the literature and the arts (*munye*; 文藝) [He was not focused on the more important things such as scholarship, learning and writing].

Please hear me out. Your Majesty, in the palace, you have newly constructed a falcon enclosure [and dog kennel], and many hawks and hounds are gathered there. Senior [experienced] slaves (*sangno*; 上奴) have been selected to take care of them. Rice from T'aech'ang [government storage] is used to feed [these slaves, instead of feeding other members of society]. Hawks [can be seen] perched on the falconry gloves [of their handlers] travelling from the royal palace park (*kŭmwŏn*; 禁苑) to their cages, and packs of wild dogs [can be heard] barking in the main hall of the palace – in the eyes of others, these events are troublesome. If Your Majesty raises these animals, where do you intend to use them? When it is the right time for a royal sacrificial offering, then the whole country would benefit to the utmost [from offering these beasts]. But how are we to raise these things [hawks and hounds] later? Are we to contribute our meals [to feed the many slaves, who care for these animals and keep them trained and alive]? If [these beasts] become playthings, and one treats them with love (*wihŭiwan chigu*; 爲戲玩之具), then this is a sign of unsophistication and [could result in the king] galloping off to hunt (*ch'ibing chŏllyŏ*; 馳騁田獵) without a [second] thought. You should keep such matters distant from you. It is inappropriate to raise [animals] nearby [within the palace walls] . . . I hope Your Majesty will [heed my warnings and] not raise wild beasts. We hope you reject [breeding and raising them] by all means possible.[1]

The same year, Chief State Councillor Han Ch'ihyŏng (1434–1502; 韓致亨) repeated Sŏng's objections.

Many hunting dogs (*yŏpku*; 獵狗) are raised in the royal palace. They bounce around and come and go during morning meetings [in the court]. How can we just gaze upon all of this [without remonstrating against these scenes]? Moreover, over the past few days, drought [in the countryside] has intensified. At the time of King Sejong, he prohibited consumption of alcohol when spring returned. This [not consuming alcohol and by so doing limiting hunting excursions that often ended in feasting and drinking] has always been a means to look out for heavenly admonitions. I beg you to prohibit wine and pray for rain [or, in other words, take your responsibility as king seriously].

---

[1] *CWS*, 13:439. Wei Zheng was a popular Chinese figure officials referenced during the reigns of King Sŏngjong and Yŏnsan'gun as an example of a dedicated minister.

Court officials pleaded with King Yŏnsan'gun to abandon hunting and to decrease the number of dogs he held in the royal palace. The king agreed to do what he could to pray for rainfall and maintain fewer.[2]

As we have seen in earlier chapters, the bureaucracy begrudgingly tolerated the king's involvement in hunting, both the royal military Kangmu hunt and the king's private hunting trips. However, in this chapter I argue that the king's presentations of animals at court, especially dogs, went too far. A growing number of tutors and officials advocated for a Neo-Confucian ideology that insisted the king remain in the palace. According to their interpretation of Confucian doctrine, when the ruler occupied the palace heaven and earth were properly ordered. When the king travelled away from the palace therefore, he risked not only his own safety but also the cosmic order. Added to this was the rule that those leaders were supposed to be men who prized civil discourse over martial activities, a rule not everyone accepted. Confucian scholars viewed hunting as being a means to perfecting skills, which at best were not needed and, at worst, were dangerous to the ruler. Yet we have seen that fifteenth-century kings did not agree and now, King Yŏnsan'gun was bringing animals into the palace, which in their minds, upset the order and physically threatened court officials with the potential violence these hunting animals represented and could unleash.

With an eye on the sixteenth century, in this chapter I pull together many threads of the argument introduced throughout the book. Specifically, I weave together four interrelated sections. The first examines factional politics and the second probes into the personal, private hunts and the royal Kangmu military hunt under King Yonsan'gun. The third surveys the intense debates at the court surrounding the creation of royal hunting parks. The final section teases out the complicated relationships between disease outbreaks, animals as medicine, and state attempts to limit hunting.

Animals at the Court

The slow burning political crisis, which began in the 1450s between the throne and the bureaucracy, ignited during the reign of King Yŏnsan'gun, and animals and the hunt were manifestations of this crisis. In the eyes of the scholarly class, King Yŏnsan'gun was a problematic leader. Hardcore Confucians accused him of being radical, thoughtless, selfish, incompetent and angry. Yŏnsan'gun may have inherited some of this behaviour from his great-grandfather, King Sejo. King Sejo had come to the throne 'improperly'. In short, following the deaths of King Sejong in 1450 and King Munjong in 1452, Sejo staged a

[2] CWS, 13:443.

bloody coup against his nephew King Tanjong to take the throne for himself. Having come to power through force, Sejo had refused to follow patrilineal succession. This created a crisis according to the court. When kings died, the court issued them an ancestral name, a title that marked their position in the royal ancestral line. Sejo should not have acquired the position of king in this manner and as such was in a generational conflict with his nephew.

From a Confucian perspective, the dramatic and deadly ascension of King Sejo in 1455 was a clear crime, one that violated the rules set forth for ancestral relationships. Based on Confucian principles of paternal, rather than lateral, succession, ancestral rituals could not be performed by or for the same generation. In other words, King Sejo could not, according to Confucian doctrine, perform rituals for his nephew (deceased King Tanjong), a younger generation than Sejo, which upset the celestial order of the kingdom. In protest of Sejo's actions, some officials, often explained in terms of a faction that opposed the new political order in the capital, fled the court and went into hiding in the countryside, demonstrating the level of revulsion and panic some in the bureaucracy felt about the coup. They began returning during Sŏngjong's reign and occupied senior posts that ignited political factional struggles.

Sejo's sons, grandsons, and great-grandsons, including Yŏnsan'gun, maintained and protected Sejo's legacy, which was their responsibility as descendants of Sejo. When Yŏnsan'gun witnessed members of the literati posthumously criticising his great-grandfather Sejo, he attacked them. In 1498, spurred by factional struggles for the first time, King Yŏnsan'gun executed a number of scholars in what was referred to as a 'literati purge', actions that sparked a climate of fear within the court.[3] Later, the repercussions for Sejo's actions included the confiscation of the property, wives, daughters and family members of officials who had opposed Sejo. In some cases, these women and other family members were turned into slaves. Yŏnsan'gun's other issues (discussed below) may have stemmed from his parents. Yŏnsan'gun was the son of King Sŏngjong and Queen Yun (1455–82; 尹碩輔). Sŏngjong divorced Queen Yun after she had been accused of misbehaviour. Disgraced, the court sent Queen Yun into exile where officials subsequently poisoned her. In response, King Yŏnsan'gun extended his assault through another literati purge in 1504, when he executed additional scholars whom he believed had criticised him or had supported his mother's killing.

These political acts of violence, in which the king veered from Confucian norms and morality as a survival tactic against the very people advising him, mirrored what some officials saw as being one of the reasons for the

[3] For more on the struggle between Yŏnsan'gun and the bureaucracy, see Edward K. Wagner, *The Literati Purges: Political Conflict in early Yi Korea* (Cambridge, MA: East Asia Research Center and Harvard University Press, 1974), 42–50, 58–69.

breakdown of norms in the wider society. Those officials already saw a world in decline and ascribed the root cause to the king's poor behaviour. Rather than harbour concern for the social good, people were more interested in personal gain, which undermined the foundation of the society. These debates over proper conduct also involved animals. In 1495, the Board of Rites discussed one report submitted to the court from the governor of Ch'ungch'ŏng Province. In it, the governor accused a group of Buddhist monks (*ch'iryujido*; 緇流之徒) of harming the country by raising many hawks and hounds and openly training them. To tend their animals, these groups had confiscated land from others, places where oxen and horses were being raised and 'took advantage of and enticed the ignorant people'.[4] Court officials combined the raising and training of hawks and hounds with that of other scandalous activities including that of sex and financial corruption. The same report noted that men and women 'mixed together, fornicating with each other without fear . . . destroying social customs'. Among the accused was a 'monk who raised hawks and hounds (*ch'ugŭng kyŏnsŭngin*; 畜鷹犬僧人)'. According to the state, all of these actions were crimes. In response, the court had the monks and others involved apprehended, interrogated, found guilty and punished. Officials demolished an illegally constructed Buddhist monastery and had all the slaves and animals confiscated.[5] Examples like this probably demonstrate a long-standing social custom that officials were attempting to eradicate, that the king and the elite were not the only ones to search out wild beasts and tend domestic animals. While apparently tolerated at the court (see Figure 9.1), people risked their class statuses and lives to raise them, especially dogs, for the social, economic and political benefits the animals could bring.

The early history of dog breeds on the Korean peninsula, including how or where people raised and trained them, is hazy. Much of our knowledge of Korean dog breeds has been derived from advancements in genetics.[6] Contextualising

---

[4] CWS, 12:666.
[5] CWS, 12:666.
[6] Modern dog breeds protected by the South Korean government as national treasures are the Chindo (Jindo), the Tonggyŏng, the Sapsali and the P'ungsan. P'ungsan dogs are also considered a national treasure in North Korea. The Cheju dog is another indigenous species. For more on the history and science of Korean dog breeds, see Chandigma Gajeweerra, *et al.*, 'Genetic Diversity and Population Structure of the Sapsaree [Sapsali], a Native Korean Dog Breed' *BMC Genetics* 20, no. 66 (2019): 1–11. There is a strong genetic relationship between Korean and Chinese dog breeds suggesting ancient Chinese ancestry is present in Korean breeds. Further, Korean breeds have a high genetic divergence from each other, giving each dog breed distinct characteristics. See Bong Hwan Choi, *et al.*, 'Genome-Wide Analysis of the Diversity and Ancestry of Korean Dogs', *PLoS One* 12, no. 11 (November 2017): 1–20.

TAMING WILD ANIMALS AND BEASTLY MONARCHS   241

Figure 9.1 Yi Am (1499–?; 李巖), *Mother and her Pups* (*Mogyŏn to*; 母犬圖), c. 1500–20. Paper. While depicting a moment of bonding between a mother and her puppies, this painting is also significant because it portrays successful dog breeding. The surviving litter appears energetic and the mother healthy. Courtesy of the National Museum of Korea.

these studies with the Koryŏ and Chosŏn dynasties' primary sources suggests there may be important clues to be found about early canine–human interactions. Hunting dogs (*ku*; 狗) of this era, such as in Figure 9.2, were apparently bred for their calmer temperaments. Dogs with calmer temperaments were capable of concentrating on particular tasks more efficiently. This characteristic is common to at least one breed, the Sapsali. These medium-sized, long-haired dogs, resemble the English sheepdog.[7] Dogs similar to the Sapsali joined their human companions on both royal Kangmu events and private hunts. Handlers trained dogs like

---

[7] One study finds that contemporary Sapsali carry genes that allow them to concentrate on tasks more efficiently, which makes them better military working dogs than other contemporary breeds. See Hee-Eun Lee, *et al.*, 'Polymorphism Analysis of Tyrosine Hydroxylase Gene Variable Number of Tandem Repeats in Various Korean Dogs', *Genetics and Genomics* 37 (2015): 257–61. Further, the Sapsali shares no ancestry with the other indigenous Korean dog the Chindo, which is a purely indigenous species. See Ryong Nam Kim, *et al.*, 'Genome Analysis of the Domestic Dog (Korean Jindo) by Massively Parallel Sequencing', *DNA Research* 19, no. 3 (June 2012): 275–88.

Figure 9.2 Artist unknown, *Painting of a Dog* (*Kyŏndo*; 犬圖), date unknown. c. 1700–1900. Paper.
Courtesy of the National Museum of Korea.

the Sapsali and other breeds to flush out deer, wild boar, foxes and other animals more effectively than human chasers or beaters, which increased the chance hunters would have opportunities to kill prey. At times, the Chosŏn court would gift hunting dogs to foreign kings and envoys. Chosŏn royalty gave five dogs to Ming envoys in 1408 and twenty in 1468. A Korean envoy transported a pair of hunting hawks and an unspecified number of dogs to Japan in 1410.[8] When Japanese envoys arrived on the peninsula, they expressed their eagerness to acquire dogs.[9] Gifting hunting dogs, both within Korea and to foreign rulers, was common in the reigns of both King T'aejong and King Sejong. This was especially true for dogs raised and trained in the northern provinces, perhaps because they, like falcons, were considered hardier breeds capable of traversing mountain terrain. Chief Royal Secretariat Kim Yŏji (?–1425; 金汝知) and Governor of P'unghae (Hwanghae) Province Sim On (?–1444; 沈溫) each gave King T'aejong a hunting dog in 1412.[10]

---

[8] CWS, 1:543 and 8:185.
[9] CWS, 1:459.
[10] CWS, 1:626.

It is uncertain whether individuals raised dogs and presented them as gifts or if officials procured them from other sources, such as the Buddhist monasteries or from the monk mentioned earlier, who was arrested for raising animals in Ch'ungch'ŏng Province. According to tutors and officials who opposed interacting with live animals, it did not matter if the animals were presented as gifts, kept as pets, or trained as hunting companions, they represented overindulgence and potential criminality. One example of such misconduct was the behaviour of senior official Hong Yuryong (?–?; 洪有龍) who had fallen out of favour with the court. Senior civil officials accused him of corruption in addition to other crimes. His charges included that of dipping into government funds to support two *kisaeng* female entertainers and twenty hunting dogs. Officials also accused Hong of criticising Yŏnsan'gun's hunting habits even though Hong himself had taken part in the hunts.[11] Knowledge of animals, like that of knowing how to handle hawks and hounds, was threatening to bureaucrats who feared the economic and moral consequences of dealing with these animals. Allowing the king or others to have close proximity to beasts conflicted with the wider ideals these officials espoused.

Wilfully ignoring the concerns of advisors around him, Yŏnsan'gun openly displayed his fondness for dogs. While court officials begged him to end this interest in hunting animals, their pleas went unheeded. On one occasion, he demanded ten dogs join him along with a group of soldiers, probably the trainers and handlers of the animals.[12] By 1502, senior officials again complained about what they saw as a grave moral peril – the king's hunting dogs. 'This morning when all the officials were standing in order at the court, the hunting dogs rampaged around them. In particular, a trade envoy from Japan gazed upon this scene in discomfort. From now on, please do not set your hunting dogs loose.' To deflect personal blame for this diplomatic gaffe, the king simply called for an investigation into those responsible for securing the dogs.[13]

For these scholars, dogs and other animals were distractions. Officials like Ch'oe Suksaeng (1457–1520; 崔淑生) believed that the long era of peace the country was experiencing encouraged more and more luxuries that 'could not be sustained'.[14] He argued that things like horses, hawks and hounds were luxury items, hinting that the lifestyle of the king, who should set a moral example for the people, promoted human interaction with animals. In other

---

[11] CWS, 2:7.
[12] CWS, 13:441.
[13] CWS, 13:471.
[14] CWS, 3:350.

words, the government needed to conserve expenses to endure times of future hardship. He went on,

> Moreover, horses are vital for the army and government and must not be given up [reduced because of expenses], but hawks and hounds should not be bred or raised. These days, Your Majesty decrees, 'Give twelve bags of rice to the palace falconers.' But this year, the people are dying, and fathers and sons are unable to take care of each other. Things like hunting dogs (*talgu chiryu*; 獺狗之類) are not suitable for raising inside the palace. An old expression [of Mencius] states, 'This encourages beasts to devour people.'[15]

Ch'oe alluded to a passage of Mencius where Mencius argues that the king's poor governance resulted in the people growing hungry, weakened and vulnerable to wild animal attacks. Horses, hawks and hounds found prominence in the lifeways of many Koreans, not just the king. A portion of scholarly officials were railing against contemporary customs among a portion of fellow elites and then linking it to their ongoing tension with the king.

To reinforce Ch'oe's philosophical argument against royal involvement with animals, Song Chungdon (1463–1529; 孫仲暾), an official from the Office of Inspector General, also tapped into Chinese historical examples. To illuminate his point, Song stated,

> Since ancient times, raising hawks and hounds is not virtuous for the people or rulers. At the time of Tang Dynasty China, the founder of the Tang, Emperor Gaozu (566–635; 高皇帝), concealed a sparrowhawk close to his chest. Over a long period of time, the statesman Wei Zheng [in an attempt to remonstrate against the king's actions] wrote a memorial about [the king handling this bird]. The sparrowhawk unexpectedly died on the founder's chest. Emperor Gaozu had not listened to anything Wei Zheng had said because Wei Zheng was reluctant to speak the truth.

Yŏnsan'gun said nothing in return.[16] Song's story pointed to the futility and potential dangers of raising animals. Even powerful rulers like the Tang founder did not know how to tend wild beasts. Clutching the creature close to the imperial body to protect it and demonstrate his ownership of it killed the animal. The story, meant to dissuade the king from raising animals, made

---

[15] CWS, 3:350.
[16] CWS, 13:560.

no impression on Yŏnsan'gun who paid little attention to scholarly demands. In fact, his frustration brought added insistence that he spend time away in the wilderness, on hunts, distant from the watchful eyes of close officials who sought to restrain and constantly assault his royal actions and authority.

Hunting, Rites and the Animal Frontier

By the end of the fifteenth century, Korea began witnessing more dramatic weather events from the Little Ice Age. Given the geography of the peninsula – high mountain ranges in the north, with strong continental weather patterns and delicate agricultural fields in the south, often hit with seasonal monsoons from the Pacific Ocean – the peninsula was a barometer for the shifting climate that unfolded over the next century. As the subsequent storyline attempts to flesh out, hunting, royal access to animals and hunting grounds, and the question of stability along the frontiers, all themes explored in previous chapters, converge over the question of royal authority and legitimacy as the state became more bureaucratic in nature and strengthened counterbalances to royal power.

After the death of his father, King Sŏngjong, King Yŏnsan'gun continued traditions he, his royal family members and other elites practised. He took part in small-scale hunts and royal military Kangmu events around the capital. In the summer of 1495, for instance, he attempted to view a hunt, but unexpected heavy rain forced him to cancel.[17] Minister Yun P'ilsang noted, 'The wild animals have already been driven nearby into the shooting fields (*sajang*; 射場). Standing in a circle to watch them is possible.' The advisor Yi Kŭkpae simply demanded the troops stop. Minister Yun P'ilsang believed the 'the king's precious body cannot remain in the fields for long in the rain'.[18] To help appease the spirits and prevent calamity to the people, Yŏnsan'gun ordered the troops to capture a fox to offer as a sacrifice. On another occasion, the king hunted with soldiers on a mountain behind Yŏnhŭi Palace, just outside the western wall of the capital, where the attending guards hunted non-dangerous game such as hare and foxes.[19] These smaller, personal hunts gave the king a taste of the outdoors and took him away from the overly demanding officials and his enemies at the court.

In the autumn of 1497, Yŏnsan'gun announced his plan to spend more time in the field, away from the court. 'In ancient times, there were hunts in the spring, summer, autumn, and winter. I too wish to go on hunts.' The Royal

[17] CWS, 12:682.
[18] CWS, 12:682.
[19] CWS, 13:329.

Secretariate responded, 'If so, why don't you do it once in September and once in October?' The king replied that after September, he would go on four hunts.[20] Advisors recommended he attend a circle hunt at Mt Chasan (慈山) in South P'yŏngan Province after which he should visit the Shrine of Confucius. The king, not wanting to wash himself ahead of time for fear of catching a cold, decided to skip the worship ceremony at the shrine. Washing before such ceremonies was a ritual obligation. Instead, he insisted, 'I'll go hunting without a bath.'[21] Other officials argued that he should take part in the ritual, saying, 'Going hunting first is inconvenient [unproper].' The king argued that catching a cold was not only harmful to his health, but also detrimental to the country if he were to become weak, so he would worship at the Shrine of Confucius next year.[22]

More officials opposed this breach of protocol. Inspector General Chŏng Sŏkkyŏn (?–1500; 鄭錫堅) evoked memories of other moments when King Yŏnsan'gun hunted without concern for the weather on his health. That included many instances when the king spent days outside in the royal palace garden watching soldiers unleash arrows and other times when he went on short personal hunts. '[When the king] only does such things as crafts [archery] and hunting, we officials cannot bear this [lack of royal leadership] and ache in pain.' Worried that the king may injure himself with archery, officials begged him to give up these kinds of activities. Injuring himself would be an affront to the king's parents, a Confucian belief based on filial piety. They continued to warn the king not to go hunting. Undeterred, and perhaps in an attempt to upset them more, Yŏnsan'gun suggested that he would conduct a walking tour hunt (yujŏn; 遊畋), where he would travel the country and remain away for 100 days. 'How can I give up watching archery just because of the words of [a few] senior officials?'[23]

If Yŏnsan'gun's intention was to shock court officials, he succeeded. Chŏng Sŏkkyŏn and other scholar officials were upset by the king's words. Chŏng responded, 'Yesterday, you said you would go out hunting and not return for one hundred days. [You] resemble Tai Kang, the third king of the Xia Dynasty (2070–1600 BCE; 夏朝) . . . He engaged in play [hunting excursions] for a long time and never returned.' Officials asserted that if Yŏnsan'gun insisted on leaving the palace and the capital for 100 days, he would never come back. Moreover, they expressed their displeasure in the king engaging with officials

[20] CWS, 13:274.
[21] CWS, 13:274.
[22] CWS, 13:274.
[23] CWS, 13:275.

this way. They argued that it was improper for kings to compete with them in games such as archery. 'Kings are to shoot bows alone and not with teams. If the king watched archery with other royal family members [that would be fine and] they could certainly do so in teams.' Arguments like this point to the power balance between Chosŏn kings and civil officials in central government ministries and bureaus. The king, never in full control, clashed verbally and sometimes violently with close officials around him.

Yŏnsan'gun noted that he no longer hunted as past kings once had. He reminded them that now there were only spring and autumn hunts because of restrictions due to agricultural seasons and the fear of disrupting crop production. On top of that, if he began watching archery with his royal relatives, he asserted, officials, over time, would abolish that too.

> If I watched archery day after day, I'm sure that what you say is right, but [I watch it] only a few times a year . . . [To respond to your story of] the Xia and King Zhou, I am ordinary and stupid [compared to him] and cannot do it [step back from governing]. Now, bring some wine and meat. Let's consume as much as we can and then go back [to the court].[24]

It is important to remember that despite the heated rhetoric at the court, kings also enjoyed recreation, such as music, food, drink and hunting. They continued to share food and drink with their close officials and family members and met daily, discussed matters of the state, and sometimes travelled together. For those who did not hold such common values, like Chŏng, they were in constant struggle to change the perspective of monarchs.

Chŏng Sŏkkyŏn reminded the king that the court did not sanction four hunts a year, only two, and they were for military practice.

> Further, the animals killed on these hunts are to be presented to the royal ancestral shrines (hŏn'gŭm ŏjongmyo; 獻禽於宗廟). This is an extraordinarily ancient system. These days, the circle hunt (t'awi; 打圍) is a touring hunt (yujŏn; 遊畋). It is not an ancient winter hunt (susu 蒐狩) [one of the seasonal hunts held four times a year]. Now Your Majesty has abandoned the royal Confucian lectures (kyŏngyŏn; 經筵) and instead observes archers releasing arrows [every day].

Suggesting that the king was loitering around, he explained to King Yŏnsan'gun that ministers were obligated to advise the ruler concerning the teachings of

---

[24] CWS, 13:276.

the ancient sage kings and that a ruler was required to listen to his advisors and receive their advice. Chŏng invoked the previous ruler, King Sŏngjong, Yŏnsan'gun's father, as an example of excellent leadership. Sŏngjong was brilliant, Chŏng insisted, and was imbued with a heavenly nature. However, Chŏng stressed, King Sŏngjong had had scores of people who provided him guidance inside and outside of the palace. 'From the beginning to the middle of his reign, the former king did not conduct any hunts . . . and governing was beautiful and illustrious.' Chŏng went further, identifying what he considered part of the problem. 'Now, there are no former queens inside the royal palace to provide you with assistance [as in the early days of King Sŏngjong] and no great ministers outside the palace to deter your unseemly rulership. Therefore, over these past few days, Your Majesty's political situation has turned upside down and is in disorder.' King Sŏngjong achieved sagely virtue in his final years, Chŏng asserted, while Yŏnsan'gun appeared to have no interest in governing and merely observed the shooting of arrows and handling dogs and hawks. 'Your Majesty is too young to see it now. You will see it only later in your final years.'[25] Chŏng's pleas went unheeded. Yŏnsan'gun ignored the advice and continued to prepare for his hunting excursion.

Many memorials, petitions and admonitions flooded into the court regarding King Yŏnsan'gun's decision to hunt and to halt his attendance at state rituals. Officials planning this trip inquired as to why the king insisted on attending four hunts when they were uncertain if he would attend one. 'I'm going to give circle hunting a go one more time (*t'awi tangsiilto*; 打圍當試一度)', he countered, before handing the responsibility of planning the trips to other officials. The king sought to abandon his responsibilities with regards to training the military and simply hunt.[26] Officials at the royal lectures, which he continued to attend, illuminated the differences between military training in the field and the hunt. 'Practicing military skills in the spring and autumn cannot be abolished. [It is necessary to protect the country from invaders.] Things like hunting, however, are mere entertainment.' The king, in return, emphasised that 'hunting was not the same as other kinds of entertainment'.[27] Senior advisors and ministers hoped to reason with the king to give up hunting, but he adamantly refused. They pointed out the impropriety of a king not carrying out the necessary ceremonies at the state shrines and instead galivanting around the country hunting.[28] If a natural disaster or a bad harvest struck, the king

[25] CWS, 13:276.
[26] CWS, 13:277.
[27] CWS, 13:277.
[28] CWS, 13:282.

declared a compromise, 'I would end the royal military Kangmu hunts but still go on a circle hunt [on a much smaller scale].'²⁹ Frustrated by the restrictions placed on the hunt and the diminishing locations for hunting, Yŏnsan'gun complained, 'If royal tombs are sacred locations where one is not permitted to hold a circle hunt, then I will travel all the way to China to hold one!'³⁰

Officials could be found on both sides of the issue. When Ch'anggyŏng Palace suffered fire damage in 1498, officials called for the suspension of the royal review of the troops (*yŏlmu*; 閱武). The court considered cancelling the event altogether. A dispute broke out over what constituted a national emergency, the immediate destruction of a symbol of governance or the imaginary dangers of a future military threat? One scholar expressed his concern that the dynasty would not be prepared. 'For a long time, there has been no large-scale royal review of the troops . . . as ancient people used to say, "There's no concern when you're ready."' Another minister opposed this line of reasoning, 'Now, there is a calamity [a fire in the palace], so inspecting the troops is inappropriate.' Yŏnsan'gun agreed that military troop inspections should continue. In fact, he reiterated that royal military hunts should be conducted, not twice, but four times, seasonally. Rather than harming the country, the king explicitly stated that these hunts assisted the common people, presumably by eradicating agricultural pests, such as birds, deer and foxes, from farmland, while simultaneously preparing the military to protect the people from disorder and invasion.³¹ Most officials did not seem to be convinced by this line of reasoning.

Questions over royal authority and access to the lands around the capital extended to close family members. In the late fifteenth century, despite the criticism of officials, royal family members still hunted. In the spring of 1497, royal family member Hong Sang, a brother-in-law who had married Sŏngjong's sister Princess Myŏngsuk (1456–82; 明淑) in 1466, travelled to the hunting area of Kap'yŏng, forty-two kilometres (26 mi.) northeast of the capital where the plains met the mountains, with three hunters (*sasuja samin*; 射獸者三人) to hunt. Censorate P'yo Yŏnmal (1449–98; 表沿沫) criticised Hong for taking part in a hunt at the beginning of the farming season. 'He [Hong Sang] leads horses and men who trample the fields. All the officials find this unpleasant.'³² The next day, P'yo Yŏnmal petitioned the king about the matter of Hong Sang and the re-establishment of a falconer post (*ŭngbang*; 鷹坊). Yŏnsan'gun defended Hong, who was, according to the king, a meritorious subject and

---

²⁹ *CWS*, 13:278.
³⁰ *CWS*, 13:282.
³¹ *CWS*, 13:331.
³² *CWS*, 13:201.

falconer declaring, 'King Sejong did not abolish all falconers. He only did away with peregrine falcons (*haedongch'ŏng*; 海東青). Establishing the position of falconry is not solely for me. Establishing this position is for the royal palace (*sangjŏn*; 上殿). Do not exile Hong Sang!'

In a gesture to Confucian ritual obligations, P'yo Yŏnmal explained the importance of the spring and autumn state ceremonies. 'They are not meant to be for celebration, but rather these rituals are matters of past precedent.' During the reign of former King Sŏngjong, P'yo went on, the palace retained a position called the 'inner palace falconer' (*naeŭngbang*; 內鷹坊). Rightly or wrongly, P'yo explained that he had never heard much about this position. P'yo also noted that during the previous dynasty, the court had stripped those who avoided military service of their ranks and grouped them with the falconers (where they had no significant service obligations). These demotions, P'yo insisted, 'destroyed the state' (*imangguk*; 以亡國), suggesting not only were they a drain on finances, but also undermined Confucian state identity.

During the reign of King Ch'unghye of the Koryŏ Dynasty, P'yo elaborated, '[the king heard] the cry of a lone rooster [and declared that this] was extremely sad, and that when you chose to gaze upon it, your shoulders would ache with pain [from sobbing], because this [crying rooster] was to be fed to the falcons', presumably disturbed because of his Buddhist beliefs. P'yo continued,

> [Koryŏ's] King Ch'unghye felt sorry for the roosters and ordered an end to falcon hunting. Ch'unghye was an ordinary ruler . . . so how can you [King Yŏnsan'gun], Your Majesty, reestablish falconry now? There are few live animals (*saengmul*; 生物) in the capital region of Kyŏnggi Province. How can you be certain that after establishing falconry Your Majesty will be filial [attend to your duties as king and son]? When your ministers gaze upon you, your attention to trivial matters will undo you (*wanmul sangji*; 玩物 喪志). [In other words, distractions from governance undermine the state and threaten your monarchy.] We ask you to end these affairs.[33]

Put simply, P'yo warned the king that if he did not give up falconry, he risked his own legacy and may be remembered as worse than the notoriously bad rulers of the Koryŏ era.

Angered, King Yŏnsan'gun responded, 'If I listen to everything you say, what am I going to be able to do? While there is precedent [for removing falcons from the palace], you all also offer up your opinions to win your points [gain my favour] – how can this be? You say, that "Your attention to trivial

---

[33] CWS, 13:201.

matters will undo you." Excluding falconry, what do you find problematic when you watch me? When I'm inside the palace, I don't want you to watch me. Do you know how demoralizing it is (*hahwan ŏsangjiho*; 何患於喪志乎) [to be constantly under observation]?"[34] Much as his father, the former king, had objected, Yŏnsan'gun was most concerned about the restrictions to his movements and actions. Yet, another petition presented by the Censorate implored the king to abandon falconry to preserve the dynasty.

> Koryŏ established falconry and searched widely for birds. [At that time] the rich and powerful people and commoners (*hobu yangjŏng*; 豪富良丁) outside the capital came from far away in an attempt to save themselves and be exempted from corvée labor [by raising and training birds of prey] ... this later caused great damage [to the dynasty]. In Your Majesty's early governance, if you grant official titles and salaries to men who catch small birds (*p'ojagin*; 捕雀人), then later generations will rely on the graces of the court [and this will continue to drain the finances of the state].

The petition concluded by warning the king that if he was not careful, his people would grow corrupt like those from Korea's past. If Yŏnsan'gun did not abolish falconry, officials cautioned, then commoners from 'near the capital and throughout the countryside would fall over each other to join in, and Chosŏn's falconry practice would share the same misfortune as Koryŏ'. Somewhat moved by this argument, Yŏnsan'gun agreed to strive to control his falcons and falconers but promised nothing more.[35] Debates like this give us a sense of the human psychological drama of the court and its complex relationships between the king and his officials.

A year after the Ch'anggyŏng Palace fire in 1499, Yŏnsan'gun openly questioned the private hunting practices of elites, including royal family members, ministers and hunting park officials. These men had been hunting privately in the woodlands outside the walls of the capital where many birds and animals lived. Even though they were known to have hunted in such places, he observed they had not been able to present much game as tribute to the court. (Implying that they were keeping the meat for themselves.) Concerned about the impact such hunting had on animal populations, the king decided to ban private hunting in these locations. 'If anyone commits the crime [of private hunting],' he warned, 'he will be dismissed from office.'[36] His threat

[34] *CWS*, 13:201.
[35] *CWS*, 13:209.
[36] *CWS*, 13:376.

now extended to elites and members of the royal family to control who hunted and where.

Later in 1499, an anonymous petition reached the court criticising these and other government hunting practices.

> On the twenty-ninth day of this month, a hunt was planned on the mountain behind Ch'anyŏng [a mountain close to the capital]. These days, there have been frequent hunts, but without any seeming pleasure [in other words, the hunt was not pleasurable because only a few animals were killed]. Despite this, [another hunt is planned] once again. The previous day, someone said, 'Now, hunting is unjust because it is a year of famine.' So how do you know in later years there will be no famine? There is no one saying, 'I enjoy hunting.'

With a wider lens that also took into consideration the military needs of the dynasty, the Royal Secretariate defended the king, countering, 'Soldiers practice the circle hunt every month to sharpen their skills. This cannot be called "enjoying the hunt".'[37]

To many of these and other court officials, hunting in the capital region or the agricultural fields distracted the king from his duties of governance and potentially threatened the ruler with injury or death, and thereby endangered the dynasty as a whole. Such dangers extended well beyond the capital to the frontier of the country to include questions of royal authority, hunting and military preparedness. In the north, Jurchen hunting parties continued appearing along the Yalu River, especially when the river was frozen, giving them easier access to lands the Jurchen claimed as hunting grounds. Like in previous reigns, the appearances of these Jurchen along the frontiers rattled northern military commanders.[38] However, the growing number of encounters between the Jurchens and Chosŏn subjects of all statuses intensified because of the expanding number of people in the north and the shifting weather conditions in the region that spurred Jurchen south. In 1496, for example, the court expressed concern about Jurchen parties crossing into P'yŏngan Province. From spring to autumn the Jurchen 'ride their horses and hunt as an excuse'.[39] To Chosŏn officials, the Jurchen hunting parties were simply a pretext for nefarious activities such as spying on the conditions of the country. This was seen as a national threat. The Jurchen carried 'large bows' as they strode along

---

[37] CWS, 13:383.
[38] CWS, 13:57.
[39] CWS, 13:153.

the riverside, implying that they were holding armaments of war, not weapons for hunting game. This appeared distressing and put Korea on the defence.[40]

To repel these Jurchen, one Chosŏn plan the court debated was to sneak across the border and launch a raid of their own while they were on the 'hunt'. However, not all officials agreed with the military option. Military leader Yi Kŭkton (1435–1503; 李克墩) realised this would lay the blame on Chosŏn.[41] He wondered if the Jurchen threats were overstated: 'The places where Jurchen live are far from our frontiers and since the Jurchen move along the rivers, they will not reveal much about Chosŏn's state of affairs.'[42] The Jurchen 'covet hunting, and they spend a long time along the riverside carrying large bows'.[43] The imposing bows they carried vexed officials, who feared they would cross over into Chosŏn. However, such bows were necessary for killing the formidable game found in the north, such as elk, tiger and moose. Combined with their hunting tactics of moving 'along the riverside' – a technique which proved easier and faster for hunters to traverse than denser forests and mountains and a place where game would congregate – these Jurchen hunters were mistaken as a military risk.

Recognising a more fluid border defined not by permanent geographical separation of the two states, but rather by the need to access animals, Yi Kŭkton and Yun Hyoson (1431–1503; 尹孝孫), another military leader, called for compromise. 'Our lands and their lands are already separated. What's the crime in hunting on each other's lands? We can forbid it. But even if you outlaw it, and they don't obey it, only our prestige will suffer.'[44] In other words, hunting grounds between the Jurchen and Korean could overlap without consequence. A shared need for game appears to have softened the political boundaries between the Jurchen and Chosŏn. The court held a diversity of views on the matter.

Jurchen hunting triggered the debate about the royal Kangmu hunts and military preparedness via the northern frontier. In 1499, Counsellor on the Left Hong Kwidal (1438–1504; 洪貴達) submitted a petition to King Yŏnsan'gun. Linking his argument to the Jurchen presence in the north, Hong questioned the need for royal Kangmu hunts. Hong suggested that the court was wasting time, money and resources on a performance when there was a real concern to the border. He went on to subtlety critique the Kangmu.

---

[40] *CWS*, 13:136.
[41] *CWS*, 13:128.
[42] *CWS*, 13:123.
[43] *CWS*, 13:136.
[44] *CWS*, 13:139.

To Hong, the royal Kangmu hunts were unnecessary. He believed they weakened the country because the extensive events pulled troops away from the important locations in the north that were responsible for defending against the Jurchen and other potential invaders. Instead, Hong argued, the king should only rely upon the troops from Hanyang, non-military personnel and lower-class nonprofessionals from the surrounding provinces to perform the Kangmu hunt. While helping to stabilise the frontier, the cancellation of the Kangmu promised other consequences. In particular, it would further erode the connection the king had with the military arts. Fewer Kangmu hunts undermined the king's involvement in military planning and organisation, skills that were decidedly martial and not scholarly. Hong suggested that some of the military personnel come from outside the conventional army, many from the lower strata of the Chosŏn social system and the least powerful – and least dangerous – members of society. Hong associated Jurchen action in the north with the need for state military preparedness and pointed out the central role of animals as sacrifice at state altars. These sacrifices were made to help preserve the country by appeasing the spirits and cosmic order at times of frontier instability and to honour the Chosŏn people the Jurchen had killed or kidnapped. Yŏnsan'gun did not follow Hong's advice.[45]

Other officials agreed with Hong Kwidal's argument that the Kangmu's purpose was mainly to provide game, which was then offered as sacrifice at the state altar. But despite this need, more officials expressed concern that such hunts presented an unacceptable level of danger to all involved. 'Now soldiers, those who act as chasers, are injured by evil beasts. Some are crushed by rocks falling from cliffs. This [outcome] is not [good] for these people. Tomorrow, you want to ride to a mountain [housing the royal tomb of secondary members of the royal family] at a location called Kanŭng (恭陵) [25 km (16 mi.) northeast of the palace].' Officials believed that the chasers would trample the tomb mounds. 'Your Majesty has killed a lot of animals, a sufficient amount for making offerings. Please stop [these hunts].' Yŏnsan'gun simply agreed to change the location of the hunt to two other mountains. Later he postponed it only after an outbreak of heavy rain made it impossible to continue.[46]

Officials subtly, and not so subtly, hoped to shame the king into giving up the hunt. By 1500, Secretary of the Royal Lectures An Ch'ŏsŏn (?–?; 安處善) criticised Yŏnsan'gun for displaying more interest in martial notions than scholarship during the royal Confucian lectures. 'Royal military training in the spring and autumn is [an] ancient [tradition]. However, circle hunts

---

[45] CWS, 13:377.
[46] CWS, 13:379.

have nothing to do with the way of governing. Even though there have been heavenly changes [omens, during the king's hunting events, such as political upheaval, natural calamities, or disease], [I believe] the heavenly heart of Your Majesty is benevolent. [And so I find it necessary to] remonstrate and then inform Your Majesty [about the importance of giving up the hunt].' The king deflected these accusations. He questioned Secretary An Ch'ŏsŏn about the connection between his participating in hunting and bad omens: 'How is it possible for the circle hunt to bring about heavenly change [dynastic misfortune]?'[47] On another occasion, an inspector from the Inspector General's Office simply stated, 'Your Majesty is about to stage another circle hunt. I'm afraid the people will say you like hunting.' Yŏnsan'gun was not amused, 'Why are you saying things that are contrary to reason? A long time ago, there used to be examples of royal Kangmu hunts that lasted sixteen days. In one year, I've attended one or two circle hunts. Why is this a problem? From now on, do not say these kind of things!'[48] Yŏnsan'gun ignored their protests and continued to plan royal Kangmu hunts. In an attempt to surpass even the hunts conducted by earlier kings, Yŏnsan'gun facilitated a military review (taeyŏl; 大閱) in Kaesŏng that rallied 30,000 men.[49] He desired to recreate the hunts of earlier reigns, when the events were displays of complete royal power and authority, which he seemed to keenly feel was slipping away and could only be regained through dramatic measures.

A Park for the Disappearing Beasts

Since the founding of Chosŏn (and perhaps even earlier), leaders understood that China had established hunting parks and Korea had not. King T'aejong noted in 1403, 'Our country does not have a royal hunting park.'[50] A royal hunting park was an expansive contiguous area, enclosed by walls or other barriers, different from the patchwork of separate royal Kangmu grounds. Korean ideals of what a Chinese hunting park was were inspired by classical Chinese philosophers and histories. Chinese writers recorded animal hunting grounds in early texts, as celebrated in the works of Huananzi and Mencius for instance.[51] The histories told about the Zhou, Wei and Han dynasties also

---

[47] CWS, 13:429.
[48] CWS, 13:431.
[49] CWS, 13:659.
[50] CWS, 1:280.
[51] Edward H. Schafer, 'Hunting Parks and Animal Enclosures in Ancient China', *Journal of the Economic and Social History of the Orient* 11, no. 3 (1968): 318–43.

fed popular elite imagination about Chinese parks' sizes and their abundance of animals. Accordingly, China was thought to have had vast lands set aside by the government for the use of the imperial family, elites and commoners.

By 1406, T'aejong contemplated creating one of these parks on the peninsula asking, 'Shall we establish a royal hunting park close to the capital?'[52] He argued against the abolishment of the royal Kangmu hunting grounds because a royal park could not replace all these hunting locations. Instead, he insisted that kings still must hunt on Kangmu lands.[53] By 1450, however, the royal family's concept of a royal hunting 'park' expanded to become synonymous with the many royal Kangmu hunting grounds located throughout the peninsula.[54] As King Sejo expressed in 1457, 'Royal hunting parks are not to be locations where kings play and enjoy themselves. Rather, [the royal hunting parks and Kangmu hunting areas are to be places where] kings hold ritual sacrifice and practice military arts.'[55] By 1481, however, defending his idea based on classical texts, King Sŏngjong had begun to contemplate building a royal park that would be available to the commoners and the elite: 'Isn't there an old saying [of Mencius] that goes something like this, "The grass cutters and the firewood gatherers had the privilege of entering [the king's park], the catchers of pheasants and hares did too [ensuring the common people had access to the park]."'[56]

Sŏngjong's son, King Yŏnsan'gun, yearned to build that park. If more officials argued to limit his mobility, he would bring the experience of the hunt closer to himself. In 1496, the censorate general submitted a document to the king outlining his opposition to a number of projects, including the expansion of a royal hunting park. 'If Your Majesty wants a sizeable park, then I say, [Your Majesty] should build a park like that of "The park of King Weng, [which] contained 70 square *li*."'[57] This was roughly seventy-five square kilometres (29 sq. mi.). By 1497, it appears that some of the park was erected. Yŏnsan'gun grew troubled that the condition, of what he called the Chosŏn royal hunting park (*wŏnyu*; 苑囿), was worse than China.

> The walls are narrow. When you release animals inside the park, they escape and run away. I was deeply distressed when I saw this. Mencius held that, 'Although he had towers, ponds, birds, and animals, how could [the

[52] CWS, 1:350.
[53] CWS, 2:127.
[54] See CWS, 6:319, 6:364 and 6:367.
[55] CWS, 7:229.
[56] CWS, 12:613. This is another direct quote from Mencius.
[57] CWS, 13:140.

ruler] have pleasure alone?' I too cannot gaze upon these wild beasts and enjoy them alone.[58]

In other words, by tapping into Mencius and other examples of the Confucian classical past (as his advisors consistently did in an attempt to control the king's actions), Yŏnsan'gun insisted that the lack of a suitable hunting park prevented him from sharing the space with others. Even nearly a decade later, in 1506, the park's condition continued to be of interest to the king. Yŏnsan'gun insisted on enhancing the park. He argued that the current era of peace was the appropriate moment to construct an addition to the hunting park. 'Even if [only] one or two people are starving in the cold out in the villages and fields, the people may still feel resentment. Not everyone can be saved.'[59] Put differently, there was already a certain level of suffering and anger at the government that could never be overcome, so he insisted on moving forward with improvements to the park because in his mind the people were going to suffer regardless.

As discussed in earlier chapters, by the 1450s, the government had eliminated most of the Kangmu hunting grounds in the outer provinces and instead established a limited number of hunting areas around the capital and in Kyŏnggi Province. King Yŏnsan'gun reversed this. Wanting to create a royal hunting area where animals were reared specifically for him to hunt, he dramatically expanded the royal hunting lands around the capital from seventy to 100 *li* (48 km [30 mi.]). He declared this area off limits, abolished the administrative borders (governing the towns, villages and counties, for instance), and forced the people living inside these areas to leave. He did all of this 'to establish a hunting ground (*iwi yuryŏp chiso*; 以爲遊獵之所)'. The king was not fooling around. Anyone found wandering inside was immediately beheaded. He also declared that there would be no farming within several hundred *li* circling the capital; the land went untended and was 'overgrown with weeds'. Most likely hyperbole to later attack Yŏnsan'gun, officials claimed that the capital region soon became 'grounds on which to try to raise beasts', rather than fields for grain or land to raise domesticated animals.[60]

Yŏnsan'gun's demand for a royal, enclosed hunting area may have been because there were few wild animals in the region to hunt. Apart from occasional harmless game, such as hares and foxes, the wildlife was so scarce that to find the nearest larger wild animals (deer, elk, bear or boar), a squad of

---

[58] CWS, 13:199.
[59] CWS, 14:35.
[60] CWS, 14: 67.

thirty soldiers had to travel to the neighbouring Kangwŏn and Hwanghae provinces. Such trips were unsustainable. Unable to carry their own supplies, the men requisitioned their grain and feed for their horses from the commoners, which caused great stress on the common people.[61] In one court session, King Yŏnsan'gun inquired simply, 'Why are there no more beasts?' Official Sŏng Chun (1436–1504; 成俊) replied, 'I heard it's because there are many private hunters.' Yŏnsan'gun responded, 'We must ban hunting because there are few animals.' Sŏng Chun replied that there were many new blacksmith homes inside the new hunting area grounds, suggesting these craftsmen disturbed the wildlife with their presence and work, and agreed with the king that they should be removed, while another official pushed back arguing that those already living on the grounds should not be removed.[62] Commoners were not the only ones infringing on the grounds. Many local magistrates privately hunted there too. 'I implore Your Majesty,' senior-official Yu Chagwang (1439–1512; 柳子光) pleaded, 'Please ban private hunting.' Both commoners and the elite hunted. They recognised that the animals were scarce. Despite the risks, they continued to enter the forbidden grounds to find game.

Yŏnsan'gun explained the reason why he believed the local magistrates, in particular, broke the law to hunt. These officials, he averred, hunted in order to submit their quarry to the state as tribute, which was part of their local villages' tax obligations. In essence, these leaders were facing two equally challenging situations. 'Their hunting on the Kangmu grounds must not be allowed,' he demanded. 'Moreover, the people share common lands in the hills and marshes (kurŭng ch'ŏnt'aek; 丘陵川澤). Shall I ban their private hunting [too]?' The areas the king was referring to here were marginal lands unsuitable for agriculture. They were not privately owned but considered communal spaces where the lower classes hunted and gathered firewood. Animals were disappearing from those areas too. Additional pressure on the populations of smaller game such as sable, squirrel, hare and ringed pheasant came from the slaves employed as falconers by powerful yangban families (sega noja chiŭngp'ae; 勢家奴子持鷹牌) who hunted as they pleased on Kangmu grounds. Their immunity angered Yŏnsan'gun. 'Birds and beasts are scarce,' he lectured, and as such he demanded an end to these illegal hunts.[63] It was also noted that extreme weather had impacted the number of animals in the southern provinces. 'Animals have frozen to death [because of heavy snow in recent years], and there are practically none left (sujok tongsat'aejin; 獸族凍死殆盡).'[64] Again, we

[61] CWS, 13:404.
[62] CWS, 13:575.
[63] CWS, 13:580.
[64] CWS, 13:541.

should remember that hunting was a long-established tradition practised by many from all backgrounds, but the government sought to regulate it and then completely ban the hunt.

Human population growth, particularly in the capital region, increased demand for land. As part of this expansion, commoners and skilled craftsmen began moving into the area, building additional homes in villages located at the base of nearby mountains. However, this policy had resulted in an increasing number of humans colliding with the habitat needs of animals and Yŏnsan'gun's ambition to expand his royal hunting area. To solve this dearth in the number of animals, Yŏnsan'gun commanded that all homes near the grounds be removed. The king determined that the people in these settlements and those who hunted animals had either killed too many animals or had scared them away. In one location, the government relocated fifty homes to an area outside the hunting grounds and erected signs that stated 'no fires and no collecting firewood' in an effort to reinforce the court's decision to strengthen control over access to the hunting grounds.[65] Rather than allow the commoners into a park, as he had earlier suggested with the story of Mencius, instead it appears that the king wanted to ban the people from going inside the area as a means to allow the animals to return.

As animals became increasingly hard to find, kill and offer up to the state as tribute, Kangmu hunts grew less about the hunting of animals or the means to practise military manoeuvers and more about entertainment. In the eyes of critical scholar officials, the king would spend his time viewing archery, listening to reed flute music (*ch'ojŏgak*; 草笛樂), consuming alcohol with his guests, and spending time with women.[66] The details of the king's habits in the sources indicate that he had become known for enjoying other facets of the Kangmu hunts. On one occasion, Yŏnsan'gun criticised the clothing he was wearing on the hunt, complaining that when he poured an official some alcohol, the tassel had fallen into the drink.[67] For one Kangmu in 1504, former Queen Dowager Chŏnghyŏn, the third wife of Yŏnsan'gun's father Sŏngjong and stepmother to the king, had presented the king with a small drinking table to use during his trips, apparently suggesting that senior women in the royal family accepted these customs. He used this table, even while claiming to be a poor drinker.[68] In the autumn of 1505, Yŏnsan'gun demanded that female musicians (*yŏak*; 女樂) be selected in advance from nearby villages to where

[65] CWS, 13:627.
[66] CWS, 13:442.
[67] CWS, 13:665.
[68] CWS, 13:674.

the Kangmu was to be held.[69] Officials spoke frequently against Yŏnsan'gun participating in the Kangmu hunt and lumped hunting animals together with other unseemly pastimes such as womanising and drinking. Others instructed Yŏnsan'gun as to the inappropriateness of hunting based on Confucian precedent, offering many stories from China's past about kings neglecting state affairs to hunt. While music, women, alcohol and material culture (his clothing and the drinking table for example) occupied his time, Yŏnsan'gun took other steps to compensate for the scarcity of game around him on the hunt.

When travelling into the mountains and forests to encounter animals grew harder to do because it was more and more difficult to find animals, Yŏnsan'gun brought the wildlife closer to the capital and the royal palace. He released game in the rear palace garden (huwŏn; 後苑) so he could mount his horse and gallop across the grounds to hunt. These human and very private moments recreated some sense of the freedom he felt while out hunting away from the capital. It appears the king despised being on display. 'He hated the guards and soldiers peering over the wall to watch.'[70] By 1505, the last year of Yŏnsan'gun's reign, the king had collected numerous rare birds and dogs and displayed them on the palace grounds. He raised geese and ducks on a nearby pond, and supplied the birds with grain, perhaps even feeding them himself.[71] To further bring wildlife to him, the court requested, on his behalf, that hawks and hounds be delivered from all of the provinces.[72] When the king could no longer encounter animals on the hunt, he surrounded himself with beasts at the court and palace grounds.

Diseases, Animals and Death

While humans hunted wild beasts, another kind of animal pursued humans. Illnesses, common on the peninsula during the Koryŏ and Chosŏn dynasties, infected kings, ministers and officials. Reported symptoms ranged from those found with mild colds, for example congestion, sore throat and cough to signs of debilitating illness or infection including chills, body aches, paralysis, fever and skin lesions that not only sickened but also killed people. Impossible to fully tease out because of gaps in the sources, the image that emerges on diseases in premodern times and their indirect association with animals and the hunt, including animal parts used for medicinal purpose, is vague and undefined.

---

[69] *CWS*, 14:20.
[70] *CWS*, 13:223.
[71] *CWS*, 14:19.
[72] *CWS*, 14:62.

Animal-borne diseases most likely sickened Koreans, and medicines from animal products helped cure them.

On a national level, the government repeatedly reported outbreaks of what appear to have been contagious zoonotic diseases throughout the fifteenth century.[73] 'Pestilence' or what was commonly described as the plague (yŏkchil [疫疾] or on occasion onyŏk [瘟疫] in the sources) referred to serious illnesses that were present throughout the society. Most likely, pestilence represented more than one type of illness. One possibility was the smallpox virus (*Variola major* and *Variola minor*). This deadly pathogen most likely jumped from rodents to humans thousands of years ago near the Egyptian Nile Valley (the first visible scars were found on 3,000-year-old mummies). Smallpox swept through the societies of both Africa and Eurasia, one strain reached East Asia by the fourth century with the earliest smallpox inoculations occurring in sixteenth-century China.[74] As in other parts of Eurasia, smallpox mutations were likely to have been present in Korea, some strains being more virulent than others.[75] With an incubation period of ten to fourteen days, small-pox-infected persons easily spread the disease through their saliva and the scabs on the body, which in turn infected their clothing and bedding. In severe cases, death occurred within fourteen days. Individual mortality rates could reach 20–40 per cent, if not higher.[76] Surviving smallpox was known to ensure immunity for life.

Another possible cause of these epidemics was the plague (*Yersinia pestis*). Like the smallpox virus, bacterial strains of the plague have ravaged human populations for at least 5,000 years. The plague first surfaced in rodents and was then transmitted to humans through fleas. Fleas are capable of biting both humans and rodents and, on these animals, remained hosts for future mutations. Humans, once contracting these diseases, can easily transmit them through contact with infected tissue or respiratory excretion. The

---

[73] Yi Chunho, 'Chosŏn sidae kihu pyŏndongi chŏnyŏmbyŏng palsaeng e mich'in yŏngyang' [The development and impact of infectious diseases in the Chosŏn Dynasty], *Han'guk chiyŏk chirihak hoeji* 25 (2019): 425–36; and Kim Yangsik, 'Chosŏn sidae chŏnyŏmbyŏng yangsang kwa t'ŭkching' [Chosŏn dynasty infectious disease trends and characteristics], *Ch'ungbok Issue and Trend* 39 (2020): 8–13.

[74] See William Wayne Farris, *Population, Disease, and Land in Early Japan, 645–900* (Cambridge, MA: Harvard University Press, 1995), 54.

[75] For an overview on smallpox, see Alexander Mercer, *Infections, Chronic Disease, and the Epidemiological Transition: A New Perspective* (Rochester: University of Rochester, 2014), 58–9.

[76] Frank Fenner, 'Smallpox: Emergence, Global Spread, and Eradication', *History and Philosophy of the Life Sciences* 15, no. 3 (1993): 397–420.

plague has an incubation period of up to a week, which, like smallpox, provides time for the host to transmit it to others unknowingly. Flu-like symptoms develop before the bacterium begins attacking the lymph nodes and the lungs. For the seemingly less severe strains of bubonic plague, mortality rates can reach 30–60 per cent, while more strains of pneumonic plague are fatal – this is high compared to the mortality rate of 2–5 per cent for COVID-19.[77] The strain that touched off the age of the Black Death across Eurasia in the fourteenth and fifteenth centuries – what is referred to as the second plague pandemic – most likely originated in the Qinghai-Tibetan plateau of central China and was then transported across Eurasia east and west through trade and travel. In China, lethal contagious diseases in the 1330s and 1350s contributed to major population loss in the northeast and along the east coast. Many of those who contracted these diseases died. Population losses in societies ranged from 20–40 per cent.[78]

These incidences of 'pestilence' most likely refer to these and other zoonotic diseases – even such viral respiratory infections caused from the droppings of infected migratory waterfowl – which may have killed thousands of people and impacted society and politics.[79]

Animals and animal pathogens shaped Korean history. As Monica Green points out, key historical agents in the transmission of these diseases across regions were animals and insects: rodents, swine, birds, ticks, mosquitos and fleas.[80] The progressive expansion of the population, the growth of villages, towns, and a new and larger capital in Hanyang brought more people into contact with convergent zones that were also home to various animals and insects. The movement of royal family members, diplomats and soldiers across the frontier – via the royal Kangmu hunts and interactions with Jurchen hunters or Japanese pirates searching for quarry – occurred simultaneously with diseases, suggesting a correlation. Most likely, a different strain of smallpox

---

[77] John P. A. Ioannidis, 'Infection Fatality Rate of COVID-19 Inferred from Seroprevalence Data', *Bulletin of the World Health Organization* 99 (2021): 19–33.

[78] Yujun Cui, *et al.*, 'Historical Variations in Mutation Rate in an Epidemic Pathogen, Yersinia pestis', *Proceedings of the National Academy of Sciences of the United States of America* 110, no. 2 (January 2013): 577–82. As George Sussman explains, scholars are uncertain about the nature and impact of disease in late Yuan and early Ming China. See George Sussman, 'Was the Black Death in India and China?' *Bulletin of the History of Medicine* 85, no. 3 (Fall 2011): 319–55.

[79] For the avian flu, see L. D. Sims, *et al.*, 'Origin and Evolution of Highly Pathogenic H5N1 Avian Influenza in Asia', *Veterinary Record* 157, no. 6 (August 2005): 159–64.

[80] Monica H. Green, 'Taking "Pandemic" Seriously: Making the Black Death Global', in *Pandemic Disease in the Medieval World: Rethinking the Black Death*, ed. Monica Green (Kalamazoo: Arc Humanities Press, 2019), 31.

emerged in the Ming Dynasty around 1454 and started popping up along the border regions with Manchuria by 1499. The disease appears to have been circulating among Chinese, Mongols and other central Asians on diplomatic and trade missions to China. Some of these people appear to have had contact with Jurchens and Koreans.[81] All of this movement contributed to the transmission of infectious diseases in the region. The number of uninfected remained high. These people came into contact with infected individuals, allowing diseases to remain active on the Korean peninsula rather than die out or the population to build immunity.

Smallpox, the plague, influenza and other infectious diseases subsumed under the term 'pestilence' began as class-based illnesses, infecting those who lived in closer proximity to each other and in closer proximity to wildlife, domesticated animals and insects that served as vectors for these diseases. The earliest report of an outbreak on the Korean peninsula occurred in 1393 at the Hoeam Monastery (檜巖寺), a Buddhist temple approximately thirty-four kilometres (21 mi.) northeast of the royal palace.[82] Monks were susceptible to the transmission of such diseases within their monasteries because of their close living quarters. Most likely, the diseases were present throughout society – possibly from domesticated animals that transmitted them or even from water contaminated with parasites or supporting mosquitoes infected with malaria that hatch eggs in standing water – but went unreported until severe enough to gain the attention of the state. We do not know the nature of the 'disease' (pyŏng; 病). As such it is difficult to argue the events were related over time and space. However, the Sillok reports more of these disease events throughout the fifteenth century. Disease in Ŭiju, the important border town for travellers and trade, killed many commoners. The northwest region of the country suffered particularly hard; disease events joined with starvation where 'thousands of people were sick'.[83] A disease outbreak also slowed the construction of the capital walls by corvée labour in 1413.[84] By at least 1422, a disease had broken out in the capital where 'many people [had] died in Hanyang and the surrounding areas'.[85] Disease events touched the

---

[81] Henry Serruys, 'Smallpox in Mongolia during the Ming and Qing Dynasties', Zentralasiatische Studien 14, no. 1 (1980): 41–63. For more on the Ming smallpox outbreak in the fifteenth century, see Liu Siyuan and Cao Shuji, 'Ming Qing shiqi tanhua bingli de liuxing tezheng' [Study on epidemic characteristics of smallpox in Ming and Qing dynasties based on epitaphs], Henan daxue xuebao 55, no. 3 (2015): 65–70.
[82] CWS, 1:42 and 1:46.
[83] See CWS, 1:583 and 1:619.
[84] CWS, 1:700.
[85] CWS, 2:477.

elite as yangban families and their slaves suffered too.[86] Soldiers also reported sickness.[87] Any movement – here the movement of troops from regions outside the capital to royal Kangmu hunts and the king's review of the troops – would have contributed to transmission. Soon, diseases like this cut across geography, gender and class. Malnutrition and failed harvests, maybe partly from malaria, may have further weakened the population making them vulnerable. The diseases did not discriminate and infected everyone from the privileged to the poor.

By the end of the fifteenth century during the reign of King Yŏnsan'gun, pestilence grew widespread, killing many people. Sometimes outbreaks were blamed on air quality, especially in the heavily forested or mountainous regions of the north. Other outbreaks killed people closer to the capital. In 1495, many soldiers performing corvée labour on Sallŭng (山陵), a mountain holding royal tombs south of the Han River, died from disease despite medical attention because of their proximity to water.[88] The location of the soldiers along the riverbanks may explain the transmission of insect or water borne diseases, such as malaria from mosquitos and dysentery from contaminated water, in areas with high densities of humans, animals (military horses urinating and defecating in the water) and mosquitos. Regardless, by this time, geographical location no longer mattered. Pestilence appeared an endemic with no end. Some explored the possibility that animals impacted human health. The consumption of meat, for instance, worried some. State laws and religious practices regulated the eating of meat. The court had enacted a sumptuary law to control spending of any kind, including purchasing meat, and to dissuade commoners from butchering animals. The state considered livestock part of the foundation of an agricultural society and banned meat consumption among the masses. Yangban and royal family members, a small percentage of society, were permitted to consume meat, but this too was regulated and occurred during Confucian ritual ceremonies or during the Kangmu or other hunting events. Based on Neo-Confucian regulations, the consumption of meat during certain ritual activities, such as mourning for parents and certain celebratory days, was taboo. For instance, while in mourning the death of his father, King Sŏngjong, Yŏnsan'gun did not eat meat. Only after the mourning period did he begin consuming it again.[89]

---

[86] CWS, 3:407.
[87] CWS, 3:338.
[88] CWS, 12:656.
[89] CWS, 13:346.

But times of illness brought the court to reconsider the consumption of meat. Animal protein was thought to endanger one's chance of recovery from disease.[90] The chance of contracting disease was another reason King Yŏnsan'gun chose to give up meat. He feared there was a connection between the consumption of animal protein and what was called 'old age disease' (nobyŏng; 老病). This illness appeared to be more than just a condition of reaching advanced age. For instance, early in Chosŏn, ministers and officials suffering from old age disease were prohibited from consuming alcohol; later, alcohol was accepted as a remedy; another remedy was acupuncture.[91] While only nineteen years old at the time, Yŏnsan'gun worried about contracting the disease at some point in his life. 'I don't suffer [now] from old age disease, [and never wish to] so how could I ever possibly eat meat [again]?'[92] Yŏnsan'gun believed that eating meat was the root cause of the sickness among the elderly elite at the court. Those who consumed it, the king ruminated, suffered from the illness, unlike the rest of the population who were spared from the disease. Meat can harbour parasites that harm the body, including attacking the brain, while another cause may have been gout.[93] Thus, in an apparent attempt to improve the welfare of the people, he decided, 'Do not ban the consumption of meat! (mulgŭmyuk; 勿禁肉)' The Royal Secretariate pushed back. 'If [the common people] begin consuming meat like this, then the people will go too far [hunt animals to extinction], so the prohibition [on hunting and consuming meat] should not be loosened.'[94] To Yŏnsan'gun, while it was potentially the cause of old age disease, the consumption of meat allowed people to live longer. Commoners never suffered from old age disease because their lives were shorter; therefore, they would not die from eating meat. The Royal Secretariate summoned elderly officials in front of the king to argue in favour of banning the consumption of meat and the importance of class distinctions and sumptuary laws limiting or prohibiting the consumption of animals. 'None of us ministers suffer from old age disease, and we cannot stand for the indulgence of eating meat.'[95]

From the spring of 1499 onward, disease intensified throughout the country. The court feared it was only a matter of time before it reached the

---

[90] For instance, see CWS, 8:59, 8:449, 10:471 and 10:472.
[91] CWS, 2:327, 13:476 and 13:365.
[92] See CWS, 12:643 and 12:647.
[93] See Harvard Health Publishing, 'More on Gout: Once Kingly, Now Common', *Harvard Medical School*, 1 April 2020. https://www.health.harvard.edu/newsletter_article/more-on-gout-once-kingly-now-common.
[94] CWS, 12:654.
[95] CWS, 12:643.

capital region again because the country was connected 'like four limbs of a body'.⁹⁶ Following this metaphor, the court described the disease with the same words, how it sickened all four limbs of the entire government body. Government response to the outbreak was first to audit the supply of animal-based medicinal ingredients required for the health of the royal family and other elites in the capital. This was to ensure that the *sadaebu* and the royal family would have enough medicine to survive the outbreak. The Bureau of Royal Rituals (Pongsasi; 奉常寺) and the Government Storehouse (Saungwŏn; 司饔院) held a year's reserve of medicine. These included ingredients from Chŏlla, Kyŏngsang, Ch'ungch'ŏng, Hwanghae, Kangwŏn and Hamgyŏng provinces. The Bureau expressed anxiety about the production of medicine because of the prevalence of disease in the country (and that it would soon attack the capital) and the dwindling supply of animals necessary to make it. These medicines 'cannot be made without roe deer and other species of deer', probably from their antler velvet, blood and other organs. The court, expressing its concern, was well aware of the different distributions of deer on the peninsula. 'There are some places where roe and deer reproduce and other places where they do not.'⁹⁷

The government, not differentiating between regional populations, mandated the same number of deer from each location. Regardless of the density of deer in a particular area, the quantity the government demanded was fixed. Curbing supply even more were the actions of local magistrates who had exploited the system by pressing commoners into hunting and submitting game as tribute to the central government. This placed an even heavier burden on the masses. 'Things [animals] are no longer reproducing, and the original amount [these regions are required to submit to the government] has not decreased; the people are in trouble [cannot locate these animals and cannot pay tribute], but there is no limit to the amount of hunting and trapping (*yŏp'oek muje*; 獵獲無際) [demanded of them].' The official suggested reducing the quantity of deer products submitted to the state to help 'revive the people in each province'.⁹⁸ In response, the court agreed to only lower the amount of products from animals (*saengmul*; 生物) required from the capital region of Kyŏnggi, one of the areas hardest hit by the decline of wildlife population.⁹⁹

While royal family members and elites accessed scarce medicines – many made from deer and bear – to prepare for and treat diseases, the outbreak of

⁹⁶ CWS, 13:352.
⁹⁷ CWS, 13:352.
⁹⁸ CWS, 13:352.
⁹⁹ CWS, 13:352.

disease also contributed to the growth of a rudimentary public health system.[100] In 1503, reports of diseased people sleeping in the streets of Hanyang, the constant moaning of the sick, and the sight of corpses were numerous. Many blamed official negligence and accused the government of being incapable of providing enough medicine to treat the people. All of this attests to an overburdened health system and the scale of the epidemic. An anonymous petition put the tragedy into perspective, 'On top of that, there are sick people near the palace walls . . . Why don't you allow those who fall ill to get treated?'[101]

To conclude the story of Yŏngsan'gun, we need to turn briefly to politics. In the midst of these social problems, Yŏngsan'gun carried out another political purge in 1504. With politics and the state sliding into disarray – at a time, comparatively, of general peace in Northeast Asia – and with the king distracted by parks, hunting and animals, meritorious elites he had not eliminated reached their limits of tolerance. In 1506, these people – enraged by the king's actions defying, attacking and killing scholarly bureaucrats and meritorious subjects who he believed opposed him – staged a coup against Yŏnsan'gun, forced him from the throne, stripped him of his royal rank and reduced him to the status of a prince.[102] The apparent lack of support for the deposed king among military leaders guaranteed his removal from power. In choosing Yŏngsan'gun's successor, the court brought Yŏnsan'gun's half-brother, King Chungjong (r. 1506–44; 中宗), the second eldest son of former King Sŏngjong, to the throne and unleashed a political purge of royal family members and pro-Yŏnsan'gun officials. Within weeks of his exile into the mountains of Kanghwa Island, Yŏnsan'gun's fears of disease materialised as he grew increasingly ill. Suffering terribly, he was unable to drink water or open his eyes. Chungjong, the new king, pitied him, and instructed court physicians to provide the deposed king with medical attention.[103] The following day, however, Yŏnsan'gun died at the age of thirty-one. Attacked for his fondness of beasts and his execution of scholar officials and meritorious subjects, his final words reveal a very human side of him, the intimate connection he shared with his closest family member

---

[100] The East-West Bureaus for Saving People (*tongsŏ hwalinsŏ*; 東西活人署), an urban-based system established in the fifteenth century to provide medical treatment for the poor in the capital, was part of this system. The bureau was the first effort by the government to address the hardships of ordinary people. This was due in large part to the growing number of outbreaks of disease, in and around the capital, in the first half of the fifteenth century.

[101] *CWS*, 13:537.

[102] From 1451 to 1500, eighty reports of pestilence appear (averaging five a year) while between 1500 and 1550 the number jumps to 307 or twenty-one cases a year. See Yi Chunho, '1623–1800 nyŏn Sŏul chiyŏk ŭi kisanggihu hyangyŏng', 428.

[103] *CWS*, 14:94.

that his struggle over the boundaries of royal authority had obscured. 'I miss my wife, former Queen Sin (1476–1537; 慎氏).'[104]

* * *

The tensions over animals and hunting in Yŏnsan'gun's reign reflect many of the same issues from earlier in the fifteenth century. Like leaders and elites before him, Yŏnsan'gun was interested in hunts of all kinds from small-scale personal hunts to large royal, military Kangmu events. Hunting expressed his royal authority over the land, and the beasts, birds and people of the peninsula. This representation of power also extended over elites in the military and civil branches, as well as meritorious subjects. He equated the large-scale hunts with military preparedness and private hunts were times he escaped the confines of the royal palace and spent time with people, especially soldiers, who shared his love of the hunt. The link between hunting and the military preparedness of the dynasty remained a key point as Jurchen hunters crossing into the peninsula to hunt for food and fur continued to generate concern along the northern frontiers. While many elites hunted, others around the king sought to persuade him to forgo the hunt. They relied on similar moral and practical arguments we have seen in earlier chapters to dissuade his involvement in martial matters.

What differed in this era was scale. The royal court appeared to embrace animals like never before or since. The large number of animals brought into the royal palace, for instance, reflected the king's attitudes towards living beasts as they too projected images of royal power, masculinity and authority. Also, by this time, concern grew at many levels of the government over the sharp decline in animals from overhunting and loss of habitat in the capital region. In response to the decline and the constant critiques of disapproving officials, the king sought to consolidate the Kangmu hunting grounds around the capital and expand them to create a royal hunting park to realise, on a grand scale, the ambitions of earlier kings. On top of this, as noted, disease and dramatic weather events appeared throughout the fifteenth century and both intensified after 1500. The unusual weather, shifting human populations and overhunting pressured animals (especially carnivores such as tigers and leopards) to relocate into new lands that brought them into contact with people.

Different too was the level of the political response in this era. Backed into a corner, King Yŏnsan'gun's answer to the political threats, and his push back

[104] CWS, 14:95.

against the now glaringly apparent curbs on royal movement and actions, was to align with groups at the court to purge and attack enemies. As noted, he first purged officials who he felt had questioned the legitimacy of his great-grandfather (and hence, his own right to sit on the throne) and then killed those he thought had colluded to poison his mother. While extreme demonstrations of filial piety, they were filial acts none the less. Attacks against his own royal lineage triggered the purges, but more was going on under the surface as he struggled to maintain power articulated here through his love of hunting dogs, hawks and the hunt, both private and Kangmu. I believe these extreme actions represented an exasperation on the part of Yŏnsan'gun who, with the support of like-minded officials and close royal family members, continued the royal hunts that his father, great-grandfather and great-great grandfather had inherited from late Koryŏ practices. Emulating them (or following in their footsteps) was another display of filial piety. The king's desire to go out into the fields reflected traditions that many members of the elite and non-elite practised.

Ironically, the real threat to royal authority came not from hunting accidents or Jurchen invasions but from domestic politics, as powerful officials in the bureaucracy sought to contain the kingship via his access to animals and the wilds. The growing chorus of voices around him that questioned the hunt revolved around issues of legitimacy, central control and power sharing. How could rulers present themselves both as sages and as military leaders, contradictory images in the eyes of many Confucian tutors and officials? In the capital, he needed to be a sage, but along the frontier and along the coasts, border defence and national security demanded his leadership as a strong military symbol. As the Confucian bureaucracy penned him in, he found other ways to try to express his independence. The hills, mountains, valleys and plains around the capital became symbolic battlegrounds over the limits of royal authority. If I may extend the metaphor of a royal hunting park further, the merit subjects and civil officials proved that they could erect their own fences around the king, surround him and 'kill' him.

Ousting King Yŏnsan'gun reveals double standards. While officials who opposed the hunt attacked kings, often based on classical precedence, and harped against the practice because it was rooted in the Koryŏ years, they proved that loyalty between the king and court officials, one of the cardinal bonds in society, was not unbreakable. Ousting Yŏnsan'gun demonstrates another example of continuity with Koryŏ when powerful officials and military men pushed aside kings and elevated new ones of their backing. If these Chosŏn merit subjects and officials demanded kings give up vestiges of a Neo-Nomadic tradition from the late Koryŏ era (such as the hunt or uxorilocal marriages), they did not hesitate to fracture the bonds of loyalty to the king, a Koryŏ practice they rhetorically despised. Later critiques of Yŏnsan'gun, such as the description in the *Geographical Reference to Korea* at the opening of this chapter, are meant to illuminate his misdeeds and uncivilised follies by associating the ruler with animals, particularly living ones such as hawks and hounds. Just like depriving him of his royal title, associating him so intimately with living animals was another attempt by later officials and historians to punish Yŏnsan'gun and to serve as a warning to future leaders to avoid. If Yŏnsan'gun was a beast for defending his great-grandfather and mother, and for his penchant for animals and hunting, then those officials who opposed him, ousted him and banished him to death were also capable of beastly acts.

Finally, apparent at the turn of the sixteenth century was the chasm between the continual hunting practices of elites and non-elites and the growing discourse within the central government. People hunted, but the bureaucracy advocated animal management on the needs of the people. Those who opposed the hunt frequently argued it harmed the people or placed great burden upon them. The tension arises between these two conflicting points. Those who opposed the hunt argued that a pastime and occupation many people practised was in fact harmful to the masses. This argument justified curtailing a lifeway that removed animals from state use. These animals proved to be especially needed at the turn of the sixteenth century as animal parts were used as medicines to combat bodily sickness, and were offered up at state ritual altars to appease the spirits and help eradicate disease outbreaks that killed the people and calm unpredictable weather that harmed the crops. The constant limits the central government set on access to animals reflected a growing awareness of the importance of animals to the dynasty.

Conclusion: Legacies of the Hunt in Politics, Society and Empire

As we have seen, from the earliest confederacies and kingdoms on the Korean peninsula, people, including rulers, hunted. After the founding of the Koryŏ Dynasty in the late tenth century, royal and elite hunting seemed to lose popularity. This may have been due to the strong Buddhist sentiment present in the court, which adopted precepts against the killing of animals, or perhaps it was because court scribes did not deem recording such things necessary. Elite hunting re-emerged in the Mongol–Koryŏ era in the 1270s. Hunting and spending time in the field as a definer of royal authority and masculinity fluctuated over the next two centuries. Kings and their hunting parties, whether large-scale, royal military Kangmu hunts or smaller, personal hunting parties, travelled away from the capital to find game in the forests and mountains. Korean kings, royal family members and like-minded officials wanted to hunt, while other bureaucrats tried to control such pastimes and moved to end hunting by outlawing it as a royal pursuit. The maturing of Confucian institutions after the founding of the Chosŏn Dynasty in 1392 – and the diehard Neo-Confucians who staffed it – coupled with human population expansion, the outbreak of disease and a fluctuating climate, created a political and natural environment that finally pushed hunting and other wild animal encounters out of the minds of kings and the court in the sixteenth and seventeenth centuries. Domination of wild beasts through the hunt, a public symbol of monarchical power in the Koryŏ–Mongol era that survived into the early Chosŏn, shifted from the responsibility of the king to the responsibility of the bureaucracy with the death of King Yŏnsan'gun, a ruler who literally blurred the boundaries between wilderness and civilisation when he brought wild and domesticated animals into the royal palace. After him, the fate of the Kangmu, falconry and other hunting activities mainly rested in the hands of professional soldiers who hunted animals, local and provincial scholar officials who delegated tax demands (animals as tribute), and commoners and slaves who ventured onto the lands around them to hunt, trap and collect wild animals that the state needed in order to conduct business, heal bodies or calm the weather. This was especially true when it came to the animals deemed necessary for sacrifice in ritual ceremonies.

In 1507, shortly after the dethronement and death of King Yŏnsan'gun and the installment of King Chungjong, official Pak Wŏnjong (1467–1510; 朴元宗) held a discussion with military officials about the Kangmu hunting grounds. 'There are a lot of places where the Kangmu lands are not important,' he insisted. Pak then went on to request that the court send the parks administrator to these areas to investigate and to 'permit the commoners to undertake slash and burn farming (hwajŏn; 火田) on these lands'. The new king and his advisors agreed.[1] In other words, the court opened up hunting grounds in the mountains and forests of the capital region, to farming. The central government encouraged landless commoners to move into the hills, clear the forests by lighting it ablaze – a practice normally outlawed – and plant and grow crops on it. Of note here is the agreement that burning land for agricultural purposes was more acceptable than conducting a fire hunt with the sole purpose of flushing out and killing game. The government continued this trend by opening up some of the remaining Kangmu lands to 'wandering commoners' (yumin; 流民) thirty-five years later.[2]

These scholarly concerns extended to animals that represented a bygone era of courtly regalia. In 1517, King Chungjong ordered the presentation of birds of prey as gifts to the elderly parents of senior members of the royal family, three senior state councillors and other special officials – most likely a generation that understood the grand symbolism of these gifts. Officials protested that this was superfluous, and that there were too many people who had died of starvation. 'Even in Hwanghae Province [presumably where many of these birds originated], elderly women beg in the villages. [The court] has eliminated useless tribute items [such as hawks, yet] every province is forced to submit hawks and hounds ... Why [should this be done when it places an extra burden on the people during hard times]?'[3] Here, when the king wanted to celebrate the older generation around him with extravagant gifts of falcons, the officials reminded him that elderly members of the same generation lived in the provinces and were suffering from hardship. Carrying out his request, court officials declared, only burdened them more. The subject of hawks and hounds appear in only a few

[1] CWS, 14:116.
[2] CWS, 18:499.
[3] CWS, 15:250.

moments during his reign, attesting to its diminished status, and the court abolished the position of falconer in 1541.[4]

Beginning with King Chungjong, fewer references to royal and elite hunting appear in the official sources. The era of Chungjong was one of both the suppression of royal hunting activities and the expansion of domination over the land and animals by the throne. That King Chungjong pushed aside hunting and hunting grounds, with the encouragement of the officials around him, is understandable. When presented in the context of disease running rampant throughout the country and the aftermath of a political coup, the king and court had other pressing concerns. Instead, they shifted their definition of legitimacy away from martial matters, like hunting, to one of sagely rulership, where the king would spend his time in the capital and royal palace to steady the state.

While a few Chosŏn kings attempted to assert domination over the bureaucracy, beginning in the sixteenth century, little could be done to control these scholar officials. Through several political purges, the court officials gained power, and kings struggled to control competition among bureaucratic groups. The political balance shifted as the bureaucracy came to nearly dominate the king, igniting political tension and conflict. Then the hunt faded as the new state and bureaucracy, created in the first century of Chosŏn, rooted out what it considered 'improper' practices, especially among the royal family and elites. This included personal hunting parties, royal military Kangmu hunts, falconry and hunting dogs.

Through an examination of the hunt, this book has attempted to shed light on human–animal connections, an underexplored topic in Asian Studies. This work has focused mainly on the royal family and elites due to the limitation of the sources. Commoners and slaves in Korea did not write about themselves in premodern times. Still, state officials and elites noted the involvement of non-elites in hunting events and their care of animals for ritual and for sport, thus providing a more rounded, though still incomplete, snapshot of the era. Decisions that the state made to promote agricultural production, the expansion of the human population and farming settlements, the continual centralisation of authority, and, tellingly, the expansion of Confucian rites all impacted how people interacted with animals and, in turn, how animals interacted with people.

This study has also demonstrated that the energies of premodern Korea were not just consumed by scholarship and Confucianism. Kings, members of the royal family, even other elites (sometimes the scholar officials themselves)

---

[4] For instance, see a case in 1528 (*CWS*, 17:10) and in 1541 (*CWS*, 18:441).

had another side, one that was active outside the royal palace, libraries, Confucian academies and homes. Time was spent in the wilderness, in a place that was external to domestic affairs. In other words, these men found the time to engage and interact with the landscape and with animals. While the study of Confucian texts and the expansion of Confucian rituals and bureaucratic laws consumed a large part of the attention of the ruling elites in the capital, interaction with and concerns about animals reveal another aspect of the state and society.

I have partly defined this engagement with animals through the hunt as a martial tradition. While defining it this way is helpful in discussing it in the context of other practices, calling it a 'martial tradition' has problems too. As has been demonstrated throughout the book, the early Confucian take on hunting was mixed. Those who supported it argued the activity prepared the country for war. Meanwhile, members of the extreme view denigrated the hunt and lumped it together with all 'problematic' forms of entertainment and activities that they argued distracted kings from governing and studies, drained limited resources from the country, and imperiled the security of the state along the frontier. On top of that, an activity such as the chase endangered the lives of everyone from commoners to the king, who went out into the wilds in search of beasts to kill. Confucians themselves dubbed it a military matter. This allowed them to rationalise state usurpation of the hunt, removing it from one of the duties of the king – both private hunts and the royal military Kangmu hunts – and then the court eventually suppressed it. I have attempted to reveal the human side of kings in particular and why they enjoyed riding horses, shooting bows and arrows, and engaging with falcons and hunting dogs outside and even inside the capital. These activities were something practised not only by kings, but also by non-scholars and gruff military men – the lower status of the yangban order – and were not considered inferior to scholarship and learning. These lifestyles were not incompatible.

Perhaps scholar officials lumped the hunt together with military and barbarian practices because it differed dramatically from the societal norms they espoused. These norms were aspirational and did not describe actual lifeways of most contemporaries. As officials engaged in politics in the centre – first in the Koryŏ capital of Kaegyŏng and then in the Chosŏn capital of Hanyang [Seoul] – they lost touch with their rural roots and their connection to the countryside and the animals on it. Living in the capital and engaged in power politics with the king and other *sadaebu* (super elite) leading officials, they did not have time to hunt or appreciate the value of the chase. They justified co-opting the hunt and then the suppression of the hunt by claiming Confucian moral high grounds as a means to strengthen their own power and control something they feared – engagement with animals. They also wanted to downplay the Mongol era of Korea's past, an era that experienced a rise in the popularity of hunting practices among many segments of society. This was a spin on the story of an unyielding minority that through constant agitation sought to transform broader values.

Confucians were not considerate of animal welfare nor did they care about the ethical purposes of animal rights. As this book has tried to argue, Confucian scholar officials, like some of their predecessors, embraced an identity of animal violence through the butchering and offering of animals, both wild and domestic, to the altars of the state and private family homes of the Confucian elites. They did not argue for saving wild animals from the blade of the hunter out of ethical concerns for wild beasts but rather as means to protect the ritual needs of the state. They recognised the importance of conserving resources and that overhunting might deplete the animal population, which materialised by the second half of the fifteenth century. But these discussions touched on another ethical question: how does the depletion of wildlife impact the state's agricultural policies? Through their rhetoric of helping the people, they established guidelines that expanded agriculture, considered the economy of a civilised state. To officials, it was this issue (arguing policy based on helping the people) that legitimised their rule over the peninsula and their constraints on the monarchy. These policymakers were a civilising force extending from the capital throughout the peninsula and beyond.

As the sources suggest, and as hunting in other parts of the world and in different eras reveal, hunting was not just a military matter, regardless of what Confucians argued. Non-military men hunted, and it is understandable that hunting was popular among the military – they had the skills, weapons and mobility necessary to enter forests and mountains and to locate and kill game. Hunting is not an easy affair, as anyone who has hunted or tried to hunt can attest. Hunting in the fifteenth century – without camouflaged clothing, anti-scent sprays, range-finding binoculars, portable tree stands, anti-tick and mosquito clothing, and any other of the modern inventions that make hunting a more accessible activity today – was not an easy task. Let alone not having access to firearms. While the military used gunpowder and firearms for defence in Korea during the fifteenth century, firearms were most likely not adopted as hunting weapons until their technology improved – size, weight and reliability – after the early seventeenth century when the central government began developing firearms in the wake of Japan's invasion. During the fifteenth century, hunters hunted with bows and arrows, sometimes released from the ground, other times from horseback. Hitting an animal – a non-stationary target – took practice. Men with military backgrounds often had that. Men with the time to develop such skills, and those who had the time to set up targets to practise, included kings, royal family members, elites, commoners and even slaves living in the countryside.

As noted, in the context of the Mongol Empire, the hunt and how people interacted with animals emerged as an important definer of royal authority and elite masculine identity. The Mongols – recognised for their lifestyle which valued animals – relied on wildlife as their only means to live on the steppe and governed their empires by adhering to those values. They demanded horses for war, for instance, searched for pasture lands (finding them on Cheju Island, well known for its steppe-like meadows appropriate for horse husbandry), and hunted animals for sport and for food in newly conquered lands, all of which partly defined Mongol masculinity. As part of the Mongol Empire, Korean royalty and elites recognised the importance of hunting to the Mongols and responded. Hunting never disappeared as an activity on the Korean peninsula, but its popularity during the thirteenth century cannot be denied. All of this came at a time when Korean royal family members and elites around the king interacted heavily with the Mongol imperial centre at Daidu in Yuan Dynasty China. These interactions involved intermarriage of the royal family with daughters of the imperial clan. Some Korean elites also intermarried with the Mongols. For all of these men, spending time in the field on the chase was a valued part of male camaraderie.

To the dismay of hardcore Confucian officials, Koreans seemed to have had more in common with the Mongols than they wanted to admit. This included an uxorilocal family system and foundation myths that, like the Korean stories of Tan'gun and Chumong, centred around animals. The *Secret History of the Mongols* – the first record of Chinggis Khan (1158–1227), the Mongol leader who united the tribes on the steppe lands and began campaigns of conquest that his sons and grandsons realised – notes the animal origins of the Mongol people, 'The first ancestor of [Chinggis Kahn] was a grey wolf, sent from heaven, chosen by destiny; his spouse was a white hind.'[5] Identifying with animals and 'barbarian' people disturbed many scholar officials who believed in the civilising power of Chinese classical learning, a belief that found a competing form of masculinity in sagely learning and the studies of the Confucian classics.

---

[5] Other northeast and central Asian tribes claim similar animal foundation myths that involve wolves and deer. See Mircea Eliade, Alf Hiltebeitel and Diane Apostlos-Caappadona, *History of Religious Ideas, Volume 3: From Muhammad to the Age of Reforms* (Chicago: University of Chicago Press, 2013), 288.

Within the framework of the Mongol Yuan–Chinese Ming transition, I have partly argued that as the Korean bureaucracy suppressed the royal and elite hunt, the state grew more engaged with debates over wild animal populations. As this work demonstrates, from the late thirteenth through the beginning of the sixteenth centuries in particular, Korean elites increasingly applied Neo-Confucian policies to better understand the world around them, including the place of animals and the relationships between humans and animals. Through Neo-Confucian texts, these officials justified suppressing the hunt and royal contact with wild beasts. I have also tried to show that these views were not accepted completely. Kings and royal family members continued to hunt, despite the rebuke of Buddhists and Confucians. Commoners, slaves, yangban elites and even some officials at the court 'trespassed' on hunting grounds to hunt wild animals or to capture and train birds of prey despite the Confucian laws of the state that prohibited such activities.

The fight between kings and their courts over hunting and animals can help us better understand why the Chosŏn Dynasty was unprepared for war against Japan at the end of the sixteenth century and why they could not better resist the Jurchen-Jin and Manchu-Qing invasions in the first half of the seventeenth century. With the court regulating the hunt and limiting access to animals after 1506, the military declined symbolically and literally. Uncertainty over the need for the king's involvement in the hunt became tied to debates over the usefulness of a military prepared for war in times of peace. While there was no clear unified opinion about the matter, the lack of unity allowed those who opposed the chase to restrict resources and eventually remove the king's direct involvement in the royal hunt. A lack of sustained royal attention diluted the readiness of the military. While the king remained the de facto leader in times of war, military policy became reactive, rather than proactive.

Like the people, animals adapted to changes taking place on the peninsula as part of their instinct to survive. Habitats receded. Natural predators declined. The climate fluctuated. Humans became more of a presence in the mountains and forests. Slash and burn farming in the hills destroyed vegetation and animal habitats. Invasive species were introduced to Korea (Chinese swine) or hitchhiked in as organisms (new strains of diseases) on travellers, who, in turn, interacted with neighbouring peoples through trade or combat. Viruses, bacteria and other organisms thrived as they fed on a new population of human hosts. Many animals fled populated areas or adapted to live side by side with people out of harm's way. Much like the humans around them, these wild animals sought food, shelter, company, mates and offspring and preferred to live and die in their home territories. They shared a common sphere of life.

The habitats of wild animals and people often overlapped, as they shared food and water and sources of comfort (trees, for example). They also unleashed violence against each other. This violence was mostly one way (human toward animal), although tigers were a problem for mountain travellers as they would stalk and kill humans as prey. Animals could bother and, when threatened, attack people, but people were more than nuisances to the beasts of the wild. As the human population grew, the state extended its control over mountainous regions, forests and coastal islands. Animal–human encounters increased, usually to the detriment of the animal, a situation that only accelerated in the years that followed.

Stories of the hunt and state interactions with wild animals thread their way through Korea from premodern to contemporary times. Removed from the dangerous and violent nature of wild animal encounters, such as tigers and leopards, scholars romanticised these encounters. By the late seventeenth and eighteenth centuries, for instance, the 'barbarian hunting screen' depicting the Manchu hunt grew popular among scholar officials. Poets and writers elevated animals, such as the crane, into symbols of moral certainty and natural beauty, while others in the eighteenth and nineteenth centuries began writing more detailed descriptions of wild beasts. Some elites continued falconry and painted artwork about it (Figure C.1). Others relied on professional mountain men and hunters to harvest pieces of animals, such as deer antlers, bear paws and gallbladders, and blood for medicinal purposes or trade.[6] At the turn of the twentieth century, hunting had become part of Korea's colonial experience. Hunting and the ecology of the peninsula fell within reach of foreigners again. Westerners and Japanese colonial officials hunted in the Korean mountains. In 1915, the American missionary Horace H. Underwood (1859–1916) described one hunting expedition:

> Once, when stupid farmers, acting as beaters, had bungled things, an old gentleman of over seventy, a famous hunter in his day, offered to guide us and apparently found no great difficulty in climbing the hills and beating through the brush. Most of them are good trackers; one big fellow over six feet, hardly stooped to look at the tracks but strode along as though he was following a path. I saw them track a boar back and forth over the hills for the greater part of three days without being seriously at fault once, and they told me of trackers who could estimate to within an ounce or so the weight of a stag's horns from its tracks.[7]

---

[6] Underwood, 'Hunting and Hunters' Lore in Korea', 41.
[7] Underwood, 'Hunting and Hunters' Lore in Korea', 23–4.

Figure C.1 Kim Hongdo (1745–1806?; 金弘道), *Noble Falcon Hunt* (*hogwiŭngnyŏp to*; 豪貴鷹獵圖), date unknown. This painting depicts the ideal late Chosŏn Dynasty falcon hunt. Of note is the social nature of the outing attended by men and women, the elite and non-elite. The elite man (which we assume was Kim Hongdo himself) sits astride his mount and observes the successful kill from a distance. Birds of prey, hunting dogs, horses, pheasants (alive and dead with their tailfeathers protruding from backpacks) and humans interact intimately in the wild.
Reproduced by permission from Kansong Art Museum.

Underwoods' criticism of farmers who lacked hunting skills contrasts with his praise of professional hunters. In 1917, one Japanese tiger hunting group noted: 'In the end, there were only two tigers [taken] in a month. Of course, there are many other beasts, such as bears, leopards, wild boar, and water tigers (*suiko*) [a cross between a leopard and a tiger].'[8] In a photo caption of the expedition, one Japanese hunter smiles while standing above his squatting Korean guide and two tiger corpses neatly arranged on their sides. Hunting depicted domination and the quieting of disorder and danger, but it also suggested dependence. The Americans, Japanese and others who came to the peninsula to hunt were not familiar with the terrain and required the skills of Korean hunters who deeply understood not only the land but also the whereabouts of the creatures that inhabited it.

[8] Isaburo Yamamoto, *Seikoki* [Diary of a Tiger Expedition], (Tokyo: Ryutaro yoshiura, 1918).

The end of Japanese colonialism in 1945, the destruction of the Korean War from 1950 to 1953, and the continual separation of the peninsula into North and South held important consequences for the environment and Korean ecology. The Demilitarized Zone (DMZ) or 'no-man's land', between the two countries, has been saturated with landmines, unexploded ordnances and sharpshooters, making it uninhabitable for humans but a haven for wildlife. Less than a decade after the ceasefire, US personnel began describing the DMZ as the 'world's largest game preserve'.[9] However, these prime hunting grounds were off limits to the US army. By the early 1960s, roughly 8,000 privileged South Koreans had become licensed hunters. Social critics demanded a limit on the number of hunting licenses, because hunters or the animals fleeing from them damaged the crops of farmers, complaints echoing criticism from the Chosŏn period.[10]

As in other parts of the world, hunting was an elite sport in South Korea and, for the most part, a gendered and politically motivated pastime dominated by male supporters of President Park Chung Hee during his presidency from 1961 to 1979.[11] Of the 30,000 registered hunters taking part in the opening of hunting season in November 1971, that ran through February, among them were nearly 6,000 hunters from the Seoul area; only eight of them were women.[12] One of the most visible members of the South Korean hunting elite was Yi Pŏmsŏk (1900–72), former prime minister of South Korea and president of the Korea Hunting Society (Suryŏphoe) who explained, 'You can find game almost anywhere in this country, because of the variety of terrain.' The few hunters in the South pursued pheasants, ducks, deer and wild swine. Hunting was class and status driven and seen as a 'luxury . . . [as] few people can afford to buy guns, have automobiles, own a dog, and above all, have time to go hunting'.[13] Such patterns were replicated in the North during the Cold War where access to hunting weapons was tightly restricted and limited

---

[9] *Stars and Stripes–Pacific*, 6 March 1961.
[10] For instance, see 'Kaejŏng suryŏp myŏnjŭng sinch'ŏngbŏp' [Revising the application law for hunting], *Kyŏnghyang sinmun*, 30 September 1958: 1.
[11] Park appreciated hunting – even if he did not take part as president – expressed by his support of such tournaments as the international hunting competition on Cheju Island. Competitors from six Southeast Asian countries and the United States and the United Kingdom hunted pheasants, competing for the President Park Chunghŭi Cup. See *Tonga ilbo* [Tonga daily news], 17 January 1967: 1 and *Maeil kyŏngje* [Daily economic news], 10 October 1967: 3.
[12] *Kyŏnghyang sinmun* [Kyŏnghyang newspaper], 11 November 1971: 7.
[13] *Stars and Stripes–Pacific*, 6 March 1961. See also *Chosŏn ilbo* [Chosŏn daily news], 10 August 1966: 1. The ownership of foreign hunting breeds, such as the pointer, also helped display wealth and status. For example, see newspaper images and descriptions in *Tonga ilbo*, 3 October 1962: 8 and 27 February 1964: 8.

to a handful of elites in the regime. At times, North Korean soldiers hunted while on patrol. The first leader of North Korea Kim Il Sung (r. 1948–94) was rumoured to hunt in special hunting parks. Hunting was most likely permissible even among non-elites as some were arrested for violating various hunting regulations. Until the 1980s, foreign representatives and elite expats had some access to hunting. Soviet diplomats, on escorted trips, hunted in the countryside, but they also used those opportunities to surveille conditions – much like Jurchen hunting groups had been accused of doing. Also, certain travel agencies in China recently promoted hunting tours in North Korea, probably to chase deer.[14] These are just a few of the myriad of examples of the intersections among animals, people and the hunt on the Korean peninsula in terms of class, status and ideals of masculinity.

In this book, I have expanded the historical eye to include debates over animals and the hunt that shaped court politics and the military, economic and social practices from the late thirteenth to the beginning of the sixteenth century. This era saw the rise and fall of the royal hunt. What was at stake during this period was not just the balance of political authority fought over hunting excursions, hunting grounds and access to wild animals. What people at the court fought over was how all kinds of animals – from domesticated animals and hunting animals and pets (hawks and hounds) to wild beasts – defined central authority and the identity of the country. Animals were exchanged in regional trade, part of the tax burden of commoners, and sought after as symbolic enemies to flush out and kill in order to sharpen military skills. Animals contributed to experiences that connected people together when hunters gathered, ate and drank over their kills. Animals spurred stories that were imagined, remembered, told and retold to shape concepts of identity, masculinity and political authority. They were prized and sought after, sold for profit and raised or acquired as status symbols. At times, they were showered with attention and care. Finally, animals were not just passive objects. In the wild, they were active agents of their own lives. Their presence motivated people to pursue them, as well as to propel debates at the court by those who sought them or wished to regulate access to them.

---

[14] I am indebted to Professor Andrei Lankov of Kookmin University for sharing with me his insight and anecdotes he heard about hunting in North Korea.

Bibliography

Primary Sources

Chosŏn wangjo sillok (CWS) [Veritable records of the Chosŏn Dynasty]. 48 vols. Seoul: Kuksa p'yŏnch'an wiwŏnhoe, 1955–8.

Chŭngbo munhyŏn pigo [Documents for reference, revised and updated]. 250 vols. Seoul: Tongguk munhwasa, 1971.

Daisheng, and Liu Zhangjiang. *Liji* [Book of Rites]. Beijing: Zhong guo gong ren chu ban she, 2016.

Iryŏn. *Samguk yusa* [Memorabilia of the Three Kingdoms]. 3 vols. Seoul: Han'guk chŏngsin munhwa yŏn'guwŏn, 2003.

Jorgensen, John, ed. *Anthology of Stele Inscriptions of Eminent Korean Buddhist Monks*. Translated by Patrick Uhlmann. Seoul: Jogye Order of Korean Buddhism, 2012.

Kim Chongjik. *Kim Chongjik chakp'umjip* [Collected works of Kim Chongjik]. P'yongyang: Munhak yesul ch'ulp'ansa, 2017.

Kim Pusik. *Wŏnmun Samguk sagi* [History of the Three Kingdoms]. Kyŏnggido P'ajusi: Han'guk haksul chŏngbo, 2012.

Koryŏsa (KS) [History of the Koryŏ Dynasty]. 3 vols. Seoul: Asea munhwasa, 1990.

Koryŏsa chŏryo [Essential history of the Koryŏ Dynasty]. 5 vols. Seoul: Minjok munhwa ch'ujinhoe, 1968.

Kyŏnghyang sinmun [Kyŏnghyang newspaper].

Kyŏngguk taejŏn [Administrative code of the Chosŏn Dynasty]. Seoul: Han'guk pŏpche yŏn'guwŏn, 1993.

Kyujanggak, eds. *Taemyŏngnyul chikhae che-16 kwŏn* [Great Ming code directly explicated]. Seoul: Sŏul Taehakkyo Kyujanggak, 2001.

Lee, Peter, trans. *Songs of Flying Dragon*. Cambridge, MA: Harvard University Press, 1975.

Maeil kyŏngje [Daily economic newspaper].
Muller, A. Charles, ed. *Doctrinal Treaties: Selected Works*. Translated by A. Charles Muller and Richard D. McBride II. Paju: Jogye Order of Korean Buddhism, 2012.
Muller, A. Charles, ed. and trans. *Exposition of the Sutra of Bramna's Net*. Seoul: Jogye Order of Korean Buddhism, 2012.
Pak Sun, and Kim Sanghŏn. *Saamjip* [Collected works of Saam]. Chosŏn original manuscript, Ch'ŏlchong year 8, 1857. Held at Columbia University.
Sach'uksŏ samok [Guidelines for Office of Sacrificial Animals]. Early Chosŏn Dynasty, original document, Kyujanggak Library, Seoul National University.
Sinjŭng ŭnggol pang [New and augmented methods for falconry]. 1 vol. Shinpei ogura [Showa 1930 edn].
Tonga ilbo [Tonga daily news].
Tongguk yŏji pigo [Geographical reference to Korea]. Seoul: Sŏul t'ŭkpyŏl sisa p'yŏnch'an wiwŏnhoe, 2000.
Tripitaka. SAT Daizokyo Text Database. https://21dzk.l.u-tokyo.ac.jp/SAT/index_en.html.
Underwood, Horace H. 'Hunting and Hunters' Lore in Korea'. *Transactions of the Korea Branch of the Royal Asiatic Society* 6, no. 2 (1915): 23–44.
Whitfield, Roderick, and Young-Eui Park, eds and trans. *Seon Poems: Selected Works*. Seoul: Jogye Order of Korean Buddhism, 2012.
Yang Boujun and Yang Fengbin, eds. *Meng zi* [Mencius]. Zhangsha: Yue lu shu she, 2019.
Yi Chehyŏn. *Kugyŏk Ikchae chip* [Collected works of Ikchae]. 2 vols. Seoul: Minjok munhwa ch'uljinhoe, 1997.
Yi Chu. *Manghŏn sŏnsaeng munjip* [The collection of Manghŏn's work]. Hwasan: Pan'gyujŏng, Toju myŏnggye sŏwŏn, [kapchae 1804], original manuscript.
Yi Kok. *Kajŏngjip* [Collected works of Kajŏn]. Edited by Sŏng Nakhun. Seoul: Tonghwa ch'ulp'ankongsa, 1972.
Yi Sango. *Suryŏp pihwa* [Secret stories of hunting]. Seoul: Pagusa, 1965.
Yüan shi [History of the Yuan Dynasty]. 15 vols. Beijing: Zhong hua shu ju, 1992.
Zong, In-Sob. *Folk Tales from Korea*. London: Routledge and Kegan Paul, 1952.

Secondary Sources

Agoston, Gabor. 'Firearms and Military Adaptation: The Ottomans and the European Military Revolution, 1450–1800', *Journal of World History* 25, no. 1 (March 2014): 85–124.

Ahn, Juhn. *Buddhas and Ancestors: Religion and Wealth in Fourteenth-Century Korea*. Seattle: University of Washington Press, 2018.

Allison, Thomas. *The Royal Hunt in Eurasian History*. Philadelphia: University of Pennsylvania Press, 2006.

Ambros, Barbara. *Bones of Contention: Animals and Religions in Contemporary Japan*. Honolulu: University of Hawai'i Press, 2018.

An Myŏngsu, 'Hanjungil ŭi siksaenghwal munhwa pigyo yŏn'gu 14–19 segi, chirijŏk, yŏksajŏk hwan'gyŏng kwa siksaeng kwallyŏn sŏji rŭl chungsim ŭro' [Study on the comparison among Korean, Chinese, and Japanese food culture from the fourteenth to the nineteenth century, focusing on the environments of geography, history, and bibliographies], *Han'guk siksaenghwal munhwa hakhoeji* 12, no. 3 (1997): 353–64.

Atwell, William S. 'Time, Money, and the Weather: Ming China and the "Great Depression" of the Mid-Fifteenth Century', *Journal of Asian Studies* 61, no. 1 (February 2002): 83–113.

Austin, Dennis. *Mule Deer*. Logan: Utah State University Press, 2010.

Baillie, Jonathan, et al. *Mongolian Red List of Mammals*. London: Zoological Society of London, 2006.

Baker, Donald. 'Rhetoric, Ritual, and Political Legitimacy: Justifying Yi Seonggye's Ascension to the Throne', *Korea Journal* 53, no. 4 (Winter 2013): 141–67.

Beinart, William. 'Empire, Hunting, and Ecological Change in Southern and Central Africa', *Past & Present* 128 (1990): 162–86.

Black, Jeremy. *Military Power and the Fate of the Continents, 1450–2000*. New Haven: Yale University Press, 1998.

Bohnet, Adam. *Turning Toward Edification: Foreigners in Chosŏn Korea*. Honolulu: University of Hawai'i Press, 2020.

Brantz, Dorothee. *Beastly Natures: Animals, Humans, and the Study of History*. Charlottesville: University of Virginia Press, 2010.

Breuker, Remco E. *Establishing a Pluralistic Society in Medieval Korea, 918–1170*. Boston, MA: Brill, 2010.

Bull, Jacob, and Tora Holmberg. 'Introducing Animal Places'. In *Animal Places: Lively Cartographies of Human–Animal Relations*, edited by Jacob Bull, Tora Holmberg and Cecilia Asberg, 1–14. New York: Routledge, 2018.

Canepa, Matthew. *The Iranian Expanse: Transforming Royal Identity through Architecture, Landscape, and the Built Environment, 500 BCE–642 CE*. Oakland: University of California Press, 2018.

Cartmill, Matt. *A View to a Death in the Morning: Hunting and Nature through History*. Cambridge, MA: Harvard University Press, 1993.

Ch'a Munsŏp. *Chosŏn sidae kunje yŏn'gu* [Research into the Chosŏn military structure]. Seoul: Tan'guk taehakkyo ch'ulp'anbu, 1973.

Chen, Huaiyu. 'A Buddhist Classification of Animals and Plants in Early Tang Times', *Journal of Asian History* 43, no. 1 (2009): 31–51.
Choi, Bong Hwan, et al. 'Genome-Wide Analysis of the Diversity and Ancestry of Korean Dogs', *PLoS One* 12, no. 11 (November 2017): 1–20.
Choi, Chang-Yong, and Hyun-Young Nam. 'Diet of Peregrine Falcons (*Falco peregrinus*) in Korea: Food Items and Seasonal Changes', *Journal of Raptor Research* 49, no. 4 (December 2015): 376–88.
Chŏng Taham. 'Chosŏn chŏn'gi ŭi chŏngch'ijŏk chonggyojŏk chilbyŏngkwan ŭi yak ŭi kaenyŏm pŏmju kŭrigo ch'iyu pangsik' [Political and religious concepts of disease and medicine in early Chosŏn], *Han'guksa yŏn'gu* 146 (2009): 119–57.
Chŏng Yongsŭng, and Kim Haksŏng. 'Hanbando sanmaek ŭi chejosa wa pullyu mit taegi hwan'gyŏng e mich'inŭn yŏnghyang' [Classification of mountains on the Korean peninsula and the influence of the atmospheric environment], *Han'guk chiguhak hoeji* 37 (2016): 21–8.
Chosŏn ilbo [Chosŏn daily news].
Cockram, Sarah, and Andrew Wells, eds. *Interspecies Interactions: Animals and Humans between the Middle Ages and Modernity*. New York: Routledge, 2018.
Connell, Robert. *Masculinities*. Berkeley: University of California Press, 1995.
Cui, Yujun, et al. 'Historical Variations in Mutation Rate in an Epidemic Pathogen, *Yersinia pestis*', *Proceedings of the National Academy of Sciences of the United States of America* 110, no. 2 (January 2013): 577–82.
Deuchler, Martina. *The Confucian Transformation of Korea: A Study of Society and Ideology*. Cambridge, MA: Harvard University Press, 1995.
———. 'Rites in Early Chosŏn'. In *King Sejong the Great: The Light of Fifteenth-Century Korea*, edited by Young-Key Kim-Renaud, 35–40. Washington, DC: International Circle of Korean Linguistics, 1992.
———. 'The Tradition: Women during the Yi Dynasty'. In *Virtues in Conflict: Tradition and the Korean Woman Today*, edited by Martina Deuchler and Sandra Mattielli, 1–48. Seoul: Royal Asiatic Society, Korea Branch Samhwa Publishing Company, 1977.
Do, Hyeon-chul. 'Analysis of Recently Discovered Late-Koryŏ Civil Service Examination Answer Sheets', *Korean Studies* 41 (2017): 152–72.
Drucker, D. G., et al. 'Evolution of Habitat and Environment of Red Deer (*Cervus elaphus*) during the Late-Glacial and Early Holocene in Eastern France (French Jura and the Western Alps) Using Multi-Isotope Analysis (δ 13C, δ 15N, δ 18O, δ 34S) of Archaeological Remains', *Quaternary International* 245, no. 2 (December 2011): 268–78.

Duncan, John. 'Confucianism in the Late Koryŏ and Early Chosŏn', *Korean Studies* 18 (1994): 76–102.

———. 'Maintaining Boundaries: The Military and Civil Branches in the Koryŏ and Early Chosŏn', *Taiwan Journal of East Asian Studies* 8, no. 1 (June 2011): 21–50.

———. *The Origins of the Chosŏn Dynasty*. Seattle: University of Washington Press, 2000.

Durand, John D. 'The Population Statistics of China, A.D. 2–1953', *Population Studies* 13, no. 3 (March 1960): 209–56.

Eaton, Richard M., and Philip B. Wagoner. 'Warfare on the Deccan Plateau, 1450–1600: a Military Revolution in Early Modern India?', *Journal of World History* 25, no. 1 (March 2014): 5–50.

Eberly, Lee. 'Glossary of Falconry Terms', *Raptor Research News* 3, no. 3 (July 1969): 58–67.

Eliade, Mircea, Alf Hiltebeitel and Diane Apostlos-Cappadona. *History of Religious Ideas Volume 3: From Muhammad to the Age of Reforms*. Chicago: University of Chicago Press, 2013.

Farris, William Wayne. *Japan's Medieval Population: Famine, Fertility, and Warfare in a Transformative Age*. Honolulu: University of Hawai'i Press, 2006.

———. *Population, Disease, and Land in Early Japan: 645–900*. Cambridge, MA: Harvard University, 1995.

Fenner, Frank. 'Smallpox: Emergence, Global Spread, and Eradication', *History and Philosophy of the Life Sciences* 15, no. 3 (1993): 397–420.

Fiskesjo, Magnus. 'China's Animal Neighbours'. In *The Art of Neighbouring: Making Relations Across China's Borders*, edited by Martin Saxer and Juan Zhang, 223–36. Amsterdam: University of Amsterdam Press, 2017.

———. 'Rising from Blood-Stained Fields: Royal Hunting and State Formation in Shang China', *Bulletin of the Museum of Far Eastern Antiquities* 73 (2001): 48–192.

Freeman, Carol C. *Considering Animals*. Burlington: Ashgate Publishing, 2011.

Gajeweerra, Chandigma, et al. 'Genetic Diversity and Population Structure of the Sapsaree, a Native Korean Dog Breed', *BMC Genetics* 20, no. 66 (2019): 1–11.

Geist, Valerius. *Deer of the World: Their Evolution, Behavior, and Ecology*. Mechanicsburg: Stackpole Books, 1998.

Golden, Peter. '"I will giveth the people unto thee": The Cinggisid Conquests and Their Aftermath in the Turkic World', *Journal of the Royal Asiatic Society* 10, no. 1 (2000): 21–41.

Grayson, James H. *Korea: A Religious History.* New York: Routledge Press, 2002.
———. 'The Myth of Tan'gun: A Dramatic Structural Analysis of a Korean Foundation Myth', *Korea Journal* 37, no. 1 (Spring 1997): 35–52.
———. *Myths and Legends from Korea: An Annotated Compendium of Ancient and Modern Materials.* New York: Routledge, 2001.
———. 'Tan'gun and Chumong: The Politics of Korean Foundation Myths', *Folklore* 126, no. 3 (December 2015): 253–65.
Green, Monica H. 'Taking "Pandemic" Seriously: Making the Black Death Global'. In *Pandemic Disease in the Medieval World: Rethinking the Black Death*, edited by Monica Green, 27–62. Kalamazoo: Arc Humanities Press, 2019.
Haboush, JaHyun Kim. *Heritage of Kings: One Man's Monarchy in a Confucian World.* New York: Columbia University Press, 1988.
Hall, Andrew, Kendrix Evans and Shea Pribyl. 'Cold Injuries in the United States Military Population: Current Trends and Comparison with Past Conflicts', *Journal of Surgical Education* 67, no. 2 (2010): 61–5.
Hamilakis, Yannis. 'The Sacred Geography of Hunting: Wild Animals, Social Power, and Gender in Early Farming Societies', *British School at Athens Studies* 9 (2003): 239–47.
Han Chŏngsu. 'Chosŏn T'aejo-Sejong tae sup kaebal kwa chungsong chŏngch'aek' [The development of forests and the formation of policies for cultivating pine trees from Chosŏn kings T'aejo to Sejong], *Sahak yŏn'gu* 111 (September 2013): 41–91.
Han Hŭngsun. 'Sijang chuŭijŏk koch'al kwa kŭe tahan pigyo: Chosŏn hugi sallimjŏngch'aek mit sallim hwangp'ehwa' [Forest policies and forest devastation in the late Chosŏn: A review of the market principal critique], *Han'guk chiyŏk kaebal hakhoe* 20, no. 2 (June 2008): 169–92.
Han Hyŏngju. 'Chosŏn sidae kukka chesa esŏŭi hŭisaeng sayong kwa kŭ unyŏng' [Use and operation of sacrifices of Chosŏn period national rites], *Yŏksa minsokhak* 52 (June 2017): 47–75.
Han Myŏngju. 'The Establishment of National Rites and Royal Authority during Early Chosŏn', *International Journal of Korean History* 9 (December 2005): 89–131.
Han Sŏngju. 'Chosŏn kwa yŏjin ŭi ch'op'i kyoyŏk sŏnghaeng kwa kŭ yŏnghyang' [The sable trade between Chosŏn and Jurchen and its impact], *Manju yŏn'gu* 25 (2018): 9–42.
Hamilton, Angus. *Korea.* New York: C. Scribner's Sons, 1904.
Harvard Health Publishing. 'More on Gout: Once Kingly, Now Common', *Harvard Medical School.* 1 April 2020. https://www.health.harvard.edu/newsletter_article/more-on-gout-once-kingly-now-common.

Hejtmanek, Milan. 'The Elusive Path to Sagehood: Origins of the Confucian Academy System in Chosŏn Korea', *Seoul Journal of Korean Studies* 26, no. 2 (December 2013): 233–68.

Henthorn, William E. *Korea: The Mongol Invasions*. Leiden: Brill, 1963.

Hicks, Michael. *English Political Culture in the Fifteenth Century*. London: Routledge, 2002.

Hŏ Wŏn'gi. 'In'gan tongmul kwan'gyedam ŭi saengt'aejŏk yangsang kwa ŭimi' [The meaning of the ecological aspect of human-animal relations], *Tonghwa wa pŏnyŏk* 23 (2012): 255–82.

Hong Hyŏngsun. 'Hwan'gyŏngsa kwanjŏm esŏ pon Chosŏn sidae kunggwŏl e pŏm kwa p'yobŏ ŭi ch'ulmul' [The emergence of tigers and leopards in the royal palace in the Chosŏn Dynasty from an environmental perspective], *Han'guk chŏnt'ong chogyŏng hakhoeji* 36, no. 3 (September 2018): 1–15.

Howorth, Henry H. *The Mongols Proper and the Kalmuks*. New York: B. Franklin, 1964.

Hughes, Julie. *Animal Kingdoms: Hunting, the Environment, and Power in the Indian Princely States*. Cambridge, MA: Harvard University Press, 2012.

Hunter, Luke. *Wild Cats of the World*. London: Bloomsbury Publishing, 2015.

Hurn, Samantha. *Humans and Other Animals: Cross-Cultural Perspectives on Human–Animal Interactions*. New York: Pluto Press, 2012.

Hwang Kyŏngsun. 'Illum muhyŏng yusan taep'yo mongnong 'maesanyang' kongdong tŭngjae ŭi t'ŭksŏng kwa ŭiŭi' [The significance of the joint inscription of falconry to the intangible cultural heritage of humanity], *Munhwajae* 51, no. 4 (2018): 208–23.

Ioannidis, John P. A. 'Infection Fatality Rate of COVID-19 Inferred from Seroprevalence Data', *Bulletin of the World Health Organization* 99 (2021): 19–33.

Jo, Yeong-Seok, John Baccus, John Koprowski and Yo-han Ji. *Mammals of Korea*. Seoul: Life Science Publishing Company, 2018.

Kang, H. W. 'Institutional Borrowing: The Case of the Chinese Civil Service Examination System in Early Koryŏ', *Journal of Asian Studies* 34, no. 1 (November 1974): 10–25.

Kang, Sook Ja [Kang Sukcha]. 'The Role of King Sejong in Establishing the Confucian Ritual Code', *The Review of Korean Studies* 9, no. 3 (2006): 71–102.

Kang Sukcha. *See* Kang, Sook Ja.

Karlsson, Anders. 'Confucian Ideology and Legal Developments in Chosŏn Korea: A Methodological Essay'. In *The Spirit of Korean Law: Korean Legal History in Context*, edited by Marie Seong-Hak Kim, 83–103. Boston, MA: Brill, 2016.

Kim Anesŭ. 'Koryŏ sidae kaegyŏng iltae myŏngsan taech'ŏn kwa kukka chejang' [Great mountains and streams and national ritual rites in the Koryŏ capital], *Yŏksa wa kyŏnggye* 82 (2012): 1–45.
Kim, Baek Jun, and Sang-Don Lee. 'Home Range Study of the Korean Water Deer (*Hydropotes inermis agyropus*) Using Radio and GPS Tracking in South Korea: Comparison of Daily and Seasonal Habit Use Pattern', *Journal of Ecology and Field Biology* 34, no. 4 (2011): 365–70.
Kim Chaeho. 'Chosŏn sidae ŭi in'gu-changgi pyŏndong' [Population estimates during the Chosŏn era], *Han'guk kyŏngje* 19 (May 2014): 18. https://www.hankyung.com/news/article/2014051670741.
Kim Chingt'aek, Kim Kŏnjung and Kim Hyŏnch'ŏl. 'Myŏlching wigijong Han'guk sahyang noru ŭi sŏsikchi chosa' [Investigation of the natural habitat for Korean musk deer], *Han'guk kach'uk wisaeng hakhoeji* 30, no. 3 (2007): 459–66.
Kim Chinsu. '13-segi mal Haptan'gun ŭi ch'imgong e taehan Koryŏ ŭi taeŭng' [The Koryŏ response to the thirteenth-century invasion of Haptan's army], *Kunsa* 77 (2010): 87–115.
Kim Ch'ŏlung. 'Koryŏ kukka chesa ŭi ch'eje was kŭ t'ŭkching' [Organization and characteristics of Koryŏ state ritual], *Han'guksa yŏn'gu* 118 (2002): 135–60.
Kim Chongsu. 'Imjin waeran chŏnhu chungan'gunje ŭi pyŏnhwa' [Changes to the command system of the central army after the Imjin War], *Kunsa* 84 (September 2012): 85–115.
Kim, Haek-Jun, Dae-Hyun Oh, Seung-Hoon Chun and Sang-Don Lee. 'Distribution, Density, and Habitat Use of the Korean Water Deer (*Hydropotes inermis agyropus*) in Korea', *Landscape and Ecological Engineering* 7, no. 2 (2011): 291–7.
Kim, Hwansoo. 'Buddhism during the Chosŏn Dynasty (1392–1910): A Collective Trauma?', *Journal of Korean Studies* 22, no. 1 (Spring 2017): 101–42.
Kim Hyŏlla. 'Koryŏ Ch'ungnyŏl wang tae ŭi Yŏ Wŏn kwan'gye ŭi hyŏngsŏng kwa kŭ t'ŭkching' [The special characteristics and formation of Koryŏ–Yuan relations at the time of King Ch'ungnyŏl], *Chiyŏk kwa yŏksa* 24 (2009): 195–224.
Kim, Jisoo. *The Emotions of Justice: Gender, Status, and Legal Performance in Chosŏn Korea*. Seattle: University of Washington Press, 2015.
Kim, Jongmyung. 'Kings and Buddhism in Medieval Korea', *Korean Studies* 41 (2017): 128–51.
Kim Kwangŏn. *Han Il Tong Siberia ŭi sanyang: Suryŏp munhwa pigyoji* [The hunt of Korea, Japan, and Eastern Siberia: Comparative notes of their hunting cultures]. Seoul: Minsogwŏn, 2007.

Kim Kyŏngnok. 'Hongmuyŏn'gan Myŏng ŭi pongjŏn chŏngbi wa Cho-Myŏng kwan'gye' [Ming–Chosŏn relations and preparations of the conferral ceremony during the years of the Ming Hongwu Emperor], *Chungguksa yŏn'gu* 106 (February 2017): 59–94.

Kim Myŏngok. 'Tan'gun sinhwa insik e taehan yŏksajŏk koch'al' [Historical examination of the awareness of the Tan'gun myth], *Yŏksa wa yunghap* 3 (2018): 45–86.

Kim, Nan-ok. 'Low-Class Commoners during the Koryŏ Dynasty', *International Journal of Korean History* 6 (December 2004): 87–111.

Kim Pangul. 'Maesayuk kwa maesanyang ŭi wihan chich'imsŏ *Ŭnggolbang ŭi yŏjŏng*' [The journey of the *Guidebook on Falconry*], *Muhyŏng yusan* 8 (2020): 161–84.

Kim Pyŏngju. 'Yongmaek kwa sugu ro pon Chosŏn hugi toso ipchi hwan'gyŏng ŭi pyŏnhwa yŏn'gu' [A study on the location of village settlements in the late Chosŏn as reflected in the mountain ranges and watersheds], *Taehan kŏnch'uk hakhoe nongminjip* 31 (2015): 111–21.

Kim Pyŏngju, and Yi Sanhae. '"*Taedong yŏjido*"rŭl t'onghae pon Chosŏn sidae ssijok maul ŭi ipchi hwangyŏng' [Location and natural environment of lineage villages in the Chosŏn Dynasty based on the *Taedong yŏji*], *Taehan kŏnch'uk hakhoe nongmunjip kyehoekkye* 22, no. 1 (2006): 155–66.

Kim, Ryong Nam, et al. 'Genome Analysis of the Domestic Dog (Korean Jindo) by Massively Parallel Sequencing', *DNA Research* 19, no. 3 (June 2012): 275–88.

Kim Sangjun, ed. *Yugyo ŭi yech'i inyŏm kwa Chosŏn* [Confucian ideology and Chosŏn]. Kŏnggido P'ajusi: Chŏnggye ch'ulp'ansa, 2007.

Kim Sŏnp'ung. 'Han'guk sanyang sŏrhwa ŭi sangjingjŏk ŭimi' [The symbolic meaning of Korean hunting fables], *Chungang minsokhak* 11 (2006):11–49.

Kim Sumin. 'P'yŏngyang chiyŏk Koguryŏ pyŏkhwa suryŏpto e poinŭn saengsagwan' [View of life and death in Koguryŏ paintings of the hunt in the area of P'yŏngyang], *Koguryŏ yŏn'gu* 15 (2003): 165–88.

Kim, Sung-Eun Thomas. 'Perception of Monastic Slaves by Scholar Officials and Monks in the Late Koryŏ and Early Chosŏn Periods', *Journal of Korean Religions* 7, no. 1 (2016): 5–34.

Kim Taehong. 'Uri nara kkwŏng kogi choribŏp ŭi yŏksajŏk koch'al' [Historical study of pheasant cooking in Korea], *Han'guksik saenghwal munhwa hakhŏeji* 11, no. 1 (1996): 83–96.

Kim Taehyŏn. *Koguryŏ ch'ogi sahoe esŏ sanyang ŭi yuhyŏng kwa kinŭng* [The pattern and function of hunting in early Koguryŏ society]. Unpublished MA thesis, Graduate School of Education. Korea National University of Education, 2003.

Kim Tongjin. 'Chosŏn chŏn'gi nongbonjuŭi wa p'oho chŏngch'aek' [Agrarianism and tiger catching policies in early Chosŏn], *Yŏksa wa tamnon* 41 (September 2005): 71–113.

———. 'Chosŏn chŏnjŏn'gi Kangmu ŭi silhaeng kwa p'oho chŏngch'aek' [Operation of the Kangmu and tiger hunting policies in the early Chosŏn], *Chosŏn sidaesa hakpo* 40 (March 2007): 93–131.

———. '15–19 segi hanbando sallim ŭi min'gan kaebang kwa sup ŭi pyŏnhwa' [Fifteenth- through nineteenth-century open door policy on the forests of the Korean peninsula and the transformation of forests], *Yŏksa wa hyŏnsil* 3 (2017): 77–118.

———. '17 segi huban 18 seigi ch'o hosokmok hyŏkp'i wa chejŏng unyŏng ŭi pyŏnhwa saengt'ae hwan'gyŏng kwa kukche chŏngse pyŏnhwa rŭl chungsim ŭro' [Impact of the changing environmental and international situation during the late-seventeenth and early-eighteenth centuries, focusing on the abolition of the tiger skin penalty], *Saengt'ae hwan'gyŏng kwa yŏksa* 1 (December 2015): 45–86.

Kim Ŭna. 'Chosŏn chŏn'gi chaesan sangsok pŏpche esŏ yŏsŏng ŭi chiwi' [The position of women on inheritance laws in early Chosŏn], *Pŏphak yŏn'gu* 28 (2007): 207–26.

Kim Yangsik. 'Chosŏn sidae chŏnyŏmbyŏng yangsang kwa t'ŭkching' [Chosŏn Dynasty infectious disease trends and characteristics], *Ch'ungbok Issue and Trend* 39 (2020): 8–13.

Kim, Youngjin, Soyeon Cho and Yeonsook Choung. 'Habitat Preference of Wild Boar (*Sus scrofa*) for Feeding in Cool-Temperate Forests', *Journal of Ecology and Environment* 43, no. 30 (2019): 297–304.

Ko Ŭnbyŏl. 'Han'guk kodae tongmul hŭsaeng ŭirye ŭi t'ŭkching Samguk sidae Silla punmyojŏk ŭl chungsim ŭ ro' [Animal sacrifice rituals in ancient Korea centring on Silla tombs of the Three Kingdoms], *Haebu saengmul illyuhak* 33, no. 2 (2020): 69–77.

Kong, Gee Soo, et al. 'Characteristics of the East Asian Summer Monsoon in the South Sea of Korea during the Little Ice Age', *Quaternary International* 286 (2013): 36–44.

Kong, Man-Shik. 'A Reconsideration of Koryŏ Meat-eating Culture', *Seoul Journal of Korean Studies* 33, no. 1 (2020): 99–126.

Kwak Nakhyŏn. 'Chosŏn chŏn'gi sŭpchin kwa kunsa hullyŏn' [Military training methods in the early Chosŏn], *Tongyang kojŏn yŏn'gu* 35 (2009): 359–84.

Kwŏn, Yŏnung. 'The Royal Lecture and Confucian Politics in early Yi Korea', *Korean Studies* 6 (1982): 41–62.

Lancaster, Lewis R., and Chai-Shin Yu. *Buddhism in the Early Chosŏn: Suppression and Transformation.* Fremont: Asian Humanities Press, 2002.

Lee, Hee-Eun, et al. 'Polymorphism Analysis of Tyrosine Hydroxylase Gene Variable Number of Tandem Repeats in Various Korean Dogs', *Genetics and Genomics* 37 (2015): 257–61.

Lee, John S. 'Postwar Pines: The Military and the Expansion of State Forests in Post-Imjin Korea, 1598–1684', *Journal of Asian Studies* 77, no. 2 (May 2018): 319–32.

Lee, Kang Hahn. 'Koryŏ Trade with the Outer World', *Korean Studies* 41 (2017): 52–74.

Lee, Song-Chong, ed. *The Role of Meaning of Religion for Korean Society*. Internet Resource. https://www.mdpi.com/books/pdfview/book/1266.

Li Sha, 'Jin sanshi nianlai Yuan dai renkou yanjiu zonshu' [A summary of population research in the Yuan Dynasty over the past thirty years], *Yindo xuekan* (2007): 43–8.

Licoppe, A. M. 'The Diurnal Habitat Used by Red Deer (*Cervus elaphus* L.) in the Haute Ardenne', *European Journal of Wildlife Research* 52, no. 3 (2006): 164–70.

Lim, Jaesoo, Jin-Young Lee, Jin Cheul Kim, Sei-Sun Hong and Dong-Yoon Yang, 'Relationship Between Environmental Change on Geoje Island, Southern Coast of Korea, and Regional Monsoon and Temperature Changes during the Late Holocene', *Quaternary International* 344 (2014): 11–16.

Liu Siyuan, and Cao Shuji. 'Ming Qing shiqi tanhua bingli de liuxing tezheng' [Study on epidemic characteristics of smallpox in Ming and Qing dynasties based on epitaphs], *Henan daxue xuebao* 55, no. 3 (2015): 65–70.

Loo, Tina. 'Of Moose and Men: Hunting for Masculinity in British Columbia, 1880–1939', *Western Historical Quarterly* 32, no. 3 (Autumn 2001): 297–319.

Lovins, Christopher. *King Chŏngjo: An Enlightened Despot in Early Modern Korea*. Albany: State University of New York Press, 2019.

Macdonald, David, and Andrew Loveridge. *The Biology and Conservation of Wild Felids*. Oxford: Oxford University Press, 2014.

Mahabal, Anil, et al. 'Colour Aberrations in Indian Mammals: A Review from 1886–2017', *Journal of Threatened Taxa* 11, no. 6 (2019): 13690–719.

Mandala, Vijaya. *Shooting a Tiger: Big-Game Hunting and Conservation in Colonial India*. New Delhi: Oxford University Press, 2019.

May, Timothy. *The Mongol Empire*. Edinburgh: Edinburgh University Press, 2018.

———. 'The Training of an Inner Asian Nomad Army in the Pre-Modern Period', *Journal of Military History* 70, no. 3 (July 2006): 617–35.

Mercer, Alexander. *Infections, Chronic Disease, and the Epidemiological Transition: A New Perspective*. Rochester: University of Rochester, 2014.

Mertes, Kate. 'Aristocracy'. In *Fifteenth-Century Attitudes: Perceptions of Society in Late Medieval England*, edited by Rosemary Horrox, 42–60. New York: Cambridge University Press, 1994.
Mikhail, Alan. 'War and Charisma: Horses and Elephants in the Indian Ocean Economy'. In *Asia Inside Out: Connected Places, Volume 1*, edited by Eric Tagliacozzo, Helen Siu and Peter Perdue, 128–68. Cambridge, MA: Harvard University Press, 2015.
Min Sŭnggi. *Chosŏn ŭi mugi wa kabot* [Weapons and military uniforms of Chosŏn]. Seoul: Karam kihoek, 2004.
Moon, Seungsook. *Militarized Modernity and Gendered Citizenship in South Korea*. Durham, NC: Duke University Press, 2005.
Nongbri, Natasha. 'Elephant Hunting in Late Nineteenth-Century North-East India: Mechanisms of Control, Contestation, and Local Reactions', *Economic and Political Weekly* 38, no. 30 (2003): 3189–99.
Nunn, Patrick D. 'The AD 1300 Event in the Pacific Basin', *American Geographical Society* 97, no. 1 (January 2007): 1–23.
O'Hanlon, Rosalind. 'Manliness and Imperial Service in Mughal North India', *Journal of the Economic and Social History of the Orient* 42, no. 1 (1999): 47–93.
Onev, Sergei Ivanovish. *Mammals of Eastern Europe and Northern Asia*. Volume 2. Jerusalem: Israel Program for Scientific Translations, 1962.
Owens, J. B. 'Diana at the Bar: Hunting, Aristocrats, and the Law in Renaissance Castile', *The Sixteenth Century Journal* 8, no. 1 (1977): 17–36.
Pak Chongch'ŏng. 'Sangjeryeŭi Han'gukjŏk chŏn'gae wa yugyo ŭi yeŭi munhwajŏk yŏnghyang' [Historical change of funerary and ancestral rites and cultural influence of Confucianism], *Kuk'ak yŏn'gu* 17 (December 2010): 365–96.
Pak Kyŏngja. '15 segi kongmul ŭi unsung pangbŏp kwa punch'ŏng sagi myŏngmun ŭi chiyŏkbyŏl t'ŭkching' [Transportation methods of tribute items to the central government and the different regional properties of letter markings in the fifteenth century], *Yŏksa wa tamnon* 47 (September 2007): 215–54.
Palais, James B. *Confucian Statecraft and Korean Institutions: Yu Hyŏngwon and the Late Chosŏn Dynasty*. Seattle: University of Washington Press, 1996.
Palmer, Spencer J. *Confucian Rituals in Korea*. Berkeley: Asia Humanities Press, 1992.
Park, Eugene Y. *Between Dreams and Reality: The Military Examination in Late Chosŏn Korea, 1600–1894*. Cambridge, MA: Harvard University Press, 2007.
Park, Jae Woo. 'Early Koryŏ Political Institutions and the International Expansion of Tang and Song Institutions', *Korean Studies* 41 (2017): 9–29.

Park, Jong-ki. 'The Characteristics and Origins of Koryŏ's Pluralist Society', *Korean Studies* 41 (2017): 202–3.

Paul, Michael. 'Military Revolution in Russia, 1550–1682', *Journal of Military History* 68, no. 1 (January 2004): 9–45.

Perlo, Katherine Wills. *Kinship and Killing: The Animal in World Religions*. New York: Columbia University Press, 2009.

Peters, Richard, and Xiaobing Li. *Voices from the Korean War: Personal Stories of American, Korean, and Chinese Soldiers*. Lexington: University of Kentucky Press, 2014.

Pu, Chengzhong. *Ethical Treatment of Animals in Early Chinese Buddhism: Beliefs and Practices*. Newcastle upon Tyne: Cambridge Scholars Publishing, 2014.

Putnam, Aaron, et al. 'Little Ice Age Wetting of Interior Asian Deserts and the Rise of the Mongol Empire', *Quaternary Science Reviews* 131 (2016): 33–50.

Pyŏn T'aesŏp. *Han'guk t'ongsa* [Outline of Korean history]. Seoul: Samyŏnsa, 2000.

Reed, Carrie E. 'Tattoo in Early China', *Journal of the American Oriental Society* 120, no. 3 (2000): 360–76.

Ro, Myoung-ho. 'The Makeup of Koryŏ Aristocratic Families: Bilateral Kindred', *Korean Studies* 41 (2017): 173–99.

Robinson, David M. *Empire's Twilight: Northeast Asia Under the Mongols*. Cambridge, MA: Harvard University Press, 2009.

———. *Korea and the Fall of the Mongol Empire: Alliance, Upheaval, and the Rise of a New East Asian Order*. New York: Cambridge University Press, 2022.

———. *Martial Spectacles of the Ming Court*. Cambridge, MA: Harvard University Press, 2013.

———. 'Why Military Institutions Matter for Ming History', *Journal of Chinese History* 1, no. 2 (July 2017): 297–327.

Robinson, Kenneth. 'From Raiders to Traders: Border Security and Border Control in Early Chosŏn, 1392–1450', *Korean Studies* 16, no. 1 (1992): 94–115.

———. 'Organizing Japanese and Jurchens in Tribute Systems in Early Chosŏn Korea', *Journal of East Asian Studies* 13, no. 2 (May–August 2013): 337–60.

———. 'Pak Tonji and the Vagaries of Government Service in Koryŏ and Chosŏn, 1360–1412', *Korean Studies* 40, no. 1 (2016): 78–118.

———. 'Residence and Foreign Relations in the Peninsular Northeast during the Fifteenth and Sixteenth Centuries'. In *The Northern Region of Korea*, edited by Sun Joo Kim, 18–36. Seattle: University of Washington Press, 2010.

Sahin, Kaya. 'The Ottoman Empire in the Long Sixteenth Century', *Renaissance Quarterly* 70, no. 1 (2017): 220–34.
Schäfer, Dagmar, Martina Siebert and Roel Sterckx. 'Knowing Animals in China's History: An Introduction'. In *Knowing Animals in China's History: Earliest Times to 1911*, edited by Roel Sterckx, Martina Siebert and Dagmar Schafer, 1–19. New York: Cambridge University Press, 2020.
Schafer, Edward H. 'Hunting Parks and Animal Enclosures in Ancient China', *Journal of the Economic and Social History of the Orient* 11, no. 3 (1968): 318–43.
Serpell, James. 'Animals to Edible: The Ritualization of Animals in Early China'. In *Animals through Chinese History: Earliest Times to 1911*, edited by Roel Sterckx, Martina Siebert and Dagmar Schafer, 46–63. New York: Cambridge University Press, 2019.
_____. *In the Company of Animals: A Study of Human-Animal Relationships*. New York: Cambridge University Press, 2014.
Serruys, Henry. 'Sino-Mongol Relations during the Ming (III) Trade Relations: The Horse Fairs (1400–1600)', *Melanges chinoises at bouddhiques* 17 (1975): 9–275.
_____. 'Smallpox in Mongolia during the Ming and Qing Dynasties', *Zentralasiatische Studien* 14, no. 1 (1980): 41–63.
Seth, Michael. 'Myth, Memory, and the Reinvention in Korea: The Case of Tan'gun', *Virginia Review of Asian Studies* 10 (Fall 2007): 55–67.
Shin, Gi-Wook. *Peasant Protest and Social Change in Colonial Korea*. Seattle: University of Washington Press, 1996.
Shultz, Edward J. *Generals and Scholars: Military Rule in Medieval Korea*. Honolulu: University of Hawai'i Press, 2000.
Sim Sŭnggu. 'Chosŏn sidae sanyang ŭi ch'ui wa t'ŭksŏng' [The special characteristic and development of hunting in the Chosŏn Dynasty], *Yŏksa minsokhak hoe* 24 (2007): 165–97.
Sim Sŭnggu, Im Changhyŏk, Chŏng Yŏnhak and Cho T'aesŏp. *Sanyang ŭro pon sam kwa munhwa* [Seeing life and culture through hunting]. Kyŏnggido kwach'ŏnsi: Kuksa p'yŏnch'an wiwŏnhoe, 2011.
Sims, L. D., et al. 'Origin and Evolution of Highly Pathogenic H5N1 Avian Influenza in Asia', *Veterinary Record* 157, no. 6 (August 2005): 159–64.
Sin Yŏngju. 'Kihoek chuje: Chungse ŭi tongmul e taehan inskik kwa munhakjŏk hyŏngsang: Chosŏn sidae chisikindŭl ŭi tongmul aeho wa munhakchŏk hyŏngsang-ŭng, kyŏn, hak, ma rŭl chungsim ŭro' [Planning subject: The perception and literary form of animals in the Middle Ages: Focusing on falcons, dogs, cranes, and horses], *Tongbang hanmunhak* 1 (2014): 55–87.

Smith, G. Rex. 'Some Remarks on the Economics of Hunting in Medieval Islam', *Journal of the Economics and Social History of the Orient* 23, no. 1–2 (April 1980): 205–6.

Son Pyŏnggyu. 'Chosŏn wangjo ŭi hojŏk kwa chaejŏng kirok e taehan chaeinsik in'gu wa kajok ŭi kyŏngje sujun ch'ujŏk kwa kwallyŏnhayŏ' [A new understanding of household register and financial records of the Chosŏn Dynasty], *Yŏksa hakpo* 234 (June 2017): 155–94.

Song Ungsŏp. 'Chosŏn Sŏngjong ŭi Munmyo chunghaeng kwa kungwang ŭro sŏŭi kwŏnwi ch'angch'ul' [The Munmyo ritual ceremony of Chosŏn King Sŏngjong and the creation of royal authority], *Yŏksa wa tamnon* 85 (January 2018): 123–56.

Sramek, Joseph. '"Face Him like a Briton": Tiger Hunting, Imperialism, and British Masculinity in Colonial India, 1800–1875', *Victorian Studies* 48, no. 4 (2006): 659–80.

Stars and Stripes–Pacific [US military newspaper].

Steinhart, Edward. *Black Poachers, White Hunters: A Social History of Hunting in Colonial Kenya*. Athens: Ohio University Press, 2006.

Steinhardt, Nancy Shatzman. 'Imperial Architecture Along the Mongolian Road to Dadu', *Ars Orientalis* 18 (1988): 59–93.

Sterckx, Roel. 'Transforming the Beasts: Animals and Music in Early China', *T'oung Pao, Second Series* 86, Fasc. 1/3 (2000): 1–46.

Storey, William K. 'Big Cats and Imperialism: Lion and Tiger Hunting in Kenya and Northern India, 1898–1930', *Journal of World History* 2, no. 2 (1991): 135–73.

Suh, Soyoung. *Naming the Local: Medicine, Language, and Identity in Korea Since the Fifteenth Century*. Cambridge, MA: Harvard University Press, 2017.

Sun, Weiguo. 'Legend, Identity, and History: The Historiographic Creation and Evolution of Tangun Choson and Kija Choson', *Chinese Studies in History* 44, no. 4 (Summer 2011): 20–46.

Sussman, George. 'Was the Black Death in India and China?', *Bulletin of the History of Medicine* 85, no. 3 (Fall 2011): 319–55.

Tak, K., Y. Chun and P. M. Wood. 'The South Korean Forest Dilemma', *International Forestry Review* 9, no. 1 (June 2007): 548–57.

Tani, Mitsutaka. 'A Study on Horse Administration in the Ming Period', *Acta Asiatica* 21 (1971): 73–97.

Teiser, Stephen. 'The Wheel of Rebirth in Buddhist Temples', *Arts Asiatiques* 63 (2008): 139–53.

Tilson, Ronald, and Philip Nyhus. *Tigers of the World: The Science, Politics, and Conservation of Panthera tigris*. Amsterdam: Academic Press, 2010.

Vermeersch, Sem. 'Views on Buddhist Precepts and Morality in Late Koryŏ', *Journal of Korean Religions* 7, no. 1 (April 2016): 35–65.
Wagner, Edward K. *The Literati Purges: Political Conflict in Early Yi Korea*. Cambridge, MA: East Asia Research Center and Harvard University Press, 1974.
Walraven, Boudewijin. 'Confucians and Shamans', *Cahiers d'Extrême-Asie* 6 (1991–1992): 21-44.
Wang, Sixiang. 'What Tang Taizong Could Not Do: The Imperial Koryŏ Surrender of 1259 and the Imperial Tradition', *T'uong Pao* 104, 3–4 (2018): 338–83.
Wang, Yuan-kang. *Harmony and War: Confucian Culture and Chinese Power Politics*. New York: Columbia University Press, 2010.
Wechsler, Howard J. 'The Confucian Impact on Early T'ang Decision-Making', *T'oung Pao* 66 nos. 1–3 (1980): 1–40.
White, Sam. *The Climate of Rebellion in the Earl Modern Ottoman Empire*. Cambridge: Cambridge University Press, 2012.
Wu Mingwei, 'Gaoli xiang Yuanchao renkou qianyi zhong de yinyue wenhua jiaoliu' [Population migration of Korea and the Yuan dynasty music cultural exchange]. *Fujian shifan daxue xuebao* 5 (2015): 104–11.
Yamamoto, Isaburo. *Seikoki* [Diary of a tiger expedition]. Tokyo: Ryutaro yoshiura, 1918.
Yi Chongsŏ. '"Chŏnt'ongjŏk" kyemogwan ŭi hyŏngsŏng kwajŏng kwa kŭ ŭimi' [The formation of traditional views on stepmothers and its meaning]. *Yŏksa wa hyŏnsil* 51 (2004): 135–63.
Yi Chunho. 'Chosŏn sidae kihu pyŏndongi chŏnyŏmbyŏng palsaeng e mich'in yŏngyang' [The development and impact of infectious diseases in the Chosŏn Dynasty], *Han'guk chiyŏk chirihak hoeji* 25 (2019): 425–36.
———. '1623–1800 nyŏn Sŏul chiyŏk ŭi kisanggihu hyangyŏng' [Weather and climatic environment of the Seoul region from 1623–1800], *Han'guk chiyŏk chiri hakhoeji* 22, no. 4 (2016): 856–74.
Yi Hongdu. 'Chosŏn ch'ogi Suwŏn tohobu ŭi mamokchang sŏlch'i yŏn'gu' [Research on the installation of horse ranches in Suwŏn tohobu during the early Chosŏn], *Kunsa* 106 (March 2018): 329–59.
———. 'Homa ŭi chŏllae wa Chosŏn sidae homa mokchang ŭi sŏlch'i [The importation of Manchurian horses and the installation of Manchurian horse ranches during the Chosŏn Dynasty], *Kunsa* 99 (June 2016): 113–44.
Yi Hyesun. *Chosŏn chunggi yehak sasang kwa ilsang munhwa: Chuja Karye rŭl chungsim ŭro* [Mid-Chosŏn study of rites and Zhu Xi's family rituals]. Seoul: Ehwa yŏja taehakkyo ch'ulp'anbu, 2006.

Yi Hyŏnsu. 'Chosŏn ch'ogi Kangmu sihaeng sarye wa kunsajŏk kinŭng' [The military function and practices of the Kangmu in the early Chosŏn], *Kunsa* 45 (April 2002): 233–64.

Yi, Ki-baek. *A New History of Korea*. Translated by Edward Wagner. Seoul: Ilchokak, 1988.

Yi Kyŏngju, T'ak Chonghun and Pak Sŏnil. 'Urinara kosoktoro esŏ yangsaeng tongmul rodek'il e kwanhan sigongan ch'ui punsŏk' [Spatial and temporal patterns of wildlife roadkill on highways in Korea], *Han'guk imsangsuŭihak hoeji* 31, no. 4 (2014): 282–7.

Yi Kyŏngsik. '16-segi chijuch'ŭng ŭi tonghyang' [Trends of the landlord class in the sixteenth century], *Yŏksa kyoyuk* 4 (1976): 139–83.

Yi Pyŏnghŭi. 'Koryŏ sidae kŏsa ŭi saenghwal pangbŏp kwa kŭ ŭimi' [Buddhist votary of the Koryŏ era and their significance], *Sahak yŏn'gu* 116 (December 2014): 197–242.

Yi, Sangheon and Ju-Yong Kim. 'Pollen Analysis at Paju Unjeong, South Korea: Implication of Land-Use Changes since the Late Neolithic', *The Holocene* 22 (2011): 227–34.

Yi Sŭngho. 'Tan'gun: Yŏksa wa sinhwa, kŭrigo minjok' [Tan'gun: history, myth, and nationalism], *Yŏksa pipyŏngsa* 117 (November 2016): 224–51.

Yi Taejin. 'Sobinggi (1500–1750) ch'ŏnbyŏnjae yŏn'gu wa *Chosŏn wangjo sillok*' [An interim report of the little ice age (1500–1750) based on the records of the *Veritable Records of the Chosŏn Dynasty*], *Yŏksa hakbo* 149 (March 1996): 203–36.

Yun Eŭnsuk. 'K'ubillai k'an ŭi chungang chipkwŏnhwa e taehan tongdo chewangdŭl ŭi taeŭng: "Nayan pallan" ŭl chungsim ŭro' [Kublai Khan's central power in relation to the Eastern princes' response: Focusing on the Nayan rebellion], *Chungang Asia yŏn'gu* 8 (2003): 29–50.

_____. 'K'ubillai wa Koryŏ' [Kublai and Koryŏ], *Yŏksa pip'yŏng* 90 (2010): 334–55.

Yun Hunp'yo. 'Chosŏn ch'ogi kapsa ŭi t'ongsol ch'egye' [The private army command system of the early Chosŏn], *Yŏksa wa sirhak* 17 (January 2000): 8–9.

_____. *Yŏmal Sŏnch'o kunje kaehyŏk* [Military system reform in the late Koryŏ and early Chosŏn]. Seoul: Hyean, 2000.

Yun, Peter. 'Mongols and Western Asians in the Late Koryŏ Ruling Stratum', *International Journal of Korean History* 3 (2002): 51–69.

Zhambal, A. *13–14 zuuny Mongolyn uls toriin setgelgeenii zarim asuudal* [Research on the political thought of the Mongols in the thirteenth and fourteenth centuries]. Ulaanbaatar: Bembi san, 2006.

Zhang, Mingming, et al. 'Hydrological Variation Recorded in a Subalpine Peatland of Northeast Asia since the Little Ice Age and Its Possible Driving Mechanisms', *Science of the Total Environment* 772 (2021): 1–15.

Zhang Shengda, Pei Qing and Zhang David Dian. 'Xiao bingqi sichou zhi lu diqu qihou bianhua yu zhanzheng guanxi de dingliang fenxi' [A quantitative analysis of the relationship between climate change and war along the Silk Road regions during the Little Ice Age], *Di si ji yanjiu* 42 (2022): 250–60.

Zurndorfer, Harriet. 'Polygamy and Masculinity in China: Past and Present'. In *Changing Chinese Masculinities: From Imperial Pillars of State to Global Real Men*, edited by Kam Louie, 13–33. Hong Kong: Hong Kong University Press, 2016.

Index

Ach'a, Mt, 118, 148, 197, 230, 231
Africa, 62, 103, 261
agriculture, 9–10, 69, 103, 130, 272
    Chosŏn state and, 121, 190
    and climate events, 106–7
    expansion of, 275
    government promotion of, 223, 275
    hunting grounds converted to, 4–5, 14
    Kangmu hunts, 147, 176, 178–9, 180–1, 258
    in north, 105–6, 120
    predators, control of, 145
    slash and burn, 272, 277
    spring and autumn hunts, 143–4, 247
    see also farmers
alcohol
    and foreign relations/diplomacy, 133
    on the hunt, 19, 112, 117, 144, 179, 216, 259
    prohibitions on, 237, 259, 265
Amur leopards (*Panthera pardus orientalis*), 41; *see also* leopards
An Ch'im, 172, 203, 204
An Ch'ŏsŏn, 254, 255
An Yunson, 178, 227
ancestral rites/lands, 69, 78, 126–7, 135, 171–2, 180, 201–7

animals
    decreasing numbers from overhunting, 120, 147, 198, 218, 251, 258–60
    as diplomacy, 12, 18, 42, 64, 89, 101, 121, 128, 133, 186, 191, 196, 208, 209, 242
    disregard for, 8, 50
    in folktales, 51–3
    kindness toward, 45–9, 53, 194, 250
    as living tribute to the court, 228, 234
    as medicine, 127, 189–191, 266–7
    as pets, 7, 8, 9, 42, 243, 281
    policies over, 105, 120, 121, 148, 221, 223, 259
    in political and religious texts, 11, 43–4
    as portents and omens, 51
    in regional trade, 101, 105, 121, 186, 189–90, 220, 278
    as ritualized enemies, 112–13, 149–50
    as sacrifice in Chosŏn, 122–35
    as sacrifices in Koryŏ, 78–80, 110–14, 122–9
    shortage of, 126, 134–5, 198
    as social comparisons, 44, 49, 51, 159, 278

INDEX

see also ancestral rites/lands; insects; rituals; specific animals
animal skins *see* fur; pelts
animal studies, 7–10, 121–2
animal tribute *see* tribute
Anp'yŏng, Prince (Yi Yong), 171, 221
Ansu wanghu, Queen, 1, 135
archery, 57, 66, 72, 75, 77, 90, 174, 175, 246, 247, 259
aristocracy *see* bureaucracy; scholarly elites
armies *see* military elite; military training/skills
art, hawking as, 212, 213, 220; *see also* falconry
Asiatic bear (*Ursus thibetanus*), 39

Baker, Donald, 114
Batu Khan, 165, 166
  as Chinggisid legacy, 167
bears, 35, 120, 121, 279
  medicine, 39–40, 42, 189, 190, 267, 278
Beijing, 18, 25, 85, 133
  see also Daidu
birds, 38–9
  birding manuscripts, 209–10
  and Confucianism, 44–5
  and disease, 262
  see also falcons/falconry; fowl; individual animals
Board of Rites, 21, 107, 113, 122–3, 124, 130, 131, 133, 155, 240
Book of Rites, 64, 79, 110, 123–4, 129
Book of Songs, 49, 178, 223, 236
borderland frontiers
  animal tribute, 101
  cooling climate, frozen rivers, and hunters, 157–9, 162, 252
  expansion to, 104–6
  Mongol-Ming challenges, 94–5

northern, conflict between hunters, 134, 151–62, 252–3
  thriving wildlife zones, 106, 147–8, 190–1
bows and arrows, 111, 117, 160, 191, 196, 218, 274, 275
Britain, and the hunt, 62
Buddhism, 19, 50, 195
  animals depicted in art, 8
  decline of, 97–8, 100
  and hunting practices, 76, 118, 194
  Koryŏ and, 68, 96
  liberating beasts, 45, 226
  non-killing of animals, 46
  perceptions of animals, 44–6, 47–8, 57, 58, 234, 271
  private practice of, 100
  on the royal hunt, 63
  reincarnation, 53, 57
  state support for, 97
  see also monasteries/monks; *Tripitaka*
bulls, 123, 127, 128
bureaucracy
  on ancestral rites, 171, 198, 203, 204, 246
  centralisation and control of the provinces, 99
  challenges the Kangmu hunt, 168–9, 172, 176, 253–4
  and corruption, 21, 74, 175, 198, 240, 243
  domesticated animals, 120, 243
  falconry, restrictions on, 220, 221
  gift-giving, 73–4, 191, 243, 272
  hunting restrictions, 37, 218, 219, 259
  institutions, 21
  opposition to falconry, 219, 250–1
  opposition to the hunt, 215, 216, 224–6, 227–9, 260
  outlaws private armies, 141

bureaucracy (*cont.*)
  private hunts, resistance and restrictions, 194–6, 197–201, 203–7, 218
  record-keeping challenges, 60, 68, 134, 217, 229
  toleration/defence of royal hunting, 177, 238
  worldviews, 67–8
  see also Neo-Confucianism/Neo-Confucians; scholarly elites
butchers, 129; *see also* slaughter

captive animals, Buddhism on, 47
Cartmill, Matt, 62
Ceremonial Animal Office, 126, 127–8
Ceremonial Stable Bureau, 123, 124, 125–6, 130
Chang Sullung, 76
Chickens, 43, 121, 133, 134, 211
  for state ritual, 123, 124, 126, 130, 131, 132
Cheguk, Queen, 73, 82, 83, 170
  hunting with family, 84
China/Chinese
  disease, 103, 261, 262, 263
  hunting, 62–3
  hunting and military, 61, 72
  hunting parks, 254–5
  Kija and, 55
  population increase, 102–4
  rebel groups, 95, 121; *see also* Red Turbans
  trade with, 22, 101, 105, 121
  tributary system with Ming, 101, 189, 190
  worship ritual of, 126
  see also Confucianism; Ming Dynasty; Neo-Confucianism/Neo-Confucians

children, 24, 52, 70, 71, 82, 159
  attacked by animals, 41
  as offspring of human–animal unions, 54–5, 276
Chin'gam, 47
Chinggis Khan, 81, 167, 276
Chinyang, Prince (King Sejo), 165–6; *see also* King Sejo
Chiri, Mt, 26, 47, 56
Cho Chisŏ, 173, 232, 233
Cho Chun, 92
Cho Wi, 226
Ch'oe Anto, 91
Ch'oe Ch'unghŏn, General, 23–4
Ch'oe Kwan, 175
Ch'oe Pu, 117
Ch'oe Suksaeng, 243–4
Ch'oe Yŏng, 92
Ch'oe Yuŏm, 83
Chŏlla Province, 153, 175, 188
  animal tribute, 221, 222, 266
  Kangmu hunting grounds, 146
Chŏng Ch'angson, 135, 180, 203, 204, 230
Chŏng Hoea, 174
Chŏng Hyosang, 158, 194
Chŏng Kwan, 175
Chŏng Munhyŏng, 225
Chŏng Nanjong, 136, 198
Chŏng Tojŏn, 138, 141–2
Ch'ŏnggye, Mt, 29, 176, 178, 229
Chŏnghŭi wanghu, Queen, 1, 135, 169, 203, 220
Chŏngjong, King, 68–9, 115
Chosŏn Border Defence Command, 128, 131–2
Chosŏn Dynasty, 2, 12–13, 60, 271
  centralisation and control of the provinces, 20, 99, 102, 141, 189

climate events/change, 106–9, 140, 151, 176, 223, 245
falconry, 218–19, 220
founder of, 56, 98; *see also* Yi Sŏnggye
government restructuring of animal husbandry, 131–3
hierarchical society, 20–2, 119
identity formation, 14, 55, 101, 110, 122, 213, 216, 250, 281
matrilineal power, 170
military reform, 141–3
and the Ming, 101, 121, 141
moral objection to hunting, 60
and Neo-Confucianism, 3, 14, 67–8, 98–102, 110–13, 122–4
political and military reforms, 141–3
population increase and expansion north, 104–5, 151–2, 154
private hunting on royal lands, 148
spring and autumn hunts, 143–4, 247
tax revenues, 188
tribute (animals), 189–90
two royal hunting practices, 139
wildlife habitat and hunting, 28–9
see also bureaucracy; Jurchen (non-Korean tribes); scholarly elites; *individual names of kings*
Chumong legend, 55–6, 187
Ch'ungch'ŏng Province, 142, 188, 240
animal tribute, 222, 266
gift-giving on royal hunts, 73
hunting practices, 174
Ch'unghye, King, 89
and compassion towards animals, 250
Chungjong, King, 267
decline of royal hunts, 273
presentation of falcons, 272

Ch'ungnyŏl, King, 2, 60, 71, 81, 82–3, 83–4, 125
annual hunts, 89
authority as a militarised monarch, 86, 88
Buddhist contradiction, 76
compensation to farmers, 74
falconry, 218
hunting, 73–5
and Kublai, 88–90
scholar official critical depictions of, 76–7, 86–7
references to hunting during reign of, 73
rewards favoured officials, 90
uxorilocal alliance with the Yuan court, 70, 81, 86, 170
Ch'ungsuk, King, 89
on hunts, 91
support of falconry, 90
Ch'unsŏn, King, 89
circle hunts, 170, 174, 191, 205, 213, 215–17, 229, 231, 246–9, 252, 254–5; *see also* ring hunts
civil officials *see* bureaucracy; scholarly elites
civil service examination, 19, 22, 67–8, 100
classics mat *see* Confucianism
climate events/patterns, 102, 103, 106, 151, 162, 178, 245
impact on animals, 233, 258
impact on capital region, 106–7, 196
impact on hunting, 76, 107, 134, 170, 176, 178, 196, 215, 237, 245, 254
and nomadic/semi-nomadic peoples, 108
Cockram, Sarah, 121–2
colonialism, 62, 279–80

commoners, 6, 22, 43, 112, 113, 155, 156, 173, 183, 258, 273, 276
  access to hunting grounds, 79, 112, 119, 139, 147, 148, 151, 176–8, 215, 256, 258, 259, 277
  and agriculture, 121, 154, 223, 272
  army, 142
  and disease, 263, 265
  domesticated animals, 121
  falconry, 39, 42, 212, 231, 233, 251
  government policies supporting, 203, 204, 223
  interaction with royals, 113, 149, 215–16
  land ownership, 22
  and perceptions of animals, 43, 44, 51
  sumptuary laws against meat consumption, 264
  taxation of, 22–3, 135, 192, 193, 196, 198, 266, 271, 281
  see also farmers
communication, animal–human, 53
compassion for animals, 53, 234–5
Confucianism, 3, 13, 19, 67–8, 275
  animal sacrifice, 12, 78–81, 110–14, 122–9
  and Buddhism, 96
  classics mat, 21, 225
  filial piety, 11, 96, 99, 110, 246, 269
  hagiography, 169
  Mencian model, 72
  moral objections to hunting, 50, 60, 63, 91, 203, 233, 229
  and the natural world, 50
  perceptions of animals, 44–5, 48, 49, 51
  Rules of Hunting, 110–13
  on uxorilocalism, 71, 86
  see also Book of Rites; bureaucracy; Neo-Confucianism; scholarly elites

conservation, 1, 139, 198, 275
cooking, for ritual, 80, 112, 125
corruption, 74, 175, 198, 225, 240, 243
corvée labour, 22, 188, 212, 216, 264
COVID-19, 7
creation myths, 54–6, 187

Daidu (Yuan capital, Beijing), 70, 73, 75, 81, 82, 83, 85, 90, 276
Daoism, 19, 44, 68, 195
Daoxuan, 45
deer, 11, 29, 30–5, 36, 51, 61, 73, 77, 113, 119, 121, 125, 134, 152, 156, 165, 177, 179, 205, 242, 249, 280, 281
  culled in hunts, 50, 91, 115, 117, 134, 145, 146, 164–5, 171, 230
  in fables, 51, 52–3,
  in medicine, 31, 33, 35, 189, 190, 266, 267, 278
  as tribute, 1, 34, 65, 189, 190, 192
  as sacrifice, 78, 79, 112, 124, 125, 198
  see also individual deer species
deforestation, 8, 27
Demilitarized Zone (DMZ), 280
diplomacy/diplomats, 3, 64–5, 96, 101, 121, 127, 131, 133, 160, 191, 196, 220, 226; *see also* alcohol; animals; Jurchen; Japan/Japanese; trade
disease
  animals, 131
  contemporary, 7
  old age disease, 265
  regional spread, 102–3
  royal family member, 199, 267
  various forms of 'pestilence' in early Chosŏn, 260–7, 270, 273
  zoonotic, 7, 261
divine animal births, 54–6, 187, 276

INDEX

dogs, 12, 200, 231, 236, 240–3
  breeds, 240–1
  domesticated, 260
  as gifts, 12, 75, 133, 242–3
  hunting, 42, 90, 155, 217, 218, 237–8, 269, 273, 280
  meat, 42
  as sacrifice, 123, 128
domesticated animals, 9, 43, 120–1
  for banquets, 135
  breeding, 121, 124, 126, 135, 219, 237, 241
  Chinese breeds, 127–8
  criminalisation of failure in raising, 131–2
  sacrificial offerings, 79, 80, 125–6, 130
  as state resources, 22, 137
  see also agriculture; dogs
droughts see climate events/patterns
ducks, 38, 230, 260, 280
  failure to breed, 126
  in falconry, 210, 211
  as gifts, 133
  as ritual sacrifice, 125, 130
Duncan, John, 99

economy
  decline after Mongol collapse, 105
  and growth in bureaucratic state, 216
  Koryŏ Dynasty, 22
  see also agriculture; taxes
eco-social development, 108
elites
  Chosŏn Dynasty, 71–2
  clashes between governing status groups, 23
  and Classical Chinese, 100
  falconry, 214
  increase in hunts under Mongol rule, 89

land ownership, 22, 104
masculine identities, 59
perceptions of animals, 57–8
popularity of hunt at late Koryŏ court, 90–1
see also bureaucracy; Confucianism; military elite; sadaebu; scholarly elites; yangban
elk and moose, 113, 145, 151, 152
Encyclopaedia of Government Posts, 125
environment and ecology
  islands, 24, 70, 82–4, 267
  peninsula, 26–9, 105–6, 116, 151–2, 176, 190
Europe, and critiques of the hunt, 62
eunuchs, 71, 93, 227

falcons/falconry, 12, 39, 62, 65, 90, 91, 173
  as gifts, 12, 42, 75, 272
  moral economy of, 222–33
  New and Augmented Methods for Falconry, 209–12, 219
  official resistance, 224–9, 230–3, 250–1
  and royal family hunts, 116, 117
  training and techniques, 42, 212, 218–20, 234–5
  watering and feeding, 210–12
  see also under tribute
Family Rites of Zhu Xi (Wengong), 124, 131
famine, 173, 178, 223, 224, 232
farmers, 43, 72, 74, 178, 188, 190; see also agriculture; commoners
feasting, 59, 66, 87, 123, 118, 133, 134, 173, 197, 230
firearms, 95, 275, 280
fire hunts, 65, 73, 74, 75, 134, 174, 202, 272
  prohibitions against, 92
fish, 55, 130, 134

305

fishing, 153, 162, 198
Five Rites, 126
floods *see* climate events/patterns
folk tales, 51–3; *see also* animals
food shortages *see* famine
forests, 27, 28, 106, 151
foundation myths, origins, 55–7, 100, 276
fowl, 38–9; *see also* birds
fox, 1, 5, 41, 50, 152, 173, 190, 191, 242, 245, 257
fur, 38, 41, 106, 113, 152, 190, 191

game, 30–42, 135, 183, 257–8, 260
    feasting on, 17, 66, 76, 112, 132, 237
    gift-giving, 69
    hunting, and brutality, 9, 50
    as tribute, 266
    see also feasting; *and individual names of species*
geese, 38, 121, 124, 130, 133, 210, 211, 229, 260
gender roles *see* masculinity; women
gift-giving, 69, 73–4, 133, 138, 191, 242–3, 272
goshawks, 209, 210, 219, 222, 223, 226, 228, 230
government officials *see* bureaucracy; scholarly elites
Grayson, James, 55
Green, Monica, 262
grey wolf (*Canis lupus*), 41, 276
guns *see* firearms

Ha Sukpu, 155
Han Ch'ihyŏng, 195, 237
Han Hŭiyu, 75
Han Hwak, 118
Han Myŏnghoe, 177, 180, 194, 215, 228, 230
Han River, 176, 219, 228, 264

Hamgyŏng Province, 158
    animals and animal tribute, 147–8, 189, 266
    hunting, 39–40
    mountains, 26, 190
Hanyang (Seoul), 27, 98, 145, 160, 188, 254, 262, 263, 267
hare, 1, 29, 38, 78, 113, 118, 177, 205, 210, 218, 245, 257, 258
hawks, 42; *see also* falcons/falconry
'Heavenly Maiden and the Wood Cutter', 51–3
heroic tales, 185–6, 207, 208
hides, 12, 113, 189, 190, 191, 192, 193, 194, 198
history of the Korean peninsula, overview, 19–25
Hŏ Chong, 182, 205
Hŏ Kong, 83, 85
Hong Chabŏn, 83, 85–6
Hong Kwidal, 253, 254
Hong Sang, 215, 216, 249, 250
Hong Ŭng, 157, 179, 180, 181, 182, 215, 224
Hong Yunsŏng, 201–2
Hong Yuryong, 243
Hongwu Emperor, 94–5
horns, 123, 189, 190, 278
    as medicine, 33
horses, 42, 43, 94, 120–1, 128, 189
Hunter, Luke, 7
hunting
    attendants, 65
    in colonial Korea, 278
    dogs *see* dogs
    earliest records, 3
    grounds/parks, 116, 118, 146–7, 148, 217–18
    intangibles, 9
    palaces, 73

regulations, 18, 92, 111–13, 197, 207, 218, 281
rules from *Book of Rites* and Chosŏn adoption 110–14
screens, 120, 138, 142, 150, 278
terms, 65
Hwang Hŭi, 131
Hwanghae Province, 91, 142, 221, 222, 272
  animals, 39, 147, 181–2, 194
  diseases, 181, 183
  hunting, 91, 115, 181, 183, 257–8
Hyŏnjong, King, 6, 68
Hyŏn Sŏkkyu, 172, 200, 201

India, and the hunt, 62
Inhu, 83, 84
insects
  as disease vectors, 262, 263
  as nuisances, 43, 80, 127
Insu Sohye wanghu, Queen Dowager, 1, 135, 169, 194, 195
Islamic societies, and falconry, 62

Japan/Japanese, 12, 95, 104, 153, 154, 243, 262, 275, 277, 279–80
  animals and the environment, 8
  coastal hunting parties, 151, 152, 153, 195
  diplomacy and animals, 133, 196, 209, 242
  Mongol invasions of Japan and ecological impact, 26–7
  Tsushima and the hunt, 191–2
Jin Xing, 226
Jurchen (non-Korean tribes), 5, 14, 42, 54, 83, 104–5, 133
  animal trade, 77, 105, 186, 189, 190
  clashes over hunting grounds, and debates about, 151–62, 252–4

descriptions of homelands and hunting identity, 134, 161, 252–3
  and diplomacy, 133, 134, 166, 196
  in northern Korea, 152, 153, 154, 157, 195

Kaegyŏng, 60, 70, 73, 83, 84, 188, 274
  debates on relocation, 82–4, 98
Kang Chap'yŏng, 178, 223, 228
Kang Hŭimaeng, 127
Kanghwa Island, 24, 70, 82, 83, 84, 267
Kangmu hunts, 6, 37, 113, 139, 143–51
  entertainment, 259
  Hwanghae Province, 181–4
  official resistance, 172–7, 178, 218, 253–4
  and royal hunting parks, 256–7
  stage to boast martial skills, 166–7
  see also hunting regulations
Kangwŏn Province, 34, 52, 164–5
  animals, 181, 183, 221
  hunting grounds, 146, 181
  hunts, 116, 118, 181, 202, 258
Kaya, 56
Kihwa, 48–9
Kija, 55, 100
Kim Chajŏng, 19, 192
Kim Chesin, 171, 172, 195–6
Kim Chongjik, 49
Kim Hongdo, 19, 279
Kim Hŭn, 227, 230
Kim Il Sung, 281
Kim Kukwang, 171
Kim Kyech'ang, 178
Kim Man, 133
Kim Sejŏk, 230
Kim Sŏhyŏng, 174
Kim Sŭnggyŏng, 181, 223, 224, 227, 228

Kim Yŏji, 242
kings, 42, 53, 96, 114, 185–6, 187;
    see also royal hunts; *individual names of kings*
kisaeng, 198, 243
Kojong, King, 46
Koguryŏ, 55, 56, 187
Kongmin, King, 25, 91, 92, 95, 96
    and animals, 91
    scholarly rebuke for hunting, 92
Kongyang, King, 96
    royal military Kangmu hunts, 144
Korean Amur tiger (*Panthera tigris altaica*), 40; see also tigers
Koryŏ Dynasty
    animal sacrifice, 78–81
    and Buddhism, 19–20, 96
    falconry, 90, 92, 93, 218, 220
    General Ch'oe, and military house rule, 23–4
    identity formation, 59, 61, 69, 94
    intermarriage with Mongols, 24–5, 55, 60; see also uxorilocalism
    international trade, 22
    and Japanese piracy, 95
    Koryŏ–Chosŏn transition, 94–109
    political system favouring of the bureaucracy, 59
    and the spectacle of the royal hunt, 90–1, 93, 168
    submission to Mongols, 70, 85, 103, 189
    see *individual names of kings*
Koryŏsa and *Koryŏsa chŏryo*, 89
Ku Ch'igon, 178
Ku Kyŏm, 161
Ku Sukson, 226
Kublai Khan, 72, 81–2, 84, 85, 86, 88
Kŭmjang, Mt, 117
Kungye, King, 202

Kwŏn Kŏn, 225
Kwŏn Kyŏngu, 217
Kwŏn Pin, 183
Kyŏnggi Province, 107, 149
    animals, 125, 181, 221, 250, 266
    extreme weather, 107, 196
    hunting grounds, 146, 149, 173, 176
    hunts, 117, 194, 215
Kyŏngsang Province
    animal tribute, 221, 222, 266
    extreme weather, 106–7
    hunting grounds, 146
    royal hunts, 117

land ownership, 4–5, 22, 104
leather, 191
Ledyard, Gari, 16
leopards, 29, 37, 41
Liang Hui, King, 63
Liao Dynasty, 68, 169
Little Ice Age, 102, 106, 109, 151, 245
luan (phoenix-like bird), 49
Luo Xiong, 161–2
lynx, 42, 189, 190

magistrates, local, 193–4, 198, 258
Maje, Mt, 73, 74, 75, 76, 84
Manchuria, 81, 85, 95, 153
Manchurian hare (*Lepus mandschuricus*), 38
Manchurian wapiti (*Cervus canadensis xanthopygus*), 34–5
manuals, falconry, 218–19, 235
marriage alliances, 24–5, 60, 71, 81, 86, 99
masculinity
    elite and royal, 5–6, 58, 88, 116, 139, 166, 167
    hunting as expression of, 62, 93, 150, 193, 214

living beasts and, 268
nature of elite masculinity, 5–6, 59, 167
meat, 51, 124–5, 191, 264–5;
  see also animals as sacrifice;
  game; vegetarianism; venison
medicine, 33, 42, 106
  animal-borne diseases, 261
  bears see bear as medicine
  Chinese, 37, 38
  deer see deer as medicine
  elite access to, 133, 191, 266–7
  Hamgyŏng Province and animals, 189–90
Medieval Climate Anomaly, 102, 106
Memorabilia of the Three Kingdoms, 64–5
Mencius, 63–4, 177
  on animals and social stability, 124, 244, 255, 256, 259
merit subjects, 5, 22, 96, 98, 135, 149, 214, 269
migration (people), 102–3, 157, 183, 259
military
  conscription of commoners, 22
  elites, 23–4, 73–5, 90, 114, 120, 131
  examination, 20, 142
  hunting and training/skills, 69, 72, 111–13, 139–40, 174, 175, 178, 192, 252
  kings, hunting and rulership, 114
  state reforms, 141–3
  troop inspections, 146, 249
  see also elites; heroic tales; Kangmu hunts; private hunts
Min Sagŏn, 229
Ming Dynasty, 5, 91
  animal sacrifice, 126
  clashes with Chosŏn hunters, 161–2
  disease, 263
  emperor, 101
  falconry, 219, 226–7

founder of, 94–5
gift-giving, 127, 242
kings of Korea and, 101
Ming–Chosŏn diplomatic trade relations, 121
reclaims land from Mongols, 95
rise of, 89
transition to, 94
tribute burden on Korea, 189
see also China/Chinese
Ministry of Military Affairs
  and animal tribute, 134
  hunts, 111, 146
Ministry of Rites, 110, 132
Ministry of War, 119
  and hunting grounds, 147, 177
  and Jurchen hunters, 156, 157
miscellaneous animals, category of, 119
Mokchong, King, 68
monasteries/monks, 96, 243
  critiques of the hunt, 63, 76
  and disease, 263
  raising hawks and hounds, 240
  royal visits, 76
  see also Buddhism
Mongol *darugachi*, 73, 75, 90
Mongols/Yuan Dynasty, 2, 54–5, 65 89, 276
  animals, 42, 72, 276
  arrival in Korea, 24, 70, 103
  control Jurchen land, 95
  demand for ships, 26–7
  disease, 263
  falconry, 218, 219
  fall of, 5, 89, 103, 140
  governing practices and identity, 72, 276
  hunting, 14, 61–2, 72, 90, 166
  in favour of the royal hunt, 61, 62, 109
  increase in royal/elite hunts, 89

Mongols/Yuan Dynasty (*cont.*)
  intermarriage, 24–5, 55, 60–1
  nomadic cultural practices, 93, 94
  submission of Koryŏ, 70, 85, 103
  trade with, 22
  transition to Ming Dynasty, 91, 94
  and transnationalism, 12
  tribute burden on Korea, 186, 189
  see also Kublai Khan; shamanism
moose, 113, 145, 151, 152
mosquitos, 43, 262, 264
mountain hare (*Lepus timidus*), 38
mountain ranges, 26–7, 28–9, 34
mourning, 99, 126, 194, 264
music, 135, 166, 174, 247, 259, 260
  as danger to rulership, 60, 195, 199, 204
Munjong, King (Koryŏ)
  hunting prohibition, 46, 69
Munjong, King (Chosŏn), 114, 116, 238
musk deer, 31–2, 145, 189, 190
Muŭija Hyesim, 48
Myoch'ŏng, 23
Myŏngsuk, Princess, 249
myths of rulership and hunting, 185–6, 207, 208

Nam Eŭn, 142
Namhan, Mt, 37
National Confucian Academy, 107
National Ritual Code, 127
Nayan, 81–2, 86
Neo-Confucianism/Neo-Confucians, 12–15, 95–8, 238
  Chosŏn Dynasty, 100–2, 109
  creation of a patrilineal society, 99
  early Chosŏn scholars, 141–2
  hostility towards Buddhism, 100
  on the hunt and Confucian values, 63–4, 117, 167, 170, 172, 216, 274
  Koryŏ–Chosŏn transition, 98
  on meat consumption, 124, 264–5
  see also royal lectures
No Sasin, 157, 162, 179–1, 183, 215
North Korea, hunting, 280–1

O Sun, 159
Ŏ Yuso, 179, 182
Office for Raising Animals, 131
Office of Protocol, 128, 131, 132, 133
Office of Sacrificial Animals, 128, 132–3
Office of the Censor General, 174, 223, 233
  and royal hunts, 118, 143, 173, 201
older men, and the royal hunt, 214–15, 234
oral stories, 43–4
  animal folktales, 51–3
Ottoman Empire, 140
overhunting, 13, 147, 268

Paekdu Mountain, 152
Paekdu Mountain elk, 34–5
paintings
  Kim Hongdo, 19, 279, fig. C.1
  Prince Anp'yŏng, 221, fig. 8.2
  as sources, 3, 77, 212, 220, 226
  unknown artist, 242, fig. 9.2
  Yi Am, 213, 241, fig. 8.1, 9.1
  Yi Chehyŏn, 78, fig. 2.1
Pak Ansŏng, 174
Pak Hyŏkkŏse legend, 56, 187
Pak Sungjil, 200, 201
Pak Ŭi, 75, 91
Pak Wŏnjong, 272
Pan Pokhae, 93–4
Pan Uhyŏng, 232
Pang Sinu, 89
Park Chung Hee, 280
pasture lands, 132, 276

peasants *see* farmers
pets *see under* animals
petitions (hunting), 77, 169, 172, 173, 181, 182, 193, 195, 233, 236–7, 248, 249, 251, 252, 253, 267
Pictures of Hunting Scenes in the Four Seasons, 138–9, 142, 150
political support: patronage via the hunt, 5, 22, 66, 73, 75, 90
pelts, 42, 119, 189; *see also* fur
personal hunts *see* private hunts
pheasants, 38–9, 125
piebaldism, 164
pigs, 124, 128, 132–3; *see also* swine
piracy, 95, 153
plague, 103, 261–2; *see also* disease
poaching, 148
    laws against private hunting, 176–7, 251–2, 258
poetry, Confucian critique of the hunt, 50
Pojang, Mt, 28, 117
polo, 69
Pŏp of Paekche, King, 46
Pŏphŭng, King of Silla, 46
population, animals, 13, 147, 179, 257, 266, 268
population, humans, 102–3, 104, 223, 259, 262
predators, 40–2
    and Kangmu hunts, 145
private hunts, 18–19, 251–2
    bonding with elders, 214–15
    commoners, 148
    foreign diplomacy, 196
    official resistance, 194–6, 197–201, 203–7, 218
    royal, 80, 139, 186, 191, 193–201
    royal tomb mounds, 202–3, 206–7
P'ungsu (wind and water), 28

Puyŏ *see* Koguryŏ
P'yo Yŏnmal, 249, 250
P'yŏngan Province, 75, 133, 155–6, 226
    animals, 136, 147–8, 198
    Jurchen hunting parties, 158–60, 252
    list of animal tribute, 190, 221
    royal hunts, 246

Qadan insurrection, 81–6
Qing Dynasty, 6, 277
quail, 38–9
    Queen Dowagers, 1, 221, 230; *see also* Insu Sohye wanghu, Queen Dowager

racoon dogs, 42
    record-keeping
    of animal categories, 30
    attendance on the hunt, 217, 229
    of hunting, 17, 18, 60
    see also histories, official
red deer (*Cervus elaphus*), 34, 113
red fox (*Vulpes vulpes*), 41
Red Turbans, 95, 121
reincarnation, 45, 53, 57
remonstration, 21, 62–3, 168
rice production, 106–7, 233
ring hunts, 1, 65, 73, 134, 181, 197
    rules regarding, 111, 113, 114
    see also circle hunts
Rites of Zhou, 68, 112, 126
rituals, 12, 14, 80, 96, 98, 102, 108, 111, 113, 114, 123, 124, 127, 131, 133, 138, 180, 183, 197, 198, 202, 239, 248, 250
    ritual altars, 78–80, 122–3, 127–9
    Ritual Guest and Palace Catering Service Office, 130, 132

rituals (*cont.*)
  ritual sacrifice of animals, 3, 12, 45, 51; *see also* animal sacrifice
  ritual wailing, 194
roe deer, 31, 32–3, 113, 115, 119, 125
royal families, and transnationalism, 12; *see also* elites; kings
royal hunts
  bureaucratic language and institutions, 65
  in early Mongol era, 61–2
  increase in Mongol era, 89
  official resistance to, 60; *see also* bureaucracy
  scholarly elites participation and popularity of, 59–60
  Rules of Hunting, 110–13
  see also Confucianism; Kangmu hunts; private hunts
royal lectures, 168, 174, 196, 204, 217, 224, 225, 226, 227, 230, 232, 247, 248, 254; *see also* Confucianism
royal park attendants, 197
royal tombs *see* private hunts
Rules of Hunting, 110–13
Russian armies, 140

sable (*Martes zibellina*), 37–8, 152, 185, 189, 190, 258
sadaebu, 3, 201–2; *see also* bureaucracy
Sapsali (dog breed), 241–2
scholarly elites
  and access to animals, 3, 5, 13, 243–4
  coup against Yŏnsan'gun, 267
  fissures among over hunting, 85, 169, 171, 177, 178, 198, 228
  on Kangmu hunts, 253–4
  power reinstated under Mongols, 24
  resistance to hunting, 60, 90–1, 173, 178, 182, 246–51

transnationalism, 2, 12, 25, 73, 75, 276
views on Buddhism, 97
worldviews, 59, 68, 100–1
see also bureaucracy; elites; yangban
Sejo, King (also Prince Chinyang), 114, 142, 158, 166, 203, 215, 238–9
  depiction of hunting acumen, 165–6
  and falconry, 220, 228
  hunts with family members, 117
  royal Kangmu hunts, 144
  views on hunting parks, 256
Sejong, King, 28, 114, 133, 153, 168, 237
  adoption of Five Rites and state animal sacrifice, 126
  altars, repair of, 128–9
  falconry, 118, 219, 220, 228, 250
  gift-giving of animals, 133, 200, 242
  government institutional reforms, 129–30, 168, 188
  hunts with family members, 116, 117, 118
  Kangmu hunts, 144, 146, 164–5, 180
settlements, human, 27–8, 38
sexuality: beastiality taboo, 47
shamanism, 12, 44, 53, 57, 78, 119, 122
Shanglin Park, 126
Shang Dynasty China (1600–1027 bce), 61, 100
sheep, 132
  Chinese breed, 127–8, 133
  costs, 133
  as ritual sacrifice, 79, 123–5, 127, 130–2
Shinto art and literature, 8
sika deer, 34, 35, 113, 119
Silla Dynasty, 63, 66, 78, 128, 141
Sillok, 107, 263
Sim Han, 156
Sim Hoe, 177, 230

Sim Hyosaeng, 142
Sim On, 242
Sim Yang, 76
Sin, Queen, 268
Sin Ch'ŏng, 90
Sin Chongho, 233
Sin Sukchu, 134–5
Sin U, King, 88, 89, 91
   hunting practices, 92–4, 144
six animals (of Zhou Dynasty), 123
slaves (*nobi*), 11, 22, 71, 108, 191, 240, 264
   animal sacrifice, 79, 124, 126, 131
   care of altars, 129
   comparisons to animals, 51, 58
   encounters with animals, 43–4
   falconry, 42, 212, 237, 258
   hunting practices, 19, 79, 119, 258
   and perceptions of animals, 43
slaughter, 53, 122, 129
   Buddhist precent against, 46, 47, 69
   and Confucianism, 51, 80, 112, 124, 264
   and shamanism, 58
smallpox, 261, 262–3; see also disease
snakes, 43, 51, 192
snares and traps, 42
   for tigers and leopards, 40–1, 198
snowfall see climate events/patterns
Son Sunhyo, 182
Song Chil, 227
Sŏng Chung, 258
Song Chungdon, 244
Sŏng Hyŏn, 201, 236–7
Sŏngjong, King, 1, 29, 46, 169, 239
   ancestral rites, 204–5
   bonding with commoners on the hunt, 215–16
   bonding with elders on the hunt, 214–15
   Buddhist influences against killing animals, 195
   death of, 234
   falconry, 220–33
   the hunt of Tsushima, 191–2
   hunts with family members, 1, 169–70, 214, 230,
   and hunting on the frontiers, 161
   and Hwanghae Province, 181–4
   Kangmu hunts, 149, 169–71, 172, 175, 178–80
   official depiction of, 248
   private hunts, 173, 193, 196, 202–4, 206, 216–18
   storytelling and the hunt, 214
   and Prince Wŏlsan, 199–201
Songs of Flying Dragons, 187
South Korea, hunting as a sport, 280
spotted deer (*Cervus nippon mantchuricus*), 34
spring and autumn hunts, 143–4, 192, 247
   debates over, 175, 248, 254
squirrels, 118, 190, 258
state altars and ceremonies, animal sacrifice, 127
steppe lands
   climate impact, 108
   foundation myths and legends, 276
Sterckx, Roel, 54–5
storytelling
   as a martial legacy, 214, 278
   see also myths of rulership
Sugang Palace, 'Palace of Longevity and Good Health', 73
superintendents of hunting parks, 217–18
swine
   for ceremonial rites, 134–5
   Chinese imports of, 277

swine (cont.)
    as common domesticated animal, 121, 124, 262
    costs of, 133

T'aebaek mountain range, 26, 35
Taehyŏn, 47
T'aejo, King (Yi Sŏnggye), 95, 98, 119, 138
    display of martial skills, 114–15, 185–6, 187, 190
    falcons, 228
    hunting with family members, 116, 117
    Kangmu hunts, 144, 145, 150, 170
    land reform laws, 99
    military reform, 141, 142
    private hunts, 176, 185, 193
    sacrifice in honour of, 125, 130
    and uxorilocal practice, 99
T'aejong, King, 114, 115–16, 126, 142, 215, 220
    falcons, 116
    hunting dogs as gifts, 242
    hunting stories, 176, 202
    hunts with family, 116, 117
    Kangmu hunts, 144
    private hunts, 202
    royal hunting parks, 255, 256
'talented people', hunters, 197–8
Tang Dynasty times (618–907 CE), 45
Tan'gun legend, 54–5, 187
Tanjong, King, 114, 118, 239
taxes, 103
    animal products, 9, 188
    the elite and the community, 22–3
    game for, 135
    monastery land, 97
    tribute tax, animals, 127
    see also tribute
Temur Oljaitu Khan, 85

Three Kingdoms era, 46, 63, 64, 128
tigers, 11–12, 29, 40–1, 145, 203, 204, 279
    Buddhist monks and, 47
    hunting methods, 40–1
    importance of, 119
    rewards for killing, 119–20
    storytelling, 57, 214
Tŏkchong (Prince), 169, 204,
Tonga Wangha, 196
trade
    growth in fifteenth century, 103
    horses, and Ming–Chosŏn diplomacy, 121
transformation stories
    animal–human, 55
    human–animal, 53
transnationalism, 12
transportation of tribute products, 188, 191
traps see snares and traps
tribute, 190, 192–3, 198
    falcons, 219, 221, 226–7, 232, 234
    Mongol demands on Korea, 189
    special items, 192–3
    tax system, 188
Tripitaka, 45, 96
Tumen River 5, 26, 105, 120, 154

U Kong, 158, 161
Ŭihŭng Commandery, 142
Ŭijong, King, 69
Underwood, Horace H., 278–9
ungulates see deer, elk, moose and wild boar
Urasian moose (*Alces alces cameloides*), 35
uxorilocalism, 24–5, 71, 81, 86, 99

vegetarianism, 45, 46, 58
venison, 32, 125, 134, 152–3, 191

Wang Heng, 133–4
Wang Kŏn (King T'aejo, Koryŏ) 66–7, 68, 69
warfare
  population loss and societal/economic decline, 103
  see also military training/skills
water deer, 30
weather see climate events/patterns
Wells, Andrew, 121–2
white stags
  to hunt, 164–5
  as living tribute, 192, 194, 197, 208
wild animals, 5, 10, 11–12, 120, 121; see also game; individual names of species
wild boar, 36–7, 93–4, 113, 132, 145
wilderness, metaphor of, 50
Wŏlsan, Prince see Yi Chŏng, Prince
wolves, 29, 37, 41
women
  in early Koryŏ society, 67
  kisaeng, 198, 243
  musicians, 103, 259–60
  and Neo-Confucianism, 99, 170
  role in the hunt, 2, 6, 170, 279, 280
  status, 6
  uxorilocalism and, 71
Wŏnjong, King, 24, 70

Yalu River 5, 26, 95, 104, 105, 120, 154, 158, 160, 161, 252
Yang Ch'an, 230
Yang Sŏngji, 133, 169
yangban, 23, 43, 77, 100, 104, 122, 131, 264
Yangnyŏng, Prince, 116, 117, 133, 172, 200
Yi Am, 213
Yi Chagyŏm, 23
Yi Chehyŏn, 77–8
Yi Chijŏ, 74, 75
Yi Ch'ŏlkyŏn, 170, 171, 182, 222
Yi Chŏng, General, 74, 90
Yi Chŏng, Prince, 199–201, 214
Yi Chongyun, 226
Yi Chu, 50
Yi Hyŏ, Prince, 216
Yi Kok, 69
Yi Kŭkchŭng, 176, 178, 179, 193, 228
Yi Kŭkki, 222
Yi Kŭkkyun, 156, 159
Yi Kŭkpae, 183, 214, 215, 230, 232, 245
Yi Kŭkton, 253
Yi Maenghyŏn, 195–6
Yi Ŏ (Prince), 166
Yi Pŏmsŏk, 280
Yi Punhŭi, 90
Yi P'yŏng, 73, 75
Yi Siae, 158
Yi Simwŏn, 205, 206
Yi Sŏnggye, 56–7, 95–6, 98; see also T'aejo, King
Yi Sŭnghyu, 76
Yi Ubo, 203, 204
Yi Yong see Anp'yŏng, Prince
Yŏnsan'gun, King, 2, 234, 258
  animals and the hunt, 238, 243–51
  death of, 267–8, 272
  and disease, 264, 265
  dogs, 237, 238, 243, 244, 248, 260
  falconry, 237, 250–1
  Kangmu hunts, 245
  new hunting parks, 256–9
  official resistance to hunting, 246–51
  political purges, 239, 267, 269
  private hunts, 245
  spring and autumn hunts, 245, 247
Yu Chagwang, 258
Yu Chongsu, 194–5

Yu Su, 222
Yuan Dynasty *see* Mongols/Yuan Dynasty
Yun, Queen, 239
Yun Chaun, 17, 201, 206
Yun Ho, 179, 180
Yun Hyoson, 253
Yun P'ilsang, 157, 160, 175, 181, 214, 215, 245
Yun Sojong, 91–2
Yun Sŏkpo, 229
Yun Su, 75, 90

Zheng Tong, 227
Zhou Dynasty, 63
Zhu Xi, 96
Zhu Yuanzhang (Hongwu Emperor, Ming Dynasty), 94–5
zoonotic diseases *see* diseases

EU representative:
Easy Access System Europe
Mustamäe tee 50, 10621 Tallinn, Estonia
Gpsr.requests@easproject.com

www.ingramcontent.com/pod-product-compliance
Lightning Source LLC
Chambersburg PA
CBHW050202240426
43671CB00013B/2223